Praise for *The America*

"Charles Post's new book, *The American Road* . . . . a reference point for debates among historians and Marxists about the transformation of the English colonies into the fully developed capitalist United States. . . . It should be widely read, appreciated for its insights and rigor, and also debated."
— Ashley Smith, *International Socialist Review*

"This is a thoughtful, learned, stimulating, challenging and altogether valuable volume. It reprints a series of reflections by the Marxist sociologist Charles Post on various aspects of the rise and evolution of capitalism in North America between the colonial era and the late nineteenth century. The book is anchored in a wide-ranging study of (and it duly credits) the work of generations of historians."
— Bruce Levine, author of *Confederate Emancipation*

"Explaining the origin and early development of American capitalism is a particularly challenging task. It is in some ways even more difficult than in other cases to strike the right historical balance, capturing the systemic imperatives of capitalism, and explaining how they emerged, while doing justice to historical particularities. . . . To confront these historical complexities requires both a command of historical detail and a clear theoretical grasp of capitalism's systemic imperatives, a combination that is all too rare. Charles Post succeeds in striking that difficult balance, which makes his book a major contribution to truly historical scholarship."
— Ellen Meiksins-Wood, author of *The Origins of Capitalism*

"In *The American Road to Capitalism*, Charles Post offers a brilliant reinterpretation of the origins and diverging paths of economic evolution in the American north and south. The first systematic historical materialist account of US development from the colonial period through the Civil War in a very long time, it is sure to be received as a landmark contribution."
— Robert P. Brenner, author of *Agrarian Class Structure and Economic Development in Early Modern Europe*

"Charles Post has written an excellent book on the origins of American capitalism in the antebellum North, on plantation slavery in the Old South and on the cataclysmic conflict between them. His interpretation is bold and controversial; it will have to be considered by all scholars in the field."
— John Ashworth, author of *Slavery, Capitalism and the Antebellum Republic*

"This is the most original and provocative materialist interpretation of the origins and dynamics of US capitalism for a long time. Post combines impressive command of the historical sources with a sharp analytical understanding, not least of the centrality of agrarian questions to the development of capitalism."
— Henry Bernstein, emeritus editor, *Journal of Agrarian Change*

"Over the past three decades, Charles Post has been developing an original and powerful interpretation of the American road to capitalism. This volume brings together his most important essays in what is sure to be a landmark volume. Post brilliantly analyzes the structural basis of economic development in both the North and the South, culminating in a powerful interpretation of the social basis of the Civil War. The book is one of the best examples of historical sociology that I have seen in recent years, effortlessly melding theory and historical research. This is engaged scholarship of the highest order."
— Vivek Chibber, author of *Locked In Place*

Historical Materialism Book Series

More than ten years after the collapse of the Berlin Wall and the disappearance of Marxism as a (supposed) state ideology, a need for a serious and long-term Marxist book publishing program has arisen. Subjected to the whims of fashion, most contemporary publishers have abandoned any of the systematic production of Marxist theoretical work that they may have indulged in during the 1970s and early 1980s. The Historical Materialism book series addresses this great gap with original monographs, translated texts and reprints of "classics."

Editorial board: Paul Blackledge, Leeds; Sebastian Budgen, London; Jim Kincaid, Leeds; Stathis Kouvelakis, Paris; Marcel van der Linden, Amsterdam; China Miéville, London; Paul Reynolds, Lancashire.

Haymarket Books is proud to be working with Brill Academic Publishers (http://www.brill.nl) and the journal *Historical Materialism* to republish the Historical Materialism book series in paperback editions. Current series titles include:

THE AMERICAN ROAD TO CAPITALISM

STUDIES IN CLASS-STRUCTURE, ECONOMIC DEVELOPMENT AND POLITICAL CONFLICT, 1620–1877

CHARLES POST

Haymarket Books
Chicago, Illinois

First published in 2011 by Brill Academic Publishers, The Netherlands
© 2011 Koninklijke Brill NV, Leiden, The Netherlands

Published in paperback in 2012 by
Haymarket Books
P.O. Box 180165
Chicago, IL 60618
773-583-7884
www.haymarketbooks.org

ISBN: 978-1-60846-198-1

Trade distribution:
In the US, Consortium Book Sales, www.cbsd.com
In Canada, Publishers Group Canada, www.pgcbooks.ca
In the UK, Turnaround Publisher Services, www.turnaround-psl.com
In Australia, Palgrave Macmillan, www.palgravemacmillan.com.au
In all other countries, Publishers Group Worldwide, www.pgw.com

Cover image of *Architectonic Painting*, 1917, by Liubov Popova. Cover design by
Ragina Johnson.

This book was published with the generous support of Lannan Foundation
and the Wallace Global Fund.

Printed in Canada by union labor.

10 9 8 7 6 5 4 3 2

Library of Congress Cataloging-in-Publication data is available.

to
T, Z and RIMP

Contents

Foreword

This book is a major contribution to historical scholarship. I say this with particular emphasis, because so much that has been written about the history of capitalism has been anything but historical.

There are essentially two ways of thinking about history unhistorically. One is to posit a single, universal transhistorical law of change and development. The other is to reduce history to a welter of particularities, all detail and difference without causality or even process, just, in Arnold Toynbee's classic phrase, one damn thing after another. The history of capitalism has been subject to both these tendencies, though perhaps more the former than the latter.

Since the eighteenth century, beginning with Enlightenment-conceptions of progress and classical political economy, capitalism – or 'commercial society' – has commonly been viewed as the outcome of a general law of technological progress, typically associated with an increasing division of labour and growing commercialisation. While earlier versions of this 'grand narrative' have been refined and modified – for instance, by certain varieties of Marxism or Weberian historical sociology, or more recent demographic theories – the 'commercialisation'-model, with or without technological determinism, has remained remarkably tenacious.

The result has been to define away the need to explain the historical emergence or 'origin' of capitalism, because the capitalist system seems always to have existed, at least in embryo. It appears to be the more-or-less inevitable outcome of human practices that have existed since time-immemorial, if not embedded in the very depths of human nature, then already present in the earliest acts of exchange. Such (a)historical accounts have certainly been challenged; but, especially in recent years, the challenge has most often come from various kinds of even more ahistorical history, in 'postmodernist' or 'revisionist' form. These approaches not only reject 'grand narratives' of any kind but have little use for any explanation of historical causality or process, or, indeed, for any conception of a 'system' like capitalism, as distinct from chaotic and random collections of 'damn things'.

The position of Marxism in all this has been ambiguous. Some important strands of Marxism have, of course, been among the strongest advocates of technological determinism. But it was Marx himself who laid the foundation for a very different approach, and Marxist historians have carried on his work to great effect. Although, in his earlier works, Marx still owed much to Enlightenment-conceptions of progress, in his critique of political economy and, above all, in *Capital*, he moved far beyond conventional accounts of capitalist development. Starting from the premise that every 'mode of production' operates according to its own systemic logic, he transformed the definition of capitalism itself, so that it was no longer simply 'commercial society', or a bigger and better system of trade. Capitalism has its own distinctive social-property relations, from which derive its own unique systemic logic, its own imperatives, its own specific 'laws of motion'. Its specific mode of exploitation, in which relations between capital and labour are mediated by the market, create very specific compulsions of competition, profit-maximisation and constant capital-accumulation. Nor was it the outcome of some universal law of technological progress. In fact, the imperative constantly to improve the technical forces of production was specific to capitalism, and to posit technological determinism as a general theory of history was simply to read back into all history a drive that is a specifically capitalist imperative. This meant, too, that the origin of capitalism, as a distinctive mode of production, did indeed require a historical explanation; and what Marx proposed was not a transhistorical narrative of technological development or commercialisation but the story of a historically-specific social transformation.

While Marx certainly intended to repudiate old technological determinisms or, indeed, any idea of a single, universal 'law' of historical development, he did not simply replace them with historical contingencies. His analysis of capitalism, which remains unsurpassed to this day, depended on discovering the systemic logic or 'laws of motion' that characterise all capitalist economies, the operating principles that make them all 'capitalist', irrespective of their empirical differences. Yet, if every mode of production has its own systemic operating principles, grounded in specific social-property relations and modes of exploitation, Marx insisted that 'this does not prevent the same economic basis…from showing infinite variations and gradations in appearance, which can be ascertained only by analysis of the empirically given circumstances'. This proposition has several implications: it means, first of all, that we cannot simply read off the empirical specificities of any given society from its economic 'base', nor can we predict the outcome of social interactions and struggles that take place within the constraints of 'basic' social-property relations; but it also means that the logic of those social-property relations operates, and is discernible, throughout those empirical manifestations.

This is what it means to think historically, and it is not an easy trick to pull off: on the one hand, it means acknowledging all the particularities of history, all the empirical detail and difference, while recognising the systemic 'rules for reproduction' and the 'logic of process' that characterise a system of social-property relations like capitalism. This challenge has in recent years been very fruitfully taken up by Marxist historians, especially in explaining the emergence and development of capitalism – notably by Robert Brenner and others sometimes called, rather awkwardly, 'political Marxists'. This form of Marxist historiography does not assume that the transformation of one mode of production into another is inevitably determined by a single, universal law of history. It starts from the premise that each social form has its own systemic logic, what Brenner calls its 'rules for reproduction'. But neither are the transformations from one form into another merely random or contingent. Capitalism was not the inevitable successor to feudalism; but Brenner has demonstrated how it emerged in England out of the relations between landlords and peasants, operating according to the 'rules for reproduction' imposed by their own system of social-property relations.

This is the tradition in which Charles Post has been working. Explaining the origin and early development of American capitalism is a particularly challenging task. It is, in some ways, even more difficult than in other cases to strike the right historical balance, capturing the systemic imperatives of capitalism, and explaining how they emerged, while doing justice to historical particularities. American history has been so overwhelmed by mythologies of 'American exceptionalism' that the temptation must be very powerful either to exaggerate the specificities or to compensate by going to the other extreme, discounting historical particularities on the grounds that, after all, capitalism is capitalism is capitalism. And there is another huge and distinctive conundrum: the question of slavery, how it was, or was not, compatible with capitalism, and how slave-production shaped – and/or was shaped by – the capitalist 'logic of process'. To confront these historical complexities requires both a command of historical detail and a clear theoretical grasp of capitalism's systemic imperatives, a combination that is all too rare. Charles Post succeeds in striking that difficult balance, which makes his book a major contribution to truly *historical* scholarship.

Ellen Meiksins Wood

Acknowledgements

All intellectual work – like all human labour – is social and collective. Work that has been percolating for over thirty years owes much to the support of a great many institutions and individuals. The first phase of my intellectual journey was spent in the Graduate Program in Sociology at SUNY-Binghamton, which provided me with financial support and research-facilities between 1977 and 1983. Many of the ideas contained in the first chapter owe much to my fellow graduate-students at Binghamton and to friends and comrades in other parts of the world. I am particularly grateful to Cesar Ayala, Eric Berg, Rafael Bernabe, Mike Davis, Alex Dupuy, the late Ernest Mandel, Robert Russel, and Kevin Ryan.

I want to thank three faculty mentors who played a central role in my intellectual formation at Binghamton. James A. Geschwender was a model dissertation-advisor, combining humour, compassion, insight and integrity. Martin J. Murray's work on Indochina and South Africa provided a model of the synthesis of theoretical rigour and historical depth. Perry Anderson's intellectual support and encouragement in those years and his detailed and challenging commentary on my work were invaluable.

The second phase of the work that produced this book was spent in New York, where I taught at Sarah Lawrence College (1991–3, 2002–4) and at the Borough of Manhattan Community College-City University of New York (1994–present). The library staff at Esther Raushenbush Library of Sarah Lawrence College and the A. Philip Randolph Library of Borough of Manhattan Community College helped in locating sources. The Research Foundation of CUNY, the Professional Staff Congress-CUNY and the BMCC Faculty Development Committee provided grants that supported my research over the years. I would also like to thank the organisers and participants in seminars held by the Geography Department of the University of California, the Development Studies Programme at the School of Oriental and African Studies in London, and the Agrarian Studies Program at Yale University; and conferences organised by the American Sociological Association, the *Journal of Agrarian Change* and *Historical Materialism*.

In this latter phase, many friends, comrades and colleagues have been a source of intellectual inspiration and stimulation: John Ashworth, Liam Campling, Gavin Capps, Sheila Cohen, Peter Drucker, Sam Farber, Sue Ferguson, Eric Foner, Rebecca Hill, Michael A. McCarthy, David McNally, Kim Moody, James Perlstein, Anwar Shaikh, Kit Wainer, and Richard Walker. A special thanks must go to Sebastian Budgen, who, almost single-handedly, is responsible for my committing to writing this book.

Four individuals stand out for special thanks during my years in New York. Henry Bernstein and Terrence J. Byers, the former editors of *Journal of Peasant Studies* and *Journal of Agrarian Change*, have been a continuous source of intellectual and personal support, and helped introduce me and my work to the broader world of scholars labouring in agrarian studies. Their combination of intellectual non-sectarianism and rigour is a model to which I aspire. Vivek Chibber, at New York University, has been a reliable friend and comrade. Our shared political and theoretical commitments nurtured sharp exchanges, which have immeasurably strengthened my work. Ellen Meiksins Wood, both when she was teaching at York University in Toronto and in retirement in London, has been a consistent, reliable and insightful commentator and friend. Her impact on this book can be seen in almost every chapter.

One person has been a constant source of support and inspiration throughout this entire project. From the time we met in 1978, Robert Brenner has been a friend, comrade and colleague. This book is based on his historical and theoretical analysis of the origins of capitalism, and has benefited from his detailed and astute comments on every essay. My debt to him is enormous.

Finally, I would like to acknowledge the people with whom I shared my personal life. Mary C. Malloy (1947–2004) was my partner and intellectual collaborator for over fifteen years. While our relationship ended before she died, she helped shape my Marxism. Terésa B. Stern has not simply helped make the past decade the best of my life, but has constantly challenged me to present my ideas in ways an educated, politically committed layperson could grasp. My daughters, Rosa Malloy-Post and Zara Stern-Frazier, although probably still unclear why I spent over thirty years studying events that occurred 'back in the day', have been a source of inspiration throughout.

Finally, I would like to thank the editors and publishers of the following journals for permission to reprint the articles below:

'The American Road to Capitalism', *New Left Review* (1982) 133: 30–51.

'The Agrarian Origins of US Capitalism: The Transformation of the Northern Countryside Before the Civil War', *Journal of Peasant Studies* (1995) 22, 3: 389–445.

'Plantation Slavery and Economic Development in the Antebellum Southern United States,' *Journal of Agrarian Change* (2003) 3, 3: 289–332.

'Agrarian Class Structure and Economic Development in Colonial British North America: The Place of the American Revolution in the Origins of Capitalism in the US', *Journal of Agrarian Change,* (2009) 4: 453–83.

'Social-Property Relations, Class-Conflict and the Origins of the US Civil War: Toward a New Social Interpretation', *Historical Materialism. (Forthcoming 2011)*

Introduction

This book is a Marxian intervention into the historical debates on the structure and trajectory of the US-economy in the eighteenth and nineteenth centuries, and the causes and consequences of the US Civil War and Reconstruction. Our intervention rests on the assumption that US economic and political development, while *specific,* is in no sense *exceptional,* as many historians claim. Instead, these processes can be analysed using the fundamental concepts of historical materialism. In other words, the dynamics of production and circulation in the United States are best understood through the prism of distinctive social-property relations – relations between human beings and between human beings and nature.[1] These social-property relations and their specific rules of reproduction dictate the contours of social and economic growth and development, and create the social matrix in which political conflict is conducted. Put simply, this book is a *defence* of Marx's theory and method:

> The specific economic form in which unpaid labour is pumped out of the direct producers determines the relationship of domination and servitude, as this grows directly out of production itself and reacts back on it in turn as a determinant. On this is based the entire configuration of the economic community arising from the actual relations of production, and hence its specific political form. It is in each case the direct relationship of the owners of the conditions of production to the immediate producers – a relationship whose particular form naturally corresponds always to a certain level of development of the type and manner of labour, and hence to its social productive power – in which we find the innermost secret, the hidden basis of the entire social edifice, and hence also the political form of the

---

[1] Brenner 1977; 1985a; 1985b; 1989.

> relationship of sovereignty and dependence, in short, the specific form of the state in each case.[2]

This book seeks not merely to defend, but to contribute to the *renewal* of historical materialism. Over the past three decades, one of the most important sources of this renewal has been the critical-Marxist engagement with historical data in the forms of archival-primary sources and the best of the (predominantly non-Marxist) secondary-historical literature.[3] Historians and social scientists in various disciplines have used Marxist categories – social relations of production, labour-process, laws of motion, class-struggle, the state – to produce historically grounded analyses of concrete societies. In a period when subjectivist and idealist frameworks such as postmodernism have had a profound influence on the intellectual Left, this critical-Marxist historical research has re-affirmed that the purpose of theory is to *explain the material world*.

This engagement of critical Marxism with historical data has not only deepened our understanding of actual history, but has helped revive Marxian theory. The 'political Marxists' (I would prefer '*Capital*-centric Marxists')[4] have re-affirmed the centrality of social-property relations with strong rules of reproduction to historical materialism. They reject teleological interpretations of history, where some transhistorical dynamic – the growth of markets or the development of the productive forces – explains the transition from one form of social labour to another. Instead, political Marxism emphasises the *random* – unpredictable – outcome of class-struggles in preserving, restructuring, or transforming different forms of social labour.

The inability to grasp the roots of economic development in the specific dynamics of different social-property relations limits the existing historiography of the antebellum-US, despite voluminous empirical research. The extensive historical research has been unable to produce an effective synthesis that incorporates the logic of plantation-slavery in the South, the social character of family-farming in the North, or the trajectory of the US-economy in the

---

[2] Marx 1981, p. 927.
[3] Wickham 2007 collects some of these contributions.
[4] The best synthetic presentations of the contributions of 'political Marxism' to the renewal of historical materialism are Wood 1995 and 1999. A similar perspective on historical materialism can be found in Bensaïd 2002.

eighteenth and nineteenth centuries. As a result, most of the existing explanations of the origins of the US Civil War privilege autonomous political and ideological factors, while ignoring the deep social roots of the conflict. This book is not, to any significant extent, based on original, primary historical research. However, it exhaustively reviews the existing historical literature, uncovering conceptual and empirical inconsistencies, and suggests how a rigorous understanding of social-property relations can transcend these limits and raise new questions for further research and debate.

Together, these essays offer the outlines of an alternative explanation of the origins of capitalism in the US, and the social origins of the US Civil War. Briefly, the dominance of non-capitalist social-property relations in both the South (plantation-slavery) and North (independent household-production) produced a pattern of extensive, *non-capitalist* economic growth in British North-American colonies. While the class-struggles during and after the American Revolution revived plantation-slavery in the South, these same struggles effectively subordinated northern family-farming to 'market-coercion', forcing rural household-producers to specialise output, innovate technically, and accumulate land and tools. The result was a pronounced regional economic uneven and combined development. In the North, agrarian petty-commodity production provided a growing home-market for industrial capital. In the South, the dominance of plantation-slavery blocked the deepening of the social division of labour and industrial development. The growing sectional conflict over the future class-structure of the territories conquered from Mexico in 1844–6 was rooted in the contradictory requirements of the reproduction of plantation-slavery and capitalist agriculture and industry in the mid-nineteenth century. Ultimately, four years of Civil War destroyed plantation-slavery in the South and secured the dominance of capitalist agriculture and industry in the northern and western United States, while creating new, non-capitalist relations in the South.

These essays have been the result of over three decades of intellectual work, and thus embody the *evolution* of my thought on the origins of capitalism and the Civil War in the US. Put another way, my analysis did not emerge fully formed, but was developed through a deepening encounter with the historical and theoretical literature.

The first chapter was written in 1980 and published in *New Left Review* in 1982. 'The American Road to Capitalism' was the first approximation of my argument that the uneven and combined development of social-property relations in the antebellum-US determined the class-conflicts that culminated in the Civil War. While central elements of this thesis remain intact, the essay does reflect a particular phase of my intellectual development. The heady years of graduate-studies in historical sociology at SUNY-Binghamton from 1977 through 1983 imparted a certain Althusserian cast to some of my theoretical formulations – 'articulation of forms and modes of production', 'determination in the last instance' – while substantive issues concerning the transformation of northern household-production and the determinants of technical change under plantation-slavery remain undeveloped.

Thirteen years separate the publications of the first and second chapters. During these years, I put my scholarly work on hold, devoting most of my time and energy to political activism – opposing the bureaucracy in the United Federation of Teachers, which represent public-school teachers in New York City; and building Solidarity, a small socialist organisation in the US – and raising my daughter, Rosa. During that time, the attractions of Althusserianism – its obscure language and notion of history as a 'process without a subject' – faded, as many of its leading proponents abandoned materialism for poststructuralist and postmodernist variants of idealism.

In the early 1990s, I returned to the academy and renewed my work, focusing first on the transformation of northern household-agriculture. The result was 'The Agrarian Origins of US Capitalism: The Transformation of the Northern Countryside Before the Civil War', which appeared in the *Journal of Peasant Studies* in 1995. In this essay, I specify how the class-struggles between merchants and farmers in the 1780s and 1790s effectively transformed rural household-production, unleashing the nineteenth century northern agricultural and industrial revolutions.

Over the next years, I turned to the massive literature on comparative plantation-slavery in the Americas. The third chapter, 'Plantation-Slavery and Economic Development in the Antebellum-Southern United States' was originally published in the *Journal of Agrarian Change* in 2002. The essay marks a refinement of my understanding of the *differentia specifica* of slave- and capitalist social-property relations, greater clarity about the complex determinants of technical change and geographical expansion under plantation-slavery, and the roots of the near universal tendency of slave-owners to make their plantations self-sufficient in food stuffs and other inputs. Put another way,

I was able to establish a firmer conceptual and comparative-historical foundation for my argument that plantation-slavery was an obstacle to the deepening of the social division of labour and industrial development in the US in the two decades before the Civil War.

The next phase of my investigation of the origins of capitalism involved looking backward, reviewing the literature on economy of the British North-American colonies in the eighteenth century, in order to determine more precisely the social roots and consequences of the American Revolution. The fourth chapter, 'Agrarian Class-Structure and Economic Development in Colonial British North America: The Place of the American Revolution in the Origins of Capitalism in the US' was published in the *Journal of Agrarian Change* in 2009. There, I grapple with the historical debates on the colonial economy, and examine the process of state-building in the post-Revolutionary years, deepening my analysis of the roots of the growing uneven and combined regional development in the differential outcome of class-conflict in the North and South after the Revolution.

The fifth chapter, a version of which appears as part of a symposium on the US Civil War in *Historical Materialism*, attempts to bring together the various strands of my research into the outline of a new, synthetic social interpretation of the War. In this effort, I was fortunate to have John Ashworth's monumental two-volume work, *Slavery, Capitalism and Politics in the Antebellum Republic* as an intellectual foil. This essay reviews Ashworth's arguments, raises several fundamental criticisms and strives to integrate his insights into a new explanation of the War rooted in the specific historical path to capitalism in the United States. While reaffirming my central thesis – that four years of bloody war and revolution were rooted in the concrete-historical contradictions between the social conditions of the expanded reproduction of capitalism and plantation-slavery in the 1840s and 1850s – the essay challenges my earlier, and facile use of the notion of the bourgeois revolution to understand the Civil War. Finally, the conclusion – the only essay written exclusively for this book – utilises Ellen Wood's discussions of the contradictions and limits of democracy under capitalism to analyse the class-struggle during Reconstruction, and to encourage Marxists to jettison the notion of the bourgeois-democratic revolution.

Chapter One

The American Road to Capitalism

This essay is an attempt to examine the theoretical and historiographical debates on the development of capitalism in the United States between 1790 and 1877. The realisation of the necessary conditions for capitalist production in the United States took place through the articulation, expanded reproduction and transformation of three forms of production, and through a process of political class-struggle that culminated in the Civil War. Each of these forms of production – slavery, petty-commodity production and capitalist manufacture – has been the subject of theoretical and historiographical controversy. These debates will be reviewed in order to determine the place of each productive form in the development of US-capitalism. The Civil War's place in the history of US-capitalist development has also been the subject of well-known controversy; these discussions will be scrutinised to determine how the class-struggle that culminated in the War affected capitalist development in the United States.

I. Plantation-slavery

The overall question of the relationship between plantation-slavery as a social system and the development of American capitalism must be apprehended, first of all, through a survey of discrete historiographical debates on slavery's profitability, its relations of production, its impact on the South's social division of labour and industrialisation, and its contribution to the total volume of commodity-circulation within the boundaries of the antebellum United States. Only through a careful examination of the empirical and theoretical issues posed by each of these debates can we ultimately arbitrate in what manner slavery was either an obstacle or spur to the process of national capitalist development.

The question of slavery's profitability was initially raised in 1905 with the publication of U.B. Phillips's article, 'The Economic Costs of Slaveholding in the Cotton Belt'.[1] Arguing on the basis of price-series for cotton and prime male fieldhands, Phillips claimed that plantation-production was an increasingly unprofitable investment in the antebellum-period, and that the only profits gained from slave-owning were derived from the speculative purchase and sale of the slaves themselves. Phillips's thesis remained the orthodox view of the subject for over fifty years until it was contested by Conrad and Meyer in 1958.[2] Utilising the more sophisticated statistical tools of neoclassical economics, Conrad and Meyer asserted that slavery was actually a comparatively profitable investment compared with other sectors of the antebellum-economy. While technical questions concerning the exact rate of return on plantation-investments remain unanswered,[3] it is clear that slave-production of cotton was a profitable investment prior to 1860. However, the implications of this profitability for the social character of slavery remain open to question.

On the basis of further research into the profitability of slavery, two economic historians, Robert Fogel and Stanley Engerman, have claimed that Southern plantation-slavery was a capitalist form of commodity-production, governed by profit-maximisation and characterised by the efficient allocation of factors of production.[4] Leaving aside the massive critical literature on Fogel and Engerman's 'cliometric' techniques and use of evidence,[5] we must consider the theoretical implications of the attempt to build a concept of capitalist production on the basis of profit-maximisation and commodity-production.

---

[1] Phillips 1905.
[2] Conrad and Meyer 1958.
[3] Most of the contributions to the debate are reprinted in Aitkin 1971. See also Fogel and Engerman 1974 and Wright 1978.
[4] Fogel and Engerman 1974, pp. 67–78.
[5] David et al. 1976; and Gutman 1975.

Fogel and Engerman are not alone in conceiving of American plantation-slavery as a capitalist form of production. A number of writers from outside the tradition of the 'new economic history', including Lewis Gray, Louis Hacker and Immanuel Wallerstein,[6] have characterised plantation-slavery in the American South as a variant of capitalist production on the basis of its commodity-producing and profit-maximising character. While Wallerstein's 'world-systemic' perspective allows us to grasp the relationship of US slavery to the development of industrial capitalism in England, and in other parts of the emergent capitalist world-economy, the notion that slavery is a variant of capitalist production tends to obscure the specificity of slave- and capitalist relations of surplus-appropriation and their effects on the dynamics of their respective labour-processes.

Fogel and Engerman's arguments concerning the capitalist character of plantation-slavery bring out the problems with this conception most clearly. Fogel and Engerman locate the source of plantation-slavery's profitability in the high quality and productivity of black slave-labour, which combined with the plantation's factor-combination, made the Southern plantation equally or more efficient and productive than other forms of agriculture in the antebellum-period. The source of this high-quality, efficient and productive black labour under slavery was the internalisation by the slave-population, through numerous non-coercive incentives offered by the planters, of the 'Protestant work ethic' of the master-class.[7] Fogel and Engerman's claims concerning the nature of labour-productivity and the determinations of plantation-profits are contradicted by both their own evidence and recent research. Gavin Wright has convincingly argued that the source of the cotton-plantations' profitability was neither the high productivity of slave-labour, nor economies of scale achieved under the plantation-régime, but the demand for raw cotton by industrial capitalists in England, and the complete domination of the world-market for raw cotton by the plantations of the American South.[8] This

---

[6] Gray 1933, p. 302; Hacker 1947, pp. 280–320; Wallerstein 1976.

[7] Fogel and Engerman 1974, pp. 38–43, 144–57, 209–23. For a detailed criticism of their data on incentives and coercion in the plantation labour-process, see Gutman 1975, pp. 14–87.

[8] Wright 1978, pp. 90–106, 176–84.

produced continually high prices for raw cotton prior to the Civil War, which buoyed up the planters' profits.

In *Time on the Cross*, we are presented with a detailed description of the labour-process under slavery, which is purported to be highly efficient and productive.[9] However, when one scrutinises Fogel and Engerman's description of the plantation labour-process, one finds that it is characterised by gang-labour and the production and appropriation of absolute surplus-labour. The labour-process under slavery was organised to maximise the use of human labour in large, co-ordinated groups under the continual supervision of overseers and drivers. The instruments of production used were simple and virtually unchanged during the antebellum-period. Such a labour-process leaves only a few options to the planter seeking to increase labour-productivity: increasing the pace of work, increasing the amount of acreage each slave or slave-gang cultivated, or moving the plantation to more fertile soil. These methods of increasing labour-productivity expanded absolutely the amount of surplus-labour performed by the direct producers, while leaving the amount of necessary-labour performed constant. This stands in sharp contrast to the capitalist organisation of the labour-process, where labour-productivity is increased by the continual introduction of new instruments of production which reduce the amount of necessary labour performed in relation to surplus-labour.

Genovese and the 'irrationality' of slavery

Eugene Genovese, fully cognisant of the non-capitalist character of slavery's labour-process, has attempted to explain this by reference to slavery's non-capitalist relations of production. While making many advances over those who consider plantation-slavery a form of capitalism, Genovese's analysis remains theoretically unsatisfying. Genovese's characterisation of Southern slavery as non-capitalist rests on a comparison of the 'rationality' of capitalism with the 'irrationality' of plantation-slavery. Relying on Weber's discussion of slavery, Genovese sees four major irrational features of slavery:

> First, the master cannot adjust the size of his labor-force in accordance with business fluctuations.... Second, the capital outlay is much greater and riskier for slave labor than for free. Third, the domination of society by a planter

---

[9] Fogel and Engerman 1974, pp. 203–6.

class increases the risk of political influence in the market. Fourth, the prices of cheap labor usually dry up rather quickly, and beyond a certain point costs become excessively burdensome.[10]

These irrational features of slavery, combined with the non-bourgeois and aristocratic ideology of the planters, and their propensity toward conspicuous consumption, led to continual investment in more land and more slaves, rather than new and more productive instruments and tools, with consequent technological stagnation and low labour-productivity.[11]

Genovese's arguments remain theoretically problematic because of his failure to produce a concept of the necessary relations that constitute the slave-form of production, thereby weakening his analysis at two major points. First, the 'irrational' features of slavery he borrows from Weber are based on a comparison of the observable features of slavery with those of capitalism; no necessary relationships are drawn between the 'irrationality' of slavery and the 'rationality' of capitalism, and their respective relations of production. In particular, the inability of masters to adjust the size of their labour-force remains undetermined by the structure of the master-slave relation. This lack of theoretical specification leaves Genovese's analysis of slavery's dynamics at the level of abstracted empirical generalisation. Second, Genovese's failure to produce a concept of a slave-form of production forces him to rely on notions of 'human motivation' in his discussion of the productivity of slave-labour. Genovese relies heavily on the nineteenth-century English economist, J.E. Cairnes, for his discussion of the slave labour-process. According to Cairnes, the slave's unfree legal status deprives him of any interest in the production-process, making him a reluctant worker whose labour can be utilised only under close supervision of highly repetitive tasks. By making 'human motivation' a determination of labour-productivity, Genovese falls into a similar problematic as Fogel and Engerman. While Genovese's slaves are unmotivated labourers because of their lack of personal freedom; Fogel and Engerman's slaves are imbued with their masters' Protestant spirit which compels them to efficient labour and 'achievement under adversity'.

---

[10] Genovese 1967, p. 16.
[11] Genovese's empirical findings of a complete technical stagnation have to be revised in the light of recent research that shows a highly episodic process of technical change in the plantation-South. See Garrett 1978, Chapter 4.

By placing human motivation at the centre of their discussion of labour-productivity, Fogel, Engerman and Genovese ignore the structural determinations of labour-productivity given by the specific and antagonistic relations of
production in different forms of production.[12]

Neither the notion that slavery is a variant of capitalist production, nor
Genovese's formulations on the non-capitalist character of slavery are sat-
isfactory. Those who conceive of slavery as a form of capitalism ignore the
specificity of the relations of surplus-appropriation that define slavery and
capitalism; while Genovese fails to present a rigorous concept of the necessary relations that constitute slavery as a form of production. The conceptual
differentia specifica of slavery and capital as forms of social labour can be understood along the following lines: under capitalist social relations of production,
the direct producers are excluded from the effective possession of both the
means of production and subsistence. The direct producer enters the capitalist production-process as a *variable* element of production, capable of being
fired or replaced by machinery. This relation gives capital the powers of real
possession and the ability to introduce new techniques into the labour-process, increasing the productivity of labour and the appropriation of relative
surplus-labour. Under the relations of production that characterise slavery,
the direct producers enter the plantation-slavery production-process as *constant* elements of production, entitling them to access to the means of subsistence in order to reproduce their value as means of production. The character
of slaves as both direct producers and means of production, severely limits
the ability of the masters to regulate the size of their labour-force, burdening
the non-producers with inflexible costs of reproducing their direct producers. These structural features of slavery's antagonistic relations of production, which shape the daily economic class-struggle under plantation-slavery,
block the masters' ability to reorganise the labour-process through technical
innovation. The masters are forced to organise the production-process along
the lines of closely supervised gang-labour, making the only possible methods of increasing labour-productivity the intensification of labour and the
migration of production to more fertile soils. These forms of absolute surplus-
labour appropriation made geographical expansion (addition of more slaves
and more land) the most 'rational' mode for increasing production under

---

[12] Cairnes 1968; Fogel and Engerman 1974, pp. 258–64; Genovese 1967, pp. 43–4.

slavery – a tendency accentuated in the American South by soil-exhaustion and changes in textile-production to which slavery was subordinated.[13]

The non-capitalist character of plantation-slavery had important effects on the social division of labour and the development of industry in the antebellum-South. The 'traditional' historical interpretation of plantation-slavery's impact on Southern economic development emphasised the incompatibility of slavery with the development of industry. The advocates of this thesis pointed to several factors that posed obstacles to the industrial-capitalist development of the antebellum-South: the political hostility of the planters to the emergence of a wage-earning class, the small-scale of immigration to the South created by fears of slave-competition on the labour-market, and the shallow markets provided by the plantations for the products of industrial enterprises. Criticisms of 'traditionalism' have centred on the size of the market created by the plantations. Fogel and Engerman have challenged the notion that the plantations provided a small market for industrial goods. They claim that the 'traditionalists' estimates of per capita income in the South, including the incomes assigned to the slaves, are too low. Fogel and Engerman found that per capita income in the South was reasonably high compared with the antebellum-North and was growing at a faster rate. On the basis of these calculations, Fogel and Engerman concluded that the plantations could have provided a large and growing market for industrially produced commodities.[14]

Plantations and markets

There is a theoretical problem posed by the attempt to measure the size of the market provided by the plantations of the cotton-South with per capita income-statistics. Such an attempt obscures the fact that the size of the home-market for commodities, the depth of the social division of labour, is determined by the extent to which the means of production and means of subsistence are reproduced through commodity-circulation. In other words, the 'effective demand' generated is determined by the extent to which non-producers *purchase* objects and instruments of production, and direct

---

[13] For data on differential soil-productivity in the antebellum-South, see Foust and Swan 1970, pp. 44–5.
[14] For the 'traditional' historical approach see Parker 1970, pp. 115–26. Fogel and Engerman 1974, pp. 247–57.

producers *purchase* their means of consumption. As we have seen, slave-rela-
tions of production block the process of technical innovation, thus limiting
the demand generated by the cotton-plantation for objects and instruments
of production. This places definite limits to the development of industries
producing means of production. In addition, slaves have direct access to
means of subsistence provided by their masters. No matter how large the
amount of use-values the slaves *consume* (the basis of the various estimates
of slaves' 'per capita income'), the amount they *purchase* is negligible. This
feature of slavery's relations of exploitation block the emergence and expansion of industries producing means of consumption.[15]

In the antebellum-South, the structural isolation of the slave-plantation
from commodity-circulation was accentuated by the planters' attempts to
make the plantations 'self-sufficient' in food, clothing and tools. The slaves
produced both cotton as a commodity, and corn, livestock and certain tools
and implements as use-values.[16] This 'self-sufficiency' not only sheltered the
cotton-plantation from the fluctuations of the world cotton-market, but, by
removing the reproduction of the plantation production-unit from the sphere
of commodity-circulation, severely limited the development of the social division of labour in the South. The limitations of the development of the home-
market posed by slavery's relations of production and the 'self-sufficiency' of
the plantations had important implications for the development of non-slave
agriculture and industry in the South. The 'self-sufficiency' of the plantations
in foodstuffs meant that free farmers seeking to increase their production of
commodities found a negligible market on the cotton-plantations. This reinforced the tendency for non-cotton, non-slaveowning agricultural producers
in the South to remain outside of the sphere of commodity-production and
circulation.[17]

The shallow social division of labour in the Southern countryside, created
by the reproduction of both free farms and slave-plantations outside of the
sphere of commodity-relations, severely limited the development and diversification of industry. While industrial production did develop on the basis

---

[15] This discussion of the determination of the depth of the social division of labour
by the specificity of different relations of production is drawn from Lenin 1974,
pp. 37–43, 68–70, 184–8.
[16] Gallman 1970, pp. 2–24; Wright, 1978, pp. 55–74.
[17] Wright 1970.

of both free wage-labour and slave-rentals, the general diversification of industrial production was blocked by the shallow home-market created by plantation-slavery. As William Parker points out, the South lagged behind the North in all categories of industry, particularly the medium and large-scale production of iron, textile-machinery and agricultural implements. Industry and manufacture in the South was limited to resource-extraction (lumber, mining), plantation-auxiliary production (rope, ginning, sugar-refining), and the production of low-quality textiles and iron for the plantations' limited needs. In sum, the shallow home-market dictated by plantation-slavery left the South the least industrialised area in the antebellum-US.[18]

The 'self-sufficiency' of the plantations helps to answer questions concerning the role of the expansion of cotton-production in the expansion of commodity-production and circulation in the trans-Allegheny West. Douglas North, following upon the work of Louis Schmidt, claimed that, in the antebellum-period, the Southern plantations constituted a major market for Western foodstuffs.[19] Basing this assertion on the gross receipts of Western grain and flour at the port of New Orleans, North maintained that the expansion of Southern plantation-production was a spur to the expansion of commodity-production and circulation nationally. The first criticism of the North-thesis came with Albert Fishlow's 'Antebellum Interregional Trade Reconsidered'.[20] Fishlow began his challenge to North's thesis with a re-examination of the receipts for foodstuffs in the port of New Orleans. In disaggregating this data, Fishlow made two interesting discoveries. First, New Orleans was a major trans-shipping centre for Western foodstuffs from at least the 1830s through 1860. Approximately one-half of the Western commodities shipped to New Orleans were re-shipped to the Northeast. Second, by comparing the proportion of Western goods consumed in the South with the proportion of Western commodities shipped via New Orleans, Fishlow discovered that the South consumed no more than 20% to 25% of Western commodities. On the basis of these findings, Fishlow claimed that the plantation-South was not a major market for Western agricultural commodities, and that the major pattern of internal commodity-circulation prior to the Civil War was between the West

---

[18] Parker 1970, pp. 121–5. On the use of slaves in industrial production see Starobin 1970.

[19] North 1961. See also: Schmidt 1939.

[20] Fishlow 1965b.

and Northeast. Thus, the expansion of plantation-slavery, at least in terms of its direct effects on the development of agrarian petty-commodity production, cannot be seen as a spur to the process of capitalist development in ante-bellum-America.

What can we conclude from our discussion of plantation-slavery, concerning the place of this form of social labour in the process by which capitalist production's conditions of existence and dominance were realised? The expansion of cotton commodity-production on the basis of plantation-slavery was a spur, that was transformed into an obstacle, to the development of capitalism in the antebellum-American social formation. Moreover, the transition of commercial plantation-slavery from a spur to an obstacle was determined by the process by which merchant-capital created the conditions for its subordination to industrial capital. Northeastern merchants, who facilitated the trade of cotton with the capitalist world-market, accumulated mercantile wealth from the circulation of cotton. Cotton, as the major export of the antebellum-US, also created a favourable balance of trade and sound international credit for American merchants and bankers. The expansion of commercial slavery provided the basis for both the geographical expansion of merchant-capitalist operations (land-speculation) and the importation of money-capital from Europe for merchant-sponsored transportation-projects in the 1830s. As we shall see, the increase of commodity-production and circulation engendered through the agencies of merchant-capital brought agrarian petty production under the dominance of the law of value. This deepening of the social division of labour in the North transformed the agrarian West into the home-market for industrial capital, creating the conditions for the subordination of merchants to industrial capital in the 1840s and 1850s.

The emergence and rise to dominance of specifically capitalist production, on the basis of the expansion of agrarian petty-commodity production, transformed the geographical expansion of slavery into an obstacle to the development of capitalism. The expansion of plantation-slavery into the territories conquered from Mexico in 1845 would have posed economic and political obstacles to the dominance of industrial capital. Economically, the expansion of slavery would have stifled the development of agrarian petty-commodity production and the social division of labour, strangling the home-market for industrial capital. Politically, the expansion of slavery would have increased planter-representation in the federal government, which would have blocked the implementation of such pro-industrial capitalist state-policies as the Homestead Act and the protective tariff. In sum, the commodity-producing character of plantation-slavery was a catalyst to capitalist development as long as merchant-capital was the major agency for the expansion of commodity-production and the deepening of the social division of labour. As merchant-capital created the conditions for its subordination to industrial capital, by generalising commodity-relations in the Northern US, slavery's non-capitalist relations of production became an obstacle to the dominance and expanded reproduction of capitalist production in the US social formation.

II. Agrarian petty-commodity production

In contrast with the debates about plantation-slavery, where the crucial theoretical and conceptual issues remain embedded within historiographical controversy, analyses of agrarian petty-commodity production have found a much firmer conceptual basis. In particular, the exchange between James O'Connor and Robert Sherry,[21] though plagued by certain conceptual ambiguities, has posed the central questions concerning the concrete dynamics of family-farming in the antebellum-North and the place of this form of production in the process of primitive accumulation in the US. O'Connor's discussion of family-farming is introduced in the course of his critical review of Douglas Dowd's *The Twisted Dream*. Pointing to the deleterious theoretical effects of Dowd's reliance on Veblen's notions of 'business' and 'industry', O'Connor accuses Dowd of failing to recognise, 'the theoretical distinction between capitalism and independent commodity-production as modes of production'.[22] This conceptual failing leads Dowd to obscure what O'Connor sees as the obstacles posed by the 'independent mode' to the development of capitalism. According to O'Connor, independent commodity-production posed an obstacle to capitalist production in the antebellum-era because of its ability to provide the conditions of reproduction to the direct producers outside of the capitalist labour-market. In other words, independent commodity-production blocked the formation of a class of propertyless

---

[21] O'Connor 1975; Sherry 1976; O'Connor 1976.
[22] O'Connor 1975, p. 46.

wage-earners forced to sell their labour-power to capital in order to obtain means of consumption.

This analysis of the place of Northern agriculture in the process of capital-ist development prior to the Civil War is based on O'Connor's analysis of the laws of motion of the 'independent mode of production'.[23] According to O'Connor, the family-farms of the antebellum-Northeast and Middle West were 'subsistence' units of production. Marketing only their surplus-product, the family-farms were not dependent on commodity-circulation for the repro-duction of their means of production and subsistence. This autonomy of the 'independent mode' from the market in its economic reproduction had two consequences for this mode's relation to the development of capitalism. On the one hand, the isolation of the antebellum-farm from commodity-exchange meant that 'market-forces' alone were incapable of dislodging the direct pro-ducers from the effective ownership of the objects and instruments of pro-duction. This implies that the family-farm was a real historical alternative to wage-labour before the Civil War. On the other hand, the family-farm's logic of subsistence (which can be expressed in terms of the circuit, commodity-money-commodity; C-M-C), led to a stagnation of the productive forces. This implies that the 'independent mode's' dominance was an obstacle to the deepening of the social division of labour, the home-market for industrial capital.[24]

O'Connor concludes his discussion of the 'independent mode' with an his-torical description of the relation of this form of social labour to capitalist production.[25] According to O'Connor, the logic of subsistence governed the agricultural production of the Northern states before the Civil War, retarding the development of capitalism by robbing industrial capital of its needed sup-ply of wage-labour. Politically, the emergent industrialists needed the support of the Western subsistence farmers in their struggle against the planters. With the end of the War and the defeat of the planters, the industrialists 'betrayed' their farmer-allies and began to implement a series of state-policies designed

---

[23] O'Connor 1976, pp. 61–2.

[24] This is a consequence that O'Connor (1975, p. 48) fails to recognise when he claims that the family-farms did provide a mass-market for industrial capital.

[25] O'Connor 1975, pp. 47–52. O'Connor's analysis of pre-Civil-War Northern agri-culture and its transformation only after the War is shared by a number of authors: Kelly 1979; Merrill 1976; Luxemburg 1968, pp. 396–411.

to smash the 'independent mode of production'. Through railroad and mining land-grants, massive immigration and other state-policies, the industrial bourgeoisie destroyed the 'independent mode', opening the possibility of large-scale capitalist production in the late-nineteenth century.

Sherry's criticisms of O'Connor focus on the dynamics governing Northern agricultural production, the conceptual status of the notion of an 'independent mode of production', and the place of this form of production in the process of primitive accumulation. Sherry begins by making a basic re-assessment of the concrete dynamics governing the family-farm of the antebellum-North. For Sherry, the free farmers of the West and Northeast marketed not merely their surplus-product, but nearly their entire product. As a result, the free farmers of the antebellum-North were dependent on commodity-production and exchange for their economic reproduction, and were not governed by the circuit of subsistence (C-M-C), but by the circuit of competition and accumulation. (M-C-M'). The competitive and accumulationist dynamic forced the family-farmers to undertake the continual technical re-organisation of their labour-processes in order to survive. This process of competition, innovation and accumulation led to a process of concentration and centralisation of objects and instruments of production (tools, implements and land); a process of social differentiation into an agrarian petty bourgeoisie on the one hand, and a growing mass of propertyless wage-labourers on the other. These laws of motion, the product of the subordination of this productive form to the simplest form of the law of value,[26] lead Sherry to challenge O'Connor's notion that self-organised commodity-production constitutes a 'mode of production'. For Sherry, 'It does seem that for a social form to be elevated to the position of a mode of production, rather than being seen as an aspect of some other more encompassing mode of production, the form being considered must have an existence and a dynamic that can be isolated from those of all other social forms one considers to be modes of production.'[27] Since self-organised commodity-production shares a dynamic of accumulation with the

---

[26] On the operation of the law of the value in petty-commodity production, see Engels 1981, Mandel 1968, pp. 65–71; and Dobb 1976, pp. 60–5. While Dobb and Engels differ from Sherry on the question of whether petty-commodity production constitutes a 'mode of production', they share the view that this form of production is governed by a competitive and technically innovative dynamic.

[27] Sherry 1976, p. 55.

capitalist mode of production, Sherry rejects giving it the conceptual status of a 'mode of production'. Instead, Sherry conceives of self-organised commodity-production as a form of capitalist production, the 'petty-bourgeois form of capital'.

By recasting the laws of motion governing Northern agriculture prior to the Civil War, Sherry is able completely to alter O'Connor's interpretation of the place of this form of production in capitalist development.[28] Rather than an obstacle to capitalist development, family-farming in the North becomes a central mechanism in the emergence of manufacture and industry in the nineteenth century. The dependence of the family-farms on commodity-circulation for economic reproduction, and their continual improvement of their objects and instruments of production, made Northern agriculture into a massive home-market for capitalist produced means of production and consumption. The expansion of agricultural commodity-production stimulated the emergence of capitalist processing of agricultural produce. Nor did the Western frontier constitute an escape from wage-labour. As concentration and centralisation of farming raised the costs of establishing a viable farm, increasing numbers of ex-farmers and their children were forced into wage-labour. This interpretation transforms the petty-bourgeois farmers from a passive and foolish group, manipulated by the industrialists, into a class struggling to advance its position, by promoting the development of commodity-production and circulation.

Although Sherry's analysis marks a theoretical advance over O'Connor's notion of an 'independent mode of production', his concepts remain ambiguous in two areas: his analysis of Northern free farming as a form of capital, and his notion that the subordination of self-organised commodity-production to the dictates of the law of value is a 'natural' consequence of commodity-circulation. Sherry's analysis of Northern agricultural production as a form of capital rests on the fact that both forms of production are governed by the logic of self-expanding value, M-C-M', which Marx called the 'general formula for capital.'[29] It is only in this most general sense that self-organised commodity-production governed by the law of value can be conceived as a form of capital. The conception of capital solely as self-expanding value,

---

[28] Sherry 1976, pp. 57–60.
[29] Marx 1976, pp. 247–57.

shared by both O'Connor and Sherry, tends to obscure the fact that capital is a specific *relation*. The relation that characterises capital defines two antagonistic social classes, the bourgeoisie and the proletariat, which engage in a specific form of class-struggle. Self-organised commodity-production subordinated to the law of value defines only one class, the petty bourgeoisie. By conceiving of Northern farmers as 'capitalist' producers, Sherry runs the risk of conflating the class-location and appropriate forms of class-struggle of two distinct social classes, the bourgeoisie and the petty bourgeoisie. Such a conflation of these two classes could lead to ignoring the possible and specific antagonisms between the petty bourgeoisie and industrial capital. In the case of the political struggles in the antebellum-US, this conflation could lead to obscuring the changing class-alliances that produced the political crisis that led to the Civil War.[30] In order to maintain a clear understanding of the specific determinations of the class-location of the petty bourgeoisie and industrial bourgeoisie in their respective social relations of production, we will conceive of self-organised commodity-production governed by the law of value as petty-commodity production – a form of production, distinct from, but transitional to, the capitalist mode of production.

The second problem involved in Sherry's analysis of the dynamics of petty-commodity production is his assertion that the dependence of petty producers on commodity-production for their economic reproduction is a natural result of the logic of commodity-production and circulation. However, as Robert Brenner has pointed out, it is possible to conceive of situations where direct producers are not *compelled* to specialise and market increasingly large portions of their production.[31] In such situations, the direct producers maintain non-market access to their means of production and consumption. These producers are relatively impervious to the 'dictates of the market', and are under no competitive compulsion either to accumulate and innovate or to lose possession of their means of economic reproduction. Sherry's conception poses a dual problem. On the one hand, the possible existence of forms of commodity-production governed by a logic of subsistence is denied, making all historical forms of self-organised commodity-production merely 'moments' in the

---

[30] For the most rigorous discussion to date of the petty bourgeoisie and its specific forms of class-struggle, see Poulantzas 1975, pp. 191–336.
[31] Brenner 1977, pp. 51–5, 73–5.

inevitable and teleological emergence of capitalist production. On the other hand, Sherry's conception can lead to ignoring the specific historical mechanisms by which self-organised commodity-production is subordinated to the law of value in the process of primitive accumulation.

Demythologising the family-farm

We can conceive of the possible existence of two forms of self-organised commodity-production. One form is governed by a logic of subsistence, the result of the independence from commodity-production. This form is a variant of what Lenin and Luxemburg described as 'patriarchal peasant' or 'natural economy',[32] which poses obstacles to the development of capitalist production along the path suggested by O'Connor. The other form is governed by the law of value, the result of its production-units' dependence on commodity-production for their economic reproduction. Petty-commodity production does not pose any obstacle to capitalist development and can, in fact, be a spur to it along the lines discussed by Sherry. The question of which of these two forms of self-organised commodity-production characterised free farming in the antebellum-North can only be answered by reference to the historiographical material.

As Sherry points out, O'Connor's historical analysis of the dynamics of free farming and its place in the process of primitive accumulation in antebellum-America is based on a 'very common and ancient populist interpretation of American farmers'.[33] The major representatives of this populist historiography are Mary and Charles Beard and Fredrick Jackson Turner.[34] The research of Turner and his students found the antebellum-Northwest to be occupied by sturdy independent farmers, who, through selling a portion of their produce, were self-sufficient in foodstuffs and either made their own farm-implements or bought them from a village-blacksmith. Technological innovation in the agrarian labour-process was slow and competition among farmers was limited. Little concentration of landholdings took place, and with a vast area open to settlement, the West was a 'safety-valve' for impoverished farmers and urban workers seeking to escape permanent wage-labour. While Turner's

---

[32] Luxemburg 1968, Chapters 27 and 29; Lenin 1974, pp. 42–3, 175–90.
[33] Sherry 1976, p. 58.
[34] Beard and Beard 1927, Part I; Turner 1893.

schema did allow for the eventual subordination of independent farmers to the pressures of the market, the ever-expanding frontier allowed for subsistence-production to be continually renewed both before and after the Civil War. If Turner and the Beards' historical description of antebellum-Northern agriculture was accurate, then O'Connor analysis of antebellum-history would be substantially correct. Northern free farming would be governed by a dynamic of subsistence which would produce technical stagnation of the labour-process, the limitation of the development of the social division of labour, and would provide an escape for a large portion of the population from wage-labour. Through these processes, the development of capitalist production prior to the Civil War would be retarded, and northern agriculture, a form of 'natural economy', would stand in an antagonistic relationship with capitalism.

Unfortunately for O'Connor, research on antebellum-agriculture in the North and West since the 1930s has progressively challenged the description of the Beards and Turner. The general trend of historical research has produced a description of antebellum-agriculture more in line with Sherry's analysis: the development of Northern agriculture was governed by the dynamics of petty-commodity production, not those of 'natural economy'. By the 1840s and 1850s, at the latest, agrarian self-organised commodity-production in the Northeast and West was governed by the law of value. Merchant-capital, through the mechanisms of land-law, land-speculation and the promotion of internal improvements, was responsible for the enforced dependence of free farmers on commodity-production for their economic reproduction. In particular, federal land-policy promoted the transformation of land into a commodity through the public auction of the public domain. This policy encouraged the speculative purchasing of large blocks of land, which forced actual settlers to purchase land from large land-companies at prices well above the minimal prices charged by the federal government. The cost of land-purchases and the burden of mortgages to the land-company forced the farmers to specialise their crops and increase their production of commodities, thus becoming dependent on the sphere of commodity-circulation for their economic reproduction.[35] The merchants also promoted internal improvements projects, such

---

[35] Gates 1942.

as canals and railways in the 1820s and 1830s, which lowered the costs of commodity-circulation, further promoting commodity-production.

The subordination of free farming to the law of value unleashed a process of increasing labour-productivity, technical innovation and social differentiation in the 1840s and 1850s. This period saw a sharp rise in the productivity of the farms of the old Northwest and the eastern Great Plains. This increase in the productivity of labour was accomplished through the introduction of labour-saving farm-implements, such as the mechanical reaper, new seed-drills and new ploughs.[36] This technical innovation aided in sharpening social differentiation in the West by raising the costs of 'farm-building', the costs of establishing a commercially viable farm. This process of social differentiation not only led to the dispossession of many petty producers, but effectively eliminated any opportunity for urban workers to 'escape' wage-labour by settling in the West. For, as the critics of Turner have demonstrated, the cost of establishing a commercially viable farm in the late-antebellum West was beyond the means of even the most well-paid and thrifty skilled worker.[37]

The development and expansion of Northern agriculture was shaped by the dynamics of petty-commodity production, not those of 'natural economy'. The subordination of self-organised commodity-production to the dictates of the law of value, through the activities of merchant-capital and merchant-sponsored state-policies, had been completed by the late 1830s. From the early 1840s until the end of the nineteenth century, the expansion of petty-commodity production was the main motor for the expansion of industrial capital. The expansion of petty-commodity production deepened the social division of labour, the home-market for capitalist production of means of production and consumption. As we shall see, agrarian petty-commodity production in the antebellum-period laid the basis for the development of an 'agro-industrial complex', a series of capitalist industries producing farm-implements and supplies and processing farm-produce.[38] This process of capitalist expansion, based on the subordination of petty-commodity production to the capitalist mode of production, faced only one obstacle prior to 1860: the expansion of

---

[36] Parker and Klein 1966.
[37] Danhof 1941.
[38] Aglietta 1978, pp. 19–21; Davis 1978, pp. 218–19.

the slave-form of production, which would strangle industrial capital's home-market and block its political policies at the level of the state.

III. Capitalist manufacture and industry

Our discussion of capitalist manufacture and industry will revolve around three central problems: the process by which an industrial working class was formed; the origins of the industrial bourgeoisie; and the nature of the 'vanguard'-branches of production in the capitalist industrialisation of the US. The first two problems, the formation of an industrial bourgeoisie and proletariat, directly confront the question of the process by which the basic elements of capitalist production come into existence. The third problem, the identification of the 'vanguard'-branches of industrial production, will allow us to determine precisely how non-capitalist forms of production, such as slavery and petty-commodity production, were either obstacles or motors of capitalist development in the antebellum-US.

There is a general historiographical consensus on the formation of the antebellum-American proletariat.[39] Prior to the 1840s, the differentiation of artisan-producers and the progressive impoverishment of New-England farm-families produced an industrial and manufacturing labour-force. However, the restricted size of the available labour-force posed problems for industrial capital, especially in cotton-textile production. Various methods of securing an adequate labour-supply were introduced in cotton and other industries; the 'Waltham'-system of employing single young women and housing them in company-dormitories, and the 'Rhode Island' system of employing entire families who were paid in script redeemable at company-owned stores and housing offices. Both systems aimed to secure an adequate supply of labour-power for industrial capital, and to muffle the class-struggle between labour and capital by creating 'paternalistic' cultural-ideological bonds between the two antagonistic classes. In both respects, these systems of labour-power procurement met with only limited success. Labour-power remained scarce and costly; and trade-union organisations, albeit unstable, emerged in the cotton-industry and other branches of production in the 1820s and 1830s.

---

[39] Gutman 1973.

In the 1840s and 1850s, the obstacle to the development of capitalism posed by the shortage of labour-power was overcome by massive immigration from Europe. While immigration had taken place in the 1820s and 1830s, its volume was so small as to have little impact on the supply of labour-power to capital. In the 1840s, the volume of immigration tripled, and doubled again in the 1850s. The commercial crisis of the mid-1840s, the potato-famine in Ireland, and the active recruitment of immigrant-workers by industrial capital produced this increase in the numbers of immigrants to the US in the twenty years prior to the Civil War. This massive inflow of workers, which could be conceived as capital's response to native labour's economic militancy, made the 'Waltham'- and 'Rhode-Island' systems redundant by creating the first permanent reserve-army of labour in the US. Until the early twentieth century, European and Asian immigration would continually re-shape and supplement the American working class, giving this proletariat certain of its specific political and ideological characteristics.

In contrast to the historiographical consensus on the process by which the industrial working class was constituted, there is considerable disagreement on the origins of the industrial bourgeoisie in the US. At the centre of the debate is the question of what was the major source of industrial capital prior to the Civil War: the savings of artisanal petty producers or the wealth of merchants in the Northeastern commercial centres. While this debate has not, for the most part, been conducted within a Marxist framework, it does address certain questions raised by Marx's discussion of the 'two roads' to capitalist production in the third volume of *Capital*. According to Marx, the transition to capitalist production can proceed along two paths:

> The producer may become a merchant and capitalist, in contrast to the agricultural natural economy and the guild-bound handicraft of the medieval urban industry. This is the really revolutionary way. Alternatively, however, the merchant may take direct control of production himself. But however this occurs as a historical transition...it cannot bring about the overthrow of the old mode of production by itself, but rather preserves and retains it as its own precondition.[40]

---

[40] Marx 1981, p. 452.

The first and 'really revolutionary path' to capitalist industry is clear: the artisan becomes petty-commodity producer, competes and accumulates. The competition among petty producers leads to a process of social differentiation, where the more productive direct producers become capitalists and purchase the labour-power of their less productive neighbours who have lost the effective possession of their means of production. The second path is more problematic, for it is not a path to capitalist production proper. Historically, the second path referred to the out-work, or *verlag*, system organised by merchant-monopolists, which increased the volume of commodity-production, but preserved the relations of production and the labour-process of artisanal production. In attempting to resolve the problems presented by the 'second path', Marx offers us another variant of this path, in which, 'the merchant becomes an industrialist directly'.[41] In other words, the second path can be conceived as the process by which merchant-capital withdraws from the sphere of commodity-circulation, purchases means of production and hires wage-labourers, becoming industrial capital proper.

The historiographical discussion of the origins of the industrial bourgeoisie in the US can be seen as revolving around Marx's typology of the paths to capitalist production: the 'artisan'-road or the 'merchant'-road. The supporters of the hypothesis that merchants were the prime movers of capitalist industry in the antebellum-period, such as Lance Davis, have based their arguments on the financing of the New-England textile-industry.[42] Although small firms established by skilled artisans did dominate cotton-textile production prior to 1815, they were rapidly displaced by the development of large-scale industrial production in the late 1810s and 1820s. The cotton-factories established after the War of 1812 were financed by large merchants who sought alternative investments after the decline of the American carrying trade. As Davis has shown, merchants in cotton and other commodities were both the main purchasers of the stock of cotton-textile firms, and the major source of both long and short-term industrial credit. On the basis of the fact that cotton-textiles were the first fully 'mechanised' and capitalist industry in the US, Davis and Ware concluded that the dominant path to capitalist production was the direct transformation of merchants into industrial capitalists.

---

[41] Marx 1981, p. 453.
[42] Davis 1960.

In contrast, other historians have argued that the main path to industrial capitalist production was through the differentiation of artisanal producers. Supporters of this position (Louis Hacker and Herbert Gutman) have based their arguments on the study of industries other than cotton-textiles: iron, farm-implements, railroad-supplies and machine-making.[43] Beginning with the observation that the shift from commerce to industry was unique to a small group of New-England merchants, proponents of this hypothesis have sought the origins of the industrial bourgeoisie in the self-exploitation and accumulation of skilled artisans. Some of these skilled artisans, particularly in locomotive- and machine-production, began as skilled workers in the textile-machine shops that were part of most textile-mills prior to the 1830s. Other artisans, particularly in farm-implements and iron-production, began as blacksmiths and small-scale refiners of iron. Through self-exploitation and partnerships with well-off petty-bourgeois farmers and shopkeepers, these skilled artisans and workers were able to acquire additional objects and instruments of production, hire wage-labourers, and transform themselves into industrial capitalists. For these historians, the role of merchant-capital was marginal to the development of an industrial bourgeoisie, limited to making occasional loans and marketing commodities produced by the artisan *cum* capitalist.

The 'really revolutionary' path

Neither of these historiographical theses, either of the transformation of merchants into industrialists or the autonomous emergence of industrial capitalists from the ranks of the artisanal petty bourgeoisie, is historically complete. Those who see a variant of Marx's 'second path' as dominant, base their assertions on very shaky empirical evidence. Not only was cotton-textile production unique in the transformation of merchants into industrialists, but, as we shall see, the centrality given to cotton-textiles in the industrial revolution in the US by most economic historians is misplaced. However, those historians who see the origins of the American industrial bourgeoisie solely in the self-exploitation and differentiation of artisanal petty producers tend to obscure the complex historical relationship between merchant- and industrial capital in the antebellum-period.

---

[43] Hacker 1947, pp. 257–66; Gutman 1977.

While 'men of small means', skilled workers and artisans, were the major agents of the organisation of capitalist production in the antebellum-era, they were very dependent upon merchant-capital for both long, and short-term credit.[44] While merchants rarely took up the powers of industrial capital to allocate productive resources or re-organise the labour-process, their control of money-capital ensured their dominance over industrial capital before the Civil War. In the 1840s and 1850s, however, some manufacturers, especially those producing means of production, began to dispense with the services of merchants, as their markets became centralised with the concentration of various industries. But it was only during the Civil War that the majority of industrial capitalists were able to break from financial dependence upon merchants, and subordinate merchant-capital to the logic of industrial capital. In sum, the origins of the American industrial bourgeoisie are found in the social differentiation and transformation of artisanal petty producers, not in the direct transformation of merchants into industrial capitalists. However, the transformation of the artisanal petty bourgeoisie into an industrial bourgeoisie did not take place simply through the self-exploitation of the petty producers. Merchant-capital, as the source of money-capital in the form of credit, was able to maintain its dominance over industry until the Civil War.

In the light of the historical experience of the US, we can begin to refine Marx's cursory discussion of the first, 'really revolutionary' path to capitalist production. The path by which the direct producer becomes her/his own merchant, and is transformed into a capitalist, must not be conceived in a highly abstract manner. The emergence of an industrial bourgeoisie through the autonomous self-exploitation of artisans and skilled workers has occurred very rarely, it at all. Instead, merchant-capital intervenes in the process of the social differentiation of petty producers as the primary source of money-capital to continue and expand production. The 'revolutionary' path must be conceived in terms of the process by which the artisanal petty-commodity producers come to exercise the characteristic powers of industrial capital, those of economic ownership and real possession. This road to capitalist production implies a two-fold struggle on the part of the artisanal petty bourgeoisie *cum* industrial capital; to secure an adequate supply of labour-power, and to gain independence from, and subordinate to its own logic, merchant-capital.

---

[44] Livesay and Porter 1971.

Our discussion of the origins of industrial capital in the United States has already touched upon the question of the 'vanguard' – or leading branches of capitalist production in the antebellum-period. While certain business-historians, such as Alfred Chandler, define leading branches of industry solely in terms of innovations in the internal organisation of the firm, a more comprehensive definition is needed.[45] Leading or vanguard-branches of capitalist industry are characterised by both innovative labour-processes and by their revolutionising effects on the social division of labour. In other words, a central characteristic of a leading complex of branches of production is its ability to call forth new developments in the labour-process and create new branches of production in Department I (the department of social production producing objects and instruments of production).

The majority of the historians of antebellum-American industrialisation have drawn their explanatory model from the English Industrial Revolution.[46] Both Marxist and bourgeois historians of American industrial capital have given the 'vanguard'-role to the textile-, shoe/boot-, and railroad-industries in the American industrial revolution. According to this model, the development of textile- and shoe/boot-production were characterised by the first development of specifically capitalist labour-processes, and these industries, along with the railroads, called into existence new machine-making industries and innovations in the production of iron.[47] Such a conception has led Allen Dawley, in his study of the class-struggle in the Massachusetts shoe-industry to claim that the shoe-industry constituted a 'microcosm of the industrial revolution' in the US.[48] According to the traditional historiography of American capitalist industrialisation, the US parallels Great Britain in terms of its leading branches of production and their effects on the social division of labour. However, this traditional historiographical model is both conceptually and historically flawed. Conceptually, the adaptation of a model of capitalist development based on empirical generalisations from the British example obfuscates the concrete historical specificity of different social formations' processes of capitalist development. Historically, the 'textiles'-model

---

[45] Chandler 1965.
[46] For a thorough discussion of the specificity of the English Industrial Revolution, see Hobsbawm 1969.
[47] Dawley 1976.
[48] Dawley 1976, pp. 1–6.

fails to account for the much more central role played by the 'agro-industrial complex' in the development of capitalist industry in the US both before and after the Civil War.

The complex of industries producing farm-machinery, tools and supplies, and processing agricultural raw materials (meat-packing, leather-tanning, flour-milling and baking), were at the centre of the American industrial revolution. These branches of production were characterised by both technical innovation in their labour-process and either constituted or stimulated transformations in key branches of Department I. Farm-implement and machine-production alone made up 19.4% of all machine-production by 1860, rising to 25.5% by 1870.[49] While statistical data on the consumption of iron by different industries is not available for the antebellum-period, the transformation of northern agriculture and the formation of the agro-industrial complex was a major determinant of the technical development of the American iron-industry. Louis Hunter has argued that the centralisation of and technical innovations in the processes that constituted iron-production in the 1840s and 1850s were determined by changes in the character or the market for iron-goods.[50] The replacement of rural blacksmiths and farmers, who required high-quality and versatile bar-iron to produce a wide variety of products, by specialised industrial producers, who required lower-quality and less-versatile iron for a smaller number of commodities, was the main impetus for technical change in the late-antebellum iron-industry. This advance in the social division of labour, the transition from rural to specialised industrial producers, was the product of the subordination of agrarian production to the law of value. Commodities that farmers had purchased from local blacksmith or had made themselves were now produced by capitalist industries who purchased their raw materials from a technically-transformed iron-industry.

Thus, in the late-antebellum period (1840–60), the basis for the later acceleration of US industrial capitalism in the 'Gilded Age' was laid with the development of agrarian petty-commodity production and the agro-industrial complex. Only one obstacle stood in the way of this 'frontier-régime of accumulation': the geographical expansion of plantation-slavery. It was this economic

---

[49] Computed from US Department of Commerce 1865, pp. clxxvii–ccxvi; US Department of Commerce 1872, pp. 588–9, 614–5.
[50] Hunter 1929.

contradiction between the necessary conditions for the expansion of slavery and capitalism in the 1840s and 1850s that determined, in the last instance, the political class-struggles that culminated in the Civil War of 1861–5.

IV. Conclusion: the Civil War

It remains to briefly consider the impact of the Civil War on the American social formation.[51] Prior to the 1960s, Civil-War historiography was dominated by the belief that the War dramatically spurred the growth of industrialism. As espoused by its main representatives, the Beards and Hacker,[52] this tradition argued that the War galvanised industrial capitalism both economically and politically. On the one hand, the war-economy with its inflation, lucrative government-contracts and contract-immigration stimulated the reorganisation of industrial labour-processes and vastly increased the volume of production. On the other hand, the War allowed the political representatives of the rising industrial bourgeoisie to secure hegemony within the federal state-apparatus and to pass a series of policies – tariff- and monetary reform, unrestricted immigration, the Homestead Act, and so on – which secured the conditions for untrammelled industrial expansion.

The Beards-Hacker view of the Civil War was unchallenged historical orthodoxy until the publication of Thomas C. Cochran's 'Did the Civil War Retard Industrialization?' in 1961, which attempted to statistically demolish their interpretation.[53] Utilising new statistical series produced by the economist Robert Gallman, Cochran examined the differential performance of the American industrial economy before, during and after the War. His calculations showed that American industry as a whole, measured in terms of value added by manufacture, grew at a slower rate in the 1860s than during the 1850s. Pig-iron, textile- and railroad-production all displayed sharp declines in their growth-rates during the war-years compared to the five-year periods immediately preceding and following 1861–5. Coal-output remained more or less constant. Cochran therefore concluded that the Civil War, far from catalysing industrialisation, actually retarded its 'normal' expansion.

---

[51] A discussion of these problems is contained in Post 1983.
[52] Beard and Beard 1927, Chapter XVIII; Hacker 1947, pp. 339–439.
[53] Cochran 1961.

The historiographical debate sparked by Cochran's revisionist essay is only today coming to a close. In a recent article summarising the voluminous literature, Steven Engelbourg has concluded that the war-economy was neither an impetus to the reorganisation of the labour-process nor to increased output in strategic industries.[54] On the other hand, wartime-inflation did provide a powerful lever for changing the relationship between merchant- and industrial capital. As Livesay and Porter have pointed out, manufacturers' 'profit inflation' – manifested in an increased cash-flow and combined with wartime-rationalisation of the currency-system – allowed the industrialists to liquidate their debts to merchants and break their financial dependence upon merchant-capital (while, at the same time, opening up room for the proliferation of new banking capital).[55]

But the direct economic impact of the war on industrial capitalism was secondary to the War's *political* effects on capitalist development through the remainder of the nineteenth century. As Stephen Salsbury – one of Cochran's earliest critics – pointed out, the central thesis of Beards and Hacker was that the Civil War constituted a second phase of the American bourgeois revolution, which consolidated the hegemony of industrial capital at the level of the state.[56] Salsbury emphasised that Cochran's claims that the War retarded industrial capitalist development only confused the economic stimulants or obstacles to industrial expansion posed by the war-economy with the changes in political class-relations and state-policies that resulted from the victory of industrial capital. The effects of these political changes on the accumulation of capital are seen in the comparisons Salsbury made, again using Gallman's statistics, between the rate of growth of production in iron, coal and railroad-lines in the decades before and after the Civil War. In all three branches of production, the growth-rate in the decade 1865–75 was considerably higher than in the decade 1850–60. From these comparisons, Salsbury asserted that the state-policies implemented by the industrial-capitalist-led Republican bloc during the War removed obstacles and provided a powerful impetus to the expanded reproduction of capital.

---

[54] Engelbourg 1979. The major contributions to the debate on War's economic impact are collected in Andreano 1966.
[55] Livesay and Porter 1971, pp. 116–30.
[56] Salsbury 1966.

What were the state-policies implemented by the Republican industrial bourgeoisie during the Civil War and how did they secure the conditions for the expanded reproduction of capital in the United States? The first was the abolition of slavery, a measure forced upon the industrial bourgeoisie by military exigencies and the struggle of the slaves. Although the class-struggles in the Reconstruction-period did not result in emergence of either capitalist plantation-agriculture or the formation of a black petty-bourgeois farmer-class; the non-capitalist form that did replace slavery, sharecropping, did not pose an obstacle to the development of capitalism outside of the cotton-South. While sharecropping did pose definite limits to the transformation of the labour-process, it did not have plantation-slavery's geographically impe-rialist tendencies, which had posed an obstacle to the Western expansion of petty-commodity production. Sharecropping also eliminated plantation 'self-sufficiency', making the direct producers more dependent on commodity-circulation for their reproduction and deepening the social division of labour in the South.[57]

While the abolition of slavery removed the obstacles presented by the expansion of the slave-form; the Homestead Act, protective tariff and lib-eralised immigration-laws provided a powerful impetus to the capitalist accumulation of capital. The passage of the Homestead Act of 1862 did not provide the agrarian petty bourgeoisie with its long hoped for utopia of free land to the tiller and an end to land-speculation and engrossment. The por-tions of the public domain reserved for free settlement tended to be of the worst soil-quality and distant from the railroads. The railroads, on the other hand, were given, under the provisions of the Homestead and corollary land-grant acts, large alternating blocks of the public domain along their routes, while the federal government reserved the other blocks of land for sale at public auction. This plundering of the public domain through huge land-grants to railroads and mining companies, and the sale of government-land at public auction, provided a tremendous lever for the commodification of the land and created a permanent obstacle to 'natural economy'.[58] The mas-sive home-market created by the expansion of petty-commodity production,

---

[57] On the dynamics of sharecropping, see Ransom and Sutch 1977 and Wiener 1979.
[58] Gates 1936.

the largest in the capitalist world-economy, was unified by a transcontinental railroad-system and monopolised for American industrial capital by the protective tariffs passed during and after the Civil War. Liberalised immigration-laws allowed the continual inflow of European and Asian immigrants, who supplemented the industrial proletariat and reserve-army of labour. By the end of the Civil War and Reconstruction, the conditions for the dominance of specifically capitalist production were secured. The Civil War and Reconstruction thus marked the end of the US social formation's 'phase of transition', dominated by the process of primitive accumulation, and the beginning of the phase of industrial capitalist expansion, dominated by the capitalist accumulation of capital.

Chapter Two

The Agrarian Origins of US-Capitalism: The Transformation of the Northern Countryside Before the Civil War

The origins of capitalist development has long been a major focus of historical research and theoretical debate among social scientists. Almost from the beginning of the English Industrial Revolution, historians, economists and sociologists have attempted to locate the conditions for the emergence of capitalism. The classic discussions of these issues in Smith, Marx and Weber continue to define the basic parameters of research.[1] Whether in the original debates on the European transition from feudalism to capitalism and the crisis of the seventeenth century of the 1950s and early 1960s,[2] through the broad ranging discussions of the 'development of underdevelopment' in Latin America, Africa and Asia since the 1960s,[3] to the renewed debates on origins of capitalism in its European heartland during the 1970s and 1980s,[4] social scientists have weighed the relative importance of the growth of

---

[1] Smith 1937, Book I, Chapters 1–3; Book III; Marx 1976, Chapters 26–30; Marx 1981, Chapters 20 and 47; Weber 1958 and 1981.

[2] See Hilton 1976; and Aston 1967.

[3] Among this voluminous literature, see: Cardoso and Faletto 1979; Furtado 1971; Frank 1967; Laclau 1977; Murray 1980 and 1982; Rhodes 1970; Warren 1980.

[4] Aston and Philpin (eds.) 1985; Brenner 1977; Smith 1991; Wallerstein 1974.

trade and the division of labour, the alteration of class-relations, and the transformation of cultural values to the origins and dynamics of capitalism.

A consistent theme in these varied discussions is the central importance of the transformation of countryside in the process of industrialisation. Whether conceived as the result of the expansion of the market, the development of new social-property relations or the emergence of new values and norms, there is a consensus that an agrarian revolution is a necessary precondition of an industrial revolution. Perhaps the most rigorous presentation of the rural roots of capitalist industry is made by Robert Brenner.[5] For Brenner, the elimination of non-market ('extra-economic') restrictions (serfdom, slavery, etc.) on the mobility and productive activities of rural labour and the emergence of new forms of agricultural production in which direct producers are separated from their means of production and subsistence renders them dependent upon the market and makes them subject to market-discipline. Because the direct producers are brought under the constraints of competition, their economic action results in the systematic growth of productivity as the result of productive specialisation, the systematic accumulation of surpluses, and technical innovation. The growth of the productivity of agricultural labour 'frees' a growing portion of the population to work in manufacturing and industry, while simultaneously facilitating a growing demand for industrially produced consumer- and producer-goods. The creation of classes of farmers whose possession of the means of production must be reproduced through commodity-production and of workers lacking both means of production and means of subsistence deepened the home-market, a crucial precondition for industrialisation in England in the eighteenth century, the rest of Europe, North America and Japan in the nineteenth century and the 'newly industrialised countries' (Brazil, Mexico, South Korea, Taiwan, etc.) in the twentieth century. Conversely, the survival of agricultural social structures resting on non-market coercion or 'subsistence'-production remain the major obstacle to economic development in many parts of the so-called 'Third World'.[6]

While the 'transition to capitalism' is a central issue in the economic and social historiography of the rest of the world, it has been only recently been

---

[5] Brenner 1977, 1985a, 1985b.

[6] For an interesting application of Brenner's thesis to the contemporary 'Third World', see Harris 1987.

discussed seriously among US historians. The idea that 'capitalism came in the first ships' to the North-American colonies, producing 'the mentality of an independent entrepreneur' in all of the colonies' white inhabitants became the orthodoxy of the dominant-'consensus' school of US historical writing during the 1950s.[7] The notions that Northern agriculture was profit-oriented from the early eighteenth century, and that world-market production on the basis of plantation-slavery was essentially capitalist blocked serious consideration of the problem of the transition to capitalism in the US.[8] Since the 1960s, the equation of the absence of a 'feudal past' with an 'eternal capitalism' has been challenged from two directions. First, the work of Eugene Genovese on the slave-South has raised serious questions about the 'capitalist' character of plantation-slavery.[9] Despite challenges to aspects of his empirical research and theoretical approach,[10] Genovese's basic thesis that Southern slavery was a non-capitalist form of production remains convincing. Second, the past fifteen years has seen a burgeoning literature on the nature and dynamics of agriculture in the Northern US before the Civil War. Path-breaking research into probate- and tax-records and farmers' account-books has given rise to a new debate on the social character and logic of antebellum rural production and exchange. At the centre of the debate is the relationship of family-farmers to markets for farm-products, wage-labour and capital. While the participants in this debate draw upon a variety of theoretical sources (neoclassical economics, Weberian sociology, cultural anthropology and various strands of Marxism), we can, following Alan Kulikoff, distinguish two major positions.[11] While the 'market-historians' (Rothenberg and Lemon)[12] defend the older thesis that Northern farmers were profit-maximisers who enthusiastically engaged in

---

[7] The first quotation is from Degler 1959, p. 1; the second is from Hartz 1955, p. 89.

[8] On the commercial and capitalist character of Northern colonial agriculture see: Bushman 1967; Grant 1961; Loehr 1952; Lemon 1967; Schumacher 1948. The best statement of the 'planter-capitalism' thesis is Gray 1933, I, pp. 302.

[9] Genovese 1967.

[10] Garret 1978, Chapter 4 presents evidence that plantation-slavery did not produce complete technical stagnation, but a highly episodic process of technical change. Gallman 1970 presents evidence that plantations, especially the larger ones, were able to use slave-labour to produce corn and livestock for consumption. For Marxian criticism of Genovese's concept of slavery, see Hindess and Hirst 1975, pp. 148–56; and pp. 10–13 below.

[11] Kulikoff 1989, pp. 122–6.

[12] Rothenberg 1981, 1985, 1988; Lemon 1980a.

market-production when opportunities were presented, the 'social historians' (Merrill, Clark, Henretta, Weiman)[13] tend to emphasise the persistence of non-commercial production and exchange in the Northern countryside.

This chapter will review and assess the debate on the rural origins of US capitalism in light of the theoretical insights generated by the discussion of the transition to capitalism in Europe. As Kulikoff commented:

> ...the debate over the transition to capitalism in rural America has generated substantive new historical evidence, insight, and questions. But it has remained remarkably insulated from other theoretical frameworks. It needs to incorporate insights from the European debate over the transition from feudalism to capitalism...[14]

This theoretical insularity prevents either the 'market'- or 'social' historians from effectively synthesising the enormous volume of new historical evidence into a coherent explanation of the specifically US path to capitalism.

Before embarking on a detailed analysis of the US debate, we must first define precisely what is meant by 'capitalism' and what elements of the European 'transition'-debate are relevant to the analysis of the transformation of the antebellum-Northern countryside. Briefly, capitalism is a form of social production in which capitalists, a class of non-producers, owns and controls productive property (land, tools, machinery, etc.), buy the capacity to work (labour-power) of wage-workers, direct producers who do not possess means of production, and organise the latter in a labour-process to produce commodities (products for the market). While the capitalists pay the wage-workers the value of their capacity to work (the monetary equivalent of those commodities that the workers need to survive day to day and reproduce themselves inter-generationally), capitalists are able to extract a surplus-product (surplus-value) through their command of the labour-process, which allows them to force workers to produce commodities in excess of the value of their wages. Since both the capitalists' means of production and the workers' labour-power take the form of commodities, the continued economic survival of both capital and labour requires successful competition in the market-place. The social-property relation between capital and wage-labour makes possible (through capital's ability to adjust the size of the labour-force), and inter-

---

[13] Clark 1990, Henretta 1991a and 1991b, Merrill 1983, Weiman 1989.
[14] Kulikoff 1989, p. 132.

capitalist competition makes necessary (through the need to minimise costs) the specialisation of production and the continuous investment of surpluses in new productive technology (labour-saving machinery). Thus, capitalism's unique social-property or 'surplus-extraction' relationship shapes a labour-process that is the basis of industrialisation and its attendant social changes.[15]

The relative unimportance of wage-labour in the Northern US country-side before the Civil War makes much of the discussion of the development of capitalist agriculture in Europe and other parts of the world irrelevant to our analysis. While rural waged work was more common in the late eighteen and nineteenth centuries than once believed, it was not an essential feature of Northern agriculture. Even after the 1820s, when the number of poor and landless farm-families increased with the intensified commercialisation of agriculture, rural wage-labour did not become a permanent class-situation for a large portion of the population of the North. The poorest rural families more commonly engaged in capitalist 'outwork' or migrated to the burgeoning urban-industrial centres. Nor did wage-labour ever provide the majority of labour even for the most 'market-embedded' farmers. Throughout the nineteenth and twentieth centuries, despite the major transformations in rural class-structure, household family-members were the chief source of labour for Northern agriculture.[16]

Nor is the concept of feudalism particularly useful to an analysis of ante-bellum-Northern agriculture. Despite the existence of large tenant-farmed estates in the Hudson Valley of New York state in the eighteenth century and the development of agricultural tenancy in some parts of the middle west in the mid-nineteenth century, the vast majority of farmers legally owned their farms. Not only did the relative ease of obtaining land in the Northern US severely limit the development of a landlord-class, but the ground-rent appropriated by landlords was commercial rent. Different costs of production, as shaped by disparate soil-fertility and geographical locations, rather than 'custom', 'tradition' and the relative strengths of landlords and peasants

---

[15] Our conception of the necessary relations and processes of capitalist production are drawn primarily from Marx 1976 and 1981.

[16] Schob 1975 discusses the extent of agricultural wage-labour in the antebellum-period. Dublin 1979 and 1991 discusses rural 'outwork' and the migration of female labour from farm to factory in New England. Mann 1990, pp. 256–88 presents a Marxian explanation of the obstacles to wage-labour in agriculture.

determined the level of rents. In other words, the 'market-historians' are quite correct when they claim that the US has no 'feudal past'.[17]

While the dynamics of feudalism and specifically capitalist agriculture are not of immediate relevance to an analysis of rural social structure in the US before the Civil War, the problems of different forms of household-based agriculture and their relationship to the emergence of industrial capitalism certainly are. 'Peasant-economies', rural social structures based on family-farms with only limited relationship to external markets, have been a central theme in the debates on post-serfdom agriculture in Western Europe and the discussions of capitalist penetration in the so-called 'Third World'. The theoretical and historical insights these debates provide into non-commercial family agriculture – its reproduction-requirements, its retardation of capitalist development and the role of merchants, land-speculators and capitalist state-agencies in its replacement by commercial family-farming – will be central to our assessment of the debate on the rural origins of US capitalism.

Our discussion of the recent literature on antebellum-Northern agriculture is divided into three parts. First, we examine how various 'market'- and 'social' historians analyse the socio-economic structure of rural production before the Civil War. Specifically, we assess how different historians determine the extent to which the needs of household- and community-consumption (use-values) or market-prices (exchange-values) determine the economic behaviour of family-farmers in the eighteenth and early nineteenth centuries. Second, we examine how the participants in the US debate explain the transition from 'non-commercial' to 'commercial' agriculture in the nineteenth century. Finally, we will offer an outline of an alternative analysis the transformation of Northern rural social-property relations in the antebellum-period, whose purpose is to provide suggestions for further research and discussion.

I. Rural class-structure in the North before the Civil War

Before the Second World War, US historians generally regarded Northern farmers in the late eighteenth and early nineteenth centuries as subsis-

---

[17] Verthoff and Murrin 1973, pp. 256–88; and Kim 1978, Chapters 5–8 discuss tenancy in the eighteenth-century North. Atack and Bateman 1987, pp. 109–11; and Gates 1943 and 1960, pp. 66–9 and 197–8 describe tenancy in the mid-nineteenth century.

tence-producers. Following the lead of Percy Bidwell,[18] historians viewed the family-farmers and rural artisan-farmers as successfully providing the overwhelming majority of their needs through their own labours, rather than market-exchange. In the eyes of the 'progressive' historians, the rural households had limited if any contact with the market, and certainly were not subject to the demands of price competition. In the 1950s, the 'consensus'-historians assailed this perspective as rural romanticism.[19] Where the 'progressive' historians saw self-sufficient farmers content in their isolation from the risks of the market, the 'consensus'-historians saw commercially-oriented, profit-maximising rural entrepreneurs maximising their marketable output and constantly seeking new ways to bring their product to market. The historiographical pendulum began to swing back in the other direction in the 1970s and 1980s, as the first 'social historians' of Northern agriculture began to argue that the rural communities of the colonial and early national period were basically self-sufficient.[20] Despite the sale of 'surpluses', non-commercial exchange among neighbours sheltered Northern farmers from the effects of market-competition.

Winifred Rothenberg rigorously interrogated the claim that the consumption-requirements of family and community, rather than market-prices and potential profits systematically determined the production decisions of north-eastern farmers.[21] Applying sophisticated econometric techniques to data gathered from hundreds of farmers' account-books and probate-records, she demonstrated that Massachusetts family-farmers increasingly produced for competitive commodity-markets, invested in a variety of financial instruments and employed wage-workers (whose wages were set in competitive labour-markets) in the decades after 1790–1800. The most important evidence for the dominance of the 'market-process' in Massachusetts agriculture is the increasing convergence of prices for key agricultural commodities after the last decade of the eighteenth century.[22] In neoclassical-economic theory, price-convergence indicates that 'perfect competition' exists in a given market. In 'perfect competition', a large number of small firms confront one another in

---

[18] Bidwell and Falconer 1925, I, pp. 126–44.
[19] Bushman 1967, Grant 1961.
[20] Clark 1979; Henretta 1991a; Merrill 1976; Mutch 1977 and 1980.
[21] Rotherberg 1981, 1985, 1988.
[22] Rothenberg 1981, pp. 300–5.

a market. The number and size of firms prevent any firm from effecting the 'equilibrium-price' (toward which all prices necessarily converge), reducing all producers to passive 'price-takers'. Any firm's attempt to change its productive technique, lower costs and under-cut or possibly drive out its competitors is ultimately futile, because all other firms will rapidly adapt the new technique and the market will quickly and painlessly re-establish the 'equilibrium-price'. Put simply, 'perfect competition' establishes and maintains uniform conditions of production in a market. Ironically, neoclassical economics' notion of 'perfect competition', by ignoring how the long turnover-periods of existing fixed capital block the ability of all firms to adapt immediately new cost-cutting techniques, envisions a world without real capitalist competition.[23]

In a Marxian framework, price-convergence is *one* indication that producers are subject to the 'law of value' – to real competition. Competition compels producers to seek ways of producing commodities *below* the 'socially-necessary average labour-time' which is manifested in the price around which all the other prices for a given good or service tend to oscillate. Those producers who produce above the social average, whose costs of production and prices are too high, are penalised by shrinking market-shares, falling profit-margins and possible bankruptcy. Those producers who produce at or below the social average, whose costs of production and prices are low, are rewarded by growing market-shares, rising profit-margins and growth in the scale of their operations (accumulation). Price-convergence around a 'centre of gravity' (which changes with technological innovation, alterations in aggregate and market-demand, input-prices, etc.), provides producers with the price-information ('market-signals') they need in order to decide whether to enter or leave a market. Thus, increasing price-convergence around a 'centre of gravity', which is very different from the mythical 'equilibrium-price' of neoclassical economics, allows the equalisation of profit-rates for 'regulating capitals' (those units whose labour-processes set the conditions for successfully entering a market) across markets in the longrun. In other words, the operation of the 'law of value' – 'the discipline of the market' – forces producers to

---

[23] Our discussion of 'perfect competition' is drawn from Botwinick 1993, pp. 124–33; Shaikh 1978; Shaikh 1980.

raise the productivity of labour, either through the intensification of labour or mechanisation.[24]

Family-farmers are subject to the operation of the law of value only when they are compelled to complete successfully on the market in order to maintain their possession of their key means of production – landed property. If family-farmers pay minimal mortgages, rents or taxes, they are do not have to 'sell to survive.' In capitalist production, where the transformation of capital (means of production) and labour-power (labour-services) into commodities bought and sold on the market creates a situation of 'generalised commodity-production', the economic survival of both capitalists and workers depends upon successful production for the market. Marxian economics also recognises a form of household-based production that is subject to the operation of the law of value – *petty-commodity production*. In situations where household-producers (independent artisans or family-farmers – usually the eldest male – organising the labour of women and children and occasional wage-labourers) depend upon production for the market for their survival as small property-owners, a dynamic of specialisation, competition, accumulation and technical innovation similar to capitalism ensues.[25]

From a Marxian viewpoint, the price-convergence described by Rothenberg is only one, albeit crucial, indication of the dominance of petty-commodity production in Massachusetts agriculture after 1790–1800. Massachusetts farmers, while continuing to rely primarily on family-labour, became progressively subject to the 'dictates of the market'. Despite their ultimately futile attempts to produce the bulk of their own subsistence while dedicating larger and larger segments of their labour-time to commodity-production, family-farmers were constrained, eventually, to specialise output, to organise their labour-process to increase labour-productivity, and the like in order to lower production-costs and to compete effectively with other petty-commodity producers. Those that failed to lower costs faced difficulties paying debts, mortgages and taxes and the possible loss of landed property, while those

---

[24] Our conception of the law of value is drawn from Marx 1976, Chapters 1–3 and Mandel 1968, I, Chapter 2; and our understanding of role of price-convergence in the process of the equalisation of profit-rates across markets is drawn from Botwinick 1993, Chapter 5.

[25] On petty-commodity production, see Engels 1981; Friedmann 1980, pp. 161–4, 167–70; and Mandel 1968, I, pp. 65–71.

who succeeded in lowering costs accumulated surpluses that allowed them to expand production through the purchase of their less fortunate neighbours' land and labour-services. This process of social differentiation both freed capital and labour for the developing manufacturing sector; and made the farmers, as specialised commodity-producers, a market for factory-produced consumer- and capital-goods. In short, the emergence of agrarian petty-commodity production in rural New England in the last decade of the eighteenth and first decades of the nineteenth century was the basis of the growth of a 'home-market' for capitalist industry during the nineteenth century.

The Massachusetts farmers' need to compete successfully on the market in order to maintain possession of their farms, did not mean either that the farmers immediately specialised production, ceased producing a portion of their own subsistence, or began to buy and use new and more effective tools and implement immediately after 1790–1800. Instead, the transition to the dominance of petty-commodity production took various *intermediary forms* as rural household responded to the new requirements of commodity-production while simultaneously attempting to preserve their independence form the 'dictates of the market'.

Christopher Clark mistakenly interprets western-Massachusetts farmers' continued production of a part of their own consumer-goods and the reorganisation and intensification of their families' labour before 1820 as evidence of 'agricultural involution' and the persistent autonomy of the countryside from the 'market-process'.[26] However, two new developments, amply documented by Clark, illustrate the progressive dominance of petty-commodity production in this region after 1790–1800.[27] Farmers began to devote ever-larger portions of their and their families' labour-time to the production of marketable goods (flax, livestock, broomcorn, dairy, eggs, wheat). As a result, even the largest farmers began to purchase *some* new consumer-goods previously produced in the household or community. Second, farmers reorganised household labour-processes in order to increase their output of commodities per person-hour without introducing new technologies – through the intensification of labour. In sum, farmers in western Massachusetts devoted greater

---

[26] Clark 1990, Chapter 3.
[27] Clark 1990, Chapters 5–8.

and greater quantities of human labour to the production of exchange-values rather than use-values.

Additional evidence for increasing market-dependence in the early nineteenth century comes from Thomas Dublin's work on capitalist rural 'outwork' in environs of Fitzwilliam, New Hampshire.[28] Farm-households in this region responded to the new competitive requirements of land-ownership by increasing the production of non-agricultural commodities. Before 1820, better-off farm-households utilised female and child-labour to produce cloth at home for sale on the market. After 1820, local merchants paid poorer farm-women and children to fabricate palm-leaf hats in their homes, which the merchants then sold to farmers and planters in the west and the south. Whether they sold the products of their labour or their capacity to labour, these farm-families were devoting more and more labour-time to the production of commodities in order to survive economically. In sum, while New-England farmers did not specialise output, introduce new tools and implements, and purchase more and more store-bought flour, cloth, until the early 1820s, the 'turning point' in these farmers' subordination to 'market-discipline' came much earlier, in the 1790s and 1800s.

The question remains, if price-convergence for crucial agricultural commodities in Massachusetts (and possibly other parts of the northeast) after 1790–1800 indicates the growth of systematic production for the market (petty-commodity production), what do the price-divergences before 1790 indicate? Clearly, price-divergence for agricultural commodities denotes an absence of competition among suppliers in a market. In Marxian terms, the disparities in prices manifest the absence of a socially-average necessary labour-time for the production of agricultural goods among a set of producers. The absence of market-discipline over the farmers in this period is an indication of the sporadic and irregular character of market-exchange. As Alan Kulikoff put it 'to write of increasing market embeddedness and increasing price convergence as Rothenberg does, after all, suggests a time...when market exchange was less common'.[29]

The dominance of non-commercial family-farming in the northeast during the late eighteenth and early nineteenth century is, of course, the central

---

[28] Dublin 1991.
[29] Kulikoff 1989, p. 128.

thesis of the 'social historians'. There is a consensus among these historians regarding the main features of the social structure of rural self-sufficiency in the North. While individual farmer or artisan-farmer households (organised along a strict sexual and generational division of labour) did not produce all the food or handicrafts needed for household-subsistence, most rural communities were 'self-sufficient'. Exchanges between farmers, and between farmers and artisans while quite extensive, did not take the form of commodity- or market-exchange. Most 'neighbourly exchange' took the form of barter. Most frequently, the labour-services of poorer farmers were exchanged directly for food produced on the farms of better-off farmers. Debts between neighbours and extended family-members, including local merchants and artisans, were payable in labour, produce or cash, often ran for years before being partially or wholly forgiven, and interest was rarely if ever charged on unpaid balances. While most farmers and merchants assigned monetary values (derived from urban markets) to the exchanges of goods and services with neighbours recorded in their account-books, custom, not 'supply and demand' (or, in Marxian terms, socially-average labour-time or relative costs of production), determined the proportions exchanged.[30]

Non-commercial farmers only sold 'surpluses' (that portion of their output over and above what was consumed by family and neighbours) in local and long-distance markets. Cash was needed only for the limited number of commodities that could not be produced locally (salt, gunpowder, coffee, tea, glass, patent-medicine), and to buy additional land for the farmers and their sons in order to ensure the inter-generational maintenance of the farm-household. As a result, social inequality among farm-households corresponded to the age of the eldest male in non-commercial agriculture, rather than the soil fertility, technique, location and other factors shaping costs of production in petty-commodity or capitalist production. Older farmers, with fewer depen-

---

[30] Pruitt 1984 provides considerable evidence of the non-commodity/non-commercial character of exchange among farm households in the eighteenth century, despite her criticisms of Clark, Henretta and Merrill. Her claim 'that there was an operative grain market within the communities of Massachusetts' (p. 352) is based on reports of the exchange of grain for labour-services, manufactured goods and cash in farmers' account books. However, the data she cites demonstrates quite the opposite: debts based on the exchange of grain for other goods or services often ran on for years, without interest, were often forgiven and never regularly settled (pp. 351–4). See Merrill 1986, Chapters 2 and 4 for the importance of interest-free, irregularly settled debts as an indicator of non-commercial exchange.

dents tended to have the largest farms and marketed the largest surpluses; younger farmers, with the most dependents, tended to have the smallest farms, rarely marketed surpluses and often exchanged labour-services for food or manufactured goods produced in the households of better-off farmers and farmer-artisans, including those of their parents or other relatives.

Despite a general consensus concerning the description of non-commercial agriculture, the 'social historians' differ in their explanation of the necessary relations and processes of this form of production. Specifically, there is considerable disagreement about the conditions that allowed farm households to remain impervious to 'market-discipline'. Michael Merrill's theory of a 'household mode of production' is the most ambitious attempt to theorise the specific dynamics of Northern 'self-sufficient' agriculture. Merrill's concept of a 'mode of production' differs considerably from the classical-Marxist conception. Most Marxists argue that the combination of distinct 'relations of production' (relations of surplus-production and appropriation based on the distribution of means of production between producers and non-producers) and 'forces of production' or labour-processes (relations of producers to one another and the means of production in the immediate process of production) define different forms of social labour.[31] In contrast, Merrill defines a mode of production in terms of 'a necessary relation between the produced wealth and the distribution of the available social labour to produce that wealth'.[32] In other words, the mechanisms for distributing and co-ordinating labour and means of production among different productive activities provides the basis for classifying different forms of social labour.[33] Class-relations ('the distribution of the products which functions as means of production') and class-struggle ('the division of the product and labour of society, i.e., who gets what and works for whom'[34]) are effects of the different mechanisms of socio-economic co-ordination.

---

[31] See Marx 1970; Balibar 1970, pp. 199–308; Brenner 1985a, pp. 11–12.

[32] Merrill 1986, p. 27.

[33] Merrill (1986, p. 27) labels these mechanisms 'the law of value'. Unfortunately, the use of the concept 'law of value' for all forms of socio-economic co-ordination tends to deprive the concept of its specificity as the mechanism for the co-ordination of labour and means of production in capitalism and petty-commodity production. See Mandel 1968, I, pp. 560–72, for a critique of attempts to apply the 'law of value' to the postcapitalist bureaucratic command-economy of the ex-USSR.

[34] Merrill 1986, p. 32.

According to Merrill, societies have developed two basic mechanisms for co-ordinating labour and means of production in the creation of different goods and services. The first, characteristic of capitalism and petty-commodity production, is through the exchange of commodities – the unconscious, unplanned distribution of labour and means of production to different activities based on relative exchange-values (relative amounts of labour embodied in different commodities). The second, which characterises most non-capitalist social-property forms, is through direct, conscious co-ordination based on planning (in so-called 'socialist' societies like the former Soviet Union) or custom and tradition (in precapitalist economies). The property-owning direct producers of the 'household-mode of production' co-ordinated their labour through 'non-commercial exchange'. Citing 'neighbourly exchange' (governed by need rather than price, allowing long-term, interest-free debts, etc.), the direct co-ordination of labour during harvests, barn-raising, husking corn, and the like, and the role of local government in fixing prices, banning hoarding and speculating in agricultural produce, and attempting to attract needed labourers (often artisans) and to exclude ('warn out') redundant labourers (additional farmers), Merrill argues that these non-commodity-relations among rural households allowed them to avoid dependence upon the market for their basic subsistence. As a result of this community self-sufficiency in consumption, the household-producers are able to retain their autonomy from the 'discipline of the market'.[35]

The greatest strength of Merrill's theory is his insistence that social structural factors, not subjective motivations, values and the like are central to the reproduction of non-commercial household-production in the antebellum-North. According to Merrill, 'Commercial farmers need not be selfish or even individualistic, they need only pay and insist on being paid in hard cash. By the same token, non-commercial farmers need not be selfless or altruistic. They only need neither to pay nor to insist on being paid in hard cash.'[36] In other words, it is the non-commodity-relations of exchange among farmers and artisans in the household mode of production – their ability to collectively produce their own subsistence without recourse to the market – that allows them remain independent from market-forces. Farmers become sub-

---

[35] Merrill 1986, Chapter 1. This chapter is a revised version of Merrill 1976.
[36] Merrill 1986, p. 145.

ject to the 'dictates of the market' when the procurement of consumption-goods requires market-exchange, not when their 'economic culture' changes from a 'subsistence'- to 'profit'-orientation. Merrill's insistence upon the centrality of forms of exchange as objective relations among producers leads him to develop a very rigorous set of indices for determining whether agriculture is 'commercial' or 'non-commercial'.[37]

Merrill's emphasis on 'relations of exchange' (commodity- or non-commodity-exchange among households), however, produces a potential circularity in his argument. Merrill claims that households' ability to obtain subsistence without access to commodity-exchange was the key to the non-commercial character of Northern agriculture in the early nineteenth century. Clearly, farmers and artisans had to be free to devote the bulk of their labour-time to the production of use-values (items for immediate consumption) rather than exchange-values (items for sale on the market) in order to provide subsistence for themselves and their neighbours. What allowed these households to expend the majority of their productive energy producing goods for immediate consumption rather than marketable commodities? Merrill's answer appears to be the existence of non-commodity-forms of exchange among households. In other words, Merrill explains the antebellum rural artisans and farmers' autonomy from the market as the result of their autonomy from the market. Merrill succeeds in describing this form of household-production, but fails to explain its social condition of existence. An explanation of the household producers' independence from commodity-production requires placing 'relations of production' (the relation of households to the means of production – landed property) at the centre of our analysis. Non-market access to consumption-goods required non-market access to means of production. Only when rural families' possession of land was not dependent on

---

[37] Merrill 1986, Chapters 2–3. While many of Merrill's indices (particularly, long-term, interest-free debts that are settled irregularly) are quite appropriate for distinguishing commercial and non-commercial forms of household-production, his rejection of Rothenberg's use of price-convergence as an index of 'market-embeddedness' is not persuasive. Merrill 1986, pp. 135–8 cites Marshall Sahlins's findings of price-convergences in various areas of the south-west Pacific (New Guinea and Australia) in the 1940s where market-competition clearly did not exist. This comparison is very problematic. The areas studied are much smaller and much less densely populated than nineteenth-century New England. As a result, it would be much more difficult for tradition and custom to produce price-convergence in antebellum New England than in the south-west Pacific.

successful competition in the marketplace, because of the low cost of securing and maintaining possession of land, can they devote most of their labour-time to the production of use-values for 'neighbourly exchange'.[38]

Christopher Clark's analysis of the transformation of the rural economy of western Massachusetts, while not as theoretically explicit as Merrill, offers a quite different explanation of the farmers' and artisans' independence from the logic of commodity-production. A particular economic culture – a set of motivations, goals and strategies – allowed rural households to retain their autonomy from the strictures of market-competition. 'Rooted in the possession of freehold property' (legal title to land), non-commercial, non-capitalist values provided the basis for 'distinctive ways of conducting economic life'. Individual acquisitiveness, profit-maximisation and other elements of a commercial orientation did not direct the productive activities of the household producers. Instead, the desire to maintain the lineal family's landholding and to preserve their 'independence' from the vagaries of a market that could threaten land-ownership were the central goals of farmers and artisans in the eighteenth and early nineteenth century north-east: 'Families' desire to acquire and hold onto the means of controlling their own efforts and resources powerfully influenced rural economic life.'[39]

Independent household-producers pursued a 'subsistence-surplus' strategy of first ensuring the consumption-needs of the family and community before entering the market-place. Subsistence was guaranteed in two ways. First, a strict and unequal generational and gender-division of labour developed within the household, with men working in the fields and artisan-workshops, women in the house (including gardening, production of cloth and clothing for domestic consumption, preparing food, child-care), and children assisting their elders. Second, 'neighbourly exchange' provided the elements of subsistence that no single household could produce alone. Secure in their basic consumption-requirements, the independent household-producers (especially the older and larger) would produce 'surpluses' for sale in long-

---

[38] Several critics of Merrill have also pointed to how his theory of the 'household mode of production' tends to privilege relations of exchange over social-property relations. One of his critics, Christopher Clark (1978), argued that Merrill underestimated the degree of social inequality in the Northern countryside in the late eighteenth and early nineteenth century and the existence of gender- and generational conflicts within the household as a result. See also Wessman 1979–80.

[39] Clark 1990, pp. 16, 23–4.

distance markets. This 'safety-first' strategy permitted farmers to ensure the survival of the family's landholding, while attempting to obtain the means of expanding the farmstead through trade.[40]

The centrality accorded economic goals and strategies is most evident in Clark's rejection of Rothenberg's claim that the last decade of the eighteenth century marked a turning point in the Massachusetts farmers' relationship to competitive markets. Clark argues that rural producers were not subject to 'market discipline' before the 1830s, notwithstanding Rothenberg's evidence of growing price-convergence and his own evidence of an increased portion of household-labour being devoted to commodity-production. Despite these changes, Clark insists that the farmers and artisans retained their independence from the market because they continued to produce most of their consumption-goods and they sought to preserve and expand the family's landholding without regard to the demands of profit-maximisation:

> Closer examination of farmers' reasons for increasing production reveals the importance of household concerns and strategies in creating surpluses. New farming strategies developed firmly within the context of the household system. Households retained control of production and tried to make it serve their needs. Preserving independence and providing for offspring were the motives that impelled many of them. Other facets of the system, including local exchange and the rituals of 'neighbourhood', also continued to play an important role.[41]

Clark's analysis of non-commercial rural household-production marks an advance over Merrill's theory of a 'household-mode of production' in its emphasis on the interrelation of local 'neighbourly exchange' and long-distance commodity-circulation and the importance of the gender- and generational division of labour within the household. However, Clark's contention that non-commercial economic values, goals and strategies – subjective motivations – were sufficient to allow household-producers to escape 'market-discipline' is not convincing. The attempt to make 'economic culture' or *mentalités* a determinant of economic relations and actions tends to ignore how the structure of social-property relations places limits on all individual

---

[40] Clark 1990, pp. 23–44.
[41] Clark 1990, p. 87.

economic actions. As Brenner argued in the debate on the European transition from feudalism to capitalism:

> Different forms of social-property relationships made different forms of economic behaviour rational, possible and necessary for the individual economic actors and, in this way, conditioned different overall patterns of economic development/non-development.[42]

The same goals and strategies can be pursued under different social and economic constraints with quite different results. Both capitalist landlords and tenant-farmers in England and feudal landlords in Eastern Europe during the sixteenth and seventeenth centuries were inspired by an ethic of 'profit-maximisation'. However, the structure of the capitalist landlord, capitalist tenant-farmer, wage-labourer relation made specialisation, technical innovation and rising labour-productivity the necessary result of English landlords' and farmers' quest for the maximum-return on investment in the developing world-market. In contrast, the structure of the feudal lord-serf relation made diversification, technical stagnation and static or declining labour-productivity the necessary result of the Eastern-European lords' search for maximum-revenues.[43]

Clark's own research, and that of James Henretta, demonstrates that similar subjective motivations and economic strategies led to quite different results, depending upon the structure of social-property relations in the antebellum-US. In the eighteenth century, the farmers' pursuit of the goal of maintaining the lineal families' landholding through the 'subsistence-surplus' strategy led to the reproduction of independent household-production. In the early nineteenth century, under different social and economic conditions, their quest for stable family-landholding through a 'safety-first' approach to the market led to a quite different set of results – the rise of commercial and capitalist agriculture.[44] Thus, the key to understanding the preservation (and eventual destruction) of the farmers and artisans' independence from the market cannot be their subjective motivations and values, but the structure of social-

---

[42] Brenner 1985b, n. 167, pp. 300–1.
[43] Brenner 1985a, pp. 36–54; 1985b, pp. 275–84; Dobb 1947, pp. 50–70; Hobsbawm 1967.
[44] Clark 1990, Chapters 2, 4–5; Henretta 1991a, pp. 100–8, 115–9. Kulikoff 1989, p. 129 makes a similar point.

property relations – particularly the social conditions for the maintenance and expansion of landholding. Specifically, independent household-production, with its extensive market-involvement (sale of surpluses) without market-dependence (the need to 'sell to survive'), rests upon the family-farmers' security in their possession of landed property. By contrast, petty-commodity production, with its market-dependence, rests on the family-farmers' fundamental insecurity in their possession of landed property.

James Henretta's main concern in his seminal contribution to the US debate on the origins of capitalism were the *mentalités* – values, norms, world-views – produced by (but not necessarily shaping) different forms of rural household-production. However, he identified three socio-economic elements that allowed Northern farmers to retain their autonomy from 'market-forces' in the eighteenth and early nineteenth centuries. Arguing against Grant and Lemon's assertion that Northern farmers were profit-oriented from the seventeenth century onward, Henretta asserted that 'environmental opportunities' profoundly shaped 'human goals':

> ...everyone was affected by the structural possibilities and limitation of the society, whatever their cultural propensities or economic aspirations. There was a direct relationship between the material environment, on the one hand, and the consciousness and activity of the population on the other.[45]

The first element of the material environment was the lack of transportation-facilities to carry their products to distant urban and international markets. 'Given the absence of an external market, there was no alternative to subsistence or semi-subsistence production'. Henretta recognises that mere physical isolation from markets was not a necessary condition for the maintenance of non-commercial agriculture and handicrafts. Although European and Caribbean markets for North-American foodstuffs grew rapidly after 1750, Northern farmers, even in the most 'commercialised' mid-Atlantic region, consumed the vast majority of their product. In other words, the growth of markets alone did not end the ability of rural households collectively to produce the bulk of their subsistence.[46]

---

[45] Henretta 1991a, p. 89.
[46] Henretta 1991a, pp. 90–2.

Of much greater importance to the preservation of non-commercial relations in the countryside were the 'web of social relationships and cultural expectations that inhibited the free play of market forces'. Ties of kinship and community (often involving shared religion, ethnicity and language) made the provision of subsistence the primary activity in the rural villages and towns of the eighteenth and early nineteenth centuries, even when opportunities for commodity-production expanded.[47] David Weiman presents a similar, but more theoretically explicit argument. According to Weiman, co-operative labour and a diversified occupational structure (farmers, artisans and merchants), common land, and obligations to provide land for male offspring limited commodity-production and the private accumulation of wealth. Not only did 'complex familial and communal obligations among petty producers' make the provision of household- and community-subsistence the first economic priority, but they also:

> ...circumscribed the productive activities of individual households and, in turn, dampened the impact of private wealth as a force in differentiating households socially and economically. Wealthier households were prevented from aggrandising themselves at the expense of their economically weaker neighbours, while communal arrangements effectively transferred wealth to those at the lower end of the distribution...differences in wealth and economic status among households depended largely on the age of the household head and reflected the transitory effects of the life cycle pattern of wealth accumulation.[48]

Clearly, ties of family and community facilitated the ability of rural producers to pursue 'subsistence-surplus' strategies and limited the development of unequal landholding. However, the significance given these relations by Henretta and Weiman are subject to many of the same criticisms of the significance given to exchange-relations by Merrill. What social and economic conditions allowed the obligation to provide subsistence to family and neighbours to assume such a great importance in the activities of rural households? What allowed these producers to devote the majority of their labour-time to providing consumption-goods as use-values? What prevented larger,

---

[47] Henretta 1991a, pp. 98–9.
[48] Weiman 1989, pp. 259–60.

wealthier farmers from appropriating the land of their less fortunate neighbours? What allowed fathers to obtain land for their sons without becoming dependent upon the logic of commodity-production? None of these questions can be answered by reference to kinship- and communal relations, which Weiman acknowledges when he describes these social relations of 'petty production' as 'transitional'. Their answers must be sought in the structure of social-property relations, in the relationship of the rural household to the possession of landed property. To be precise, the family-farmers' capacity to obtain, expand and maintain land without commodity-production was a necessary condition for the development of kinship- and communal bonds of mutual obligation.

In the course of his discussion, Henretta briefly mentions what was in fact the main condition of non-commercial household-production in the antebellum-Northern countryside. Relatively inexpensive land, continually renewed through the expropriation of native-American tribal societies, 'enabled a rapidly growing Euro-American population to *preserve* an agricultural society composed primarily of yeoman farm owning families in many eastern areas, and to *extend* these age- and wealth-stratified communities into western regions'.[49] The general ease of obtaining landed property in the eighteenth and early nineteenth centuries allowed the development of a distinctive social-property relation that provided the basis for the entire structure of non-commercial household-production in the rural North.

Robert Brenner and Harriet Friedmann point out that the need to 'sell to survive' is the condition for systematic competition. In other words, only rural producers whose continued possession of land and other means of production require successful commodity-production are subject to the 'law of value' and must specialise output, systematically reinvest surpluses and develop the productivity of land and labour through technical innovation. The absence of market-competition among household-producers is only possible when farmers and artisans are under no compulsion to sell their output in order to maintain their possession of land. In other words, *the economic survival of the farmers as independent property-owners is not conditioned upon successful sale of agricultural goods.* The expansion of market-opportunities alone were not sufficient to displace less-efficient producers – there was no economic compulsion

---

[49] Henretta 1991a, p. 81 (emphasis in the original).

for farmers to specialise production, rationalise agrarian labour-processes and raise labour-productivity. 'Independent household-production' was a social-property form capable of reproducing its independence from 'market-discipline' in the absence of profound social disruptions and conflicts. Such autonomy from the market is only possible in situations where the price of land is relatively low (because of the relative abundance of unoccupied or recently expropriated land), taxes are minimal and debts to mercantile capitalists are either small or can be paid in kind, rather than in cash.[50]

The social-property relations of 'independent household-production', or 'peasant-economy' as it is often mislabelled, provided the material basis for the rural social forms described by Henretta, Merrill, Clark and Weiman.[51] Put theoretically, the ability of the direct producers to reproduce their possession of landed property without recourse to commodity-production determined both the nature of exchange-relations with other farmers, artisans and merchants, and the importance of kinship and community in organising the social structure of the antebellum-Northern countryside. Free from the constraint to produce for the market in order to survive economically, Northern rural households in the eighteenth and early nineteenth centuries were able to devote the bulk of their labour-time to the production of consumption-goods as use-values, providing the basis for the dense web of kinship- and

---

[50] Brenner 1985a, pp. 46–63; 1977, pp. 73–5; Friedmann 1980, pp. 162–4, 167–8, 170–84. See also below pp. 20–4. This does not imply that independent household-production did not have it own 'dynamic.' In the absence of unoccupied or relatively inexpensive land, 'subsistence-surplus' agriculture tended toward stagnant labour-productivity, parcellisation of landholding and demographic crisis. This pattern was evident in western-European agriculture generally, and French agriculture specifically, in the sixteenth and seventeenth centuries. Only English agriculture, where capitalist social–property relations had become dominant, escaped this cycle. See Hobsbawm 1967; Brenner 1985a, pp. 54–63; 1985b, pp. 284–319.
Independent household-production in the Northern US was able to avoid this cycle because of the availability of unoccupied land that could come into possession of households at relatively low costs. In early eighteenth-century New England, the 'opening' (through the expropriation of the native Americans) of the 'frontier' in western Massachusetts, Vermont, New Hampshire and Maine ended the fragmentation of landholdings and averted a possible demographic crisis. See Henretta 1991c. When 'free' or 'cheap' land disappeared, in the northeast in the 1790s and in the northwest in the 1830s and 1840s, it was under conditions that compelled the rural household-producers to transform themselves into petty-commodity producers.
[51] Friedmann 1980, pp. 158–61, 164–7 makes an excellent criticism of the notions of 'peasant-economy' and 'household-mode of production'. Ennew, Hirst and Tribe 1977 make a similar criticism of the notion of the 'peasant-mode of production'.

communal relations that structured 'neighbourly' non-commodity-exchange among households. Households and communities, secure in their possession of landed property, could pursue a 'subsistence-surplus' strategy of combined use-value and commodity-exchange. Finally, the preservation and expansion of family-landholding was a perfectly rational goal in a class-structure where obtaining, maintaining and enlarging landed property did not require production for the market. As long as land remained relatively cheap and easily accessible (had not become monopolised by a class of land-speculators or landlords), appropriating sufficient land to provide for male heirs did not pose any obstacles to the reproduction of independent household-production.

Our concept of independent household-production raises questions about Merrill's description of the dynamics of the household labour-process. Merrill rejects the notion that capitalist or petty-commodity social relations of production are necessary conditions for the development of labour-productivity through technical innovation. Citing such diverse examples as the growth of labour-productivity in the USSR in the twentieth century and the slave-South in the nineteenth century, Merrill claims that 'self-sufficient' household producers sought to innovate and raise labour-productivity:

> The maximisation of profit is not the only reason for innovation. The minimisation of labor can be equally compelling, especially where the labor you save is your own, or that of the people you love. Farmers could easily be 'subsistence producers' and still look for ways to raise their productivity.[52]

---

[52] Merrill 1986, pp. 66–9, 83. Merrill's claims about the post-collectivisation Soviet and antebellum-Southern US economies are highly questionable. Clearly, labour-productivity in the Soviet Union rose from the 1930s through the mid-1950s. However, this increase in output per work-hour was on the basis of 'extensive' industrialisation. The multiplication of production-units and the proportional increase in the size of the labour-force, mostly through the transfer of former peasants from low-productivity agriculture to industry, characterised Soviet economic growth. It was not 'intensive' industrialisation – the introduction of new and more efficient means of production – characteristic of capitalist accumulation. Governed neither the by 'logic of the market' nor by the democratic decisions of the producers, the bureaucratic command-economy in the USSR began to experience stagnating and declining labour-productivity beginning in the late 1950s. This economic stagnation ultimately undermined the bureaucratic régime, issuing in *perestroika*, *glasnost* and the eventual collapse of the USSR. See Nove 1989, Chapters 7–14; Mandel 1991; Singer 1981.
   Merrill's claims about the slave-South are equally unconvincing. Merrill's case for the development of labour-productivity under plantation-slavery rests on Fogel and Engerman 1974. Fogel and Engerman do present data on increased labour-productivity among the slaves during the nineteenth century. However, these increases are the

Merrill's case for the development of labour-productivity through improved instruments of production under independent household-production rests upon his research on Ulster County, New York in the late eighteenth and early nineteenth centuries. In the period 1785–1815, which Merrill asserts is prior to the 'commercialisation' of Ulster-County agriculture, both output per farm and the percentage of farms using 'improved' ploughs grew considerably. This evidence can be evaluated in two ways. First, I would question, based on Rothenberg's research on Massachusetts and other sources, whether stable independent household-production dominated rural production in rural New York after the Revolution. Throughout the northeast, land-prices rose precipitously as the result of land-speculation in the 1780s and 1790s, making the maintenance and expansion of landholding more and more dependent upon production for the market.[53] Faced with new pressures flowing from the transition from independent-household to petty-commodity production, those farmers who did innovate and increase their output (usually the largest and wealthiest) would best be able to survive the competitive battle in the marketplace.

Even if we grant Merrill's assumption that the social-property relations of independent household-production remained dominant in Ulster County before the 1840s, we do not have to accept his argument that technical innovation is a necessary feature of non-commercial agriculture. Anderson, Brenner, Dobb and Hilton all point to the periodic introduction of new methods and implements in the feudal labour-process in medieval Europe.[54] In other words, feudalism, like slavery and other precapitalist modes of production, was not completely technologically stagnant. However, the absence of market-compulsion to specialise productive activities and lower costs per unit of output or suffer loss of landed property in precapitalist economies meant that the development of labour-productivity through the introduction of new

---

result of either intensifying of the slaves' labour by increasing the amount of work the slave is expected to perform in a given period of time, or of moving production to newer and more fertile soils. They were not the result of the introduction of new, labour-saving implements and methods. See Foust and Swan 1970; Wright 1978, pp. 90–106, 176–84; and below pp. 10–13.

[53] Henretta 1991a, pp. 106–7 for a discussion of the impact of land-speculation in the late eighteenth century on 'subsistence'-agricultural production.

[54] Anderson 1974, Chapter 4; Brenner 1985a, pp. 31–5; 1985b, pp. 228–42, 311–4; Dobb 1947, pp. 42–50; Hilton 1985.

instruments and techniques was sporadic, occasional and of a 'once and for all' character. By contrast, capitalist and petty-commodity class-relations, where the survival of both non-producers and direct producers depend upon market-competition, necessitates continuous and progressive development of new methods, tools and machinery. The independent household-producers' ability to maintain and expand their land-holdings without commodity-production put strict limits on the development of labour-productivity in agriculture and handicrafts. As a result, labour was not 'freed' from agriculture for manufacturing and industry, and the countryside did not provide a growing market for factory-produced means of production or consumption. In other words, independent household-production, where and when it shaped rural production, was an obstacle to the development of capitalism.

II. Debating the transformation of Northern agriculture

Two of the major accomplishments of the recent discussion of the US transition to capitalism have been first, to document the existence of a non-commercial, family-based form of social labour in the Northern countryside before the Civil War; and, second, to demonstrate that a transition from this form to a commercial, family-based form began during the last decade of the eighteenth century in New England and other parts of the north-east. Rothenberg's evidence, combined with other research, indicates that farmers in Massachusetts became progressively dependent upon competitive markets for commodities, capital and labour-services. The farmers' autonomy from market-coercion during the eighteenth century was the consequence of their ability to maintain their status as small property-owners without recourse to effective production for the market, and their progressive subjugation to commodity-production in the nineteenth century was the consequence of their new found need 'to sell to survive'. In Marxian terms, the transformation of Massachusetts and north-eastern agriculture generally after 1790–1800 marked the transition from independent household-production to petty-commodity production.

How do the different participants in the debate on the US transition to capitalism explain this transformation of the Northern countryside? Drawing on the work of Bushman, Lemon and other 'market-historians', Rothenberg explains the transition from independent household-production to petty-commodity production in Massachusetts agriculture as the result of a radical shift in the dominant cultural values during the mid-eighteenth century.[55] After the 'Great Awakening' of the 1740s, New-England culture became imbued with the 'antinomian notion of the individual: the individual as ultimately singular in society, as ultimately alone in worship, as ultimately the sole perceiver of reality, alone in judgement, alone in action'.[56] The dominance of these new values, systematised in a 'Lockean paradigm' of possessive individualism, were first evidenced in the privatisation of decisions that had formerly been community/parental prerogatives: the choice of marriage-partners, places of residence, names of children and the like. This culture of individualism – in which all social relations were freely contracted in the pursuit of individual self-interest – swept away such manifestations of communitarian and collectivist values as legally-fixed 'just' prices, wages or interest-rates. The 'intellectual revolution…privatised economic decision making, put the *individual* at the centre of society and wrenched ("disembedded") the expanding economy from the domination of state, crown, and church.'[57] Fully freed from the burdens of traditional culture, Massachusetts farmers transformed the universal human tendency to 'utility-maximisation' (recognition of economic choices, budgetary/resource-constraints and the ability to rank order-preferences) into market-oriented 'profit-maximisation' in the last decade of the eighteenth century.[58]

Rothenberg's arguments are, of course, quite similar to those of Max Weber. In *The Protestant Ethic and the Spirit of Capitalism*[59] and his magisterial *General Economic History*,[60] Weber attempts to account for the origins of capitalism in a world-historic shift in values.[61] According to Weber, the Renaissance and the Protestant Reformation marked the transition from 'substantive' to 'abstract' economic rationality. No longer were substantive results (i.e., the

---

[55] Bushman 1967; and Lemon 1980b. Parker 1987 presents a cultural-determinist interpretation of the industrial revolution. A similar argument for the causal role of culture in the economic transformation of the antebellum-US northwest (Ohio River valley and Great Plains) is presented in Danhof 1969, pp. 15–25.

[56] Rothenberg 1984, p. 175.

[57] Rothenberg 1992, p. 15.

[58] Rothenberg 1992, pp. 15–23, 38–46.

[59] Weber 1958.

[60] Weber 1981.

[61] My understanding of Weber's sociology in general, and his theory of the origins of capitalism in particular, owe much to Therborn 1976, pp. 270–315; and Cohen 1981.

satisfaction of immediate needs, preservation of family- or community-ties, etc.) the driving force of economic activity. Instead the abstract 'means-ends' calculation of individual self-enrichment – profit – motivates human economic action ('enterprise') in the modern era. This 'spirit of capitalism' was manifested in institutions (transformation of means of production into private property, free commodity-markets, mechanisation, calculable law, free labour, use of commercial instruments in transfer of property) that facilitated 'rational economic calculation'.[62]

It is not necessary to enter into the complex psychological and philosophical debates about human nature and motivation, but to again assert that economic culture – the choice of economic goals, needs, strategies, choices, etc. – does not depend upon values and beliefs, but on the structure of social-property relations.[63] My discussion will focus, instead, upon the adequacy of Rothenberg's notion of ideology, and its usefulness in explaining the actual transformation of the Massachusetts countryside in the late eighteenth century. The late English historian J.P. Cooper, in discussing a similar attempt to posit changes in *mentalités* as the cause of socio-economic transformations in early-modern Europe, argued:

> The whole conception of *mentalities*...stresses the absence or impossibility of certain concepts and attitudes existing in given periods. In so doing, it tends to create a uniformity which hides or denies the capacity of individuals and societies to hold contradictory or incompatible ideas and ideals simultaneously.[64]

In other words, asserting that changes in ideas and values bring about major changes in socio-economic behaviours and relationships necessarily implies that individuals, social groups and societies hold consistent and formally logical world-views at all times. Much of the confusion among both 'market'- and 'social' historians about the ideology of northeastern farmers and artisans in the eighteenth and early nineteenth centuries is the result of this problematic notion of ideology. The 'social historians', attempts to document a consistent 'familial/communitarian' farmer-ideology is as futile as the 'market-historians' efforts to document a consistent 'individualist' rural

---

62 Weber 1981, pp. 275–8.
63 The best elaboration of this view remains Godelier 1972.
64 Cooper 1985, p. 140.

world-view. Neither are successful because ideologies are not formally logical sets of ideas and values 'with a life of their own'. In the words of the US historian Barbara Jeanne Fields:

> Ideology is best understood as the descriptive vocabulary of day-to-day existence, through which people make rough sense of the social reality that they live and create from day to day. It is the language of consciousness that suits the particular way in which people deal with their fellows. It is the interpretation in thought of the social relations through which they constantly create and re-create their collective being, in all the varied forms their collective being may assume: family, clan, tribe, nation, class, party, business enterprise, church, army, club, and so on.[65]

From this perspective on ideology, it should come as no surprise that the world-view of eighteenth-century New-England farmers who were both small property-owners commanding the labour of family-members and labourers themselves, both involved in the market and sheltered from its discipline, contained elements of *both* 'possessive individualism' and 'communitarianism'. Daniel Vickers, in his path-breaking essay, analyses the commonly held eighteenth- and early nineteenth-century ideal of 'competency':

> the possession of sufficient property to absorb the labors of a given family while providing it with something more than a mere subsistence. It meant, in brief, a degree of comfortable independence.[66]

'Competency' proved to be a world-view perfectly compatible with either co-operative or competitive economic behaviour. In a sense, it was the 'natural ideology' of the antebellum-Northern farmers and rural artisans. No other ideology could provide an adequate mental 'road-map' to the highly contradictory reality of their lived social relations.

Temporarily granting some of Rothenberg's assumptions will demonstrate other, more profound problems inherent in her explanation of the transformation of New-England agriculture. While Rothenberg does not present the precise mechanisms by which the new 'Lockean paradigm' altered the behaviour of family-farmers, the 'market-historian' James T. Lemon did so in his essay

---

[65] Fields 1990, p. 110.
[66] Vickers 1990, p. 1.

'Early Americans and Their Social Environment'.[67] According to Lemon, a minority of farmers adopted new individualist, wealth-seeking values in the aftermath of the 'Great Awakening' and adapted their agricultural practices to their newly found worldview. While a minority, these farmers (and their allies among wealth-seeking merchants) became the dominant social groups and made these values the basis of the northern colonies' status-esteem hierarchy. Put simply, the rest of the farmers must adapt these new values, and the behaviour that corresponds to them, or lose social esteem.

While the bulk of the farmers would stand to lose social honour if they failed to adapt a 'market-orientation', *they would not be in any danger of losing possession of their farms.* Independent household-producers as a class were not dependent upon successful market-competition for their economic survival. A significant minority of farmers could act on the basis of 'abstract economic rationality' (specialising production in response to market-signals, reorganising their labour-processes, etc.), but their more recalcitrant neighbours would be under no economic compulsion to do so – they would not face any of the usual market-penalties (loss of market-share, unsold product, and the possible loss of landed property) for their failure. Those who continued to act on the basis of 'substantial economic rationality' could ignore market-signals and still keep their farm, as long as they could sell enough of their output to pay minimal mortgages and taxes. As a result, the land and labour-power of the 'subsistence-oriented' majority would not become available to the 'market-oriented' minority. The ability of the enterprising farmers to consolidate landholdings large enough to use new fertilisers, crop-rotation methods or implements, to hire their poorer neighbours; and to raise the productivity of agriculture sufficiently to allow an ever growing portion of the population to work in industry would be severely limited.[68] In sum, the development of market-production, technical innovation, rising labour-productivity and the like were not the result of the value-driven choices of groups of producers. Instead, the source of these momentous social and economic changes must be sought in the destruction and construction of social-property relations in the struggle between social classes.

---

[67] Lemon 1980, pp. 118ff. A similar 'entrepreneurial-leadership' thesis is presented for the antebellum north-west in Danhof 1969, pp. 280–90.

[68] This point is made by Brenner 1977, pp. 73–5. A similar argument is presented in Luxemburg 1968, Chapters 27 and 29; and Bernstein 1977.

The 'social historians', according to Kulikoff, tend to see the process of transition to commercial agriculture and capitalist industry 'not [as] an automatic process but one fraught with conflict and violence'.[69] Unfortunately, there is neither little consensus among the 'social historians' on the transition in the Northern countryside, nor a clear emphasis on class-conflict. While Merrill provides no explanation of the transformation of north-eastern agriculture, Clark presents a detailed historical analysis of the transition in western Massachusetts. The disappearance of unoccupied land in western Massachusetts with the completion of settlement between 1720 and 1760, combined with population-growth and growing inequalities in landholdings in the 1750s and 1760s, produced rising land-prices in the decades after the Revolution. The rising cost of providing land to male heirs forced rural households to engage in new economic activities in order to maintain the lineal family-landholding in the 1780s and 1790s. First, rural households cleared unsettled lands in their possession, and brought these new lands into intensive cultivation to produce commodities for sale in distance-markets (cattle for meat and dairy, hay and other grasses to feed cattle and other livestock, and broomcorn). Second, the labour of rural women and children was directed to the production of shoes, linen and other textiles as commodities. Nearly one in every five or six households engaged in rural manufacture of both use-values for local consumption and exchange-values for the northern urban and southern plantation-markets. Finally, households attempted to use the mechanisms of 'neighbourly exchange' to obtain long-term, low or no interest-loans from local merchants to finance the purchase of additional land.[70]

These new economic practices, whose goal was the preservation of the household's 'independence', created a crisis of rural production-relations in the 1820s that completed the subordination of the households to market-discipline. On the one hand, augmented rural manufacture for both consumption and exchange radically increased the burdens on rural women, adding highly labour-intensive tasks to their domestic responsibilities to make cloth, sew clothing, prepare foodstuffs and care for children. On the other, borrowing cash for land-purchases from merchants through the mechanisms of 'neighbourly exchange' began to break down as local storekeepers, themselves under pressure to pay debts from urban merchants, began demanding the

---

[69] Kulikoff 1989, p. 123.
[70] Clark 1990, Chapter 3.

prompt and regular payment, with interest, of debts after 1800. These pressures spawned a new set of priorities in the deployment of household-labour. Cloth and several other consumption-goods previously produced by rural women were now purchased on the market, and household-labour was expended in activities that could produce a cash-income to pay debts, taxes and to purchase new 'store-bought' commodities. Wealthier households began to specialise in the production of agricultural commodities such as wheat, meat, dairy and eggs; while poorer households began to provide labour-power to local merchants who were organising capitalist 'outwork'-production of buttons, palm-leaf hats and other manufactured goods. The deepening dependence of rural households on the market for their consumption-requirements and the resulting changes in their labour-processes in the 1830s completed the transformation of the western Massachusetts countryside. Larger, better-located farmers specialised in the production of tobacco because competition from western farms undermined the production of wheat, cattle and broomcorn. Smaller, less well-located farmers intensified their dependence on 'outwork' or became wage-workers in the region's growing manufacturing and industrial centres.[71] In sum, western Massachusetts had been transformed from an area populated by independent household-producers into a region dominated by agrarian petty-commodity production and industrial capitalism.

For Clark, the development of commercial agriculture and capitalist manufacture in the north-eastern US was a 'process of accretion, rather than a single 'transition'. He claims, further, that the two decades after the Revolution were not the turning point in rural social development. Clark argues that farmers and artisans 'had succeeded in retaining effective control of rural production and the patterns of exchange' well into the nineteenth century. No single factor had any greater importance than any other in determining the course social change in the north-east:

> Demography, land shortage, the 'market', household strategies, or capital accumulation were not single, outstanding motors of change, but came together, taking different forms at different periods, to alter the character of rural New England profoundly and relatively rapidly....The search for livelihoods and security was a crucial driving force for change'.[72]

---

[71] Clark 1990, Chapters 4–8.
[72] Clark 1990, pp. 15, 54–5, 318.

Despite Clark's commitment to causal pluralism and an analysis emphasising a gradual transition from non-commercial to commercial agriculture and manufacture, his own empirical research points to the centrality of the social conditions of land-ownership and to a sharp discontinuity in development before and after the Revolution and Constitutional Settlement. It is quite clear that land-prices, taxes and debts rose sharply in the late eighteenth century. Clark attributes rising land-prices to population-pressure on land. Nonetheless, he provides evidence of a social causation for this phenomena – the speculators' social monopoly of land. Land-speculation on the New-England frontier (north-western Massachusetts, Vermont, New Hampshire, Maine) began to raise land-prices in the 1740s and 1750s, and intensified during and immediately after the Revolution. Clark dismisses land-speculation as 'marginal' to production, missing its effects on the relationship of rural households to their major means of production. Heightened land-speculation and other social disruptions of the Revolutionary period led to major social conflicts in the 1780s and 1790s, whose outcomes fatally undermined independent household-production in the north-east. In sum, Clark profoundly underestimates the impact of the Revolution and its aftermath on the north-eastern countryside, when he claims that Shays' Rebellion and other rural revolts of the period 'did little to alter the real balance of power'.[73]

David Weiman provides another, more theoretical,[74] analysis of the transition from independent household-production (in his terms, 'petty production') to simple commodity-production. Inherent in independent production is a tension between 'kinship/communal' relations ('neighbourly exchange' and the like) and production of goods for long-distance markets. Growing involvement in the market on the part of older and wealthier households promoted the development of a merchant-class, which sought to expand commodity-production through investments in transportation-infrastructure (roads, canals, railroads) and land (speculation and mortgage-lending). While the increasing dependence of larger farmers upon the market was a necessary condition for the breakdown of independent household-production, it was not sufficient. Arguing that the development of commercial agriculture was not a 'market-process', Weiman

---

[73] Clark 1990, pp. 42–3, 49, 54–5.
[74] Weiman 1989, 260–1. Weiman's (1985, 1987, 1988) empirical research concerning non-slaveholding farmers in the Southern US will not be reviewed here.

asserts that the merchants and the richer farmers engaged in political struggles over taxation, construction of 'internal improvements', use of common lands and the like in order to replace 'kin and communal bonds with contractual relations based solely on the exchange of private property'. Once kinship- and communal relations were uprooted, households became increasingly dependent on commodity-production to obtain needed consumer-goods (no longer available through non-commodity 'neighbourly exchange'), and market-integration of the petty producers became 'an irreversible process'.[75]

Weiman's analysis is distinguished by the importance it accords to the economic activities of merchants, particularly their role in land-speculation, and to class-conflicts in the transformation of rural household-production. His emphasis on the incipient class-divisions among the independent producers goes a long way to help explain the divergences in political behaviour among farmers in the late eighteenth and nineteenth centuries. However, Weiman's claim that there is an inherent tension in non-commercial agriculture between the demands of 'kinship and communal relations' and commodity-production and exchange is highly problematic. Like Rothenberg and Lemon, Weiman tends to ignore how the social-property relations of independent household-production – the ability of the direct producers to maintain their landholding without recourse to commodity-production because of the low costs of appropriating land – shield all the farmers and artisans from the logic of market-competition. As Brenner put it:

> ...the peasant [or independent household producer – C.P.] was under relatively little pressure to operate his plot as profitably and effectively as his potential competitors in order to survive, for there were no direct means for such competitors to 'defeat' him. In other words, the peasant did not have to be competitive, because he did not really have to be able to 'hold his place' in the world of the market.... Unlike the independent artisan [or family-farmer with a large mortgage or debts – C.P.], he did not have to be able to produce cheaply enough to sell good profitability at the market place – or else go out of business. All that was necessary for survival for the peasant proprietor...was sufficient output to provide for his family's subsistence and to pay his taxes...[76]

---

[75] Weiman 1989, pp. 260–1.
[76] Brenner 1985a, pp. 59–60.

On the one hand, wealthier households could participate in the market without risk. If agricultural prices and their revenues fell, richer farmers could redeploy most of their household-labour to the production of use-values without danger of losing their farms. On the other, the successful commodity-production of richer households could not threaten the poorer households' possession of land. Secure in their ownership of their farm, poorer farmers could ignore price-signals and still keep their farm. In sum, there was no necessary tension between use-value and exchange-value production in independent household-production that made it 'an inherently transitory system of economic and social relations'.[77]

In Weiman's defence, one could argue that he does not hold to a 'Smithian' notion of an immanent tendency toward commodity-production among all economic actors because he emphasises the role of political conflict in undermining 'kinship-communal' relations and replacing them with 'contractual relations'.[78] However, Weiman's discussion of class-conflict is open to related criticisms. As I argued above, 'kinship- and communal relations' are not the source of the independent producers' ability to withstand the demands of market-competition. Instead, these relations rest upon the ability of the 'non-commercial' farmers to obtain, maintain and expand their landholding without recourse to commodity-production. Similarly, 'contractual relations' are the product of the householders' need to successfully compete on the market to preserve their farm. Since he provides no discussion of how the class-struggle between merchants and wealthier farmers, on one hand, and poor and middling farmers, on the other, changes the conditions for the reproduction of the farmers' possession of landed property, Weiman's analysis remains highly problematic.

Alan Kulikoff attempts to explain the transformation of the countryside as the result of the spread of commodity-production that accompanied the development of industrial capitalism. According to Kulikoff, the transformation of the Northern countryside during the nineteenth century can best be understood in terms of how capitalist development changed the conditions

---

[77] Weiman 1989, p. 260.
[78] Such a 'Smithian' argument is found in Levine 1975, pp. 52–8, one of Weiman's theoretical sources. For a thorough critique of the notion that commodity-circulation has an inherent tendency to undermine non-capitalist forms of production, see Brenner 1977, pp. 33–41; and Wood 1999, Chapter I.

in which 'yeoman'-farmers (independent household-producers) attempted to maintain land-ownership:

> The strategies yeoman pursued to achieve economic independence – what crops they grew, how deeply they committed themselves to market production, what tools they purchased, how often they hired workers – were shaped by capitalist expansion.... As industrial capitalist replaced the petty manufacturers of the late eighteenth century, yeoman were forced into greater indebtedness by financial capitalists or railroad magnates and saw their sons and neighbours adopt capitalist agriculture or fall into wage-labor.[79]

Specifically, there were two major mechanisms through which capitalist development in the urban areas drew 'yeomen'-farmers and artisans into petty-commodity production. First, the development of capitalist production outside agriculture created markets for food and other agricultural products:

> ... wherever capitalists (even the early hand 'manufacturing' capitalists before the machine age) invested their profits and created new markets, an important minority of farmers rushed to invest and participate, and soon entire communities found themselves dependent on markets and forced to share profits with distant capitalists.[80]

Second, the development of manufacturing and industry undermined household-production by drawing labour-power (especially female and juvenile labour-power) out of the household, providing cash-income and encouraging the purchase of consumer-goods previously produced in the household.[81] In sum, it was the development of capitalism and commodity-production outside of agriculture that transformed the countryside in the nineteenth century.[82]

---

[79] Kulikoff 1989, pp. 141–2.
[80] Kulikoff 1989, pp. 134, 139.
[81] Kulikoff 1989, p. 135.
[82] In a later collection of essays, Kulikoff (1992, pp. 43–7, 147–51, 211–17) does recognise that land-speculation undermined the 'easy availability of inexpensive land' necessary to the preservation of 'yeoman'- or independent household-production. However, the main thrust of Kulikoff's arguments remains the transformation of Northern agriculture as the *result* of industrialisation and the growth of urban markets.

The weight Kulikoff assigns to the growth of urban manufacture and industry and its attendant demand for food-stuffs and labour-power is reminiscent of Paul Sweezy's and Immanuel Wallerstein's analyses of the European transition from feudalism to capitalism. For both Sweezy and Wallerstein, the growth of medieval cities was the central cause of the decline of feudalism in the western-European countryside. Not only did these cities provide a market for the output of the peasants' and lords' lands, but they provided a 'refuge' for runaway-serfs, undermining the lords' authority and promoting the decline of serfdom in the fourteenth and fifteenth centuries.[83] Unfortunately, Kulikoff's argument suffers from the same shortcomings as Sweezy's and Wallerstein's.

As Brenner pointed out in his critique of Sweezy and Wallerstein, the growth of commodity-circulation can only promote the transformation of agriculture if three conditions exist, first:

> the potential 'mobility of labour-power' in response to the market – which is, however, bound up with the degree of freedom/unfreedom and with the economic dependence/independence of the direct producers; 2. the potential for developing the productivity of labour through separation and specialisation of tasks – which is, however, bound up with the possibilities of developing co-operative labour in connection with growing means of production; 3. the potential for enforcing continuing pressure to develop labour-productivity – which is, however, bound up with the survival and reproductive needs of the direct producers and exploiters in relation to their access to the means of subsistence and production.[84]

None of these three conditions were present in the independent-household social-property relations that structured agricultural production in the late eighteenth and early nineteenth century. The ability of 'yeoman'-farmers to preserve their landholdings without recourse to successful commodity-production meant, first, there was no economic necessity for even the most inefficient household-producers to leave agriculture for urban industry. Second, there was no market-mechanism to allow the more efficient farmers to gain access to the land and labour-power of their less productive neigh-

---

[83] Sweezy 1976a and 1976b; Wallerstein 1974, Chapter 2.
[84] Brenner 1977, p. 34.

bours, blocking the reorganisation of the agricultural labour-process. Third, there was no competitive compulsion for any, even the most productive, wealthy and market-oriented minority of 'yeomen'-farmers to continuously develop labour-productivity. In other words, the transformation of rural social relations – making 'yeoman'-farmers incapable of maintaining their landholding without commodity-production – was the necessary *precondition* for the development of capitalist manufacture and industry. Only when rural households were subject to the 'dictates of the market' (law of value) were they forced to innovate and develop labour-productivity to survive, compelling the growing portion of the rural population who lost the competitive battle to work in manufacture and industry, and providing a growing market for factory-produced means of production and consumption.

III. The transformation of the Northern countryside, c. 1776–1861

The key to the transformation of Northern agriculture before the Civil War from independent household-production, a social-property form relatively impervious to market-forces, to petty-commodity production, a social-property form dependent upon competitive markets, is located in the outcome of class-struggles between merchants (including local storekeepers, larger town and urban wholesales, land-Speculators, etc.) and the bulk of the 'yeomanry' over the social conditions for appropriating, maintaining and expanding the central agricultural means of production – land. European settlement of the northern British colonies began in the seventeenth century, after Native Americans were forcibly removed from the eastern seaboard. The goal of the British-colonial administrations, representing large landholders and merchants, was to promote commodity-production in the colonies. To this end, they attempted to establish private-property rights in land in North America through two forms of land-grants. In New England, colonial governments granted land to groups of settlers in the form of townships. These original settlers, or 'proprietors', divided land among themselves as freeholds and common lands. Later settlers, faced with the proprietors' possession of the most fertile and best located land and their exclusive use of commons, were forced either to buy or lease land from the original settlers. In the 'middle colonies', the colonial governments of New York, Pennsylvania and New Jersey granted land to large mercantile companies, who in turn sold land to large landowners, who leased land to tenant-farmers. Despite growing social inequalities in land-distribution and the rapid increases in the size of agricultural 'surpluses' (grain, timber, meat and dairy, and 'home-spun' cloth) sold to the Northern cities and towns and the plantations of the Southern colonies and the Caribbean in the 1740s and 1750s, the 'yeomanry' of the northern colonies retained their autonomy from 'market-discipline'.[85]

The existence of unoccupied land within easy reach of poor and 'middling' settlers undermined the ability of land-owners to create a social monopoly of land in the eighteenth century. However, the eighteenth-century frontier was not a 'Turnerian' utopia of independent 'free-holding' pioneers. Settlers in the 'interior' found urban merchants had invested their revenues from the colonial trade in large tracks of land, which the latter hoped to sell to 'enterprising' farmers for a considerable profit. Unable to obtain legal title to land, prospective farmers and artisans (often migrating with groups of co-religionists, kin, or former neighbours) illegally occupied ('squatted') the speculators' lands. As long as the colonial militia could not and, after the 1763 Proclamation forbids colonial settlement west of the Alleghenies, the British authorities would not enforce the land-speculators' private property-rights on the frontier, farmers and rural artisans could establish, maintain and expand their landholding without extensive commodity-production.[86]

In New England, settlers took up illegal occupation on lands in the Connecticut River valley and in uninhabited areas of Vermont, New Hampshire and Maine. Some pioneers eventually established legal 'freehold'-rights to these lands at minimal cost with inflated bank-notes issued by 'land-banks' these farmers organised in the 1740s and 1750s. New waves of illegal occupations kept land-prices relatively low throughout New England before the Revolution. In the 'middle colonies', settlers 'squatted' on lands far removed from the coastal settlements, undermining the ability of landlords to impose capitalist landlord-tenant relations in the settled, seaboard-regions. The 'rent-wars' of the mid-eighteenth century scuttled the landlords' attempts to collect 'quit-rents' and impose market-discipline on the household-producers in the mid-Atlantic region. Tenancy was abolished almost completely in the north-east

---

[85] Bidwell and Falconer 1925, I, pp. 49–62, 115–7, 126–33; Henretta 1991b, pp. 211–31; Main 1965, pp. 8–30.
[86] Friedenberg 1992, Chapters 5, 6 and 8–14; Henretta 1991b, pp. 216–17; Noble 1989, pp. 647–50, 654–6; Rasmussen 1969.

during the Revolution, when many landlords (mostly British sympathisers) were expropriated and their lands distributed among their former tenants.[87]

By the time of the Revolution, 'free-holding' independent farmers and artisans with minimal mortgages and other expenses (taxes, debts, etc.) populated the northern-colonial countryside. While able to reproduce themselves economically without recourse to the market, these farmers engaged in exchange-relations with local and regional merchants. Small 'country-merchants', often in partnership with more substantial merchants in the larger inland-towns (e.g., the 'River Gods' of the Connecticut-River valley), gathered together the farmers' scattered 'surpluses' of grain, timber, cattle and dairy-products for shipment to the major coastal urban markets of New York, Philadelphia and Boston. These rural and small-town entrepreneurs also sold imported manufactured and agricultural goods (glass, iron, gunpowder, medicine, tea, sugar) that could not be produced in the self-sufficient rural communities. Local merchants continually encouraged farmers to buy more items of consumption in order to widen their scale of operations and enrich themselves. However, the farmers' and rural craftsmen's non-market access to land enabled them to produce the bulk of their own subsistence, and prevented them from being drawn into dependence upon the market.[88]

The Revolution and its immediate aftermath radically altered the relationships between the 'yeomanry' and the merchants and land-speculators.[89] State-governments and the Continental Army began to purchase food, cloth and other supplies from farm-households throughout the North at extremely high prices. In order to meet the requisitions and support the revolutionary-war effort, the 'yeomanry' were forced to devote more and more family labour to the production of commodities. Unable to produce the variety of goods previously manufactured in their self-sufficient communities, rural households borrowed from local store-keepers to purchase the output of US urban artisans and manufacturers during the War and British manufacturers after the War. In the aftermath of the War, these debts became particularly burdensome, as the Northern state-governments began to raise taxes (mostly land-taxes which fell heavily upon farmers and rural artisans) to fund the

---

[87] Countryman 1976; Hacker 1947, pp. 106–44; Main 1965, pp. 8–30; Spark 1932, Chapters 4–5.
[88] Nobles 1990, pp. 5–12; Nobles 1989, pp. 655–6; Szatmary 1980, pp. 12–18.
[89] Kulikoff 1992, pp. 100–51.

mushrooming public debt accrued during the War. The combined growth of debts and taxes forced Northern households to market larger and larger portions of both their 'subsistence'- and 'surplus'-output in order to keep their land in the 1780s.[90]

The Revolution simultaneously strengthened the position of land-speculators on the frontier. Urban and small-town merchants were able to garner tremendous 'wind-fall' profits from the War's disruption of commerce. The British naval blockade of their former mainland-colonies closed off legal trade with Europe and the Caribbean, allowing urban merchants to make enormous returns on smuggling and privateering. Similarly, the collapse of the British-backed currency- and banking system presented new opportunities for mercantile profit-making. As the new central and state-governments began to issue a torrent of paper-money and bonds to cover the public debt, merchants amassed huge fortunes in currency- and financial speculation. The favoured venue for the investment of these revenues was land on the frontier, now open to settlement with the abrogation of the British 'Proclamation of 1763' banning colonial settlement beyond the Allegheny Mountains. These absentee-landlords hoped that a US victory would rapidly open the 'west' to settlement and help create new political institutions that could enforce their private property-rights in land. The wake of the War saw increasing inequalities in landholding on the frontier (including the growth of tenancy in western Pennsylvania) and rapidly rising prices for land throughout the north-east. The speculators' engrossment of land on the frontier, together with the growing burdens of taxes and debts, seriously undermined independent household-production immediately after the Revolution. By the mid-1780s, farmers and rural artisans found themselves needing 'to sell to survive' – to participate successfully in competitive markets in order to keep their farms.[91]

The crisis of independent household-production in the north-eastern US spawned a major social explosion in western Massachusetts in 1787. In 1784–5, the simultaneous closing of the British Caribbean to US merchant-shipping and a glut of British manufactures on the US market led to a 'strangling chain of debt collection'.[92] As British manufacturing wholesalers pressed their

---

[90] Henretta 1991b, pp. 231–48; Jensen 1969, pp. 113–21; Kulikoff 1989, pp. 130–1; Nobles 1990, pp. 12–13; Szatmary 1980, pp. 19–23.
[91] Friedenberg 1992, Chapters 17, 19, 25–7, 29; Henretta 1991b, pp. 254–5; Slaughter 1986, pp. 64–70, 78–88.
[92] Szatmary 1980, p. 26.

merchant-clients in Boston for speedy repayment, the Boston merchants in turn solicited their clients in the rural towns, who in turn demanded that local farmers pay their debts in specie, rather than devalued paper-money. The result was a marked growth in the number of law-suits for the collection of debts in central and western Massachusetts. The least efficient farmers, hard pressed by falling prices and rising taxes, faced the possibility of losing their land through foreclosure. Their demands for debt-relief ('stay'-laws to delay the collection of debts, property-exemptions from seizure for debt, inflationary paper-money) and the reduction of land-taxes were rebuffed by the merchant-dominated Massachusetts General Assembly in 1786. In response, farmers and their allies in western Massachusetts began to harass tax-collectors and close courts involved in foreclosure-proceedings before launching an unsuccessful revolt in early 1787.[93]

Shays' Rebellion has often been misinterpreted as either 'a fist shaken at impending change' by the 'market-historians' or 'an economic conflict exacerbated by a cultural clash between a commercial society and a rural, subsistence-oriented way of life' by the 'social historians'.[94] Instead, it was part of a cycle of class-struggles during the 1780s and 1790s which initiated the transition from independent household-production to petty-commodity production in the north-eastern countryside. In addition to Shays' Rebellion, independent farmers and artisans contested tax-collectors, merchant-creditors and land-speculators over the conditions of their economic survival in Maine (the 'White Indians' or 'Timber Pirates'), Vermont (the 'Green Mountain Boys'), Pennsylvania ('Whiskey Rebellion' and the lesser known 'Fries Uprising') and Ohio (the destruction of 'squatter'-settlements in Ohio in 1785–6).[95] The turning point in this cycle of class-conflict was the Constitutional Settlement of 1787, which established the political dominance of the mercantile capitalists and created state-institutions (a corps of tax-collectors and a federal army) capable of implementing pro-merchant state-policies.[96] The victory of the merchants and their allies in these struggles did not reduce the family-farmers to tenancy

---

[93] Szatmary 1980, Chapters 2–6; Brooke 1989.
[94] Rothenberg 1992, p. 236; Szatmary 1980, p. 18.
[95] Cayton 1986, Chapter 1; Jensen 1969, pp. 121–2; Nobles 1989, pp. 664–9; Slaughter 1986; Taylor 1989.
[96] On the Constitutional Settlement, see Friedenberg 1992, Chapters 30–1; Kulikoff 1992, pp. 141–51; Lynd 1967, pp. 135–213; Main 1973, pp. 135–67; Mayer and Fay 1977; Szatmary 1980, Chapter 7.

or wage-labour. Instead, by closing off access to cheap or inexpensive land on the frontier, levying burdensome taxes and enforcing the payment of debt in specie, the merchants' political hegemony ensured that the farmers marketed both the 'surplus' and portions of their 'subsistence'-output. In other words, the farmers became dependent upon successful market-production for their economic survival – they became agrarian petty-commodity producers.

There is considerable evidence of the north-eastern 'yeomanry' attempting to meet the new conditions for the acquisition, maintenance and expansion of landholding while continuing to produce the bulk of their 'subsistence' during the first two decades of the nineteenth century. Increased and reorganised labour devoted to the production of marketable 'surpluses' was not limited to western Massachusetts or New England. From around 1790 until the commercial crisis of 1819, north-eastern farmers noticeably expanded their output of grain, meat and other agricultural commodities for sale in US urban and European markets. In the mid-Atlantic region, increased commodity-production in response to the changed social conditions of economic survival led many farmers to reorganise their agricultural labour-processes. 'Up and down husbandry', the crop-rotation method between fields, pastures and meadows that allowed the interdependent growth of animal- and arable output associated with the development of capitalist agriculture in England in the seventeenth century, radically increased labour and soil-productivity in the north-eastern US in the early nineteenth century. As in seventeenth-century England, the subordination of the rural population to 'market-coercion' promoted the consolidation of landholding and relative product-specialisation required for 'up and down husbandry'.[97]

The growth of handicraft commodity-production in the north-eastern countryside accompanied the farmers' and artisans' unsuccessful attempt to revolutionise agricultural production without abandoning the production of 'subsistence' in the household. The production of woollen, linen and other cloth, both for household- and community-consumption and increasingly for sale, grew markedly before 1820 in both New England and the mid-Atlantic region. This increase took place primarily on the basis of a *Kaufsystem* of 'proto-

---

[97] Appleby 1982, pp. 838–44; Clemens and Simler 1988; Henretta 1991d. On the importance of 'up and down husbandry' in the development of capitalist agriculture in north-western Europe in the seventeenth century, see Brenner 1985b, pp. 308–10, 315–16; and Kerridge 1969, pp. 109–10, 124–7, 257–8, 274–8.

industrialisation' in which the households continued to own their means of production (looms). These producers enjoyed a much greater autonomy from merchants and manufacturers, whose role was limited to supplying raw material and buying up finished products, than the *de facto* wage-labourers of the *verlag* or capitalist form of 'proto-industrialisation'. Nonetheless, there is evidence of growing intra-regional specialisation, with some townships becoming centres of craft-production and others become centres of agricultural production in the late-eighteenth and early-nineteenth centuries. In other words, the growth of handicraft-output for market in this period was not a by-product of a thriving independent-household economy of 'subsistence-surplus' production, but was evidence of the growing dependence of north-eastern households on commodity-production for their economic survival.[98]

The commercial depression of 1819–21, with its falling commodity-prices, created a crisis for the 'yeomanry's' attempt simultaneously to increase the amount of labour devoted to the production of commodities and to continue to produce the bulk of their own subsistence. There is evidence of the increasing demands on rural women to produce cloth and to carry out their 'traditional' tasks of child-rearing, house-cleaning, food-preparation, gardening, dairying and the like becoming intolerable by the early 1820s. These intra-household conflicts were resolved through the shift of female labour from weaving cloth to dairying and other commodity-producing activities.[99]

As household-production of cloth was abandoned, the 'yeomanry's' dependence upon the market deepened in the 1820s and 1830s. The results were increased specialisation in agricultural products that could be sold in distant urban and foreign markets, and the growth of capitalist domestic outwork. The capacity to work of women and children in poorer rural families, unable to raise sufficient cash to pay mortgages, taxes and other debts through agricultural production, became available to merchants and manufacturers who organised a *verlag*-system of 'proto-industrialisation' in the northeast. The merchants and manufacturers no longer traded with essentially independent

---

[98] On the growth of household-based handicraft commodity-production, see: Clark 1990 Chapter 3; Dublin 1991, pp. 538–48; Henretta 1991b, pp. 248–54. On the concept of 'proto-industrialisation', see: Medick 1976; Mendels 1972; Quataert 1988. For the classical analysis of the relationship of domestic production to capitalist manufacture and industry, see: Marx 1976, Chapters 14–15.

[99] On the role of gender-conflict in the reorganisation of household-labour, see Clark 1990, Chapter 4; Jensen 1986, pp. 87–92; Kulikoff 1989, pp. 138–40.

producers, but instead provided both raw materials and tools and machinery to rural wage-workers who produced finished or semi-finished products owned by the 'proto-industrial' capitalist. While the merchants in palm-leaf hat-manufacture operated autonomously, organising a self-contained production-process carried out entirely in rural households; those in button-, shoe-, boot- and other capitalist domestic manufacture were often partners of manufacturers, who organised a centralised labour-process in a small workshop and 'put out' parts of the production-process to workers in the countryside.[100]

The defeat of the small producers in the north-east in the last two decades of the eighteenth century, while sealing the fate of independent household-production in the original area of colonial settlement, did not spell the end of this social-property form in the US. In the South, independent household-production flourished in the interstices of plantation-slavery. In the 'upcountry' and 'pine barrens' of the South, farmers were able to remain relatively isolated from the 'market-process' as a result of the low cost of their less desirable land (the planters monopolised land in the more fertile 'piedmont'-regions) and the farmers' alliance with the planters that kept state-government expenditures (on schools, roads, and the like) and taxes on land to a minimum.[101] In the Ohio Valley and Great Plains, independent production developed as Native Americans were forcibly 'removed' and white settlers took initial possession of land in most areas for little or no cost. Although federal land-law promoted the transfer of the massive 'public domain' into the hands of private land-holders, 'squatters' (settlers who took possession of land *prior* to federal land-auctions) were often able to defend their landholding against the claims of land-speculators and investors before the 1830s. Nearly two-thirds of all farmers in Illinois were 'squatters' in 1828, and, in some communities, 40% of all farmers were still 'squatters' in 1840. 'Claims-clubs' of settlers on public lands without legal title, including some who had laid claim to lands in excess of their personal needs, usually to provide land for male heirs, successfully 'warned off' urban land-companies and later arriving farmers and secured land for a minority of settlers at federal minimum-prices. Generally, land-speculators

---

[100] Clark 1990, Chapter 4–6; Dawley 1976, pp. 25–30; Dublin 1991, pp. 548–68; Hazard 1921, pp. 42–8; Taylor 1951, pp. 207–20.
[101] Hahn 1983, Part I.

did not attempt to bid on 'squatters' lands, instead buying up the huge tracks of unoccupied lands in sparsely settled regions at federal land-auctions.[102]

At least temporarily secure in their possession of land without recourse to production for the market, the 'yeomanry' of the middle west were able to re-establish crucial elements of independent household-production in the early nineteenth century. While there is relatively little detailed research on 'self-sufficient' household-production in the antebellum-west, there is some evidence of both rural 'subsistence-surplus' production and non-commercial exchange between farmers and artisans and local storekeepers. Through the 1830s, the bulk of rural households and communities in the Ohio Valley and Great Plains appear to be self-sufficient in food and many handicraft-items. Farmers grew a wide variety of goods for consumption by their families and neighbours, and marketed only about 30% of their total output in the 1820s and 1830s. Clarence Danhof, a prominent agricultural historian, estimates that only those farms marketing 40% or more of their output became dependent upon commodity-production for their economic survival.[103] Secure in their basic foodstuffs, many households also engaged in extensive craft-production of tools, implements, utensils and clothing (but not cloth) for local consumption. Locally-produced 'general-use' implements and the inexpensive oxen, although less efficient than manufactured tools or horses, fit into the logic of 'self-sufficient' household-production:

> The choice between the two animals [oxen and horses – C.P.] was determined by the importance of speed in accomplishing necessary tasks as contrasted with the costs involved. In subsistence agriculture there were few if any operations where speed was of critical importance. The needs of the typical subsistence farmer for a wide variety of self-produced goods required that a minimum of effort be given to any single item among the variety of products desired. Maximum economy was achieved by the production of items of multiple use, even at substantial sacrifice of quality or convenience, since capital was thereby conserved. This was as true of draft animals as of implements and crops.[104]

---

[102] Bogue 1958; Bogue 1963, pp. 31–8; Faragher 1986, Chapter 7, pp. 175–6; Swierenga 1968, pp. 11–17, 214–5.
[103] Danhof 1979, pp. 129–33.
[104] Danhof 1969, p. 142.

The spread of transportation-facilities (roads and canals) facilitated the circulation of rural 'surpluses' as commodities bound for urban markets, but did not change the rural households and communities' relationship to their land and their ability to produce the majority of their subsistence as use-values before 1840.[105]

The deficiency of research using the account books of western farmers, artisans and merchants deprives us of a detailed knowledge of the exchange-relations among north-western rural households before 1840. However, Lewis E. Atherton's *The Frontier Merchant in Mid-America* provides important insights into the relationship between farmers and artisans and local merchants in the early nineteenth-century middle west.[106] The exchange-relations between western households and merchants were typical of independent household-production. The bulk of the transactions involved the farmers' and artisans' exchange of 'surpluses' for a limited number of store-bought commodities (tea, coffee, sugar, flour, liquor, and by the 1820s and 1830s, cloth):

> Farmers exchanged their crops for groceries and dry goods and thereby evaded the need for currency. Furs, meat, wheat, beeswax, flax, hemp, honey, whiskey, ginseng – anything of value – could be exchanged for goods at the neighbourhood store. Through barter, the storekeeper could dispose of his wares to a population that lacked ready cash with which to buy. All over the West this pattern of bartering goods for produce existed, the merchant serving as a middleman between producer and manufacturer or wholesaler. He consigned the farm crops he took in exchange for goods and shipped them to commission merchants in the larger Western cities and in New Orleans, and with the proceeds from the sale settled his bills to the eastward.[107]

The relationship between the rural households, local merchants and urban wholesalers was no more harmonious in the west than it was in the east. Farmers and artisans in the west maintained long-term, irregularly settled and interest-free accounts with local merchants, who were under constant

---

[105] Atack and Bateman 1987, pp. 202–7; Birch 1985; Danhof 1969, pp. 3–15; Faragher 1986, Chapters 8, and 14; Gates 1960, pp. 48–50.

[106] Atherton 1971, pp. 13–20, 51–80, 125–36, 142–53.

[107] Atherton 1971, pp. 18–19. Atherton's description of exchange-relations between merchants and independent household-producers is very similar to Merrill 1986, pp. 37–51.

pressure from their urban suppliers for rapid, regular and interest-bearing settlement of debts. Despite various attempts to induce farmers and artisans to pay cash (including considerable discounts for cash-purchases) and a growing number of law-suits for repayment of debts with interest, the country-storekeepers of the middle west were unsuccessful in their attempts to put trade on a 'cash-basis' before the 1840s. A fairly typical example was a small-town merchant in St. Helena, Missouri who listed only one-third of his accounts as 'cash-accounts'. However a careful examination of these revealed that the vast majority of 'cash-customers' paid in farm-produce.[108]

Although independent household-production developed in the antebellum Ohio Valley and Great Plains, the outcome of the class-conflicts of the 1780s and 1790s severely delimited the mid-western farmers' autonomy from commodity-production. Most importantly, the federal laws administering the distribution of the vast 'public domain' stretching from the Appalachian mountains westward, promoted land-speculation and raised the cost of landed property to the vast majority of farmers who settled the mid-west in the antebellum-era. In other words, federal land-policies radically altered the relationship of rural households to landholding, making the appropriation, maintenance and expansion of land dependent upon successful commodity-production. Conceived between 1796 and 1820, antebellum federal land-policy provided for the survey and auction sale of public land after all Native-American and foreign claims on the public domain were settled through wars of conquest and treaties. The federal government set minimum-prices and acreage to be purchased, but put no restrictions on the maximum size of purchase, allowing the operation of 'market-mechanisms' to set the maximum-price obtained at public auction. Despite reductions in minimum-price per acre from $2.00 to $1.25 in 1820, and in minimum-acreage from three hundred sixty acres to eighty acres between 1804 and 1817, no maximum-prices or acreage were set.[109]

The system of public auction of government-lands – despite the Pre-Emption Act of 1841, which ostensibly gave 'squatters' the right to purchase their land at minimum-prices directly from the federal land-office[110] – promoted

---

[108] Atherton 1971, pp. 145–6.
[109] Gates 1960, pp. 54–7, 67–9, 71–5; Opie 1991, Chapters 1–3; Robbins 1976, pp. 3–34; Hibbard 1924, pp. 56–115.
[110] On the limits of the Pre-Emption Act of 1841, see Robbins 1976, pp. 89–91.

successive waves of land-speculation in the west during the antebellum-period. In the words of the historian John Opie, 'the real beneficiary of the extraordinary transfer of the nation's sovereign wealth was speculative private enterprise'.[111] State-government land-grants for canals, roads and railways also fuelled the market for land. Land-speculation, which peaked in 1818, 1836 and 1856 – years of financial and commercial expansion in all sectors of the antebellum-economy – became a major source of mercantile profits after the collapse of the US trans-Atlantic carrying trade following the War of 1812. Land-speculation, and the construction of and speculation in internal improvements in the west also became major arenas for the investment of British loans to state-governments and private banks in the 1820s and 1830s.[112]

Speculation in land, agricultural products and transportation-infrastructure reached unprecedented heights during the 1830s. As agricultural commodity-prices (led by cotton and grain) rose, banks in the Midwest (especially the more speculative 'wild-cat' banks) borrowed money from north-eastern US and British banks, which they in turn lent to land companies and individual speculators or directly invested in public lands. The boom peaked in 1836, when the Public Land Office sold more land than at any time during the nineteenth century – more than 17.7 million acres in the north-west alone. The Bank of England's massive contraction of credit in 1837 set off a chain-reaction across the Atlantic, ending the expansion. Encouraged by deflationary federal policies (the 'Specie Circular' which required the payment of specie for land, taxes and other federal obligations), north-eastern banks sharply reduced the volume of credit. As a result, many of the weaker, speculative banks in the west collapsed, as did land-sales, commodity-prices and other indicators of commodity-production and circulation. Although land-prices and sales fell sharply during the depression of 1837–41, prospective or actual settlers were unable to garner any of the benefits of the deflation. Farmers who had purchased land before the collapse were saddled with large mortgages for land purchased 'at the top of the market' as prices for agricultural goods continued to decline. Settlers who sought to buy land at the depth of the depression

---

[111] Opie 1991, p. xi.
[112] This and following paragraphs are based upon Cole 1963; North 1961, pp. 75–96, 194–203; North 1956; Opie 1991, Chapters 4–5.

often found none for sale or rent, as speculators withheld land from the market until prices revived in the 1840s.

The speculative expansion and crisis of the 1830s and early 1840s radically transformed the class-relations of Northern agriculture. Independent speculators (often larger farmers), land-companies and railroad- and canal-companies were able to appropriate much of the best located and most fertile lands, forcing prospective settlers to purchase land from them at prices well above the federal minimum. The situation in Illinois and Iowa in the 1840s and 1850s is described by the historian Allan Bogue:

> Settlers who arrived in a sparsely settled community often found that large holders owned many of the attractive locations. The title of many pioneer farmers, therefore, was derived not from the federal government but from non-resident investors. The real estate agents, bankers, and lawyers of the struggling prairie settlements counted heavily on the fees that they received for acting as the local agents of non-resident land-owners – speculators, railroads, and railroad land companies.[113]

Land-speculators' operations were so effective that in Iowa, a relatively sparsely settled 'frontier'-region in the decade before the Civil War, 78.1% of farmers had purchased their land from speculators in 1850 and 85.7% had obtained land from speculators in 1860.[114]

Land-speculation increased the costs of 'farm-building' – the costs of establishing a viable farm – in the 1840s and 1850s. In the 1830s, the cost of developing an 80-acre farm in Illinois, including clearing and fencing the land, buying implements and livestock, and constructing housing, ranged between $500 and $600.[115] By the 1850s, the purchase-price of land in Illinois, available primarily from land-companies and independent speculators, ranged from three to ten dollars per acre, making the land-costs alone between $240 and $800 for an 80-acre farm. By 1860, eighty acres of land in Illinois had risen to $1,345. These prices were usually greater than the cash-resources of most perspective settlers, who also had to make considerable investments in fencing, seed, livestock, housing, farm-implements, and, on the prairies, expensive soil-

---

[113] Bogue 1963, p. 39.

[114] Bogue 1963, pp. 40–6; Faragher 1986, pp. 182–5; Gates 1942; Swierenga 1968, pp. 48–50, 100–23; Tinzmann 1986, pp. 53–70.

[115] Bogue 1963, pp. 169–70.

preparation ('sod busting') and drainage. As a result, the great majority of farmers seeking fertile and well-located land in the mid-west during the 1840s and 1850s had to borrow money to purchase land and capital-equipment.[116]

The most common credit-arrangement for purchasing land in the three decades before the Civil War was the 'time-entry' system. Land-speculators or their agents would purchase ('enter') the land under their name from the Federal Land Office. The farmer-settler would have one year to pay the entire price of the land, plus interest ranging from 20% to 50%. This arrangement forced the new farmers to specialise output in 'cash-crops' in order to earn enough cash to meet this large obligation. Additionally, all but the most well-off farmers – those who had sold farms in the north-east and had considerable capital – required short-term loans to purchase implements, seed, fencing and other capital-goods. Local merchants, bankers, and real-estate agents offered such short-term loans at rates of interest ranging from 10% to 25%, compounded monthly. By the 1850s, mortgage-loans became more common, as established farmers used their land to obtain credit and purchase additional land and new farm-machinery.[117]

Younger settlers, unable to secure any form of land-credit, and older farmers in densely settled regions found farm-tenancy a means of securing or expanding possession of landed property in the 1840s and 1850s. By 1860, approximately one in five farmers in the mid-west were tenants of large land-companies, railroads and wealthy farmers. Rents, whether in the form of cash- or share-rents, established the same sort of 'partnership' between landlord and tenant in the Northern US in the mid-nineteenth century that had emerged in seventeenth-century England. While English tenants-farmers did not see their 'increased revenues resulting from their capital-investments confiscated by the landlords' rent increases',[118] Northern US tenant-farmers saw their rents reduced when they increased their contributions to the fixed-capital of the farm (implements, work-animals, live-stock, etc.) Short leases (one to five years in length) created 'competitive rents',[119] allowing tenants to seek

---

[116] Atack and Bateman 1987, Chapter 8; Bogue 1963, Chapter IV; Danhof 1941; Danhof 1969, Chapters 4 and 5.

[117] Bogue 1951; Bogue 1976, pp. 73–84; Bogue 1963, pp. 170–9; Severson, Niss, Winkelman 1966; Swierenga 1968, pp. 107–23, 215–16; Tinzman 1986, Chapter V.

[118] Brenner 1985, pp. 49–50.

[119] Brenner 1985b, pp. 301–2.

better arrangements frequently and landlords to rid themselves of unco-oper-
ative tenants quickly. Leases, especially share rentals, often included detailed
instructions on the type and methods of agricultural commodity-production.
These 'commercial' forms of ground-rent allowed tenant-farmers to achieve
similar yields per acre, invest similar amounts of capital, and earn similar
rates of return as equivalent (in size, location and crop) owner-operated farms
before the Civil War.[120]

US agricultural historians have long disputed the impact of land-speculation on mid-western agriculture.[121] Paul Gates and other 'populist' historians
argue that land-speculation slowed settlement in the Ohio Valley and Great
Plains. Speculators purportedly withheld land from the market in the hopes
of raising prices and promoted farm-tenancy that was less productive than
owner-operated farms. Robert Swierenga, Donald Winters and other 'neoclassical' economic historians have produced powerful empirical criticisms
of Gates's claims that speculators withheld land and that tenancy was less
economically efficient than owner-operated farms. However, they tend to
see land-speculation and tenancy as 'market-responses' to a given allocation
of wealth and income. Swierenga and Winters assert that land-speculation
and tenancy arose to promote the rapid transfer of public lands to farmers
who often lack the cash to buy and improve the land themselves. Unfortunately, the neoclassical economic historians assume, rather than explain the
distribution of resources that gave rise to speculation and tenancy in the
mid-west. Land-speculation was the product of merchant-inspired capitalist
state-policies (federal land-law) that transformed land in the trans-Allegheny
west into a commodity. 'Land-engrossment' did not slow or distort settlement in the mid-west, but ensured that only farmers with capital could obtain
land and that they would be compelled by debts, mortgages or rents to 'sell
to survive'. In sum, the creation of a social monopoly of land in the 1830s
made successful commodity-production a necessary condition for the acquisition, maintenance and expansion of landed property; establishing agrarian
petty-commodity production throughout the Northern countryside in the
two decades before the Civil War.

---

[120] Atack and Bateman 1987, p. 111; Bogue 1963, pp. 55–66; Newman 1988, Chapters
3–4; Winters 1978, Chapters 2, 3 and 5.
[121] Gates 1973; Swierenga 1968; Winters 1978.

The rising cost of land-acquisition coincided with sharp increases in property-taxes in the wake of the commercial crisis of 1837–42, further weakening independent household-production in the Ohio Valley and Great Plains. The 1820s and 1830s were decades of large-scale construction of transportation-infrastructure, especially in the west and adjacent regions of the north-east. Nearly three quarters of the 3,326 miles of canals and almost two fifths of the 3,328 miles of railroads built between 1820 and 1840 were located in New York, Pennsylvania, Ohio, Indiana and Illinois. While the vast majority of canals and railroads were privately owned and operated, state-governments subsidised almost all transportation-construction through the sale of state-bonds in the financial centres of New York, Philadelphia, London and Amsterdam. By 1838, the state-governments of New York, Pennsylvania, Ohio, Indiana and Illinois had accumulated bonded liabilities for canal- and railroad-construction of $66,310,000, 77.9% of their total public debt. The leaders of these state-governments expected that the private canal- and railroad-companies would easily repay these debts with revenues from transporting agricultural and manufactured commodities. However, the collapse of the speculative boom of the 1830s and its attendant collapse of commodity-circulation produced numerous bankruptcies and reduced profits for most transportation-corporations.[122]

The commercial depression of 1837–42 created a fiscal crisis for most US state-governments, as the revenues needed to fund the enormous public debt plummeted. By 1842, Louisiana, Maryland, Pennsylvania and Indiana had failed to make at least one interest-payment. Foreign and domestic bond-holders, including some of the largest bankers and merchants in the US and Britain, initially hoped that the federal government would assume the state-government debts. However, when plans to use federal revenues to fund state-government bonds were defeated in 1841–2, primarily through the opposition of the political representatives of the planters and farmers, the bond holding merchants and bankers began to pressure the state-governments to restructure their tax-systems to raise sufficient revenue to pay interest and principle.

---

[122] Statistics on canal- and railroad-mileage from Taylor 1951, p. 79. Statistics on state-government debt from US Department of Commerce 1884, VII, p. 523 cited in Ratchford 1941, p. 88. See Taylor 1951, Chapters III and V for general information on canal- and railroad-construction; and Scheiber 1969 for an examination of the role of state-governments in financing transportation-infrastructure construction.

While a number of southern state-administrations (Florida, Mississippi and Arkansas) repudiated their debts in the early 1840s as the result of planter- and 'yeoman'-farmer opposition to any increase in land- and property-taxes, Michigan was the only Northern state-government to renounce its financial obligations to the eastern and British merchants and bankers.[123]

The other state-governments sold off any equity held in railroads and canals and attempted unsuccessfully to impose taxes on banks and other corporations to meet interest-payments. None of these measures proved adequate, and:

> Finally most state were forced to lean heavily on general property taxes and, as a consequence, to give some attention to improving the administration of this tax. The older system of collecting a fixed sum an acre or a unit had been gradually abandoned as higher rates led to insistent demands for more refined methods of valuation.[124]

Western state-governments did not merely increase the number of tax-collectors and assessors in the wake of the inflation of land-prices in the 1830s, they also sharply raised property-tax rates throughout the west to guarantee the payment of interest and principle to mercantile bondholders. In Illinois, property-taxes stood at 20¢ per $100 of assessed value in 1841. Faced with growing debts and declining revenues, the Illinois state-government raised taxes from 20¢ per $100 in 1841, to 58¢ per $100 in 1845, and 67¢ per $100 in 1848, a jump of over 70%. Ohio's property-tax rates rose 188% in the 1840s, from 12.5¢ per $100 assessed value in 1836 to 17.5¢ per $100 in 1841, to 30¢ per $100 in 1846, to 36¢ per $100 in 1851. In Iowa, property-tax rates increased 66%, from 76¢ per $1,000 assessed value in 1854 to $1.25 per $100 in 1860. The combination of new land-assessments at the inflated prices of the late 1830s, the sharply increased tax-incidence and the improved administration of collection led to a massive growth in the total amount of tax-revenues. The Ohio state-government, for example, collected real-estate taxes (the bulk of which fell on agricultural land) of $90,292.38 in 1836, $176,490.65 in 1841, $329,821.80 in 1846, and $956,524.22 in 1851, a total increase of 959%. Property-

---

[123] McGrane 1935, pp. 6–58, 64–82, 133–9, 143–66; Taylor 1951, pp. 372–8.
[124] Taylor 1951, 376. On the restructuring of state-property tax-assessment and collection in the 1840s and 1850s, see: Brindley 1911, Chapters 1–2; Haig 1914, Chapters 3–4; Sowers 1914, Chapter 3.

taxes collected in Illinois rose from $117,779 in 1840 to $695,236 in 1850, to $2,460,425 in 1860, an increase of 199%.[125]

Increased land-prices and property-taxes in the late 1830s and early 1840s made the north-western 'yeomanry' dependent upon the market for their economic survival. To ensure their continued and expanded possession of land, north-western farmers in the 1840s and 1850s had to pay growing land-debts, operating loans and taxes. Rural households could only obtain sufficient cash to meet these obligations through successful competition in the agricultural market-place. Two prominent agricultural historians working in the tradition of neoclassical economics have argued:

> Once established, most farmers ultimately would face that common dilemma in antebellum American agriculture: the difficult choice between independence and self-containment, on one side, and market participation to gain a cash income, on the other.... Before the Civil War, however, our evidence indicates they deliberately sought to produce for the market and to move away from the generalists' life of self-sufficiency toward specialisation. *Debts incurred to establish and maintain a farm often forced that choice upon them.*[126]

The rapid transformation of land into a commodity and rising taxes subordinated the bulk of north-western rural households to the 'logic of the market' or, in Marxian terms, the law of value.

The transformation of the north-western farmers from independent household- to petty-commodity producers during the two decades before the Civil War did not produce the visible sharpening of class-conflicts that marked the transition to 'commercial' farming the north-east during the last two decades of the eighteenth century. There is evidence of 'squatters' confronting the representatives of large land-companies at public land-auctions in the 1830s and 1840s, most of which ended with land-companies either lending the settlers the cost of purchasing the land they occupied or bidding on unoccupied lands.[127] However, there were no large-scale, insurrectionary uprisings on the order of Shays' or the Whiskey Rebellion. Two factors explain the absence of

---

[125] Statistics on Illinois from Haig 1914, pp. 122–3; on Ohio from Bogart 1912, pp. 206 and 220; and Ely 1888, pp. 134–7; and on Iowa from Bogue 1963, p. 189.
[126] Atack and Bateman 1987, p. 271 (emphasis added).
[127] Bogue 1958; Gates 1960, pp. 67–8, 72–4.

mass-action against land-speculators or tax-collectors in the 1840s and 1850s. First, the merchants and speculators had consolidated their political power nationally during the Constitutional Settlement of 1787, and had successfully used the new federal army against rebellious independent householders in the 1780s and 1790s. This historically established 'relationship of forces', continually reinforced through the presence of the federal army, land-surveyors, land-office officials and a growing corps of state-government tax-assessors and collectors allayed any co-ordinated attempt to disrupt auctions, harass tax-collectors or block foreclosures for failures to pay taxes or mortgages.

Second, the physical pattern of settlement in the Ohio Valley and Great Plains militated against large-scale collective action on the part of rural households. While rural villages and towns in the New-England and mid-Atlantic regions never developed the dense network of self-governing institutions that characterised the medieval western-European village, the existence of common lands and streams and the close proximity of rural residences did promote some level of rural solidarity against 'outsiders' – be they land-speculators, tax-collectors or prospective settlers to be 'warned out'. In contrast, the extremely dispersed settlement-patterns in the Midwest bore a greater similarity to those of medieval eastern, rather than western Europe. The much weaker traditions of common use of land (woodlands used to pasture hogs and cattle), and the markedly greater distances between residences in the Ohio Valley and Great Plains blunted the ability of rural households to take collective, class-action in defence of their independence from the vagaries of the market.[128]

The development of petty-commodity production in the Ohio Valley and Great Plains in the two decades before the Civil War spawned an 'agricultural revolution' – the growth of the size and proportion of output produced as commodities, increasing specialisation in cash-crops, rising labour-productivity with the introductions of new seeds, fertilisers and improved implements and machinery, and growing social inequalities among rural households. While antebellum-farmers in the 'old north-west', like thoroughly

---

[128] On the importance of 'public rights' to land- and water-use in the north-east, see Kulik 1985. On the dispersed character of settlement in the Midwest, see Faragher 1985 and 1986, pp. 131–5, Chapter 15. On the relation of settlement-patterns, common lands and village self-government to peasant-class organisation in medieval Europe, see Brenner 1985a, pp. 40–6.

commercial farmers today, continued to produce elements of their own subsistence (meat, dairy, eggs, vegetables and some hand-tools), they radically re-oriented their productive activity toward the production of marketable 'surpluses' during the 1840s and 1850s. Rural households not only increased the size of their commodity-output, but shifted the proportions of production for immediate consumption and for sale. By 1860, north-western farmers were selling approximately 60% of their total yield, well over the 40% that usually marked the transition from 'subsistence'- to 'commercial' agriculture. In other words, these farmers were marketing not only their 'surplus'-product but a major proportion of their 'necessary' product, necessitating the purchase of elements of their subsistence, and making them increasingly dependent on the sale of commodities for their economic survival.[129]

The necessity to compete effectively in order to survive economically compelled farmers throughout the Northern US to specialise production in cash-crops best adapted to their soil-types. Farmers in the Ohio Valley and Great Plains found that their soils allowed wheat or corn (used primarily to feed hogs and cattle for market) to be grown at lower costs of production than in the east. Faced with competition from lower-cost producers of grain, pork and beef in the west, farmers in the mid-Atlantic and New-England regions expanded cultivated acres and specialised in market-garden crops (peas and beans, fruit, potatoes), dairy-products, tobacco and oats (for horses) for sale in the growing urban centres of the north-east. By contrast, dairy-farming and market-gardening in the Midwest was limited to areas adjacent to the burgeoning metropolis of Chicago (Northern Illinois and Wisconsin) in the 1850s. By the late 1840s, the volume of grain being shipped to Chicago allowed the emergence of specialised grain-merchants and millers in both rural towns and in Chicago. By the early 1850s, grain-merchants and warehousemen had begun to store grains until prices rose in the eastern US cities or Europe.[130]

A final indication of the reallocation of rural labour to commodity-production in the Midwest in last two antebellum-decades was the decline of household-manufacture of items for family- and community-consumption. Between 1840 and 1860, per capita household-output of such goods as cloth,

---

[129] Atack and Bateman 1987, pp. 202–4, 208–25; North 1961, pp. 146–53.
[130] Atack and Bateman 1987, Chapters 9–10; Bell 1989, pp. 457–63; Clark 1990, pp. 295–309; Danhof 1969, pp. 144–53; Ferris 1988, Chapter 1.

tools, implements, fencing, packed or processed meat and grain (flour) and the like in the Northern US fell from $1.34 to $.36, a drop of 73%. While independent-household craft-production fell most rapidly in the northeast, from $1.16 per capita in 1840 to $.28 per capita in 1860, a drop of 76%; it also declined consistently in the north-west, from $1.11 per capita in 1840 to $.39 per capita in 1860, a drop of 65%.[131] Additional evidence of a growing separation of crafts from agriculture is the drop in the proportion of all improvements to productive capacity made up of agricultural improvements produced with farm-materials from over 50% in 1834–43 to only 2% in 1899–1908.[132] In other words, there is evidence that goods (implements, tools and the like) that had been produced in rural households for immediate consumption were being purchased on the market-place in the 1840s and 1850s. In the case of meat-packing and farm-implements production, their separation from farm-households led to the industrialisation of their labour-processes and their relocation in the urban centres of Chicago and Cincinnati.[133] The decline in use-value production undermined 'neighbourly exchange' in the mid-west in much the same way it did in the north-east. While farmers in the Ohio Valley and Great Plains continued to exchange labour and goods with one another in the 1840s and 1850s, careful records were kept, interest accrued on unpaid balances and payment was made in cash.[134]

Cash-crop specialisation under the impact of the 'market-imperative' allowed for a very rapid and continuous rise in labour-productivity in agriculture from the 1840s and 1850s. While economists and historians debate the precise rate of growth of labour-productivity (estimates range from 2.0% to 2.6% per annum for wheat and from 1.5% to 2.15% for corn for the period 1840–60 to 1900–10), there is a general consensus that the rate of growth of productivity in Northern US agriculture matched or surpassed other branches of production. The introduction of superior implements and machinery accounts for approximately 50% of the improvements in rural labour-productivity, the

---

[131] Statistics for household-manufacture drawn from Tyron 1917, pp. 308–9 and Atack and Bateman 1987, p. 205. For our purposes, the northwest included Illinois, Indiana, Iowa, Michigan, Ohio and Wisconsin; and the northeast included Connecticut, Maine, Massachusetts, New Hampshire, New Jersey, New York, Pennsylvania, Rhode Island and Vermont.

[132] Gallman 1966, p. 24.

[133] Pudup 1983, pp. 47–71, 104–8; Ross 1985, Chapters 4–5.

[134] Bogue 1963, pp. 185–6; Okada 1985.

rest resulting from improved fertilisers, seeds and methods of crop-rotation.[135] Technical innovation in antebellum-Northern agriculture tended to be concentrated in the soil preparation-planting and harvesting phases of grain-growing, the phases requiring the greatest and most intensive labour. Before 1840, cast-iron ploughs pulled by oxen prepared the soil and seeds were hand-broadcast in planting. While cast-iron ploughs made deeper and more regular furrows than the wooden ploughs used in the eighteenth century, improving soil-yields, they worked poorly on the hard prairie-soils that came under cultivation in the late 1830s and 1840s. The use of the slow-working oxen and hand-sowing seeds also placed severe limits on the development of yields and labour-productivity. Pressures to lower costs in the two decades before the Civil War led to the rapid diffusion of the horse-drawn 'self-scouring' steel plough (originally developed by John Deere) and a variety of seed-drills that together improved soil- and labour-productivity.[136]

Perhaps the most dramatic improvements in rural labour-productivity came with the mechanisation of grain-harvesting. Prior to the introduction of the mass-produced McCormick mechanical reaper, the main tool for harvesting wheat and other grains was the wheat-cradle, a hand-tool. With a cradle, one person could reap two to three acres per day, with additional labour being expended raking and gathering the cut wheat. The horse-drawn, mechanical reaper combined the tasks of reaping and raking, increasing the acreage a single person could harvest to twelve acres per day, an increase in labour-productivity of approximately 75%. Along with the reaper, the mechanical thresher, which separated the wheat from the chaff, also radically reduced the amount of labour needed to prepare grain for the market. The thresher's cost was usually well beyond the means of all but the most wealthy commercial farmers, promoting the development of independent 'specialists' who travelled throughout the Midwest preparing grain for milling.[137]

---

[135] The statistics on the rate of growth of labour-productivity drawn from Atack and Bateman 1987, pp. 188–94; and Parker and Klein 1966. Weiss 1993 presents new evidence of a marked increase in output per worker in grain- and corn-production after 1850. For a description in improvements in fertiliser and soil-rotation methods in the 1840s and 1850s, see Danhof 1969, pp. 251–77.

[136] Bogue 1963, Chapter VIII; Danhof 1969, pp. 142–4, 189–203, 206–17; Faragher 1986, Chapter 19; Gates 1960, pp. 280–2.

[137] Atack and Bateman 1987, pp. 194–200; Danhof 1969, pp. 221–49; David 1971.

The fact that 95% of the farmers adopting the reaper cultivated far less than the 78 acres of wheat that would make the mechanisation of harvesting a cost-efficient decision has led to an extensive debate among economic historians.[138] While they weigh the questions of whether the north-western family-farmers were 'profit'- or 'utility-maximisers', most of the participants in the 'reaper-debate' ignore the realities of market-competition and the natural obstacles to capitalist social relations in agriculture. When producers are compelled 'to sell in order to survive', competition necessarily produces a variety of conditions of production (and different rates of return) among producers in a given branch of production. Contrary to the neoclassical economists' idealised world of 'perfect competition', the long turnover-periods of existing fixed capital in industrial capitalism and the costs of obtaining contiguous land (through purchase or improvement) in agrarian petty-commodity production prevent all producers in a market from rapidly adopting the same technique or scale of production. While the producers with less than the 'state of the art' technique and scale of production are faced with eroding market-shares and declining revenues, they are able to survive, particularly during periods when the market for their commodity is growing.[139]

The 1850s were a period of rapidly rising wheat-prices (the results of numerous crop-failures in Europe, the Crimean War and the growth of the US urban population) for Midwestern farmers. Between 1850 and 1854, real (inflation-adjusted) prices for wheat jumped nearly 60%. Despite a sharp price-drop after 1855, the real price of wheat remained over $1.50 per bushel through the decade.[140] According to Paul Gates, 'with wheat prices well above the dollar mark from 1853 to 1858, Illinois, Wisconsin, Iowa and Minnesota farmers enjoyed real prosperity and were in a position to buy and pay for reapers'.[141] Specifically, the high price of wheat allowed those farmers who adopted the reaper at less than the cost-efficient threshold of 78 acres in wheat to pay their mortgages and debts, and to purchase or improve additional land for wheat-production. In other words, the growing market for wheat allowed a large number of farmers whose conditions of production were not 'state of the art'

---

[138] David 1971; Olmstead 1975; Fleisig 1976; Headlee 1991.
[139] Botwinick 1993, pp. 124–33; Shaikh 1980.
[140] US Department of Commerce 1976, Part I, p. 201.
[141] Gates 1960, p. 287.

(reaper and 78 acres in wheat) to survive the competitive battle and possibly achieve a 'profit-maximising' scale of production.

While the growing wheat-market made the diffusion of the reaper by farmers with less than 78 acres in wheat *possible*, the natural obstacles to capitalist social relations in agriculture made the adoption of the reaper *necessary*. As Susan Mann has pointed out, the natural features of agriculture prevent the widespread use of wage-labour.[142] Specifically, the disjunction between labour-time (planting and harvesting) and 'production-time' (the naturally determined growing season) creates a situation where 'labor is forced to be idle during the excess of production time over labor time' which 'gives rise to serious labor supply and recruitment problems'.[143] The longer the 'slack season' and the shorter the planting and harvest-seasons, the greater the problems in securing adequate labour at the necessary times, as potential wage-workers migrate to areas where employment is more steady (urban-industrial centres, transportation-construction, etc.) and farmers compete fiercely for a finite pool of labour during the relatively brief planting and harvest-seasons. As a result, farmers, even when compelled 'to sell in order to survive', tend to avoid the use of wage-labour. The disjunction between labour- and production-time is particularly conspicuous in wheat-cultivation. Wheat has one of the longest growing ('slack') seasons of any crop, averaging 40–4 weeks for midwestern winter-wheat. Most of the labour-requirements in wheat-planting and harvesting are concentrated in a ten to twelve-week period, September for planting and July for harvesting.[144] The harvesting period for wheat is especially short. According to Gates, 'wheat, when ripe, could not stand for long before it began to shed its grain, it had to be harvested at the right time or the loss would be heavy'.[145] This two-week 'window of opportunity' made the extensive use of wage-labour extremely risky. In late August, all of the farmers in a location would compete for the available pool of labour-power in order to bring in their harvest before the grain was spoiled, and the major

---

[142] Mann 1990, pp. 28–46.
[143] Mann 1990, p. 39.
[144] Mann 1990, pp. 56–8.
[145] Gates 1960, p. 287.

source of cash to pay mortgages and debts and to buy or clear additional land disappeared.[146]

By 1860, the Ohio Valley and Great Plains was no longer, if they had ever been, an egalitarian utopia of small producers. Wealth (land, structures, implements, etc.) was much more equitably distributed among rural petty producers in the North than between planters, slaves and slaveless farmers in the South or industrialists, merchants, professionals and wage-workers in the Northern urban-industrial centres. However, there was considerable social differentiation among the Northern agricultural population, with five per cent of the Northern rural households commanding thirty one per cent of the wealth. Wealth-distribution tended to follow age. Older farmers' accumulation of wealth under independent household-production gave them superior access to the credit needed to purchase the best located and more fertile lands, seeds, draft-animals, tools and machinery. While a prosperous agricultural petty bourgeoisie was able to appropriate a disproportionate share of land and tools, a growing portion of the rural population found themselves without access, through either purchase or rental, to adequate land to survive. Slightly over one in four inhabitants of the Northern countryside (541,719 of 2,056,286) were farm-labourers in 1860. Although wage-labour never became the main source of labour for Northern agriculture – there was no transition from petty-commodity to capitalist production – competition among rural households spawned a class of propertyless rural wage-earners. Simultaneously, the rising cost of establishing a farm during the two decades before the Civil War effectively eliminated the possibility of even the most well paid and thrifty urban worker escaping wage-labour by settling on the land.[147]

Our explanation of the transition from 'subsistence'- to 'commercial' household-based agriculture in the Northern US, with its emphasis on social-property relations and the role of class-conflict in their transformation, sheds

---

[146] The importance of natural conditions (the brief 'window of opportunity' to harvest wheat successfully) to the mechanisation of agricultural production comes clear when we compare wheat- and corn-farming in the 1840s and 1850s. Corn, used mostly to feed swine and cattle, could be left to ripen on the stalk for months without significant losses. Lacking the 'strenuous urgency' of the wheat-harvest, corn-harvesting was not mechanised in the antebellum-period. See: Bogue 1963, pp. 129–33; Faragher 1986, pp. 202–4.

[147] Atack and Bateman 1987, Chapter 6; Bogue 1963, pp. 241–3; Danhof 1941; Danhof 1970, pp. 219–27; Faragher 1986, Chapter 18; Gates 1960, pp. 272–9.

some analytical light on important economic and political developments in the antebellum-US. The pace and pattern of industrial development in the US is directly linked to the transformation of Northern family-farming. While there continues to be considerable disagreement among economic historians about the precise rate of growth during the antebellum-period, there is some consensus that the two decades before the Civil War saw accelerated growth in general, and quickened growth of industry in particular.[148] The most enduring explanation of the timing of the US industrial revolution remains that of Douglas North. While the expansion of cotton-exports from the plantation-South fuelled economic growth in the 1820s and 1830s:

> ...a major consequence of the expansive period of the 1830's was the creation of conditions that made possible industrialisation in the North-east. Transport facilities developed to connect the East and West more efficiently; a new market for western staples developed in the rapidly industrialising East and, sporadically, in Europe. The dependence of both the North-east and the West on the South waned.[149]

Albert Fishlow's research revealed important empirical flaws in North's claims that the completion of transportation-infrastructure (canal- and railroad-system) during the 1830s shifted inter-regional trade from a west-south to west-east flow, sparking rapid industrial growth in the 1840s and 1850s. Fishlow demonstrated first, that the bulk of western foodstuffs marketed during the 1820s and 1830s were destined for eastern urban markets; and second, that investments in railroads and other transportation-facilities tended to follow, rather than lead to increased commodity-production in agriculture.[150] North's thesis that the timing of industrialisation in the US resulted from changes in the direction of commodity-circulation resulting from improved transportation-facilities was untenable empirically.

Our analysis of the transformation of Northern agriculture provides a quite different explanation for the increased pace of industrialisation during the 1840s and 1850s. The subjugation of western family-farmers to the law of value created a massive and growing home-market for industrial capi-

---

[148] Among the contributions to the ongoing discussion of the rate of growth of total output, see: David 1967; Gallman 1972; North 1961, Chapters 7, 9, 11, and 15.

[149] North 1961, pp. 69–70.

[150] Fishlow 1965a, Chapters 3–4 and 1965b.

talist produced means of consumption and production. As family-farmers specialised in the production of agricultural goods, they were compelled to purchase a wide variety of consumer-goods they previously produced for themselves or obtained through 'neighbourly exchange'. Similarly, as rural householder sought to reduce production-costs through the technical innovation, they sought to purchase 'cutting-edge' machinery, tools and the like, rather than make these implements themselves or procured them from local blacksmiths.

The impact of the transformation of the rural class-structure on industrialisation in the 1840s and 1850s can be seen directly in the growth of an 'agro-industrial' complex in US industry. The industries producing farm-machinery, tools and supplies, and processing agricultural raw materials (meat-packing, leather-tanning, canning, flour-milling, baking, etc.) were at the centre of the US industrial revolution. Farm-implement and machine-production alone made up 19.4% of all machine-production in 1860, rising to 25.5% in 1870.[151] Further, these industries experienced important developments in their labour-processes (e.g., mechanisation of flour-milling, the development of the first 'disassembly' line in meat-packing, and the use of standardised parts in the construction of reapers) and stimulated technical transformations in other crucial industries.[152] For example, the formation of the 'agro-industrial complex' spurred technological innovation in the antebellum iron-industry. Specialised industrial producers (who needed lower-quality and less-versatile iron) replaced rural blacksmiths and farmers (who needed high-quality and versatile iron to produce a wide variety of products) as the main consumers of iron, providing the impetus for the centralisation of iron-production and the use of coal, rather than charcoal, in the smelting process.[153]

The transition from independent-household to petty-commodity production in Northern agriculture after the 1830s also illuminates the social basis of key political and ideological developments in the antebellum-period. Merrill's contention that an analysis of household-based production's structure and dynamics is essential to understanding both the ambiguities of Republican ideology and the origins of the radical social movements of the Jacksonian

---

[151] See materials cited in Footnote 53.
[152] For a more detailed discussion of the 'agro-industrial complex', see Post 1983, pp. 121–6. See also: Pudup 1983 and 1987; and Headlee 1991, pp. 28–38.
[153] Hunter 1929.

period is correct. Clearly, Republicanism's simultaneous embrace of absolute equality and the subordination of women, African-American slaves and (by the mid-nineteenth century) wage-workers flows from the 'lived experience' of married, adult male property-owners who faced one another as equals in the marketplace, but commanded the labour of juvenile and female members of their household.[154] Merrill is also quite correct when he argues that 'anti-bankism, Fourierist socialism, Mormonism and Land Reforms all were specific, distorted but energetic attempts to ward off the impending eclipse of the household mode', in the 1830s and 1840s. However, an understanding of the role of land-speculation in destroying independent household-production reveals the contradictions in the 'self-sufficient' farmers and artisans' attempt to preserve their autonomy from the market by embracing the Democratic Party and its opposition to the Second Bank of the United States. The Democratic Party was not the party of the 'common man' committed to a 'hard-money' policy that would limit inflation and speculation, securing the property of independent- household-producers. Instead, the very land- and currency-speculators who were undermining 'subsistence' agriculture in the west dominated the Democratic Party. The abolition of the central bank promoted 'wildcat'-banking, plentiful credit and paper-money and the largest wave of land-, currency- and commodity-speculation in the history of the US.[155]

Finally, the transition to commercial family-farming in the Ohio Valley and Great Plains in the 1840s and 1850s helps untangle much of the confusion concerning the social origins and timing of the US Civil War. Since the Beards' thesis was discredited in the 1950s, US historians have not produced a convincing explanation of the causes of the US Civil War.[156] The 'revisionist' historians have trivialised the roots of the conflict, claiming it was the result

---

[154] Merrill is mistaken when he links Republican ideology, with all of its contradictions, to 'self-sufficient' household-production. There is considerable evidence that 'commercial' family-farmers and artisans (petty-commodity producers) found radical Republicanism an adequate 'mental road-map' for their lived experience. See Foner 1970, Chapter 1.

[155] Merrill 1986, pp. 60–3. On the role of land-speculators in the Jacksonian democracy and the effects of the abolition of the Second Bank of the US on economic activity in the 1830s, see Hammond 1957, pp. 233–8, 306–456.

[156] Beard and Beard 1927, Chapters 14, 15, 17, and 18. The most important critics of the Beards include: Foner 1941; Sharkey 1958; Unger 1964.

of political demagoguery and paranoia in both sections.[157] Marxian historians (Eric Foner and Eugene Genovese) have demonstrated the incompatibility of plantation-slavery and industrial capitalist development, restoring a social basis to the conflict over 'slavery-expansion'. However, the existing Marxian historiography does not explain why this issue became explosive and irreconcilable in the 1840s and 1850s, but not before. Foner and Genovese tend to posit an immanent conflict between industrial capitalism and plantation-slavery throughout the antebellum-period, with the development of 'mass-politics' (universal white male suffrage, development of modern political parties) in the 1830s actualising this conflict in the 1840s and 1850s.[158]

The social origins and historical timing of the political crisis that culminated in the Civil War can be located in the transformation of plantation-slavery from a spur into an obstacle to the development of capitalism in the US, as the result of the transition from independent household- to petty-commodity production in the north-west in the late 1830s and early 1840s. As long as the activities of mercantile capitalists (merchants, bankers and speculators), rather than those of industrial capitalists,[159] were the main stimulus to the expansion of commodity-production and circulation, plantation-slavery's commercial character was a spur to the development of capitalism. Merchants in New York facilitated the trade of slave-produced cotton with Europe, accumulating considerable mercantile wealth. Even more importantly, cotton, as the major export of the antebellum-US, created sound international credit for US merchants and bankers. The expansion of commercial slavery provided the basis for the geographical expansion of mercantile operations – most importantly land-speculation – and for obtaining foreign capital to finance the construction of canals and railroads in the 1830s.[160]

The fruit of mercantile enterprise in the west in the 1830s was the subordination of family-farming to 'market-discipline' in the 1840s and 1850s. The 'commercialisation' of household-based agriculture in the Ohio Valley and Great Plains created a growing home-market for industrially produced capital

---

[157] Craven 1966; Holt 1978; Randall and Donald 1961.

[158] Foner 1980; Genovese 1967.

[159] The distinction between merchant- and industrial capital is derived from Marx 1981, Chapter 20. See also the perceptive discussion of merchant-capital in Fox-Genovese and Genovese 1983, pp. 3–25.

[160] North 1956.

and consumer-goods, providing the major precondition for the domination of industrial capital over merchant-capital. As industrial capitalism expanded rapidly in the two decades before the Civil War, plantation-slavery's non-capitalist class-structure became an obstacle to the development of capitalism in the US. On the one hand, the master-slave relation of production prevented the use of new, labour-saving machinery and implements, limiting the market for factory-produced capital-goods. On the other, the attempt of slave-owners to make their plantations 'self-sufficient' in food-stuffs, cloth and other items, limited the market for factory-produced consumer-goods. Together with the dominance of independent household-production in the non-plantation districts, plantation-slavery restricted the depth of the home-market and made the South the least industrialised region in the antebellum-US.[161] The geographical expansion of plantation-slavery, an unavoidable feature of this social-property relation, into the west would have stifled the development of agrarian petty-commodity production and the home-market for industrial capitalism in the 1840s and 1850s. The emergence of the conflict between the requirements of the development of plantation-slavery and of industrial capitalism made the question of the future class-structure of the west (slavery or capitalism and petty-commodity production) the central and irresolvable political issue of the 1840s and 1850s. Ultimately, a bloody four-year Civil War decided the issue, securing the conditions for the rapid expansion of industrial capitalism in the 'Gilded Age'.[162]

---

[161] Genovese 1967, pp. 13–39, 157–79, 243–74; Gallman 1970; Hahn 1983, Part I; Parker 1970.

[162] For a detailed explication of this thesis, see Post 1983.

Chapter Three

Plantation-Slavery and Economic Development in the Antebellum-Southern United States

From the moment that plantation-slavery came under widespread challenge in Europe and the Americas in the late eighteenth century, its economic impact has been hotly debated. Both critics and defenders linked the political and moral aspects of slavery with its social and economic effects on the plantation-regions of the Americas and the world-market. Critics of slavery condemned bonded-labour as immoral and economically inefficient, limiting economic growth in the Caribbean, the southern US and in the emerging centres of industrial production in Britain and western Europe. Defenders of slavery presented it as a beneficial political and cultural institution that had made New-World slave-owners and European merchants and manufacturers wealthy.[1]

The debate on the economic effects of plantation-slavery continued over the next two centuries. Currently, there is some consensus about the role of New-World plantation-slavery in creating the world-market that was one precondition of the British industrial revolution. While historians still disagree about the impact of industrialisation on the trajectory of the slave-economies in the nineteenth century,

---

[1] Davis 1966; Davis 1975.

there is little disagreement that the 'triangular trade' linking together Africa, the New-World plantation-zone and Britain was a central motor of the 'Atlantic economy'. The markets created by the African slave-trade and the plantation-economies for British manufactured goods as diverse as iron, textiles, glass, and china were important stimuli for the growth of industrial capitalism in Britain.[2]

Current scholarly controversy centres on plantation-slavery's impact on economic development in the regions where it was the dominant form of social labour. Focussing primarily on the southern US, historians and social scientists have debated whether slavery was a stimulus or an impediment to technical innovation in agriculture, to the deepening of the social division of labour ('home-market'), and to the growth of industry.

Scholarly discussion of plantation-slavery and economic development has produced two broad interpretive models. The advocates of what can be called the 'planter-capitalism' thesis,[3] whose most articulate spokespersons are Robert Fogel and Stanley Engerman,[4] argue that, despite the unfree legal status of slave-labourers, plantation-slavery was a variant of capitalism. The planters' ability to organise their slave-labourers in a centralised labour-process allowed the planters to maximise profits in the production of staple-crops, sugar, tobacco, cotton, etc.) for a competitive world-market. According to the 'planter-capitalism' model, plantation-slavery was highly efficient, productive and profitable, and allowed rapid economic growth in the regions where it was dominant. The relative absence of industrial and urban development in the southern US and the Caribbean was simply the result of these regions' 'comparative advantages' in agricultural production.

---

[2] The contemporary discussion of the relationship of New-World slavery to industrialisation begins with Williams (1944). For recent evaluation of the 'Williams thesis' and evidence for the growing consensus on the positive effects of slavery on the growth of the world-market and industrial development in Britain, see: Solow and Engerman 1987; Blackburn 1997, Chapter XII; and Inikori and Engerman 1992. On the continuing debate on the impact of the Industrial Revolution on slavery in the New World, see: Drescher 1986; and Tomich 1988.

[3] Fogel 1989; Aufhauser 1973; Coclanis 1989; Fleisig 1976; Gray 1933; Knight 1970; Oakes 1982; Wallerstein 1974.

[4] Fogel and Engerman 1974.

Opposing the 'planter-capitalist' thesis is what can be broadly defined as the 'non-bourgeois civilisation' thesis.[5] According to this model, whose most important advocate is Eugene D. Genovese,[6] the slaves' unfree legal status gave rise to a number of social-institutional characteristics that distinguish slavery from capitalism. For a variety of reasons, but, most importantly, the slaves' purported lack of motivation and the resulting need for their close supervision in simple, repetitive and unskilled tasks, slavery was an obstacle to technical innovation in agriculture. The failure of an 'agricultural revolution' in the New-World plantation-regions meant that the 'home-market' for industrially produced capital and consumer-goods of the sort that provided a mass-market for industrialisation in the northern US, Europe and Japan never developed. As a result, plantation-slavery was an obstacle to industrial development in the southern US and the Caribbean through the nineteenth century.

While both models capture facets of the dynamics of plantation-slavery in the Americas, neither the 'planter-capitalist' nor 'non-bourgeois civilisation' models provide an adequate basis for understanding slavery as a distinct form of social labour inserted into the expanding capitalist world-market. Ultimately, the failure of both models stems from their shared assumption that 'economic rationality' – the organisation of production, technical innovation, the depth of the social division of labour and the trajectory of economic development – is simply the reflection of the subjective motivations of key economic actors abstracted from their social and economic context. For the 'planter-capitalism' model, the masters' goal of profit-maximisation made plantation-slavery an 'efficient' and 'rational' form of capitalist production. For the 'pre-bourgeois civilisation' model, the slaves' unfree legal status made them recalcitrant labourers, placing severe limits on the economic activity of their masters and giving rise to a society that eschewed market-rationality.

Neither of the dominant interpretive models places the structure of social-property relations – class-relations – at the centre of their analysis. Class-structure is viewed either as incidental to the planters' goal of

---

[5] Ashworth 1995; Moreno Fraginals 1976; Oakes 1990; Wade 1964. James Oakes's inclusion as a representative of both interpretive models is the result of his shifting from a spirited defence of the 'planter-capitalism' thesis (1982) to a thoughtful presentation of the 'non-bourgeois civilisation' thesis (1990).

[6] Genovese 1967, 1972, 1983.

profit-maximisation or as a manifestation of the slaves' lack of economic motivation. It is the central thesis of this article that attempts to explain the dynamics of plantation-slavery in the New World without reference to class-structure
are fundamentally flawed. Ultimately, it is the structure of the master-slave
relation that defines what constitutes economic 'rationality' and shapes the
broad patterns of economic development in the plantation-regions. Following
Robert Brenner, we define class-structure as having:

> ...two analytically distinct, but historically unified, aspects. First, the
> relations of the direct producers to one another, to their tools and to the land
> in the immediate process of production – what has been called the 'labour-
> process' or the 'social forces of production'. Second, the inherently conflictive
> relations of property – always guaranteed directly or indirectly, in the last
> analysis, by force – by which an unpaid-for part of the product is extracted
> from the direct producers by a class of non-producers – which might be
> called the 'property relationship' of the 'surplus-extraction relationship'. It
> is around the property or surplus-extraction relationship that one defines the
> fundamental classes in a society – the class(es) of direct producers on the one
> hand and the surplus-extracting, or ruling, class(es) on the other...different
> class structures, specifically property relations or surplus-extraction relations,
> once established, tend to impose rather strict limits and possibilities, indeed
> rather specific long-term patterns, on a society's economic development.[7]

Put simply, it is our contention that the objective structure of the social-
property/surplus-extraction relation between master and slaves – not the
subjective desires of either – shaped and limited both technical innovation in
plantation-agriculture and broader patterns of economic growth and development in the plantation-regions of the Americas.

To make our argument more concrete, we first interrogate the arguments of
the leading proponents of both explanatory models in light of the comparative
development of slavery in both the ancient and modern worlds. This comparative perspective, we hope, will highlight the limited explanatory power of
both models. We then develop a theoretical model of slavery's specific social-
property relations, and demonstrate our model's analytical potential through
an analysis of the development of plantation-slavery in the southern US.

---

[7] Brenner 1985, pp. 11–12.

I. The 'planter-capitalism' model

The plantation as capitalist enterprise

The central claim of the 'planter-capitalism' model is that the slave-plantations of the New World were highly efficient, productive and profitable enterprises producing commodities for a competitive world-market. The 'planter-capitalism' model recognises, correctly, that the slaveholding planters of the Americas faced what Ellen Meiksins Wood calls 'market imperatives'.[8] Despite attempts to make the plantation 'self-sufficient' in food and some tools, staple-producing planters had to accrue debts to purchase land and slaves. Unlike the grain-exporting lords of Eastern Europe in the sixteenth and seventeenth centuries, whose possession of land rested on non-market power, the master classes of the 'New World' did not have the option of withdrawing from the world-market when prices fell below their costs of production.[9] To meet their debts and avoid the loss of their land and slaves, the planters were compelled to 'hold their place' in the world-markets for sugar, tobacco, rice, indigo, coffee and cotton through cost-reduction.[10]

For the proponents of the 'planter-capitalism' model, the master-classes of the Americas responded to this 'market-coercion' in the same ways other capitalists responded – through productive specialisation and technical innovation. According to Lewis Gray, '[t]he plantation was a capitalistic type of agricultural organisation in which a considerable number of unfree-labourers were employed under unified direction and control in the production of a staple crop'.[11] The planters, 'hard, calculating businessmen' committed to individual effort, upward social mobility, and the accumulation of wealth,[12] successfully utilised command of slave-labour in the pursuit of profits on the world-market.

On sugar- and cotton-plantations in the Caribbean and the southern US, the work of slave-gangs was 'as rigidly organised as in a factory'.[13] Unlike tobacco-cultivation, where small teams of slaves were given fixed tasks that were to

---

[8] Wood 1999.
[9] Brenner 1977, pp. 70–5; Kula 1976, pp. 100–20.
[10] Price 1991; Woodman 1968, Chapters 3–6.
[11] Gray 1933, I, p. 302.
[12] Fogel and Engerman 1974, p. 73; Oakes 1982, Chapter 1.
[13] Fogel and Engerman 1974, p. 203.

be accomplished each day,[14] sugar- and cotton-production were amenable to a division of tasks where slave-gangs performed simple and repetitive tasks under the command of masters and overseers. In sugar-production, gangs of slaves prepared the soil and planted and cultivated (weeded) sugar-cane using hoes and other hand-tools. At the harvest, the slaves would be again organised into gangs to cut the cane with machetes and transport the cane to be crushed, boiled, and evaporated into powdered sugar. Cotton-production involved an even more 'factory-like' labour-process. In the planting and cultivation of cotton, slaves were organised into labour-gangs with a detailed technical division of labour and a high degree of co-ordination and interdependence, which 'as on an assembly line...generated a pressure on all those who worked in the gang to keep up with the pace of the leaders'. While an assembly-line-like division of tasks was not possible during the harvest, the prudent use of rewards and prizes promoted competition between harvest-gangs, maximising the slaves' effort and output. The slave-plantation labour-process, resting upon the organisation of gang-labour, allowed the planters to achieve economies of scale (greater output per input of labour, capital and land) than family-farmers in the northern and southern US.[15] The division and simplification of tasks, the co-ordination of the work of the gang and other 'capitalist' features of plantation-slavery's work-régime led one proponent of the 'planter-capitalism' model to argue that New-World planters' management-practice anticipated Frederick Winslow Taylor's theory of 'scientific management'.[16] The planters' rigorous management of gang-labour led the slaves 'to produce, on average, as much output in roughly 35 minutes as a farmer using traditional methods, whether slave or free, did in a full hour'.[17]

Fogel and Engerman assert that the 'capitalist' organisation of slave-labour on large cotton- and sugar-plantation not only made plantation-slavery a profitable investment in various parts of the New World during the eighteenth and nineteenth centuries, but was the basis for rapid economic growth in those regions as well. Expanding and refining the path-breaking work of Conrad

---

[14] Gray 1933, I, Chapters 10, 24.
[15] Fogel and Engerman 1974; Fogel 1989, Chapters 2–3.
[16] Aufhauser 1973.
[17] Fogel 1989, p. 79, Chapters 3–6; Fogel and Engerman 1974, pp. 38–43, Chapter 4.

and Meyer[18] on the profitability of slavery, Fogel and Engerman[19] convincingly demonstrate that slave-production of cotton earned returns comparable to other investments in 1860. Clearly, the profitability of plantation-slavery in the antebellum-South in the mid-nineteenth century and various parts of the Caribbean in the eighteenth and nineteenth centuries is no longer open to empirical challenge.[20] However, the advocates of the planter-capitalism model go further, asserting that profitable slave-based plantation-agriculture promoted rapid economic growth in the Caribbean and southern US as well. Fogel and Engerman's data for the southern US in the two decades prior to the Civil War show southern per capita income growing at a slightly more rapid rate than northern per capita income between 1840 and 1860 (1.7% per annum versus 1.4%).[21] While average southern per capita income remained lower than average northern income in 1860 ($103 versus $141), incomes in the rapidly expanding south-western frontier (Texas, Oklahoma, Arkansas and Louisiana) were higher ($184) than in any sub-region of the north. Southern per capita incomes were much higher than any contemporary independent nation, with the exceptions of Australia and Great Britain.[22]

While providing important insights into the organisation of the plantation labour-process and its insertion into a competitive, capitalist world-market, the central claims of the 'planter-capitalism' model's concerning the 'capitalist' character of plantation-slavery are subject to several important criticisms. Fogel and Engerman's statistics on profitability and economic growth in the antebellum southern US, the plantation-region in the Americas where the most systematic data has been collected, is an artefact of world cotton-market conditions in 1860. Gavin Wright[23] and others[24] have produced a convincing critique of Fogel and Engerman's claim that the planters' high profits and the growth of per capita income in the South were the result of the 'efficient' organisation of slave-labour in plantation-agriculture. Instead, the rapid growth of demand for raw cotton on the part of industrial capitalists in Great Britain and the US North, combined with the US South's near complete domination of

---

[18] Conrad and Meyer 1958.
[19] Fogel and Engerman 1974, Chapter 3.
[20] Fogel 1989, Chapters 3–4; Ward 1978.
[21] Fogel and Engerman 1974, pp. 247–55.
[22] Fogel 1989, Chapter 4.
[23] Wright 1976; 1978, pp. 90–7, 102–6.
[24] David and Temin 1976.

the world's supply of raw cotton, account for both the high rates of return in slave-based cotton-production and the growth of Southern per capita income. According to Wright, 'southern incomes from cotton growing were primarily governed by demand and not by production'.[25] Eugene Genovese and Elizabeth Fox Genovese found similar patterns in other slave-plantation regions in the New World.[26] Consistently, 'prosperity' and 'stagnation' in these regions were determined externally, by the global demand for their staples, rather than internally, by the organisation of plantation-production.

In addition, Wright demonstrates that Fogel and Engerman's claims concerning alleged economic superiority of the slave-plantation compared with family-farming are flawed as well. Fogel and Engerman argued that the greater intensity, duration and efficiency of slaves' labour under the supervision of the master accounted for the greater output of cotton per work-hour on the plantation than on family-farms in the South.[27] Wright shows that the higher outputs of cotton and other cash-crops per capita were the result of the planters' ability to direct the majority of the slaves' labour into production of marketable commodities.[28] In contrast, Southern family-farmers, whose acquisition, maintenance, and expansion of landholdings did not require successful market-competition, devoted the vast majority of their labour to the production of food and handicrafts for household- and community-consumption. Put simply, the 'relative efficiency' of slave-labour was not the result of the superior, 'capitalist' organisation of the slaves' labour, but of the planters' capacity to devote a large proportion of the slaves' labour into commodity-production.

Episodic labour-saving technical change in plantation-slavery

A careful examination of Fogel and Engerman and other proponents of the 'planter-capitalist' model's description of the plantation labour-process actually contradicts their claim that the planters responded to competitive market-imperatives in the same way as capitalists. The labour-process under slavery was organised to maximise the use of human labour in large, co-ordinated

---

[25] 1978, p. 98.
[26] Genovese and Fox-Genovese 1983, pp. 45–9, 156–62.
[27] Fogel and Engerman 1974, Chapter 6.
[28] Wright 1978, Chapter 3.

groups under the continual supervision of masters, overseers, and drivers. As we shall see, the tools slaves used were simple and virtually unchanged. Even with a detailed division of tasks in planting and cultivation, such a labour-process left the masters few options to increase output per slave. Planters could either increase the pace of work through punishments or rewards, increase the amount of acreage each slave or slave-gang cultivated, increase the number of slaves working by tapping the capacities to work of female and juvenile slaves, or move the plantation to more fertile soil.

All of these methods of increasing output expanded *absolutely* the amount of surplus-labour performed by the slaves, while leaving the amount of necessary labour performed constant. As Brenner[29] and others[30] have pointed out, this sort of *extensive* growth based on the absolute growth of surplus-labour is typical of non-capitalist forms of social labour. By contrast, there is little evidence of gains in productivity through replacing labour with new and more complex tools and machinery, the increase in *relative* surplus-labour extraction that typifies capitalist agriculture and industry. While capitalists continuously attempt to increase absolute surplus-labour extraction by increasing and intensifying the pace of work (speed-up), it is relative surplus-labour extraction through mechanisation that distinguishes capitalism from all previous forms of social labour. The capitalists' ability to introduce, in a relatively continuous manner, labour-saving tools and machinery is the basis for capitalism's unique capacity to shift labour progressively from agriculture to manufacturing and services.

Technical innovation under plantation-slavery did not display the relatively continuous introduction of new and more complex tools and machinery that has allowed capitalist agriculture and industry to 'expel labour' from the production of material goods over the past two centuries. Instead, labour-saving technological change in slave-economies had a highly episodic character. The introduction of techniques that fundamentally altered the ratios of labour, land and tools were 'once and for all' processes, corresponding to the introduction of new crops or the expansion of plantation-slavery to new regions of the Americas. The technical change that did occur more regularly in response to competitive market-pressures was essentially what Moses Finley

---

[29] Brenner 1977.
[30] Marx 1976, Parts Three and Four; Shaikh 1978.

called 'cheese-paring'[31] – economising in the use of raw materials or increasing yields without altering the fundamentally labour-intensive features of the slave-labour process. While this 'cheese-paring' did produce important increases in output and reductions in costs, this process of technical innovation did not lead to the systematic and continuous replacement of human labour with machines that was typical of capitalist agriculture and industry in the past four centuries.

The shift from tobacco- to cotton-production and the geographical expansion of cotton-production to the Lower South (Georgia, Alabama, Mississippi, Louisiana, Texas) fuelled the most important wave of technical change in the antebellum-Southern US. Not only did the development of cotton-production allow for the replacement of task-labour with gang-labour, but it also led to the introduction of a number of labour-saving tools and seeds. Hoes and light ploughs had been the basic implements used by slaves planting and cultivating tobacco in the US south-east. When cotton displaced tobacco as the main crop in the region in the late eighteenth century, planters all along the south-eastern coast from Virginia to Georgia simply continued to use hand-held hoes and light ploughs in cotton-planting and cultivation. In the 1820s, the heavier, mule- or horse-drawn 'sweeper'-plough was introduced throughout the cotton-South. The new plough produced deeper furrows and higher yields per acre and reduced the amount of human labour required both to prepare the soil for planting and to cultivate the growing cotton plants. While never completely replacing hand-hoeing in cultivation, the sweep-plough and other horse- or mule-drawn implements allowed the planters to increase sharply the amount of acreage each slave-gang could plant and cultivate. The cotton-harvest remained labour-intensive, with slaves working in gangs picking cotton by hand. However, the geographical expansion of cotton-production to the Lower South in the 1820s and early 1830s brought with it the introduction of a new cotton-variety, the 'Petit Gulf'. Replacing the older 'Georgia upland' variety, 'Petit Gulf' was both more resistant to disease and could be picked more easily, allowing a significant increase in the number of acres slave-gangs could harvest.[32]

---

[31] Finley 1982, p. 188.
[32] Garrett 1978, pp. 107–25; Gray 1933, I, pp. 70–4, 794–6.

The historic shift in the locus of sugar-production from Jamaica and St. Domingue (Haiti) to Cuba and Puerto Rico in the nineteenth century unleashed the most dramatic wave of technical innovations in a slave-economy. Unlike tobacco- and cotton-production, sugar-production under slavery combined both agricultural (planting, cultivation, harvest) and industrial (refining cane into powdered sugar) processes in a single productive unit. From the late seventeenth through the early nineteenth century, the transport of cut cane to the sugar-refineries, the crushing of sugar-cane to extract cane-juice, and the boiling and evaporation of the cane-juice to produce powdered sugar relied on the physical strength and skill of masses of slaves organised into work-gangs often labouring day and night, in shifts, at harvest-time.

As capitalist industrialisation fuelled European and North-American demand for sugar,[33] plantation-slavery expanded into the new, 'frontier'-regions of Cuba and Puerto Rico in the 1820s and 1830s. Cuban sugar-plantations established in the nineteenth century initiated production at a much more capital-intensive technical level than their counterparts in the seventeenth and eighteenth centuries. While the agricultural phase of production remained unchanged through the nineteenth century, relying on simple hand-tools and brute human strength to plant, cultivate and harvest sugar-cane, Cuban sugar-planters introduced steam-powered milling-crushing machinery in the 1830s and 1840s. The mechanisation of rolling alone increased the amount of cane that could be processed, compelling slaves to harvest additional acreage. In the 1840s and 1850s, in newly settled western Cuban, planters replaced the wood-burning 'Jamaica train' stoves in the boiling of cane-juice with vacuum-pans that lowered the boiling point of the cane-juice and economised on the use of fuel. They also introduced centrifuges to speed the separation of molasses and water from the powdered sugar.[34] The result of these technical changes on the shifting sugar-frontier of the nineteenth century was a radical shift in the ratio of slaves to land and output. According to Phillip Curtin:

---

[33] Mintz 1985.
[34] Bergad 1990, pp. 48–56, 89–91, Chapter 7; Galloway 1989, pp. 133–42; Knight 1970, pp. 32–40, 68–75; Moreno Fraginals 1976, Chapter 4; Scarano 1984, Chapter 5; Scott 1985a, pp. 20–41; Scott 1985b, pp. 25–53; Watts 1987, pp. 482–93.

> For the old-style, eighteenth-century sugar estate the rule of thumb was one acre of land and one slave to produce one ton of sugar annually. By the 1830s, in Cuba, this had doubled. By the 1860s, production was in the range of six to eight tons per worker on the best estates and two to four tons even on the smaller or older plantations.[35]

Clearly, changes in the world-market occasioned by the growth of capitalist industry in Europe necessitated both of these episodes of labour-saving technical change in plantation slave-agriculture.[36] Both radically altered the ratio of slaves to land and tools. However, neither episode led to a self-sustaining 'agricultural revolution' in the new plantation-regions of the US Lower South or the Caribbean sugar-'frontier'. Contrary to the claims of historians in the 'planter-capitalism' school like John Moore and Franklin Knight,[37] neither the introduction of horse- and mule-drawn implements in cotton-production nor the mechanisation of sugar-refining was symptomatic of a process that continuously replaced human labour with new and more complex tools and machinery. Instead, these new methods, once adapted, became the unchanging standard for slave-production in those regions.

For the most part, the technical changes that occurred in slave-based agriculture in the Americas in response to the imperatives of world-market competition took the form of what Finley described as 'cheese-paring' – changes that increased output and reduced costs without fundamentally changing the

---

[35] Curtin 1990, p. 197.

[36] Tomich 1988, pp. 104–16.

[37] Moore (1988, Chapters 2–3) found evidence of the same technical changes that occurred in other areas of the South in the 1820s and early 1830s occurring in Mississippi in the late 1830s and early 1840s which he then labelled an 'agricultural revolution'. Rather than an 'agricultural revolution', these changes represented the adaptation of the productive standards that existed in the rest of the cotton-South in a relatively newly settled area. As Steven F. Miller 1993, pp. 161–2 points out, the use of the hand-hoe was common in cotton-production in newly settled areas, like Mississippi before the mid-1830s, because tree-roots and stumps prevented the use of ploughs in soil-preparation and cultivation. Once the roots and stumps were removed completely, frontier cotton-planters were able to adapt the horse-drawn tools that had been standard in the settled areas since the 1820s.

Similarly, Franklin Knight (1970, p. 184) argued that, in Cuba 'technology...was the salvation of the sugar industry...it made possible a substantial reduction in the work force'. However, there is evidence first, that the mechanisation of refining actually increased the number of slaves needed in agriculture, which remained unchanged technically (Bergad 1990, pp. 89–91); and second, that the introduction of new technology was concentrated in the newest Cuban plantation-regions in the 1860s and 1870s and was not generalised (Scott 1985a, pp. 20–4).

labour-intensive character of the plantation labour-process. The late seventeenth and eighteenth centuries saw numerous changes to sugar-cultivation and refining that reduced the planters' costs. The most important of these were reactions to the growing deforestation and soil-exhaustion that accompanied the spread of the sugar-plantations. The destruction of the large timber-reserves on many of the larger Caribbean islands raised the cost of the fuel used to boil sugar-cane juice in the late seventeenth and early eighteenth centuries. The increased use of bagasse (crushed sugar-cane) and the introduction of the 'Jamaica train', a series of cauldrons for boiling sugar all heated by a single fire whose heat was transferred from cauldron to cauldron through a system of internal flues, allowed substantial savings in fuel-costs.

The chronic soil-exhaustion that plagued all plantation-regions led Caribbean sugar-planters in the eighteenth century to abandon the practice of planting sugar cane in horizontal trenches which promoted soil-erosion. Planters introduced vertical 'cane holing' and extensive manuring to slow the loss of the soil's fertility. Similar patterns of 'cheese-paring' technical change continued in the nineteenth-century sugar-islands, with the introduction of new cane-varieties ('Ohati-Bourbon' cane), and in the southern US with the cotton-planters' attempts to slow soil-exhaustion through extensive manuring. These changes brought important savings in raw-materials costs, and increased, or at least slowed the decrease in, yields per acre allowing the sugar-planters who adapted these techniques to compete successfully in the world-market. However, none of these changes fundamentally altered the ratio of labour to land and tools – none reduced the quantum proportion of human labour in the plantation labour-process.[38]

As a result of the highly episodic process of technical change in the slave plantation-regions of the Americas, the relationship of slaves to land and tools remained essentially fixed for long periods of time. The ratio of slaves to land and tools remained relatively stagnant through the seventeenth and eighteenth centuries, creating a 'rule of thumb' where each slave could be allocated an acre to plant, cultivate, harvest and refine one ton of sugar. The application of steam-power to cane crushing in the early nineteenth century

[38] Galloway 1989, pp. 96–102; Garrett 1978, pp. 124–36; Gray 1933, I, pp. 800–10; Tomich 1990, pp. 140–6; Watts 1987, pp. 390–2, 429–31; Wright 1978, pp. 50–5, 74–87, 102–9.

and the introduction of the vacuum-pan in mid-century increased that ratio. However, once established in the 'new' Caribbean, this ratio remained unchanged until the abolition of slavery and the separation of agriculture and industry in sugar-production. Similarly, the ratio of slaves to land and tools remained unchanged in the cotton-South after the introduction of gang-labour and horse- or mule-drawn implements. Gavin Wright's research found that Southern planters invested much less in machinery and tools per worker than Northern family-farmers in 1860, and that investments in implements and machinery per worker may have been dropping in the 1850s. Even more indicative of a stagnant ratio of labour to land and tools, Wright found little evidence of economies of scale in Southern plantation-agriculture. In other words, the growth in the volume of slave-produced cotton involved the addition of more slaves and more land, rather than increased labour-productivity through continually improving technique.[39]

Were slaves 'cheap labour'?

Some of the proponents of the 'planter-capitalism' thesis have argued that the slave-plantations' failure to mechanise production was simply a rational market-response to the relatively low cost of slave-labour. According to Haywood Fleisig, the availability of inexpensive land in both the southern and northern antebellum-US severely limited the supply of labourers who would voluntarily sell their capacity to work to farmers, placing a 'labour-constraint' on the size and volume of agricultural production.[40] In the North, the adaptation of the mechanical reaper and other labour-saving technologies removed the 'labour-constraint' by allowing families to expand the amount of acreage they farmed without additional labour. In the South, slavery created a highly elastic supply of labour, removing the 'labour-constraint' on the scale of production. However, 'the relaxation of this constraint' through slavery 'reduced...the incentive to invent and innovate farm machinery'.[41]

---

[39] Barrett 1965; Galloway 1989, pp. 88–9, 105–10; Tomich 1990, Chapter 6; Watts 1987, pp. 390–2, 429–31; Wright 1978, pp. 50–5, 74–87, 102–9.

[40] Fleisig 1976, p. 572.

[41] Gavin Wright (1978, pp. 46–55, 106–8) made a similar argument. In his later work, Wright (1986, Chapter 5) shifts to a different explanation of the absence of technical innovation in Southern agriculture – that the planters invested all of their capital in slaves ('capitalisation of labour') rather than new and improved machinery, railroads

Franklin Knight adopts the same logic in explaining the mechanisation of sugar-refining in Cuba. The end of the African slave-trade in the early 1800s drove up the cost of slaves, 'constraining' the supply of labour for Cuban sugar-planters. The planters introduce new machinery that reduced the need for slave-labour on the sugar-plantations. According to Knight:

> Technology…was the salvation of the sugar industry. In the first place, it made possible a substantial reduction in the work force. The railroads, the use of steam, and more scientific processing enabled a higher output capacity with a lower ratio of laborers to the land. No longer did more sugar necessarily mean more land and more slaves. Nor did a larger work-gang necessarily mean the acquisition of more slaves, as Indians, Chinese, and white wage earners joined the estates. Technology, therefore, changed the nature of the sugar estate.[42]

Fleisig's thesis that slavery created an elastic supply of labour in the antebellum-South that reduced the planters' incentive to introduce labour-saving machinery is questionable. Clearly, a surplus of labour may *slow* the rate of mechanisation in certain branches of production under capitalism. Marx pointed out how mechanisation in the more capital-intensive sectors of industry reproduced the reserve-army of labour (the unemployed and underemployed), driving wages down sufficiently to allowed more labour-intensive sectors to delay replacing human labour with machinery.[43] As a particular reserve-army of labour is absorbed into the labour-intensive sectors, wages begin to rise, the retarding effects of a 'labour-surplus' on technological innovation in these sectors are reduced, and new, labour-saving instruments of production are introduced. Despite the indisputable fact that the price of

---

and industry. However, this claim does not stand up to empirical and comparative interrogation. First, Fred Bateman and Thomas Weiss (1981, pp. 74–7) demonstrate that planters' investments in slaves did not 'absorb' capital that could have been otherwise used to build factories, urban buildings, railroads and mines. Planters, especially the largest, had considerable cash-reserves, which they invested in additional land and slaves, the northern stock-and-bond markets, and land-speculation on both the northern and southern frontiers. Second, the ability of Cuban and other 'new sugar-island' planters to mechanise sugar-refining and build railroads to transport sugar to port-cities contradicts the claim that the 'capitalisation of labour' under slavery is the barrier to technical innovation and economic growth (Bergad 1990, Chapters 3).

[42] Knight 1970, p. 182.
[43] Marx 1976, pp. 590–3, 599–610.

slaves rose dramatically in the southern US during the 1840s and 1850s,[44] there is no evidence of systematic and widespread introduction of labour-saving technology in cotton-production. In other words, even as the supply of labour became *less elastic* and the cost of slaves increased, the master-class in the US was incapable of replacing slave-labour with improved farm-implements in the established cotton plantation-regions.

Knight's thesis is also problematic. First, the initial wave of mechanisation of Cuban sugar-production – the introduction of steam-powered milling in the 1820s and 1830s – corresponds to a period of 'labour-surplus'. While the African slave-trade to the southern US and the rest of the Caribbean was effectively abolished in the first decade of the nineteenth century, the African slave-trade to Cuba continued through the 1830s and early 1840s, leading to falling slave-prices though the 1840s. Second, the mechanisation of sugar-refining actually increased the need for slave-labour in planting, cultivation, and harvesting throughout the nineteenth century in Cuba because technique in the agricultural phase of sugar-production remained unchanged. Knight clearly recognises this as the case before 1840, when 'more efficient mills demanded more canes, which meant a greater area under cultivation, hence a need for more slaves'.[45] Nor did the introduction of the vacuum-pan after 1840 change the relationship between the number of slaves and land and tools. The greatest numbers of slave-labourers were to be found on the most technically advanced plantations in the newly settled regions of western Cuba.[46] Rather than an automatic response to a changing labour-market, the mechanisation of sugar-refining in the nineteenth century was only possible because Cuba remained a 'frontier'-region for sugar-cultivation through the 1870s.

Other non-capitalist 'anomalies'

Slave-owning planters, despite being subject to the competitive imperatives of the capitalist world-market, behaved differently from capitalists in two other important ways. First, planters did not specialise their productive activities and purchase their inputs from other producers. Capitalist firms increasingly specialise in the production of a single good or service, reducing costs

---

[44] Bergad, Iglesias Garcia and Barcia 1995, pp. 146–7; Gray 1933, I, pp. 665–7.
[45] Knight 1970, p. 32.
[46] Scott 1985b, pp. 28–30, 34–9.

through the purchase of inputs on the market from other specialised capital-ist producers. By contrast, planters throughout the New World struggled to make their plantations self-sufficient in food and tools. As Robin Blackburn argues:

> The resilience and versatility of the New World slave-plantation derived from the fact that it walked on two feet: that which stepped forward commercially being able to rely on that which remained fixed to the *terra firma* of natural economy. Planters generally preferred their slaves to be producing commodities for the Atlantic market; but at all times, and especially when the latter were closed, slaves could be directed to produce foodstuffs, manufactures and services – for themselves, for their masters and for the local market.[47]

Plantation self-sufficiency was accomplished either through the planters' organisation of their slaves into work-gangs to raise food-crops and raise animals, or through the slaves' working 'provision-grounds' or garden-plots independently during the time their masters did not require their labour. The staggering of sugar-planting on the eighteenth-century Caribbean sugar-islands created nearly year round demand for the slaves' labour, reaching its zenith during the five-month-long harvests with their sixteen to twenty hour work-days. With little or no time free to work either on their own or under the command of their masters in food-production, plantation self-sufficiency was difficult and contributed to the inability of Caribbean slave-populations to reproduce naturally before the nineteenth century. In the nineteenth cen-tury, sugar-cultivation outside of Cuba became less demanding and plan-tation self-sufficiency through the independent production of slaves was achieved in most of the Caribbean, with slaves producing enough food to feed themselves and the white urban populations of the sugar-islands. On the North-American mainland, the less demanding work rhythms of tobacco and cotton allowed planters to make their productive units self-sufficient in food. Tobacco- and cotton-planters took advantage of their staples' lengthy 'slack-seasons' to organise slaves into work-gangs to grow corn and raise hogs for plantation-consumption. Between corn and pork raised under the direction of the masters and the slaves' independent production of vegetables, poultry

---

[47] Blackburn 1997, p. 502.

and other food-items on small garden-plots, US slave-plantations were self-sufficient in food in the eighteenth and nineteenth centuries.[48]

The second way in which slave-owning planters acted differently from capitalists was their tendency to *increase* rather than *decrease* output over the medium term in the face of falling commodity-prices. It is true that capitalists, especially those in capital-intensive industries, will maintain production-levels in the short-run in the face of falling prices to preserve market-share. However, all capitalists over the medium to long term reduce output, either through reductions in capacity-utilisation (laying off workers) or abandoning a particular line of production, as prices fall.[49] Slave-holding planters, by contrast, consistently raised output in the face of decades-long declines in the prices of tobacco, sugar, and cotton. Only the near collapse of staple-prices as the result of new and more efficient producers entering the world-market and the possibility of shifting their slaves and other economic resources to other activities induced New-World planters to abandon their traditional staple for new crops or products, as happened with the shift from tobacco to cotton in the southern US during the late eighteenth century.[50]

Plantation-slavery in the Americas was the creature of the capitalist world-market and was subject to its imperatives of cost-cutting, but rested on non-capitalist social-property relations. Despite the planters' need to maximise profits in the production of commodities for the world-market, they were unable to achieve this economic goal in the same manner as capitalists. The planters struggled to maximise revenue and minimise costs in order to 'hold their place' in the world-market and maintain and expand their possession of land and slaves. However, they did not specialise production, smoothly adjust output to market-signals, and, *most importantly, did not increase productivity through the routine introduction of labour-saving technology*. The state of

---

[48] Berlin and Morgan 1991; Blackburn 1997, pp. 423–30, 437–9, 462–8; Gallman 1970; Genovese 1972, pp. 535–9; Hilliard 1972.

[49] Botwinick 1993, Chapter 5. Ironically, non-capitalist producers who have non-market access to land (traditional landlords, independent peasants) can most easily reduce output in the face of falling prices; redeploying most of their labour to subsistence-production. Staple-producing planters were compelled to maintain or expand output in the face of falling prices; while capitalist producers must eventually find alternative goods to produce for the market.

[50] Gray 1933 I, Chapter 12, pp. 458–61; II, pp. 496–700; Kulikoff 1986, Chapter 3; Tomich 1990, Chapter 3; Whartenby 1963, pp. 44–9.

world-market demand for tobacco, sugar, and cotton, rather than the plantations' technical conditions of production, determined the level of the planters' profits and of regional per capita income. Economic growth tended to be *extensive*, the addition of more slaves and more land in a process of geographical expansion, rather than *intensive*, with the introduction of labour-saving tools, implements and machinery. The episodic and 'cheese-paring' process of technical innovation and the planters' attempts to be self-sufficient in food and tools limited the development of the social division of labour – the 'home-market' for industrially produced capital and consumer-goods. As a result, plantation-slavery systematically stifled the development of large-scale industry and manufacturing in the regions it dominated. In sum, despite slave-owning planters and capitalists sharing the need to maximise profits in competitive markets, slavery's social and economic dynamics were fundamentally different from those of capitalism.

II. The 'non-bourgeois civilisation' model

The 'non-bourgeois civilisation' model, in a number of respects, marks an advance over the 'planter-capitalism' model of plantation-slavery in the Americas. Represented first and foremost by Eugene Genovese, the 'non-bourgeois civilisation' thesis has produced a sophisticated account of the non-capitalist character of the slave-plantation regions. Influenced by such Marxist writers as Maurice Dobb,[51] Genovese has forcefully argued that an 'agricultural revolution', the continuous introduction of labour-saving farm-implements and machinery, is an essential prerequisite for industrialisation. Genovese's research has described how plantation-slavery in the southern US prevented such a transformation of agriculture, blocking the emergence of a 'home-market' for industrially produced capital and consumer-goods.

Despite these advances, however, the 'non-bourgeois civilisation' thesis has been unable to provide a convincing explanation of *why* plantation-slavery is incompatible with continuous technical innovation that replaces human labour with new and more complex tools, implements, and machinery. Again, Genovese provides the most rigorous attempt, to date, to provide such an explanation. Genovese's depiction of plantation-slavery as a non-capitalist

---

[51] Dobb 1947.

form of social labour rests on a comparison of the market-'rationality' of capitalism (the dynamic of specialisation, technical innovation, and accumulation in response to competitive market-signals) with the 'irrationality' of slavery. Relying on Max Weber's[52] discussion of slavery, Genovese identifies four 'irrational' features of slavery:

> First, the master cannot adjust the size of his labor-force in accordance with business fluctuations....Second, the capital outlay is much greater and riskier for slave labor than for free. Third, the domination of society by a planter class increases the risk of political influence in the market. Fourth, the sources of cheap labor usually dry up rather quickly, and beyond a certain point costs become excessively burdensome.[53]

These 'irrational' features of slavery resulted in the continual investment in more land and more slaves, rather than new and more productive instruments and tools. Consequently, slavery led to technological stagnation, low labour-productivity in agriculture, and a shallow 'home-market' for industrial production.

Genovese's model of slavery, derived from Weber, prevents him from developing a consistent explanation of how slavery's social-property relations block relatively continuous labour-saving technical change. The 'irrationality' of slavery is derived from a comparison of the observable features of slavery with those of capitalism. There is no attempt to link the observed 'rationalities' of capitalism and 'irrationalities' of slavery to the structural constraints their respective social-property relations place on the actions of both non-producers and producers. Genovese never satisfactorily answers the questions of why the capital/wage-labour relation of surplus-extraction *necessarily* compels both capitalists and workers to act according to the dictates of market-'rationality', or why the master-slave relation *necessarily* compels both masters and slaves to act 'irrationally' despite their subordination to world-market-imperatives. Put another way, Genovese cannot explain why the social-property relations of slavery made 'cheese-paring' technical change and geographical expansion *rational* methods of expanding output for the

---

[52] Weber 1978, pp. 162–3.
[53] Genovese 1967, p. 16.

market. The result is an account of technical stagnation under slavery that is ambiguous and, at key points, self-contradictory.

Initially, Genovese gives explanatory emphasis, correctly in my opinion, to the planters' inability to adjust the size of their labour-force to take advantage of new tools and machinery. Genovese recognises that the use of new machinery 'would increasingly have required a smaller slave force, which in turn have depended on expanding markets for surplus slaves and thus could not have been realised in the South as a whole'.[54] Further on, Genovese argues that 'technological progress and division of labour result in work for fewer hands, but slavery requires all hands to be occupied at all times'. Thus, it would appear that the planters' inability to adjust the size of the labour-force in the face of market-imperatives is the main obstacle to the mechanisation of agriculture and the development of industry.

However, Genovese follows these insights about slavery and mechanisation with the claim that 'capitalism has solved this problem [excess workers – C.P.] by a tremendous economic expansion along a variety of lines (qualitative development), but slavery's obstacles to industrialisation prevent this type of solution'.[55] Since capitalism's ability to generate 'qualitative development' – industrialisation – is the result of its necessary dynamic of specialisation, technical innovation and accumulation, Genovese's argument becomes circular. On the one hand, the masters' inability to alter the size of his labour-force is the major obstacle to introduction of labour-saving techniques in agriculture, and to the development of a home-market and industrialisation. On the other, plantation-slavery's inability to industrialise and provide employment for surplus-slaves makes technical innovation in agriculture impossible. In sum, the master's inability to vary the size of their labour-force becomes *both* the cause *and* the effect of Southern economic underdevelopment.[56]

---

[54] Genovese 1967, p. 44.
[55] Genovese 1967, p. 49.
[56] Genovese's argument also overlooks the fact that workers under capitalism are responsible for organising their own reproduction and maintenance outside the production-process. When unemployed or underemployed, they become part of the reserve-army of labour whose presence regulates wage-rates under capitalism (Marx 1976, pp. 781–802). Under slavery, the existence of a large number of slaves 'without masters' would represent 'social chaos' (Tomich 1990, p. 136).

Slaves as 'recalcitrant' workers

In an implicit recognition of the conceptual difficulties that flow from his inability to specify how the structure of capitalist and slave class-relations shape their respective labour-processes, Genovese introduces the notion that the slave was a recalcitrant labourer with a distinctive, non-capitalist 'work-ethic'. Drawing upon the work of the nineteenth-century liberal economist J.E. Cairnes,[57] Genovese argues that the slaves' unfree legal status deprived them of any material interest in the labour-process, making them reluctant workers whose labour could be utilised only under close supervision of highly repetitive tasks. According to Genovese, '[b]ondage forced the Negro to give his labor grudgingly and badly, and his poor work habits retarded those social and economic advances that could have raised the general level of productivity'.[58] In later formulations, Genovese emphasised the unique, non-capitalist slave 'work-ethic' shaped by the day-to-day contestation with the masters.[59] Put simply, the slave's 'lack of motivation' shaped the labour-process on the plantations of the antebellum-South.

Other proponents of the 'pre-bourgeois civilisation' thesis echo Genovese's argument that the slaves' unfree legal status made them unmotivated and recalcitrant workers whose labour was incompatible with the introduction of new and more complex machinery. James Oakes locates slavery's failure to increase labour-productivity in the slaves' lack of incentives:

> Nevertheless, slavery actually provided little room for significant improvements in productivity. As laborers, the slave had little incentive to care very much or to work very hard. They had nothing like the serf's powerful claim to rights on the land. Slaves also lacked the incentives built into a wage-labor economy: the sheer need to go to work to survive, the promise of more pay for more work, and the added enticement of upward mobility in the long run. They had nothing to gain from working hard on cash crops that added nothing to their basic subsistence. The limited hierarchy of the slave community offered no real possibility of social advancement. Slave parents could work neither for their own nor their children's eventual independence. No institutional promise of future freedom provided an

---

[57] Cairnes 1968, like most nineteenth-century liberal critiques of slavery, derives his argument from Adam Smith 1937, pp. 364–6.
[58] Genovese 1967, p. 43.
[59] Genovese 1972, pp. 285–94; 1983, pp. 90–171.

incentive for slaves to work hard. So, while countless slaves took justifiable pride in their skills as nurses, managers, cooks, or artisans, the vast majority of slave-laborers, the field hands, had no good reason to care much about the success of the master's efforts to produce a 'good crop'.[60]

For John Ashworth, 'the fact that so many slaves did not wish to be slaves, did not wish to see the fruits of their labour appropriated by another, and therefore attempted, in various ways, to resist this exploitation' was the major obstacle to continuous technical innovation in the antebellum US-South.[61] Not only did slave-resistance to their unfree legal status block the introduction of new and more complex tools on the plantation, but it severely limited industrialisation and urbanisation in slave-societies. The risks associated with slave tool-breaking were even greater in industry, with its more expensive machinery, than agriculture, with its inexpensive hand-tools. The independence and autonomy that urban slaves experienced also undermined their masters' control over their labour.[62]

For Manuel Moreno Fraginals, the slaves' lack of motivation flowing from their unfree legal status placed severe constraints on the mechanisation of the Cuban sugar-industry and made the mechanisation of sugar-refining a source of profound social and economic tensions in Cuban slavery:

> Slaves showed their innate rebelliousness by slowing down on the job, doing it badly, or simply sneaking off. As machines began to be the only solution, the negativeness of slave labor made itself painfully obvious. Slaves worked badly and grudgingly, beat up the animals, ruined the tools – a trend against which handbooks and regulations were as futile as punishment. All this was reflected in the instruments of production: enormously thick and heavy machetes, spades and hoes any free peasant would have refused to work with, iron *jans* [hoes – C.P.] of vast size. If the change of implements slowed down the high incidence of breakage and damage, it also made slave labor slower and less productive. So much slovenly work resulted that in the end only the simplest physical tasks were assigned to slaves. And, as a final and insurmountable obstacle, year after year the system germinated violent rebellions.[63]

---

[60] Oakes 1990, pp. 140–1.
[61] Ashworth 1995, p. 92.
[62] Ashworth 1995, pp. 96–122; Wade 1964, Chapter 9.
[63] Fraginals 1976, pp. 134–5.

Skilled slave-labour

The notion that the slaves' unfree legal status was an obstacle to acquiring technical skills or working with complex tools and machinery, either in agriculture or industry, is empirically untenable. In both classical European antiquity and the plantation-regions of the Americas, slaves made up a large proportion of the skilled artisans. According to Westermann, 'there were few economic services which were closed to the slave class' in ancient Greece and Rome.[64] Slaves could be found among the urban and rural building trades (stone-masons, carpenters), in various metal-working crafts (sword- and shield-making; bronze, iron and goldsmiths), and in other 'handicraft-industries' (couch-makers, charcoal-burners, leather-tanners and cutters, engravers, wool-spinners and weavers, potters). All of these trades required extensive training, considerable technical knowledge and judgment, and often involved the slaves working under their own supervision.

Slaves also dominated the ranks of plantation-artisans in both the Caribbean and in the southern US. While sugar- and tobacco-plantations, with their more extensive processing and storage-facilities, required more skilled workers than cotton-plantations, slaves could be found working on almost all New-World plantations as teamsters, blacksmiths, harness-makers, boatmen, stave- and barrel-makers, sawyers, and carpenters. In the urban zones of the American plantation-regions, slave-artisans were also found among the ranks of such diverse crafts as barbers, rope-makers, shipwrights, masons, carpenters, and tailors. Cotton-plantations required fewer skilled artisans, and urban slave-artisans in the US-South faced the hostility of free, white artisans. However, Fogel and Engerman estimate that slightly over one quarter of all slaves in the US were not gang-labourers in 1860, with some 7 per cent acting as supervisors of other slaves ('drivers'), 11.9 per cent as skilled artisans, and 7.4 per cent as semi-skilled workers (boat and cartmen, domestic servants, etc.).[65] In whatever capacity they laboured, these skilled slaves, like the slave-artisans of classical antiquity, acquired and utilised extensive knowledge of their craft and often worked under their own supervision.[66]

---

[64] Westerman 1955, pp. 11, 6–7, 11–14, 67–9, 73–5, 91–6.
[65] Fogel and Engerman 1976, pp. 38–9.
[66] Berlin and Morgan 1993, pp. 17–20; Berlin 1998, pp. 134–8, 154–9; Fogel 1989, pp. 42–5, 49–52; Kulikoff 1986, pp. 396–9; Moore 1988, Chapter 11; Tomich 1990, pp. 225–7.

Highly skilled slaves effectively controlled the sugar-refining process before the introduction of the vacuum-pan in the mid-nineteenth century. The boiling and curing of sugar before mechanisation were processes that required very precise judgements concerning the use of heat and chemicals:

> From the mills, the spurting cane-juice coursed through lead-lined wooden gutters straight into the boiling house. In this steaming and smoking inferno it was crystallised by evaporation. After being held in one of several large reservoirs or 'receivers', the juice was first heated in shallow round pans called 'clarifiers', during which it was 'tempered' with lime. The calcium carbonate acted as a catalyst, causing the sediment to sink and other impurities to rise to the top of the seething liquid. This 'crust' was constantly skimmed. After tempering, the juice was boiled in a succession of progressively smaller hemispherical cast-iron 'coppers', up to five in all, until it was ready to enter the 'tache'...in which it was finally crystallised, or 'struck'.[67]

Slaves, not free workers, directed these processes in New-World sugar-plantations during the eighteenth and early nineteenth centuries, making crucial decisions based on their knowledge and experience:

> Despite growing scientific interest and inquiry, for all practical purposes knowledge of the techniques of sugar-refining remained a craft secret and could only be acquired only by long practice and experience. This knowledge was the property of the slaves....Although the white sugar master nominally oversaw the boiling house, the slave refiner was in practical control of its activities....His technical qualifications made the slave refiner indispensable to the operation of the estates, and the master was obliged to concede control over the most strategic aspect of the labor-process to this craftsman.[68]

Moreno Fraginals claimed that the introduction of the vacuum-pan in the 1850s and 1860s made sugar-refining 'too complicated for slaves' and led to the introduction of contract and free-labourers in the Cuban sugar-refineries.[69] However, recent research on the introduction of the vacuum-pan in Martinique and Cuba has shown that the new machinery actually *lowered* the level of skill

---

[67] Carton and Walvin 1970, p. 110.
[68] Tomich 1990, pp. 223–4.
[69] Fraginals 1976, pp. 112, 115–16.

and judgement required of the workers who operated it, and that slaves made up almost all of the vacuum-pan operators in mechanised sugar-refining.[70]

The slaves' legal status did not prevent them from acquiring skills and working under their own supervision in a variety of trades; nor did it prevent them from working effectively in non-agricultural pursuits. In Rome and Greece, the largest concentrations of slaves were found in mining, a relatively unskilled and highly dangerous occupation, not agriculture.[71] In the southern US, some 5 per cent of all slaves worked in industrial settings, labouring in such industries as coal, lead- and salt-mining, cotton-spinning and weaving, iron smelting and forging, leather tanning, tobacco, hemp cloth and rope making, and lumbering. According to an exhaustive study of industrial slavery in the antebellum south, these slaves worked with the latest contemporary machinery and tools and were at least as productive, in terms of output per worker, as legally free workers in the rest of the US.[72]

Free wage-labourers as 'recalcitrant' workers

The 'pre-bourgeois civilisation' historians' claim that the slaves' unfree legal status made them recalcitrant, unmotivated and untrainable workers is both empirically untenable, and tends to *idealise* the condition of legally free wage-workers under capitalism. The juridical freedom of the wage-earner under capitalism does not make her or him a motivated and willing labourer. Unlike peasants and other household-producers, neither slaves nor wage-workers have control over or interest in the production-process. Peasants and artisans organise their own labour and the labour of household-members, making all decisions about the timing, pace and technical character of the labour-process. As a result, they are 'self-supervising' and require no external 'labour-discipline' to propel them to labour.[73] By contrast, both the

---

[70] Scott 1985b, pp. 34–9; Tomich 1990, pp. 199–201, 221–5.
[71] Westermann 1955, pp. 12–5.
[72] Starobin 1970, Chapter 1, pp. 153–63; Lewis 1979.
[73] The ability of peasants to organise their own household labour-process does not imply that these households were not subject to external demands on their product, were egalitarian social organisations, or were required to technically innovate. In many cases, landlords or the agents of centralised states appropriated taxes and rents from the peasantry through non-market mechanisms, imposing some external discipline on the household-producers who, nevertheless, remained in control of their labour-process. In almost all cases, peasant-households were *patriarchal* – the eldest males effectively

slave and wage-worker confront a labour-process whose timing, pace and technical character has been shaped by the non-producers – the master or the capitalist. Thus, the problem of 'labour-discipline' – insuring continuous labour on the part of the direct producer – only becomes an issue in the labour-process under slavery and capitalism. Clearly, the forms and goals of the slaves' struggles at the workplace differed from those of wage-workers, as the slave-owners' fundamental mechanisms of 'labour-discipline' differed from those of the capitalists. However, the similarities that flow from the non-producers' command over the labour-process in both forms of social labour are striking:

> The conflict between master and slave took many forms, involving the organisation of labor, the hours and pace of work, the sexual division of labor, and the composition of the labor-force – all questions familiar to students of free workers. The weapons that workers employed in such conflicts – feigning ignorance, slowing the line, minimizing the stint, breaking tools, disappearing at critical moments, and, as a last resort, confronting their superiors directly and violently – suggest that in terms of workplace struggles, slaves and wage-workers had much in common. Although the social relations of slave and wage labor differed fundamentally, much can be learned about slave life by examining how the work process informed the conflict between wage-workers and their employers. For like reasons, the processes of production were as much a source of working class culture for slave workers as for free workers.[74]

Wage-workers' lack of motivation, their indifference to the labour-process, has not been an obstacle to the introduction of new, complex labour-saving machinery under capitalism. In fact, the division and simplification of tasks and the mechanisation of production have systematically lowered the levels of skill, knowledge, judgement, and initiative on the part of wage-

---

commanded the labour of women and children in the household. Finally, the ability of peasant-households to obtain, maintain, and expand their landholdings without successful market-competition freed these household-producers from any compulsion to specialise production and introduce labour-saving technology.
[74] Berlin 1998, p. 11. Thompson 1993 presents a path-breaking analysis of the historical struggle to impose 'labour-discipline' on workers in Britain in the late eighteenth and early nineteenth centuries. Aufhauser 1973 makes a similar point about both free industrial and slave agricultural workers' lack of motivation.

workers. While the machinery may be more complex and require a small number of technicians to service and maintain it, the level of skill required on the part of the mass of workers who operate that machinery tends to drop under industrial capitalism.[75] Thus, the slaves' lack of motivation and recalcitrance, purportedly a product of her or his unfree legal status, could not be an obstacle to the introduction of new, labour-saving technology under plantation-slavery.

While the 'pre-bourgeois civilisation' model marks an important advance over the 'planter-capitalism' model, it fails to provide an adequate understanding of the fundamental economic dynamics of plantation-slavery. Ultimately, the 'pre-bourgeois civilisation' historians fail to explain plantation-slavery's retarding effects on technical innovation, the social division of labour and economic development for the same reasons the 'planter-capitalism' historians fails. Both schools view the subjective goals and desires of key economic actors as the central determinants of economic development, regardless of social context. Genovese's slaves, lacking personal freedom, were unmotivated labourers incapable of developing the skills and self-discipline necessary to master new and more complex tools. Fogel and Engerman's 'slave-owners were hard, calculating businessmen who priced slaves, and their other assets, with as much shrewdness as could be expected of any Northern capitalist'.[76]

As we have seen, neither explanation is sufficient. New-World planters were subject to the imperatives of the world-market and were compelled to maximise profits through reducing costs. However, they were unable to pursue these goals in the same way as capitalists – through specialisation and changing output in response to price-signals and, most importantly, through the regular introduction of labour-saving tools, implements and machinery. New-World slaves were, in their majority, unmotivated and indifferent labourers. However, wage-workers under capitalism, in their majority, are also unmotivated and indifferent labourers. The wage-workers' subjective motivations were and are not an obstacle to the capitalist mechanisation of production. Rather than placing subjective motivations and goals at the centre of the analysis of the social and economic dynamics of slavery, we will focus

---

[75] Marx 1976, Chapter 15; Braverman 1974; Montgomery 1992; Thompson 1989, Chapters 4–6.
[76] Fogel and Engerman 1974, p. 73.

on how the structure of the master-slave class-relation provided the social context that shaped the organisation of production and economic development in the antebellum-southern US.

III. Class-structure and economic development in the antebellum-South

The master-slave social-property relation

To grasp the specificity and dynamic of the master-slave class-relation, we will compare it to the capitalist/wage-labourer relation.[77] Capitalist and slave-social relations of production share certain characteristics. In both capitalism and slavery, the non-producers have both legal ownership and effective possession (the ability to organise the labour-process) of the means of production – land, tools, machinery, raw materials and the like. In both forms of social labour, the direct producers are separated from legal ownership and effective possession of the means of production, and are thus compelled to labour for others. Put simply, in both capitalism and slavery, the capitalists and the masters can organise a collective, co-operative labour-process under their command. The wage-worker or the slaves confront the labour-process as 'ready-made', as a creation of the capitalist or masters. This crucial similarity accounts for the lack of interest in the production-process on the part of both the slave and the wage-worker – their shared 'recalcitrance'. Unlike various forms of household-production, where the artisan or peasant organises their own labour-process and thus requires no supervision, both slavery and capitalism require 'labour-discipline'. As we have seen, the masters' and capitalists' ability to combine labour, tools and land in a co-operative labour-process under their command also explains the strong similarities between the day-to-day conflict over the pace and organisation of work in both capitalism and slavery.

---

[77] The following paragraphs draw upon Marx's 1976 discussion of capitalist social-property relations and discussions of slave social-property relations in de Ste. Croix 1981, pp. 504–5; Hindess and Hirst 1975, pp. 125–48 and, in particular, Tomich 1990, Chapter 4.

The masters' ability to organise a co-operative, centralised labour-process under their control also accounts for the productive superiority of the plantation over household-producers of cotton, tobacco, and other staple-crops. Gavin Wright claims that there were no significant differences in economies of scale between household- (family-farms) and slave-plantation producers of cotton in the antebellum-South.[78] Clearly, the economies of scale achieved on cotton-plantations (with 20 or more slaves)[79] compared with household-production of cotton were much smaller than the gains made on sugar-plantations, where the much larger investments in tools and machinery for sugar-processing made household-production of sugar nearly impossible. However, the introduction of co-operative, centralised labour-processes (gang-labour), along with superior financial resources, gave the planters productive superiority over small farmers who owned no slaves or too few slaves to create work-gangs. Once gang-labour was established, Wright is correct that no economies of scale accrue with increased size of the slave-workforce, as the ratio of labour, land, and tools remains unchanged.[80]

The crucial difference between capitalism and slavery appears in the surplus-extractive relationship between the non-producers and the direct producers. Capitalists purchase the *labour-power*, the capacity to work, of the workers for a specified period of time. Masters, by contrast, purchase *the labourer*, the person of the worker. The purchase of the *labourer*, rather than her or his *labour-power*, has important economic effects. The purchase of labour-power allows the worker to enter the capitalist production process as a *variable* element of production. The capital invested in the reproduction of the workers, their wages, is a variable cost clearly distinguished from the constant costs of objects and instruments of production. The masters' purchase of the labourer converts the direct producer into 'means of production in human form'. The 'capitalisation of labour' requires the slave to enter the production-process as a *constant* element of production. Under slavery, the master is unable to distinguish capital invested in objects and instruments of production from that

---

[78] Wright 1978, pp. 74–87, 102–9.

[79] The figure of 20 slaves as the minimum for gang-labour in cotton-cultivation – as the dividing line between 'farms' and 'plantations' – is derived from Fogel 1989, p. 50; Gates 1960, p. 139; Genovese 1972, p. 7; and Moore 1988, p. 116.

[80] Genovese 1967, pp. 156–61.

invested in reproducing his labourers. Both the labourers and land, tools and the like appear as fixed and inflexible costs to the planter.

The 'capitalisation of labour' under slavery necessitates that slaves be maintained and reproduced, whether or not they actually labour, in order to preserve their potential market-value. Slaves who could not work were without market-value. By contrast, wage-workers receive wages that allow them to maintain and reproduce themselves only if they labour under the command of the capitalist. This fundamental difference in the structural position of slaves and wage-workers accounts for the different forms 'labour-discipline' takes in the two forms of social labour. Under slavery, physical force and violence, actual or potential, was a *necessary* element of the plantation labour-process. The 'whip of starvation', rather than physical force, is all that is necessary to ensure that wage-workers actually labour for capital. Fogel and Engerman grasp this difference:

> The hiring of free workers in the marketplace provided manager of labor with a powerful new disciplinary weapon. Workers who were lazy, indifferent, or who otherwise shirked their duties could be fired – left to starve beyond the eyesight or expense of the employer. Interestingly enough, denial of food was rarely used to enforce discipline on slaves. For the illness and lethargy caused by malnutrition reduced the capacity of the slave to labor in the fields. Planters preferred whipping to incarceration because the lash did not generally lead to an extended loss of the slave's labor time.[81]

The slaves' position as a constant element of the production-process, who must be maintained whether or not they laboured, severely restricted the masters' ability to adjust the size of their labour-force through technical innovation. Having invested in 'means of production in human form', the masters were burdened with relatively inflexible costs of reproducing their direct producers and a relatively inflexible ratio of labour to land and tools. Put simply, the masters could not readily reduce the size of their slave labour-force to adopt labour-saving technologies in the face of changing market-imperatives. Like all other precapitalist dominant classes, they were unable to 'expel' labour from production. 'Redundant' slaves had to be sold to another slaveholder in order to recoup their market-value.

---

[81] Fogel and Engerman 1974, p. 147.

Individual slave-owners or segments of the master-class might be able to sell surplus-slaves and adapt labour-saving implements and machinery, as did many planters in the 'upper' South in the nineteenth century. Only the continued geographical expansion of slavery and the resultant growth of the domestic slave-trade allowed this limited 'agrarian reform'.[82] However, at no point in the antebellum-period in the US did plantation-slavery expand rapidly enough to generate sufficient demand for slaves to allow a significant sector of the planters to adopt labour-saving tools and machinery. The domestic slave-trade reached its zenith in the 1830s, when approximately 20,000 slaves were exported from the 'upper' to 'lower' South each year.[83] While this represented some 10 per cent of the total slave-population of the 'upper' South, the domestic slave-trade accounted for less than one per cent of the total US slave-population of approximately 2.4 million counted in the 1840 census. Natural demographic increase provided the bulk of the growing slave labour-force in the US-South, limiting the market for 'surplus'-slaves made redundant through attempts to introduce labour-saving techniques into Southern agriculture. Thus, the generalised mechanisation of slave-agriculture was *impossible* – there could be no 'reserve-army' of unemployed under slavery.[84] Dale Tomich, in his study of slavery in Martinique, captures the structural roots of slavery's inability to introduce labour-saving technology:

> The contradiction between slave labor and technological innovation does not reside in the capacity or incapacity of individual workers to perform specific concrete tasks; rather, the specific character of slavery as a social

---

[82] Fields 1985, Chapter 2; Genovese 1967, Chapter 3; Tadman 1989, Part I.

[83] All data on the domestic slave-trade derived from Tadman 1989, pp. 5, 12, 44. I derived the figure of an average of 20,000 slaves sold each year by taking 70 per cent of the total slave-population exported 1830–9 (approximately 290,000) and dividing by ten. The 70 per cent figure is based on Tadman's calculation of the relative proportions of slaves sold and slaves transported by masters from the 'upper' to 'lower' South each year after 1820.

[84] Clearly like other forms of 'fixed capital', slaves are 'worn out' (no longer able to work in the fields) and lose market-value through age. As slaves age and are 'devalorised', they are 'discarded' (given light domestic tasks, caring for children, etc.) and younger slaves replace them the fields. However, this 'normal' cycle of 'human fixed capital' could not have accommodated the generalised introduction of new tools and machinery. Instead, it would have required the replacement not only of older 'devalued' slaves, but younger slaves with substantial market-value. To introduce new machinery, these younger slaves would have to be sold to other masters in order for their owners to recoup their investment in 'means of production in human form'.

relation determined the conditions under which such changes could be implemented and their consequences for social and economic development. In the slave relation, the instruments of labor did not function as capital. The reorganization of production did not save labor or reduce its cost either relatively or absolutely. Labor was not expelled from the production process, and the costs of slave maintenance remained independent of the changes in production.[85]

By contrast, capitalists can reduce the size of their labour-force to adapt new, labour-saving machinery in response to changing competitive pressures simply by laying off their 'redundant' workers and expanding the size of the reserve-army of labour. Having consumed their capacity to work for a specified period of time, the capitalists no longer have any obligation to their former workers who are 'free' to compete with one another to find other buyers for their labour-power. In sum, while capitalists have and do attempt to intensify the labour of wage-workers through speed-up and lengthening working hours, the most effective means of increasing output and reducing costs – the mechanisation of production – is available to capitalists, but not to slave-owners.

The status of slaves as a form of 'fixed capital' provided few opportunities for slave-owning planters to introduce new labour-saving technology even when such innovation would allow planters to cut costs in response to market-imperatives. The introduction of new crops or expansion to new regions provide the only opportunities for planters to break the fixed relationship between labour, land and tools through the introduction of new tools and implements. However, once the new ratio of labour, land, and tools had been established with the new crop or in the new region, it remained fixed and inflexible because of the planters' inability to adjust the size of their slave labour-force. Thus, the master-slave social-property relation necessitated episodic and 'cheese-paring' technical innovation in the slave-plantation regions of the Americas. Unable to reduce the amount of necessary labour the slave performed through mechanisation, the planters were *compelled* to organise the plantation production-process along the lines of closely supervised and co-ordinated, co-operative work that maximised the use of human labour.

---

[85] Tomich 1990, p. 201.

The only options open to planters who sought to increase the volume of production and cut costs on their plantations was either increasing the intensity and pace of work (increasing the acreage each slave-gang tilled in a given period of time), or moving production to more fertile land. In sum, geographical expansion was the *most rational* means of increasing output and reducing costs available to slave-holders embedded in the capitalist world-market.[86]

The labour-process and geographic expansion in tobacco- and cotton-cultivation

The effects of the master-slave social-property relation are clearly evident in the organisation of the labour-process in tobacco- and cotton-production. While the natural features of tobacco-production did not allow the detailed division of labour that would make gang-labour possible in sugar- and cotton-production, tobacco-planters in seventeenth- and eighteenth-century Virginia and Maryland strove to create a co-ordinated labour-process that maximised the use of human labour.[87] Tobacco-plantations were organised around the 'task-system', where the 10 or more slaves on the plantation were broken into groups of two to three and assigned daily work-quotas. White overseers would supervise the slave work-groups in seasonal tasks. During the spring, slaves would plant tobacco-seeds and cultivate the seedlings, often by hand or using simple hoes, until the seedlings were ready for replanting. The transplanting of seedlings in the summer was one of the two peak-periods of labour on the tobacco-plantation:

> After the land was cleared the ground was 'grubbed' with the 'grubbing hoe' – a kind of small mattock. Then hilling hoes, 6 to 8 inches wide and 10 or 12 inches long in the blade, were used to prepare the hills. The laborer stood with foot advanced and throws dirt from all sides around his leg, then withdrew his foot and flattened the top of the hill.[88]

---

[86] Geographical expansion was a common form of increasing output in other non-capitalist forms of social labour. According to Perry Anderson 1974, p. 31, the geographical expansion of feudalism through conquest in the medieval and early-modern period 'was probably the most *rational and rapid* single mode of expansion of surplus-extraction available for any given ruling class under feudalism'.

[87] Berlin 1999, pp. 118–9; Blackburn 1997, pp. 461–2; Gates 1960, pp. 100–3; Gray 1933, II, pp. 215–17, 545–6; Kulikoff 1986, pp. 324–5, 384–6, 408–12; Walsh 1993, pp. 172–3, 176–278.

[88] Gray 1933, I, p. 217.

Cultivation (clearing of weeds) proceeded through the rest of the summer and early autumn, with the slave work-groups using broad 'weeding' hoes to remove weeds that threatened to sap nutrients from the tobacco-plants. The harvest, the other peak-period of labour, began in the later autumn. The slaves would pick the ripened tobacco-leaves by hand, transport them to the smoking-curing house, and pack the cured tobacco in crates for market. The tools used in tobacco-cultivation, primarily hand-held hoes, remained unchanged until the shift in tobacco-cultivation to Kentucky and Tennessee in the early nineteenth century. As a result, a ratio of three acres of tobacco-land planted, cultivated, and harvested each season per slave remained unchanged through the end of the eighteenth century.

To maximise the use of human labour in the production of tobacco, the planters and their overseers utilised the labour of all their slaves. Both slave-men and women laboured together in the tobacco-fields, performing the same tasks in planting, cultivation, and harvest-seasons. Slave-children began to labour part-time in the fields at the age or 9 or 10, and became full time 'hands' at the age of 14. To maintain and increase the intensity of the work-group's task-labour, planters often appointed young male slaves to lead the group and set the pace of the group's work. This intensified pace became the basis for determining work-quotas in the task-system. Finally, by the early eighteenth century, the workday had been lengthened to 12 to 14 hours (with a two-hour mid-day break), Saturdays became a regular workday, and the number of holidays reduced to three (Christmas, Easter, and Whitsunday).

Geographical expansion, with the addition of more slaves and more land, was the most rational way for planters to increase output given the fixed ratio of labour to land and tools imposed by the social-property relations of slavery. The nearly universal tendency toward soil exhaustion in the planta-tion-regions of the Americas, resulting from the availability of inexpensive land appropriated from the Native Americans,[89] heightened the necessity of geographical expansion. Because the cost of land was less than that of pur-chasing or producing manure, most tobacco-plantations held large tracts

---

[89] Genovese 1967, Chapter 4, argued that soil-exhaustion was the direct result of the slaves' inability, as recalcitrant unfree labourers, to raise sufficient livestock for manure or to apply manure effectively. However, the record of slave-societies in the ancient world indicates no necessary relation between slave property-relations and soil-exhaustion. Hindess and Hirst 1975, pp. 162–70.

of land in reserve to allow field-rotation that slowed soil-exhaustion. Land would be planted with tobacco until yields per acre began to decline, usually within five years. At that point, the planters would move production to new lands and allow the older fields to remain fallow for 20 years. In this system, only three acres per slave would be planted at any given time, but some 20 acres per slave were needed to allow effective field-rotation. Despite these efforts, overall tobacco-yields began to decline in the Chesapeake during the early eighteenth century and tobacco-cultivation moved onto the coastal plains and into the piedmont-regions of Virginia, the Carolinas and Georgia between 1720 and 1770.[90]

The transition from tobacco to cotton as the US-South's main export-staple in the nineteenth century brought a profound transformation in the slave labour-process. First, the natural features of cotton-production allowed the development of a detailed division of labour in planting and cultivation that made possible the introduction of gang-labour on Southern cotton-plantations. The shift from task to gang-labour gave the masters' greater control over the tempo and organisation of their slaves' labour and allowed a growing scale of production, with the minimum number of slaves needed for plantation-production rising from 10 to 20. Second, the growth of cotton-production opened the way for an episode of labour-saving technical innovation in the 1820s, with the horse- or mule-drawn 'sweeper'-plough displacing the hand-hoe and the introduction of 'Petit Gulf' cotton. Taken together, the introduction of gang-labour and new labour-saving tools, seeds and implements tripled the ratio of slave-labour to land and tools, from 3 acres per slave in tobacco-production to 9–10 acres per slave in cotton-production, by the late 1830s.[91] However, once the crop-changeover was completed, labour-saving technical innovation halted, the ratio of slave-labour to land and tools became fixed, and the planters were compelled to maximise output through the close supervision of centralised work-gangs that maximised the use of human labour.

In cotton-planting, the slaves were divided into five gangs, each responsible for a specific aspect of soil-preparation and seed-placement:

---

[90] Berlin 1990, pp. 121–3; Gray 1933, I, pp. 217–18, 233–4; Kulikoff 1986, pp. 47–9, 63–4, 92–9, 142–61; Walsh 1993, pp. 172–3, 178–81.
[91] Gates 1960, pp. 136–7; Gray 1933, I, pp. 707–8; Reidy 1992, pp. 38–42.

Leading the procession were the plowmen who ridged up the unbroken earth; then came the harrowers who broke up the clods; then drillers who created the holes to receive the seeds, each hole a prescribed distance apart from the next one; then droppers who planted the seeds in the holes; and finally the rakers who covered up the holes.[92]

In cultivation, the nurturing of the cotton-plants while they grew to maturity, the hoe-gang and the plough-gang would work in close co-ordination. The hoe-gang would begin first, chopping up weeds and trimming the cotton-plants. They were followed by the plough-gang, which would stir up the soil near the rows of cotton-plants and place it back on the plants. The detailed division of labour broke down during the harvest, as undifferentiated groups of slaves would pick the cotton by hand:

> It was customary to pick the field three time, the several pickings being designated successively the 'bottom', 'middle', and 'top', crops. The middle picking furnished the largest product, and usually the best quality. The entire slave force capable of going into the field was employed. Each hand carried a sack suspended about the waist, in which the cotton was deposited as gathered, and later emptied into a basket or large sheet placed at a convenient location in the row.[93]

As in tobacco-production, the planters employed all of their slaves in the cotton-fields to maximise the use of human labour in cotton-production. Again, there was no gender-division of labour with both men and women labouring together in all aspects of cotton-production, and juvenile-labour was mobilised for minor tasks at the ages of 9 or 10 and for adult work at 14. Slaves in cotton-production worked a five and one-half day week, with Sundays and parts of Saturdays free from the masters' demand for their labour, and enjoyed the same three major holidays as slaves in tobacco-production. The slaves' work day in cotton-production varied considerably:

---

[92] Fogel and Engerman 1974, p. 203.
[93] Gray 1933, II, p. 702. Moore 1988, pp. 95–6 suggests that the introduction of horse-drawn ploughs raised the skill-level of slaves on cotton-plantations, undermined gang-labour, and brought a revival of the task-system in cultivation. This claim is not supported by any of the other studies of the slave-labour process in cotton. In fact, Reidy 1992, pp. 38–42 details the efforts of lower-South planters to completely eliminate any vestiges of the task-system so as to consolidate their command over the slave- labour-process.

The length of the solar day, seasonal weather patterns, and the variable demands of crops shaped the nature, intensity, and duration of labor. Moreover, cotton cultivation embraced two major 'slack' seasons: midsummer's laying-by time, when the cotton and corn required no further weeding prior to harvest, and winter's dead time, between the end of the harvest and the start of plowing. Both lulls provided occasions for performing routine maintenance work on the plantations, including repairing fences and ditches, removing stumps, clearing land, chopping wood, and building or repairing slave cabins and other plantation buildings.[94]

Geographical expansion was, as it had been in tobacco-production, the most rapid way cotton-planters could increase output in the face of their inability to 'expel' slave-labour from production. The tendency of cotton-production to reduce the fertility of the soil again sharpened plantation-slavery's need to expand geographically. The only systematic crop-rotation in the nineteenth-century South was between cotton and the equally soil-exhaustive corn. Cotton-planters grew very little clover, peas or other nitrogen-fixing crops and relied on manuring and the availability of inexpensive land to counter-balance declining yields. The older cotton-growing regions of upper South Carolina and middle Georgia began to experience declining yields in the 1820s. By the 1840s, segments of the Lower South were encountering the effects of soil-exhaustion on cotton-output. The larger planters owned substantial 'private frontiers' – large tracts of cultivated land – which could be brought into production when yields began to decline on the older fields. Small and medium planters had little land in reserve and were often the first to feel the impact of declining yields and the first to move.[95] For all planters moving their operations to virgin-lands, given the obstacles to altering the ratio of slave-labour to land and tools, was the most rational way for planters to increase output per slave in the cotton-South.[96]

Plantation-slavery in the antebellum-South met the growing demand for raw cotton on the part of industrialists in Britain and the northern US through geographical expansion. The centre of slave cotton-production shifted south-

---

[94] Reidy 1992, pp. 65–6.
[95] Gates 1960, pp. 142–4; Genovese 1967, Chapter 4; Gray 1933, II, pp. 910–11.
[96] Foust and Swan 1970; Whartenby 1963, Chapters 2, 5.

westerly through the early nineteenth century, from coastal South Carolina and Georgia in 1815, to western Georgia and southern Mississippi and Alabama in 1830, to Northern Mississippi and Alabama and Louisiana and Texas in 1850.[97] Between 1840 and 1860, the production of cotton in the US rose 173 per cent, from approximately 834 million pounds to 2.3 billion pounds. At the same time, cotton-acreage grew 167 per cent, from approximately 4.5 million acres to 12 million acres and the number of slaves producing cotton grew 87.5 per cent, from approximately 1.2 million to 2.25 million.[98] Put simply, the addition of more slaves and more land, combined with the intensification of the slaves' labour and increased yields per acre resulting from the cultivation of more fertile soils were the basis for expanding cotton-production in the antebellum-period. The regular introduction of labour-saving techniques was incompatible with the master-slave social-property relations, necessitating this pattern of *extensive* growth.

Plantation self-sufficiency

The slaves' place in the plantation labour-process as a constant element of production – as 'fixed capital' – also explains the near universal tendency of slave-owning planters in the Americas to attempt to make their plantations self-sufficient in food and other productive inputs.[99] In order for masters to realise their investments in slaves, the slaves must be compelled to work all year round. Agriculture, as a natural-biological process, is not well suited to providing year round, continuous work.[100] There are sharp discontinuities between the time human labour is required to plant, harvest and cultivate crops (labour-time) and the time required for natural-biological processes to bring crops to maturity (production-time). Put simply, labour-time in agriculture tends to be concentrated in the planting and harvesting of crops,

---

[97] Gates 1960, pp. 7–8, 10–11; Gray 1933, II, pp. 893–907.

[98] Hammond 1897, pp. 59–61, 74, Appendix I.

[99] Our discussion of 'plantation self-sufficiency' owes much to Anderson and Gallman 1977. However, they tend to minimise the effects of slaves as 'fixed-capital' on the plantation labour-process. For example, they tend to see 'technological obstacles' accounting for the planters' inability to introduce labour-saving machinery in cotton-production.

[100] This is one of the reasons that ancient slavery tended to be concentrated in mining and handicrafts. Jones 1956; Wood 1988, pp. 45–6, 79–80; Westerman 1955, pp. 8–9, 14–15.

which are separated by a prolonged production-time when little or no labour is required. This disjunction between labour- and production-time, which has limited the development of wage-labour in capitalist agriculture more generally,[101] posed a challenge for slave-owning planters in the Americas. All New-World planters' strove to spread their slaves' labour-time across the calendar-year. While sugar-planters had the greatest success in engaging their slaves in staple-crop production year round, the gap between production- and labour-time in *all* plantation staples created the need for planters to find other employment for their slaves during the staple-crop's 'slack season'. Thus, the possibility was opened for masters to put their slaves to work producing food and other productive inputs, either under the masters' supervision or through the slaves' independent efforts. Thus, the drive to make the slave-plantation self-sufficient and the resulting inability of the planters to specialise output was thoroughly rational and efficient given the logic of the master-slave social-property relation.

The constant need to weed tobacco-plants during their slow maturation-process from the early spring to late autumn engaged the slaves' labour for considerable portions of the year. However, except for the autumn-harvest, slaves worked fewer hours in tobacco than in sugar (10 versus 16 to 20 hours per day) and were free half of Saturday and on Sunday. In addition, 'after the crop was hung in the tobacco house', in the late autumn, 'masters had to manufacture new work for their slaves if they expected them to continue to labor'.[102] The tobacco-planters were able to organise, under their supervision, the growing of corn and the raising of hogs, allowing most of the slaves' basic food-ration (ground corn and pork) to be produced directly on the plantation rather than purchased. In addition, the masters put their slaves to work repairing and, in some cases, producing tools and equipment. The slaves were also granted garden-plots which they tilled during their 'free' time. Not only did the slaves grow a wide variety of vegetables and root-crops to supplement their diet; they produced and owned most of the fowl in Virginia and Maryland in the eighteenth century. The slaves also engaged in various craft-

---

[101] Mann 1990, Chapter 2.
[102] Kulikoff 1986, p. 412.

activities, making a variety of handicrafts, including clothing to supplement the simple clothes-provided by their masters.[103]

In cotton-production, the harvest-season (late October through November) represented the peak-period for labour-time, when slaves would work eleven hours per day, seven days per week. A lengthy slack-season followed, ending with renewed planting in the early spring. Corn, a major source of food for both slaves and plantation-livestock, was a complementary crop to cotton. According to Battalio and Kagel:

> If a plantation had a labor-force sufficient to meet the harvest requirements, it followed that a labor-surplus existed in other months that was available for other pursuits at little or no opportunity cost with respect to cotton-production. The raising of corn was ideally suited to utilising this labor supply. Corn has a short growing period which leads to a very wide range of suitable planting dates. Corn could have been planted in March before the cotton and harvested in July, or it could have been planted in June and harvested after the cotton crop was picked.[104]

The planters organised the production of corn, with the slaves working in gangs utilising the same tools (ploughs and hoes) they wielded in cotton-production. The planters also organised the raising of hogs, which were allowed to forage in the woodlands surrounding most plantations most of the year and kept in pens to fatten on corn for a few weeks prior to slaughter. Together, cotton- and corn-production kept the slaves working some 280 to 290 days per year, some 3,000 hours per year – a 60 hour week, 50 weeks per year.[105]

In addition to the planters' organisation of corn- and pork-production, which supplied most of the weekly rations slaves received from their masters, most planters granted garden-plots of approximately one acre to each slave-household in the cotton-South. On their own time (usually evenings, Saturday afternoons and Sundays), the slaves organised their own independent production of cabbage, collards, turnips, sweet potatoes and other vegetables.

---

[103] Berlin and Morgan 1993, pp. 9–11, 25–6, 29–32; Blackburn 1997, pp. 465–7; Kulikoff 1986, pp. 337–40, 392–3, 411–13.
[104] Battalio and Kagel 1970, pp. 33–4.
[105] Anderson and Gallman 1977, pp. 29–32; Battalio and Kagel 1970, pp. 26–7; Hilliard 1972, pp. 95–102.

Usually, one slave-household was able to grow enough vegetables in its garden to feed the household and provide a surplus for exchange with other slaves and for sale. Slaves in the cotton-South also raised the majority of chickens and other fowl, and engaged in hunting and fishing to supplement their diets. Slaves also produced a wide variety of handicrafts, including baskets, brooms, horse-collars, and bows both for household-consumption and sale.[106]

The masters were able to achieve a considerable degree of plantation self-sufficiency in food and tools. The successful production of corn and cotton, using slave gang-labour under the planters' direction, ensured that most plantations, at most times, were able to produce sufficient quantities of corn and pork to feed their slaves. As corn-and cotton-output rose together with the size of plantation, many of the larger planters were able to raise marketable surpluses of both corn and pork for the Southern towns and cities.[107] Not only were the planters generally able to feed the slave-population of the antebellum-South without buying food on the market, they were able to produce many of their own tools directly on the plantation. There is evidence that the larger planters owned full-time slave-blacksmiths who used wrought-iron to produce and repair the plantations' ploughs and hoes. Although small and medium-planters could not afford to purchase a full-time slave-blacksmith, they were able to lease these slaves' services from larger planters.[108] In sum, the planters were able to feed their labour-force and produce a substantial portion of their tools and implements without recourse to the market by ensuring that their slaves laboured year round. While the planters remained subject to market-imperatives to increase output and cut costs in order to maintain their possession of land and slaves, the expansion of plantation-slavery did not deepen the social division of labour through productive specialisation.

Plantation-slavery and the world-market

The master-slave social-property relation, in particular the masters' inability to alter the size or cost of their labour-force, had a profound impact

---

[106] Campbell 1993, pp. 245–6; Genovese 1972, pp. 535–6; Hilliard 1972, pp. 172–85; Moore 1988, pp. 101–15; Reidy 1992, pp. 60–1, 67–70.

[107] Batallio and Kagel 1970, pp. 31–3; Gallman 1970, pp. 18–23, Hilliard 1972, Chapters 1 and 11.

[108] Garrett 1978, pp. 64–5; Moore 1988, pp. 39–41.

on plantation-slavery's relation to the world-market. From the eighteenth century through the abolition of slavery during the Civil War, merchants organised the shipment and sale of North-American plantation-staples on the world-market, as well as provided the credit necessary for the purchase of supplies, slaves, and land. The British Navigation Acts gave British merchants a monopoly on all aspects of trade and credit with colonial Virginia and Maryland tobacco-planters. Until the 1730s, tidewater-planters sold their tobacco directly to London-merchants, who would take a commission from the final sale in exchange for shipping, storing and marketing the tobacco. The same commission-merchants would arrange the extension of credit for the purchase of plantation-supplies, slaves, and land. As tobacco-production expanded from the tidewater into the coastal plain and interior regions of Virginia and Maryland, direct shipments of tobacco became impractical. In the 1730s and 1740s, agents of Scottish merchants began to open stores in the Virginia and Maryland interior to purchase tobacco, which they would ship to agents of their firms in the coastal port-cities for shipment to Scotland and resale.[109]

During the nineteenth century, the cotton-planters consigned their crops to factors, merchants based in Southern towns and port-cities, who gathered up the cotton-crop and arranged for its shipment to England via the port of New York. In return, the factor received an average commission of 2.5 per cent of the gross price of the cotton sold. The factors also extended credit to the planters for the purchase of supplies, land, and slaves, charging an additional 2.5 per cent annual interest. As collateral for their loans, planters gave the factors both the exclusive right to sell their current cotton-crop and pledged the next year's crop. If the next year's crop fell below the amount specified in the loan-contract, the planter was charged additional interest as a penalty.[110]

The creditor-debtor relationship between merchants and planters was one factor contributing to the tendency of slave-owners in the Americas to increase rather than decrease staple-output in the face of falling prices. The merchants' mandate that planters continue producing their major staple as a condition for credit severely restrained the planters' ability to respond to falling prices

---

[109] Breen 1985, Chapters 3–5; Brenner 1993, Chapter 12; Davies 1952; Gray 1933, I, Chapter 17; Kulikoff 1986, pp. 122–31.
[110] Gray 1933, II, pp. 711–13; Woodman 1968, pp. 30–42, 49.

by shifting production to new crops. Clearly, credit is a feature of almost all commodity-production, allowing producers to purchase tools and machinery and pay workers before the sale of any finished goods. It is especially important in agriculture, where the long period between planting and harvesting creates the need for substantial credit to purchase land, seeds and tools and to secure labour long before the first crop is harvested, no less sold. For the slave-plantation, the need for credit is particularly acute because the planters have to make large outlays to purchase the person of their labourers, rather than simply purchasing their capacity to work for fixed periods of time.

Credit and debt compelled the planters to compete on the world-market in order to maintain or expand their ownership of land and slaves. However, the structure of the master-slave social-property relation compelled the slave-owning planters to increase production systematically in the face of falling world-market prices. Because the slave entered the production-process as a constant or fixed element of production, planters experienced inflexible costs of reproducing their labour-force. Capitalists can and do respond to falling prices by 'expelling labour' from production – by reducing output through lay-offs or introducing labour-saving machinery. The options for the slave-owner were much more limited:

> The planter could only respond to the market by increasing the exploitation of slave labor. This could take the form of either expanding production to marginal lands or intensifying production on the better lands. In either case, the labor component of the product could not be reduced. The planter was continuously burdened with the enormous fixed costs of slave maintenance. These costs were independent of sugar prices and had to be paid whether the slave worked or not. They thus compelled the planter to keep producing no matter what. As market conditions declined, the slave-owner could not reduce his labor-force. Instead, the need to cover the costs of slave maintenance created pressure to increase production.[111]

---

[111] Tomich 1990, p. 77.

Slavery and economic development in the US

A consistent theme in the historical and theoretical literature on the origins of capitalist industrialisation is the necessity of the transformation of the countryside. An 'agricultural revolution', that results in a dynamic of productive specialisation, relatively continuous labour-saving technical innovation and accumulation not only 'frees' a section of the rural population to work in manufacturing and industry, but deepens the social division of labour creating a 'home-market' for industrially produced goods. Rural productive specialisation creates a growing market demand for food, clothing, and other consumer-goods that rural producers formerly produced themselves, while the labour-saving technical change creates a growing market for new and more complex tools and machinery.

The master-slave social relation of production systematically blocked the deepening of the social division of labour and the creation of a home-market for industry. The masters' ownership of the slave as 'means of production in human form' and the resulting inability to 'expel labour' from the production-process created a highly episodic process of labour-saving technical innovation and a fixed and inflexible ratio of labour to land and tools. The relatively unchanging tools and implements used on the slave-plantations of the US-South, along with the attempts of planters to produce hoes and ploughs on the plantation, severely limited market-demand for capital-goods. The masters' need to keep the slaves employed continuously through out the year impelled the planters to put the slaves to work growing corn and raising hogs, making the cotton-plantations generally 'self-sufficient' in food and other consumer goods. Plantation self-sufficiency severely limited the purchase of consumption-goods to simple clothing and shoes for the slaves. Put simply, the slave-plantation provided at best a shallow and unchanging market for industrial producers in the region.

Non-slaveholding Southern farmers did not provide an alternative market for industrial producers of capital and consumer-goods. While slaveless white farmers often cleared land and initiated agriculture on the southern frontier, planters were able to supplant the 'yeoman'-farmers and engross the best located and most fertile lands. The displaced farmers settled in the southern 'upcountry' – the hill-regions and pine-barrens. Inexpensive land, few debts and low property-taxes, which planter-dominated Southern legislatures guaranteed for most of the antebellum-period, allowed the bulk of these small farmers to maintain their possession of landed property without competing on the market. Facing no compulsion to 'sell to survive', these independent producers neither introduced new technology nor specialised output, growing small amounts of cotton along with various food-crops, raising animals and producing most of their own clothing and tools. These 'self-sufficient' communities provided little market-demand for either consumer- or capital-goods.[112] Cotton-farmers in the plantation-regions who owned less than 10 to 15 slaves, and were thus unable to organise gang-labour on their farms, might have become a potential market for consumer- and capital-goods. However, the planters' growing concentration of landholdings in these areas in the 1840s and 1850s, pushed many of these farmers into the 'upcountry' and effectively short-circuited such a development.[113]

Several 'planter-capitalist' historians have challenged the notion that plantation-slavery limited the growth of the social division of labour and the depth of the home-market for industry. Fogel and Engerman, utilising data that assigned market-prices to the food, clothing, shoes and other items consumed by slaves, argue that the plantation-South provided a substantial market for low-quality consumer-goods industries. The high rates of return in cotton-production, however, explained the relative absence of manufacturing in the South:

> ...it was natural resource endowments which gave the South a comparative advantage in agriculture....To the extent that slavery permitted economies of large scale and raised agricultural productivity, it might have created an economic incentive to shift resources away from industry and into agriculture.[114]

As Wright points out, the claim that the underdevelopment of Southern industry was the result of comparative advantages is a 'tautology: goods would not be produced unless it was profitable to do so, and if it was profitable to produce these goods, the region must have had a comparative advantage in those goods'.[115] In addition, there is clear data demonstrating

---

[112] Hahn 1983, Part I; Weiman 1987; Schlotterbeck 1982; Wright 1978, pp. 62–74; Wallenstein 1985.

[113] Barney 1982; Genovese 1967, pp. 249–71; Wright 1978, pp. 24–37.

[114] Fogel and Engerman 1974, pp. 255–6.

[115] Wright 1978, pp. 111–12.

that rates of return in Southern industry were no lower than in Southern agriculture, eliminating any 'comparative advantage'.[116] More importantly, the notion that the depth of the market can be derived from data that assigns prices to the slaves' consumption is highly questionable. The size of the market depends upon the degree to which direct producers *purchase* consumer-goods and non-producers *purchase* capital-goods. No matter how large the amount of goods the slaves *consumed*, the amount *purchased* was relatively small because the plantations directly produced most of the food consumed by the slaves.

Fred Bateman and Thomas Weiss argue that the market for industrial goods was not substantially different in the South and midwest before the Civil War.[117] Specifically, they claim that both Southern and midwestern agriculture provided relatively narrow and geographically fragmented markets for industry, limiting the scale and scope of industry in both regions. They attribute the absence of Southern industrialisation to a planter-class who 'were exceptionally averse to risk'.[118] This argument is open to a number of criticisms. Bateman and Weiss ignore the differing dynamics of midwestern family-farming (petty-commodity production) and plantation-slavery. At a given historical moment, the markets in the midwest and South may appear similar. However, the midwestern family-farmers, through their search for labour-saving technology and increased dependence on the market for consumer-goods, progressively deepened, expanded and unified the 'home-market' for industrially produced commodities in the 1840s and 1850s.[119] By contrast, plantation-slavery, by blocking technical innovation and promoting self-sufficiency, left the 'home-market' shallow, small and fragmented.

Nor is there clear evidence that planters were 'risk-averse' in relation to investing in manufacturing. Planters, often in partnership with merchants, invested in iron-foundries, textile-factories, coal-mines, lumbering, rope-making, cotton-ginning, sugar-refining and various other resource-extractive and plantation-auxiliary industries which used free white workers as well as owned and 'hired' slaves.[120] Southern industry, however, lagged far behind

---

[116] Bateman and Weiss 1981, Chapter 5.
[117] Bateman and Weiss 1981, Chapters 3, 7 and 8.
[118] Bateman and Weiss 1981, p. 161.
[119] See below, pp. 42–61, 90–7.
[120] Lewis 1979; Starobin 1970.

the in the medium and large-scale production of iron, cotton-textiles and farm-implements that would fuel the Northern industrial revolution of the 1840s and 1850s.[121] This qualitatively different pattern of industrial growth was the product of the fundamentally different effects of slavery and agrarian petty-commodity production on the social division of labour and the home-markets for industrial production.

While plantation-slavery placed severe limitations on industrialisation and economic development in the South, its impact on the northern US in the nineteenth century was more ambiguous. As Eric Williams and others have pointed out, plantation-slavery simultaneously retarded economic develop-ment in the Caribbean while promoting the expansion of global commod-ity-circulation that was one precondition for the British industrialisation in the late eighteenth century.[122] Douglas North[123] made a similar argument about US-industrialisation, placing the growth and expansion of Southern plantation-slavery at the centre of economic development in the nineteenth century. Following upon the work of Louis Schmidt,[124] North argued that the expanding Southern plantation-economy exporting cotton to industrial Brit-ain constituted a major market for both western family-farmers producing grain, meat and other foodstuffs and north-eastern manufacturers producing cloth, shoes and iron before 1840. After 1840, the completion of canals, rail-roads, and roads created 'a new market for western staples...in the rapidly industrialising East....The dependence of both the North-east and the West on the South waned'.[125] Put simply, plantation-slavery was the major motor of the expansion of commodity-production before 1840; and the mutual expan-sion of Northern family-farming and manufacture became the main engine of growth after 1840.

Albert Fishlow's research revealed important empirical flaws in North's thesis.[126] Fishlow demonstrated that the bulk of western foodstuffs shipped down the Mississippi river to New Orleans during the 1820s and 1830s was reshipped and sold in the north-eastern urban centres. Fishlow concluded

---

[121] Parker 1970, pp. 121–5.
[122] Williams 1944; Solow and Engerman 1987.
[123] North 1961.
[124] Schmidt 1939.
[125] North 1961, pp. 69–70.
[126] Fishlow 1965a, Chapters 3–4; and 1965b.

that the plantation-South consumed no more than 20–25 per cent of all foodstuffs shipped through New Orleans and was not an important market for western family-farmers. He concluded that Southern food producers, who he assumed were mostly slaveless white farmers, produced enough food to make the region self-sufficient. Later research by Diane Lindstrom confirmed that little midwestern grain and meat were consumed in the plantation-South.[127] Robert Gallman[128] and Sam Bowers Hilliard[129] demonstrated that slave-plantations, not the Southern family-farms, produced the vast majority of the corn and pork consumed in both the Southern countryside and cities.

Clearly, North's claim that the growth of slave-produced cotton-exports created a market for western agriculture before 1840 is not empirically tenable. However, North presented a subsidiary thesis that does shed light on the relationship of Southern plantation-slavery to the development of Northern manufacturing and family-farming.[130] The growing exports of slave-produced cotton to Britain stimulated the activities of Northern merchant-capitalists, which bound together the diverse, sectional based, forms of social labour (plantation-slavery, capitalist manufacturing and 'subsistence'- and 'commercial' family-farming) in the US before 1840. Specifically, the growing exports of cotton allowed Northern merchants to accumulate capital directly from the cotton-trade, and to import British capital. This accumulation of merchant-capital financed the westward expansion of agricultural production in both the South and North. Northern merchants, directly and indirectly through Southern merchants and bankers, provided the capital that Southern planters needed to purchase land and slaves for the expansion of cotton-production.[131] Northern merchants and British investors provided the capital that fuelled the speculative boom in land and transport-infrastructure in the North during the 1830s.

The speculative boom of the 1830s and the subsequent depression of 1837–42 marked the completion of the transformation of Northern family-farming that had begun in the 1780s.[132] After 1840, Northern family-farmers, burdened with growing debts and taxes, had to compete successfully in the market in

---

[127] Lindstrom 1970.
[128] Gallman 1970.
[129] Hilliard 1972.
[130] North 1956; 1960, Chapter 7.
[131] Woodman 1968, Part III.
[132] See pp. 73–91 below.

order to maintain possession of their land and tools. This shift from independent-household ('subsistence'-) to petty-commodity ('commercial') production unleashed a dynamic of productive specialisation, technical innovation and accumulation that made Northern agriculture the growing home-market for Northern industrial capitalists. Thus, after 1840, the expansion of Northern family-farming stimulated the activities of industrial capitalists, which increasingly bound together the different forms of production in the US.

The transformation of the US-economy after 1840 radically altered the position of plantation-slavery and its geographical expansion. The growth of slave-produced cotton did not simply cease to be the motor of economic growth in the US after 1840. In the two decades before the Civil War, the geographical expansion of plantation-slavery became the major obstacle to the further development of capitalism in the rest of the US. As we have seen, plantation-slavery and agrarian petty-commodity production had very different social conditions of existence. In the slave-plantation regions of the Lower South, the planters used their productive and financial advantages to appropriate the best located and most fertile lands. Southern family-farmers were concentrated in the hill-regions and pine-barrens and faced no compulsion to specialise output, technically innovate, or accumulate. In no part of the antebellum-South did a dynamic, 'commercial' family-farming develop. Put simply, the geographical expansion of plantation-slavery was incompatible with the development of agrarian petty-commodity production. As a result, plantation-slavery's further westward expansion during the 1840s and 1850s would have severely retarded the development of the rural 'home-market' for capitalist manufacture and industry.

At the very historical moment when the geographical expansion of slavery became a potent obstacle to the development of capitalism in the north and west, the planters faced new pressures to expand into new territories and branches of production. Profound changes in the place and structure of capitalist cotton-textile production in Britain and the US north-east in the 1840s and 1850s, the cotton-South's main market, produced the new urgency for expansion. First, the rate of growth of global cotton demand began to slow as the cotton-industry 'matured' and fewer and fewer new consumers in the industrialising countries were substituting cotton for other cloth.[133] Second,

---

[133] Wright 1978, pp. 94–7.

the introduction of specially produced metal cotton-textile machinery reduced the labour-component, while simultaneously increasing the raw-material component of the cost of cotton-textiles. To reduce their raw-material costs, British industrialists promoted cotton-production in Egypt and Turkey during the 1840s and 1850s. Cotton-exports to Britain from these areas increased over five-fold (10.3 million pounds to 54.8 million pounds) between 1848 and 1860.[134] Together, the 'maturation' and restructuring of cotton-textile production produced increased global competition among cotton-producers.

The US-planters had few options, operating within the logic of the master-slave social-property relation, in responding to this impending crisis of profitability in slave-produced cotton. Geographical expansion of cotton-production to new and more fertile lands was one possibility. Within the boundaries of the slave-South, the best located and most fertile cotton-lands were already under cultivation.[135] New regions suitable for cotton-cultivation were not easily available within the US. As a result, US-slaveholders looked to 'frontier'-regions where they could shift to new lines of production. Some planters saw the midwestern prairies as a possible location where slaves could grow corn and raise pork. Others viewed the territories conquered from Mexico in 1848 as a region where slaves could mine metals and graze cattle and sheep. Still others hoped that the US could annex Cuba and other Caribbean islands with large reserves of uncultivated land where slaves could grow sugar, cotton, and other tropical staples.[136]

The growing contradiction between the social conditions of the development of capitalism and of slavery set the stage for the sharp class-conflicts over the social character of the expansion of commodity-production that dominated political life in the 1840s and 1850s. Put another way, the political conflicts that culminated in the US Civil War were rooted in the contradictory social requirements of the development of industrial capitalism and

---

[134] Ellison 1968, Appendix II; Landes 1972, pp. 103–8.

[135] Wright 1978, p. 132 argues that 'there is no evidence to indicate that they [the planters – C.P.] were "feeling the pinch" of land-shortage in the 1850s. Supplies of untouched cotton land were vast within the 1860 boundaries of the slave states.' As evidence, he cites the massive expansion of cotton acreage in the southern, 'ex-slave' states after the Civil War (pp. 132–3). This argument ignores that fact that the bulk of the new acreage brought into cotton-cultivation after 1865 was the less fertile soils farmed by white 'yeoman'-farmers in the pine-barrens and hill-areas. See Hahn 1983, Part II.

[136] Genovese 1967, pp. 255–64; May 1973.

plantation-slavery. The contradictory requirements led to sharpening conflicts between manufacturers, merchants, farmers, planters, and slaves over a variety of political policies, but especially the future class-structure of westward expansion, in the two decades leading to the Civil War. These sharpening class-conflicts produced the political crisis – the collapse of the 'bi-section' Whig and Democratic parties, the increasing 'sectionalisation' of political life, and the 'secession-crisis' – that culminated in four bloody years of Civil War. The outcome of the war and the nearly dozen years of tumultuous struggles during 'Reconstruction' ultimately secured the social and political conditions for industrial capitalist development in the 'Gilded Age'.[137]

---

[137] Post 1983.

Chapter Four

Agrarian Class-Structure and Economic Development in Colonial-British North America: The Place of the American Revolution in the Origins of US-Capitalism

Social and economic historians have debated whether the rapid growth of agricultural and industrial commodity-production in the post-independent United States was a *continuation of* or a *radical break with* the economic and social patterns of British-colonial North America. At issue is whether the social and economic preconditions for capitalist industrialisation existed before or emerged only after the establishment of an independent US-state. Put another way, the debate grapples with the place of the American Revolution in US-economic development. Was the revolution merely a political upheaval that had little or no impact on the dynamics of production in the US; or was the revolution a crucial turning point, at least in some regions, in US-economic development? The thirteen British colonies on the eastern seaboard of North America were predominantly agrarian societies – urban centres were relatively small, and crafts and manufactures undeveloped. Thus, considerable scholarly disagreement centres on the structure and dynamics of agricultural production in the northern and southern colonies. This chapter builds upon the arguments I make in Chapters Two and Three to determine the impact of the American Revolution on the origins of capitalism in the US.

Those historians who argue for a continuity of pre- and post-independence economic and social development before and after the American Revolution have focused on the integration of the British mainland-colonies into the expanding Atlantic economy of the seventeenth and eighteenth centuries. Bushman,[1] Gray,[2] Grant,[3] Loehr,[4] Lemon[5] and Schumacher[6] have all claimed that both family-based agriculture in the northern colonies and plantation-slavery in the southern colonies were forms of capitalist production: both family-farmers and slave-owning planters responded to market-opportunities and specialised output, accumulated land and tools, and introduced new tools and methods. More recently, 'market-historians' such as Winifred Rothenberg have used new data-sources and more sophisticated econometric techniques to assert that Northern farmers – like their Southern counterparts – were profit-maximisers who enthusiastically engaged in market-production when opportunities were present.[7]

Those who argue for a sharp economic discontinuity before and after the Revolution and the establishment of the US-state have emphasised the independence of most rural producers from the market-place. While recognising that plantation-slavery was integrated into the world-market, historians beginning with Percy Bidwell claimed that Northern family-farmers and the majority of non-slave-owning Southern farmers were essentially subsistence-producers, who provided the overwhelming majority of their needs through their own labour rather than market-exchange.[8] At best, these farmers sold surpluses to buy the handful of goods they and their neighbours could not produce themselves. In the past two decades, 'social historians' such as Clark,[9] Kulikoff[10] and Merrill[11] have examined probate records and farmers' account-books to argue for the persistence of non-commercial production and exchange in much of the northern and southern countryside through the

---

[1] Bushman 1967.
[2] Gray 1933.
[3] Grant 1961.
[4] Loehr 1952.
[5] Lemon 1967.
[6] Schumacher 1948.
[7] Rothenberg 1992.
[8] Bidwell and Falconer 1925.
[9] Clark 1990.
[10] Kulikoff 1992 and 2000.
[11] Merrill 1986.

early nineteenth century. Other historians, following Eugene Genovese, have argued that plantation-slavery, while thoroughly integrated into the world-market, was a non-capitalist form of social labour.[12]

Out of this debate, two synthetic interpretive models have emerged among historians of the colonial British North-American economy. On the one hand, McCusker and Menard have applied the 'staples-commercialisation' model to argue for the continuity of economic and social development before and after independence.[13] On the other hand, Smith has elaborated a 'demographic-frontier' model to argue for a distinct pattern of social and economic development in colonial British North America.[14]

The 'staples'-model[15] is rooted in Adam Smith's[16] claim that the expansion of the market leads all producers to seize new opportunities to 'truck and barter' through the specialisation of output, accumulation of capital, and technical innovation. In the seventeenth and eighteenth centuries, the growth of colonial exports to Britain and other parts of the burgeoning Atlantic world-economy shaped agricultural production in the British mainland-colonies. Growing demand for colonial cash-crops – staples – in the British metropolis made colonial settlement and investment profitable, and provided the framework for market-oriented colonial rural producers to organise production.

Uneven regional development in the mainland-colonies, especially the dominance of family-farms in the northern colonies and slave-plantations in the southern colonies, was the result of the particular characteristics of different staple-crops. Farm-staples like grains and livestock tended to promote the development of small-scale, relatively capital-intensive family-farms with dense linkage-networks to manufacturing and commerce. Plantation-staples like tobacco, rice, indigo and sugar led to the development of large-scale, relatively labour-intensive plantations with few linkage-networks. While responding to the growth of the Atlantic world-market in different ways, dictated by different staples, both regions experienced *intensive* economic development, manifested in rising labour-productivity and per capita incomes, which laid

---

12 Genovese 1967.
13 McCusker and Menard 1985.
14 Smith 1980, 1982.
15 McCusker and Menard 1985, Chapter 1.
16 Smith 1937.

the basis for commercial and industrial development in the US during the nineteenth century.

The 'demographic-frontier' model is rooted in Malthusian population-theories. According to Smith, the British North-American colonies experienced little *intensive* economic development despite their integration into the Atlantic world-market.[17] Output of mostly agricultural products grew together with the expansion of population and rural settlement. Put simply, the mainland-British colonies experienced *extensive* growth through the seventeenth and eighteenth centuries – the multiplication of agricultural acreage and output with little or no changes in labour-productivity or output per capita.

An extremely low labour-to-land ratio, based on the continuous reproduction of the frontier through the expropriation of Native-American populations, made possible early household-formation and marriage, relatively high fertility-rates, and little change in per capita output through the colonial period. Migration to unoccupied lands on the frontier provided a homeostatic mechanism that allowed rapid population-growth without parcellisation of landholdings or growing social inequality in the seventeenth and eighteenth centuries. Most settlers, especially family-farmers, took advantage of relatively easy access to land to engage primarily in subsistence-production for their households and neighbours. To meet subsistence-needs, most farmers engaged in non-specialised general farming with relatively little or no change in agricultural tools or methods after initial settlement of a region. In sum, the rapid and intensive growth of agricultural and industrial production in the nineteenth century represented a sharp *discontinuity* with social and economic dynamics of the colonial period.

Both the commercialisation-staples and demographic-frontier models provide insights into the development of different forms of rural social labour in British North America in the seventeenth and eighteenth centuries. However, neither approach adequately accounts for the actual dynamics of the rural economy of the British mainland-colonies, nor explains the origins of capitalist industrialisation in the nineteenth-century United States. This stems, ultimately, from the failure to root their analysis is the specificities of *social-property relations* in British-colonial North America, and the impact of class-struggle during the American Revolution on agrarian class-structure.

---

[17] Smith 1980.

As Brenner[18] pointed out in his original critique of commercialisation- and demographic accounts of European economic development before the Industrial Revolution, both approaches *assume* 'a market/supply-demand mechanism ... the response of the agrarian economy to economic pressures, whatever their source, is more or less taken for granted'. However

> ...such attempts at economic model-building are necessarily doomed from the start precisely because, most crudely stated, it is the structure of class relations, of class power, which will determine the manner and degree to which particular demographic and commercial changes will affect long- term trends in the distribution of income and economic growth – and not vice versa.[19]

Agrarian class-structure – the specific relations between producers and tools and land (labour-process) and between producers and non-producers (class- relations) – creates the 'rules of reproduction' that shape how individual producers respond to market- and population-fluctuations.[20] Put simply, only by specifying social-property relations can we effectively grasp the impact of either the world-market or demographic trends on the dynamics of agri- cultural production in British North America.

To make our argument more concrete, we first examine both the commer- cialisation-staples and demographic-frontier models in light of the actual development of different forms of rural social labour on the North-American mainland in the seventeenth and eighteenth centuries. This historical inter- rogation of both models will, we hope, highlight their limited explanatory power. We then reprise our previous analysis of agrarian social-property rela- tions and economic development in British-colonial North America, exam- ining how the structures of plantation-slavery in the southern colonies and independent household-production in the northern colonies shaped the tra- jectory of these regional economies. Finally, we will examine the processes of class-struggle and 'state-building' during and after the American Revolution and their regionally uneven impact on agrarian class-relations. This specifica- tion will allow us to analyse how the outcome of rural class-conflict in the

---

[18] Brenner 1985a.
[19] Brenner 1985a, p. 11.
[20] Brenner 2007.

1780s and 1790s reshaped rural class-structure in the North, but preserved agrarian class-relations in the South.

I. The commercialisation-staples model

In their synthetic history, *The Economy of British America, 1607–1789*, McCusker and Menard employ the staples-model to argue that colonial North America experienced the *intensive* development of commodity-production and exchange.[21] Initially developed to explain Canadian economic development, McCusker and Menard 'locate the origins of the staples approach in the *Wealth of Nations*'.[22] Like all variants of what Brenner[23] and Wood[24] have called the 'Smithian-commercialisation' model of social and economic development, McCusker and Menard see producers – whether slave-owning planters or family-farmers – responding to market-opportunities by specialising output, introducing new techniques and accumulating land and other forms of capital based on their available land, labour and capital.

The growing demand for agricultural products in Britain spurred colonial settlement in the New World, creating the Atlantic world-market in the seventeenth and eighteenth centuries. British-colonial settlers responded to these market-opportunities in a context of abundant land and natural resources but scarce labour and capital. This context gave the colonists 'strong comparative advantage in the production of resource-intensive commodities, or staples, for export'.[25] Depending upon the particular characteristics of the dominant staple-crops, different types of agricultural production units developed with different effects on the domestic colonial economy:

> Some staples have powerful 'spread effects' and encourage development in the domestic economy. Others do not ... two interrelated aspects are critical in determining the extent of an export's effects: the production function, that is, the proportions of land, labor, capital, and entrepreneurial skill required to produce a staple; and the propensity of the product to create 'linkages' by inducing investment in other parts of the economy.[26]

---

[21] McCusker and Menard 1985.
[22] McCusker and Menard 1985, p. 19.
[23] Brenner 1977.
[24] Wood 1999.
[25] McCusker and Menard, 1985, p. 20.
[26] McCusker and Menard, 1985, pp. 23–4.

Crops such as sugar, indigo, rice, and tobacco were 'plantation-crops' that encouraged the development of large-scale, labour-intensive production-units. The plantation-crop regions – the Caribbean and the southern mainland-colonies – relied heavily on different forms of legally coerced labour, either indentured servants or slaves, depending upon their relative supply and price. Plantation-staples, as a rule, 'generated few forward linkages of the sort that promoted urban development':

> Tobacco did not require much processing or elaborate storage facilities, and its relatively low bulk did not encourage an extensive internal transport network. Mercantilist restrictions and a marketing system focused on Britain kept the supply of shipping and commercial services firmly in the hands of metropolitan merchants. At best, colonial merchants functioned as factors for British firms, collecting the staple and retailing imports. Slavery also inhibited growth: it limited consumer demand, encouraged plantation self-sufficiency, and channeled entrepreneurial energies into staple production.[27]

By contrast, 'farm-staples' such as wheat and other grains and livestock encouraged the development of small-scale, more capital-intensive agriculture. In the northern farm-staple colonies – in particular the Middle Colonies of New York, Pennsylvania and New Jersey – small farms relying primarily on family labour became the dominant agricultural unit of production. The processing and shipment of grains and other farm-staples to growing markets in the Caribbean, Britain, and Europe, along with the demand for labour-saving tools encouraged forward and backward linkages with urban manufacturers and merchants.[28]

While the specific characteristics of different staples induced patterns of regional unevenness between the less urbanised plantation-regions (Caribbean, southern mainland-colonies) and the more urbanised farm-regions (New England and middle-colonies), their common integration into the expanding Atlantic world-market fuelled intensive growth throughout British North America:

> Led by a growing demand for colonial exports, linked to an expanding commercial empire, protected and promoted by a strong imperial system, and endowed with an abundance of natural resources, the British colonies

---

[27] McCusker and Menard, 1985, pp. 132–3.
[28] McCusker and Menard, 1985, Chapters 5 and 9.

prospered.... The domestic sector of the colonial economy, led by the foreign sector, organised itself to distribute imports, to produce goods for the export sector, to supply the mercantile services necessary to the movement of both, and to provide through subsistence-production goods that could not be obtained on the market. These activities became more and more profitable for the colonists.[29]

McCusker and Menard claim that output grew more rapidly than population – that productivity of labour rose – in British North America through most of the seventeenth and eighteen century, producing rising per capita income.[30] In sum, the staples-commercialisation model sees a continuity of *intensive economic development* from North America's first English settlements in the seventeenth century through nineteenth-century industrialisation.

While correctly locating the origins of British-colonial settlement in North America in the expansion of the Atlantic world-economy, historical data do not support McCusker and Menard's analysis of economic development in colonial British America. McCusker and Menard are unable to make a compelling argument for *intensive economic development* in colonial North America before the American Revolution. McCusker and Menard's claim that the seventeenth and eighteenth centuries saw rising productivity and per-capita incomes rests on an extremely shaky empirical foundation. They and other 'commercialisation'-model historians of colonial British North America also present considerable evidence that contradicts their claim that family-farmers and slave-owning planters responded to growing market-opportunities as profit-maximisers who specialised output, accumulated land and capital, and introduced labour-saving tools and methods.

McCusker and Menard claim that per capita income grew consistently in the seventeenth and eighteenth centuries – the most important indicator of *intensive economic development* before the American Revolution.[31] Their discussion of per capita income-growth begins with an acknowledgement that reliable data on colonial output does not exist. However, they construct 'surrogate measures of the colonial economy' based on a number of question-

---

[29] McCusker and Menard 1985, pp. 51–2.
[30] McCusker and Menard 1985, Chapter 3.
[31] McCusker and Menard 1985, pp. 52–8.

able assumptions.[32] First, they assume that population and output grew at the same rate, giving the colonies a much higher rate of growth (2,400%) than Britain (50%) between 1650 and 1770. Recognising that this assumption cannot sustain a claim of rising per capita income and *intensive economic development*, McCusker and Menard engage in what they admit are 'little more than guesses...that the colonial economy must have expanded at a faster rate than the population'. Their reason is that 'productivity and the standard of living in the colonies got better during the colonial era, which argues quite forcefully for real per capita growth in the economy'. They then go on to produce data based on the assumption that per capita income in the colonies must have grown at a faster rate (0.6% per annum) than in Britain (0.3% per annum) between 1650 and 1770 'if only because the colonies started out so far behind'.[33]

With no data to support their claims that per capita income and labour-productivity actually grew, McCusker and Menard merely *assume* what needs to be *demonstrated* – a real growth in labour-productivity and per capita income through specialisation, accumulation, and innovation. The geographical expansion of technically unchanging agricultural production to new and more fertile soils – a key feature of the economy of British North America in the seventeenth and eighteenth centuries – explained the rising standards of living that the majority of white settlers (but probably not African slaves) experienced during the colonial period. McCusker and Menard are unable to provide empirical data to support their claim that the British-colonial economy experienced *intensive economic development* in the form of rising labour-productivity and per capita income. Instead, they rely on 'indirect indicators' of intensive economic development: the specialisation of output, the introduction of new tools and methods, and the accumulation of land and capital.

McCusker and Menard and other market-commercialisation historians recognise that few if any agricultural producers in colonial North America, including the Southern slave-owners whose plantations were established to produce a staple-crop for the world-market, actually specialised in market-production:

---

[32] McCusker and Menard 1985, p. 53.
[33] McCusker and Menard 1985, p. 55.

Outside of a few areas – the sugar islands, perhaps the rice district of the
Lower South, and the shadow of the major colonial cities – farm units in early
British America were not fully commercialized. They did not specialize in a
narrow range of crops nor did they purchase on the market most necessary
goods and services. Rather, marketed crops and purchased commodities
accounted for only a small part of total income and expenditure. The
majority of each farm's productive resources was devoted to self-sufficient
activities...[34]

James Lemon, a 'market'-historian of colonial south-east Pennsylvania agriculture, argues that despite their proximity to Philadelphia, the largest urban
market in colonial North America, most farmers in the region 'produced
a wide range of crops and livestock for home use and for sale'.[35] These
farmers grew wheat, rye, oats, barley, buckwheat, fruit, and potatoes for
household-consumption; flax and hemp for household-manufacture of clothing and rope; and turnips, grasses, legumes and corn to feed cows, oxen,
swine and other livestock which they and their neighbours consumed.[36] At
most, the better-off family-farmers in south-eastern Pennsylvania marketed
no more than 40–50% of their total output, well below the 60% that most
agrarian historians believe indicates a high degree of market-dependence.[37]
While Northern family-farmers, especially in the mid-Atlantic region, marketed large quantities of agricultural products, they *were not dependent upon
successful market-competition for their economic survival*.

Nor is there any evidence of agricultural specialisation in the region of
British North America most integrated into the Atlantic world-market – the
tobacco-plantations of the Chesapeake. While the majority of African slaves'
labour on the plantations was devoted to producing tobacco as market-staple,
slaves spent a considerable amount of their time engaged in the production
of animals and crops for consumption on the plantation. On most tobacco-
plantations, planters organised their slaves to grow corn and raise hogs,
providing most of the slaves' basic food-ration. Many masters also granted
garden-plots to their slaves, on which they grew a variety of vegetables and

---

[34] McCusker and Menard 1985, p. 297.
[35] Lemon 1976, p. 151.
[36] Lemon 1976, pp. 150–76.
[37] Danhof 1969.

root-crops and raised large numbers of chickens and ducks during their 'free' time.[38]

The empirical evidence on the size of landholdings also contradicts the claims of the 'commercialisation'-historians that North-American colonial farmers accumulated increasingly larger landholdings. Increased population and the division of landholdings among all male heirs led to *the parcellisation of landholdings*. The parcellisation of landholdings and social differentiation among northern-colonial rural households was most pronounced in New England, where initial plots distributed to proprietors (original settlers) tended to be smaller than in the mid-Atlantic colonies. Greven[39] and Lockridge[40] detail how partible inheritance in the context of growing populations led to a progressive subdivision of landholdings and rising land-prices in older areas of settlement in two Massachusetts towns over the course of the seventeenth and eighteenth centuries. Even the Middle Colonies, where original household-landholdings were considerably larger than in New England, experienced parcellisation of landholdings in the eighteenth century. In New England, landholdings were subdivided to the point where they could no longer support a rural household and land-prices began to rise by the third generation. Rural households in south-eastern Pennsylvania experienced the effects of land-parcellisation and rising land-prices after four generations.[41] While the availability of inexpensive land expropriated from the Native Americans short-circuited the process of parcellisation and prevented demographic collapse, there is little evidence of the accumulation of capital in the form of landed property before the American Revolution.

The commercialisation-staple historians also recognise that colonial North-American agriculture experienced little technical innovation before the nineteenth century, citing 'the stubborn refusal of American farmers to adopt the progressive techniques of European agriculture'.[42] Agriculture in one of the most commercialised regions of British North America remained technically stagnant during the colonial period. Farmers in the hinterlands of Philadelphia used hand-sickles rather than the labour-saving cradle to harvest wheat,

---

[38] McCusker and Menard 1985, pp. 127–8.
[39] Greven 1970, Parts II and III.
[40] Lockridge 1970, Chapters 4–5, 8.
[41] Lemon 1976, pp. 73–6, 87–92.
[42] McCusker and Menard 1985, p. 254.

and did not adopt the Dutch fan, which removed chaff, or other labour-saving devices. These farmers engaged in *extensive cultivation*. Inadequate and improper fertilisation, primitive crop-rotation schemes, and the use of light ploughs that made shallow furrows resulted in low yields per acre. The best-off farmers in south-eastern Pennsylvania only adopted 'up and down husbandry' (the rotation of clover and grass with grains) and the systematic use of fertilisers – methods common in English agriculture since the mid-sixteenth century – in the 1780s.[43]

Tobacco-cultivation on the slave-plantations of the Chesapeake also remained technologically stagnant through most of the seventeenth and eighteenth centuries. As on the sugar-plantations of the Caribbean, the slaves on the tobacco-plantations of the North-American mainland were organised in labour-processes that maximised the use of human labour. The natural characteristics of tobacco precluded the type of gang-labour based on a detailed division of labour that developed on sugar- and cotton-plantations. Instead, slaves on tobacco-plantations worked in groups of two or three and were assigned daily work-quotas. Overseers would supervise the slave work-groups to ensure they met their daily quotas of seasonally shifting tasks. The planting and harvesting of tobacco was done by hand, and cultivation and weeding involved the use of simple hand-hoes. The resulting technical stagnation of tobacco-cultivation resulted in an unchanging ratio of three acres of tobacco planted, cultivated, and harvested per slave through the end of the eighteenth century. Unchanging tools and soil-exhaustion, encouraged by the availability of inexpensive land expropriated from the Native Americans, made the geographical expansion of slavery – the addition of more slaves and more land in a fixed ratio – the most rational way to expand output in the slave-plantation colonies of British North America.[44]

The historical realities of colonial North-American agriculture directly contradict the expectations of McCusker and Menard's staples-model. Ultimately, the inability of this model – like all variants of the commercialisation-model – to make sense of actual historical development is rooted in its *assumption* of what has to be explained. Commercialisation-models of economic development

---

[43] Lemon 1976, pp. 30, 163–78.
[44] See pp. 136–8.

...have been fundamentally circular: they have assumed the prior existence of capitalism in order to explain capitalism's distinctive drive to maximize profit, they have presupposed the existence of a universal profit-maximizing rationality. In order to explain capitalism's drive to improve labor-productivity by technical means, they have presupposed a continuous, almost natural, progress of technological improvement in the productivity of labor.[45]

With little or no evidence to support them, McCusker and Menard assume that all producers will respond to the growth of the market in the same manner – as profit-maximisers specialising output, accumulating capital, and innovating technologically. Failing to distinguish market-*opportunity* from market-*coercion*, McCusker and Menard and other 'market'-historians cannot explain why family-farmers in the northern British colonies were under no *compulsion* – and slave-owning planters in the southern colonies *were unable* – to respond to the expansion of the market through specialisation, accumulation, and innovation. Only an analysis of the specificity of the *non-capitalist social-property relations* that shaped the colonial countryside will allow us to grasp how and why agricultural producers in different regions of British North America responded to the expansion of the Atlantic market.

II. The demographic-frontier model

Daniel Scott Smith[46] drew upon the research of Greven,[47] Lockridge[48] and other historians of colonial New-England and mid-Atlantic agriculture to produce the demographic-frontier model of colonial economic development. Working within a Malthusian framework, Smith argues that demographic factors – most importantly the ratio of labour to land – shaped economic and social development in British North America. Colonial America had a very low labour-to-land ratio. The decimation of Native-American populations through force and disease made large swathes of fertile land available for English settlement. Abundance of land in relationship to labour produced

---

[45] Wood 1999, p. 3.
[46] Smith 1980.
[47] Greven 1970.
[48] Lockridge 1968, 1970.

what Smith calls an 'economic steady-state...with essentially fixed techniques of production...and no...sustained increase in per capita output'.[49]

The easy availability of land for white settlers encouraged early formation of households and nearly universal marriage for women, producing relatively high fertility-rates in British North America through most of the seventeenth and eighteenth centuries. The result was an approximately 3% per annum population-growth through natural increase rather than trans-Atlantic migration. Abundant land allowed English settlers, in both the northern and southern colonies, to engage in a technically unchanging, diversified agriculture:

> There was little, or even no economic growth in per capita terms, at least after the colonies found their economic base in the early decades of settlement. The economy grew rapidly, of course, but so did population. The principal reason for a ceiling on per-capita output or income is ironic and directly related to the Malthusian frontier man-to-land ratio: the ceiling was also a very high floor. The resource richness of the economy explains the paradox that while US per-capita economic growth rates in the nineteenth and twentieth centuries were only average compared to European rates of economic growth, the incomes of Americans were higher than those of Europeans at every date until recently.[50]

Put another way, the low ratio of labour to land after Native Americans had been 'removed' made possible the creation of a non-capitalist economy marked by extensive growth in British North America. The growth of staple-production – agricultural surpluses of grains and meat in the Northern farm-colonies; tobacco, rice and indigo in the Southern plantation-colonies – 'were not an engine of economic transformation' in the colonial period.[51]

As in all precapitalist economies, British North America experienced *some* of the Malthusian limits that resulted from growing population pressure on the land. As population grew and landholdings were divided among all surviving male heirs ('partible inheritance'), the long-settled regions of rural British North America experienced the same tendency toward the fragmentation of landholdings that marked peasant agriculture in Britain before the sixteenth century and most of continental Europe in the seventeenth and eighteenth

---

[49] Smith 1980, p. 15.
[50] Smith 1980, p. 17.
[51] Smith 1980, p. 18.

centuries.[52] However, there was no Malthusian 'B-phase' – land-parcellisation reaching a point where declining yields per acre lead to demographic crises and sharp drops in population – in any region of colonial North America. The continuing expropriation of Native-American land short-circuited the parcellisation of landholdings, preventing declining yields and demographic collapse. Continuous migration to lands made available through 'Indian removal' acted 'as a homeostatic balancing mechanism retarding the expansion of wealth inequality':

> The most effective short-run equilibrating mechanism in the Malthusian system was out-migration from the full-settled area to the frontier. Sufficient out-migration would thus reduce inequality (in income if not wealth) by raising wages and lowering land-prices in the settled region. The population would also be redistributed toward the relatively more egalitarian frontier, an environment of lower land-prices and higher wages.[53]

The 'economic steady state' of extensive growth ended in the early nineteenth century. The end of intermittent warfare, which disrupted international trade between 1689 and 1815, and the development of industrial technology initiated the transition from extensive to *intensive* economic development in the US after 1800 as labour shifted 'from lower productivity agriculture to the more productive new industrial sector'.[54]

The major strength of the demographic-frontier model of economic development in British North America is that it accurately *describes* the dynamics of colonial agriculture – the absence of specialisation, accumulation and technical innovation. However, the demographic-frontier model fails to *analyse* the structural foundation of *extensive growth* in British North America. The physical abundance of land and other natural resources is the only causal explanation of why colonial agricultural producers were able to maintain their incomes without specialising, accumulating, and innovating. Extensive growth is *assumed*, not explained, in the Malthusian framework. As a result, the demographic-frontier model cannot explain why similar demographic conditions – the low labour-to-land ratio – resulted in radically different forms of agricultural production before and after the American Revolution.

---

[52] Greven 1970, Parts II and III; Lockridge 1968; Brenner 1985a, pp. 13–18.
[53] Smith 1980, p. 19.
[54] Smith 1980, p. 18.

As Brenner points out, one of the fatal flaws of demographic explanations of economic development in pre-industrial Europe is:

> That it simply breaks down in the face of comparative analysis. Different outcomes proceeded from similar demographic trends at different times and in different areas of Europe. Thus we may ask if demographic change can be legitimately treated as a cause, let alone the key variable.[55]

In North America, a low labour-to-land ratio gave rise to safety-first family-farming and world-market-oriented plantation-slavery before independence. The same demographic conditions gave rise to a very different form – commercial family-farming – in the north-east by the early nineteenth century. With such diverse outcomes, we must again question the explanatory power of demographic trends.

Nor does the demographic-frontier model provide an adequate explanation of the shift from extensive growth before 1800 to intensive development after. Smith's[56] account of the shift relies on the growth of market through the stabilisation and growth of the world-economy after the end of the Napoleonic Wars in 1815, and the shift of labour from agriculture to industry. Put simply, the demographic-frontier model explains the end of the 'Malthusian era' as the result of changing market-conditions. Smith's analysis of the transition from extensive growth ('traditional economy') to intensive development ('modern economy') is similar to the explanations of the origins of capitalism presented by Sweezy[57] and Wallerstein[58] for Europe, and Alan Kulikoff[59] for the post-independence US. For these historians, expanding market-opportunities lead agricultural producers to specialise output, and growing opportunities for employment in urban industry leads them to introduce new labour-saving technology.

The growth of markets and industry can only promote such a transformation of agriculture if two conditions exist. First, the producers must be dependent upon commodity-production for their economic survival. Specifically, the acquisition, maintenance, and expansion of landed property *relies on* suc-

---

[55] Brenner 1985a, p. 21.
[56] Smith 1980.
[57] Sweezy 1976a and 1976b.
[58] Wallerstein 1974.
[59] Kulikoff 1992 and 2000.

cessful market-competition. Put another way, the market must appear as a sphere of coercion – forcing owners to specialise, accumulation and innovate. Second, owners must be able to expel labour from production in order to introduce new and more complex tools and machinery. If labourers cannot be deprived of means of subsistence, the introduction of labour-saving technology will be difficult, if not impossible. The existence of these conditions depends not primarily on the expansion of market-production or changing demographic conditions, but on the existence of specific, *capitalist* social-property relations. As we will see, capitalist social-property relations did not shape agricultural production in either the northern or southern British colonies on mainland North America.

III. Agrarian social-property relations in colonial-British North America

The development of different forms of agrarian social labour in British North America is historically paradoxical. The British-colonial empire was unique among the European empires that developed in the Americas in the seventeenth and eighteenth centuries. As Ellen Wood argues, 'England…first saw the emergence of a capitalist system, and it was England that first created a form of imperialism driven by the logic of capitalism…it was English colonisation…that was responding to the imperatives of capitalism'.[60] Drawing upon Brenner's[61] analysis of the emergence of the 'new' English merchants in the seventeenth century and their role in organising British overseas-expansion, Wood argues that British colonialism sought to develop profitable forms of commodity-production in the colonies rather than plundering precious metals, trading with native populations, or profiting from state-sanctioned mercantile monopolies as did other contemporary European colonial powers.[62] The British pioneered 'white-settler colonialism' and its genocidal wars against the Native Americans in the New World in order to establish agricultural commodity-production and to provide alternative employment for the growing relative surplus-population of landless former

---

[60] Wood 2003, pp. 73–4.
[61] Brenner 1993, Part One.
[62] Wood 2003, Chapters 4–5.

peasants at home. Despite the specifically capitalist impulse behind British colonialism in North America, however, they *were unable to reproduce agrarian-capitalist social-property relations in their mainland-colonies that became the US.*

The key to this paradox was the inability of British merchants and landlords and their allies among local colonial élites to establish an *effective social monopoly of landed property.*[63] The British state granted legal title to large tracts of North America to settler-colonists. Once the Native Americans had been forced into the interior – through force, fraud or disease – enterprising merchants and planters were granted land in the southern colonies, religious minorities were given townships to distribute among themselves in New England, and 'proprietors' with links to British landlords and merchants were given land grants in the mid-Atlantic colonies. While land-titles were granted and then sold to aspiring colonial landlords and merchants, the Imperial government and their colonial allies were unable to enforce these claims outside of limited areas near the Atlantic coast.[64]

Vast geographical distances and the relatively small size of the British military precluded reproducing the pattern of seventeenth-century British colonisation of northern Ireland in North America – direct colonial rule and the establishment of capitalist agriculture. Regular British troops only arrived in North America in 1754 and were stationed along the frontier to fend off attacks from the French and Native Americans.[65] Britain ruled its North-American possessions indirectly, relying on the domestic merchants, landowners, and planters who dominated the elected colonial assemblies. While the planters, merchants, and landlords sought to enforce legal claims on land in the interior, they were forced to rely on colonial militias, composed primarily of independent farmers and artisans who resisted the commodification of landed property.

While most military historians argue that the militia was effective in policing Native-American populations near areas of colonial settlement, it was ineffective in either prolonged campaigns against Native Americans or other European powers, or in preventing European settler-populations from illegally occupying lands on the frontier. Colonial assemblies routinely organised

---

[63] Wood 2003, pp. 102–9 and below pp. 73–5.
[64] Bidwell and Falconer 1925, Chapter 5; Gray 1933 II, Chapter 17.
[65] Weigly 1984, Chapter 2.

expeditionary forces made up of landless men, under the command of professional officers, for extended military campaigns to remove Native-American populations from the frontier. However, the colonial ruling groups were ineffective in policing the free, white population. Although the militias were capable of suppressing slave-revolts and conspiracies, they were rarely deployed against legally free populations. Often under the command of elected officers and composed of small farmers and artisans, colonial militias were unwilling and unable to enforce legal claims to land against other small farmers and artisans.[66]

The existence of unoccupied land in the interior, available at little or no cost other than the labour required to clear the land and begin the production of agricultural use-values, made the establishment of capitalist social-property relations impossible. The existence of this frontier was the product not simply of a low labour-to-land ratio, but the inability of the imperial and colonial authorities to effectively exclude settlers from taking up unoccupied land without payment of market-determined prices or rents.

Plantation-slavery in the southern colonies

By the 1620s, English settlers in Virginia had found a profitable staple-crop in tobacco, a weed the Native Americans had used for religious rituals.[67] Native Americans were quickly pushed back into the interior and the initial English settlers, often friends and relatives of London's 'new merchants', began a mad scramble to stake their claims in the midst of rising demand for tobacco in England and continental Europe:

> Land that would grow tobacco was everywhere, so abundant that people frequently did not bother at first to secure patents for the amounts they were entitled to. Instead, men rushed to stake out claims to men, stole them, lured them, fought over them – and bought and sold them, bidding up the prices to four, five, and six times the initial cost.[68]

While tobacco would continue to be cultivated on small farms with household-labour, large plantations quickly displaced smaller production-units in

---

[66] Cress 1982, pp. 4–11; Weigly 1984, Chapter 1.
[67] Gray 1933, I, pp. 21–2; Morgan 1975, pp. 110–15.
[68] Morgan 1975, p. 114.

the coastal tidewater-regions where the planters were able to establish a social monopoly on land. Tobacco-exports grew over eighteen fold between 1628 and 1669, from approximately 500,000 pounds to 9,026,000 pounds.[69] The only limit on tobacco-cultivation appeared to be the availability of labour for the new plantations.

With plentiful land beyond the emerging tidewater plantation-districts available for occupation at little or no cost, legally free wage-labour was effectively precluded in the tobacco-plantations.[70] Unable to enslave the Native Americans, English tobacco-planters initially brought indentured servants from England and other parts of Europe to labour on their plantations in the Chesapeake and Barbados, the first sugar-colony in the Caribbean.[71] Drawn primarily from the growing relative surplus-population of displaced peasants in England and Ireland, indentured servants, for the most part, agreed to sell their capacity to work for a period of five to seven years in return for passage to the Americas. Upon arrival in Barbados or Maryland and Virginia, the planters would purchase the servants' contracts (terms of indenture).[72] The servants' person and capacity to labour became the property of their masters for the duration of their terms of indenture. At the end of their terms, if they survived five to seven years of strenuous labour and an inhospitable disease-environment, the servants became 'freemen', collected their 'freedom-dues' (small amounts of cash, work-animals, tools, weapons), and moved to unsettled lands to become self-sufficient farmers in the Maryland and Virginia interior.[73]

The rapid shift from European servitude to African slavery in Barbados and the Chesapeake in the late seventeenth century is a subject of considerable historical controversy. Menard,[74] Galenson[75] and Beckles[76] have developed a 'commercialisation'-model of the transition from servitude to slavery in British America. The growth of production of plantation-staples like sugar and tobacco led to a proportional growth in demand for labour. Slowing population-growth and rising wages in Great Britain, combined with grow-

[69] Gray 1933, Ashworth 1995, p. 213.
[70] Domar 1970; Menard 1977; Morgan 1975, Chapter 5.
[71] Beckles 1989, Chapters 1–3.
[72] Smith 1947, Chapters 1–10.
[73] Morgan 1975, Chapters 6–8.
[74] Menard 1977 and 2006.
[75] Galenson 1981 and 1984.
[76] Beckles 1989: Chapter 5.

ing opportunities for landownership among former servants in Virginia and Maryland, reduced the supply of labour, and drove up the price of servants after 1650. The abolition of the Royal African Company's monopoly on the African slave-trade in 1698 and the growth of private slave-trading by English merchants radically increased the supply of slaves. Faced with the rising price of indentured servants and the falling price of slaves, the planters in Barbados and the Chesapeake made the rational, market-based choice to substitute the less expensive slaves for the more expensive indentured servants.

Clearly, the shifting relative prices of servants and slaves that Menard, Galenson, and Beckles document in Barbados and the Chesapeake in the late seventeenth century are undeniable. However, as in most variants of the com-mercialisation-model, they tend to explain the shifts in the relative supplies and prices of servants and slaves in terms of the *structurally unconstrained personal choices* and *opportunities* of the servants. Increased opportunities to work as wage-labourers in Britain, and for Barbadian ex-servants to opt for transportation to the mainland-colonies to become independent landowners explain the changing supply and price of servants.

A more fruitful approach would identify the class-conflict in Barbados, Virginia and Maryland as the cause of the changing options and opportunities for servants and planters.[77] Bacon's Rebellion of 1676, the multi-racial revolt of servants and ex-servants against the planters' attempts to increase the number of servants and their terms of service, made reliance on indentured servitude untenable in Virginia.[78] Faced with falling tobacco-prices and growing costs of transporting tobacco to Britain as the result of the Navigation Acts which gave British merchants a monopoly on colonial trade, planters in the 1660s and 1670s sought to reduce the cost of labour in a variety of ways. Individual planters reduced food-rations, heightened punishments for insubordination and extended servants' terms of indenture. Collectively the tobacco-planters

---

[77] Beckles 1989, pp. 98–114 discusses servant-resistance in Barbados in the seventeenth century. There was no equivalent of Bacon's Rebellion – a full-scale rebellion that radically undermined the foundations of indentured servitude – in Barbados. However, there were numerous examples of unsuccessful conspiracies and extensive day-to-day resistance (flight from the plantations, slowing down the pace of work, stealing, arson, etc.) among the Barbadian servants. Future research is needed to determine how this resistance, over time, made indentured servitude unviable, and led the planters to opt for African slaves.

[78] Morgan 1975, Book III.

dominated the Virginia assembly, which imposed poll-taxes on newly freed servants and granted legal title to large swathes of land on the frontier – often already occupied by former servants – to large landowners. According to Morgan:

> ...the servants who became free after 1660 found it increasingly difficult to locate workable land that was not already claimed. In order to set up their own households in this vast and unpeopled country, they frequently had to rent or else move to the frontiers, where they came into conflict with the Indians. Many preferred safety in the settled area even through it meant renting land from the big men who owned it.... Perhaps more important than the actual rent obtained by Virginia's landlords was the effect of the artificial scarcity of land in keeping freedmen available for hire. If a man could not get land without paying rent for it, he might be obligated to go back to work for another man simply to stay alive.[79]

Growing tensions between the planters and their servants and the armed ex-servants grew through the 1660s and 1670s. Revolts among servants broke out in 1661, 1663 and 1665, and two conspiracies involving both servants and freedmen were uncovered in 1674.[80] The spark that ignited full-scale rebellion was Governor Berkeley and the colonial assembly's concluding a peace-treaty with the Native Americans in 1676, effectively closing off much of the frontier to the former servants. Under the leadership of Bacon, a frustrated planter and land-speculator, the armed servants and ex-servants quickly overthrew the colonial authorities. The Virginia colonial militia was composed of former servants 'who would be...unlikely...to make effective instruments for suppressing the insubordination of their own kind'.[81]

In the wake of Bacon's Rebellion, indentured servitude ceased to be an effective method of supplying labour for the tobacco-plantations of the Chesapeake. African slaves became the alternative for the planters, not simply because of their relatively lower costs but because they entered Virginia and Maryland without social allies in either Britain or the colonies.[82] Whether or not slavery was a form of exploitation inherently superior to servitude

---

[79] Morgan 1975, pp. 220, 223.
[80] Morgan 1975, pp. 246–7.
[81] Morgan 1975, pp. 247–8.
[82] Fields 1990.

because it gave the planters lifetime command of the labour (and progeny), as Morgan[83] claims and Menard[84] disputes, African slavery allowed planters to cement their class-power through an alliance with former servants. By the late seventeenth century, the vast majority of non-slave-owning whites in the southern mainland-colonies were independent farmers. Most settlers of European origin were legally free property-owners and voters. Only African slaves remained unfree. For the first time in history, freedom and un-freedom corresponded to differences in physical appearance, allowing the invention of *race* as a means of justifying and explaining the unique class-position of African slaves. 'Whiteness' provided the ideological cement of this alliance of slaveholders and independent farmers through the 1850s, making non-slaveholding farmers willing to defend slavery through militia-service and participation in slave-patrols.[85]

Once slavery was established as the dominant form of social labour on the tobacco-plantations of the Chesapeake, tobacco-production expanded rapidly – growing more than tenfold from 9,026,000 pounds in 1669 to over 100,000,000 pounds each year in the 1770s.[86] This rapid expansion, fuelled by continued demand in the Atlantic world-market, proceeded on the basis of the *non-capitalist social-property relations of plantation-slavery.*[87] While capitalists purchase the *labour-power*, the capacity to work, of workers for a specified period of time; masters purchase *the labourer*, the person of the worker. The purchase of labour-power allows the worker to enter the capitalist production-process as a *variable* element of production. The masters' purchase of the labourer converts the direct producer into 'means of production in human form'. The 'capitalisation of labour' requires the slave to enter the production-process as

---

[83] Morgan 1975, pp. 297–300.

[84] Menard 1977, pp. 359–60.

[85] Morgan 1975, pp. 15–18. Menard (2006: Chapter 6) analyses how an alliance between planters and non-slaveholding former servants was cemented on the basis of 'whiteness' in Barbados. While the absence of unoccupied lands on the frontiers of the plantation-districts precluded the emergence of a class of independent farmers in the Caribbean, non-slaveholding whites were legally free, enfranchised and became overseers and supervisors on the plantations.

[86] Gray 1933, I, pp. 213–14.

[87] The following paragraphs draw upon Marx's 1976 discussion of capitalist social-property relations and discussions of slave social-property relations in Hindess and Hirst 1975, pp. 125–48 and, in particular, Tomich 1990, Chapter 4 as summarised below, pp. 131–6.

a *constant* element of production. Labourers, land, and tools all appear to the planter as fixed and inflexible costs.

The slaves' position as a constant element of the production-process, who must be maintained whether or not they laboured, severely restricted the masters' ability to adjust the size of their labour-force through technical innovation. Having invested in means of production in human form, the masters were burdened with a relatively inflexible ratio of labour-to-land and tools. Put simply, the masters could not readily reduce the size of their slave labour-force to adopt labour-saving technologies in the face of changing market-imperatives.

The status of slaves as a form of fixed-capital provided few opportunities for slave-owning planters to introduce new labour-saving technology even when such innovation would allow planters to cut costs in response to market-imperatives. The introduction of new crops or expansion to new regions provided the main opportunity for planters to break the fixed relationship between labour, land, and tools through the introduction of new tools and implements. Once the new ratio of labour, land, and tools had been established with a new crop or in a new region, it remained relatively unchanged. Unable to reduce the size of their slave labour-force through mechanisation, the planters were *compelled* to organise the plantation production-process through closely supervised and coordinated co-operative work that maximised the use of human labour.

The effects of master-slave social-property relations were clearly evident in the organisation of the labour-process in tobacco-production. Tobacco-planters in seventeenth- and eighteenth-century Virginia and Maryland strove to create a co-ordinated labour-process that maximised the use of human labour.[88] Tobacco-plantations were organised around the task-system, where the ten or more slaves on the plantation were broken into groups of two to three and assigned daily work-quotas. White overseers would supervise the slave work-groups in seasonal tasks.

Planters increased the volume of production and cut costs to compete successfully on the Atlantic world-market by increasing the intensity and pace of work and moving production to more fertile land. The nearly universal

---

[88] Berlin 1990, pp. 118–19; Gray 1933, II, pp. 215–17, 545–6; Kulikoff 1986, pp. 324–5, 384–6, 408–12.

tendency toward soil-exhaustion in the plantation-regions of the Americas, resulting from the availability of inexpensive land appropriated from the Native Americans, heightened the necessity of geographical expansion.[89]

The master-slave social-property relation also produced the near universal tendency of New-World slave-owners to make their plantations self-sufficient in food and other productive inputs. In order for masters to realise their investments in slaves, the slaves must be compelled to work all year round. Agriculture is not well suited to providing year-round, continuous work. There are sharp discontinuities between the time human labour is required to plant, harvest and cultivate crops (labour-time) and the time required for natural-biological processes to bring crops to maturity (production-time).[90] The gap between production- and labour-time in tobacco created the need for planters to find other employment for their slaves during the staple-crop's slack-season. Especially 'after the crop was hung in the tobacco house', in the late fall, 'masters had to manufacture new work for their slaves if they expected them to continue to labour'.[91] The slaveholders were able to organise the growing of corn and the raising of hogs, allowing most of the slaves' basic food-ration (ground corn and pork) to be produced directly on the plantation rather than purchased. The slaves were also granted garden-plots which they tilled during their 'free' time, growing vegetables and root-crops, and keeping chickens and ducks.[92]

While the expanding Atlantic world-market powered the expansion of commodity-production in southern British colonies, the *non-capitalist* structure of plantation-slavery's social-property relations accounts for the pattern of *extensive development* that characterised southern economic growth in the seventeenth and eighteenth century. The specific master-slave relation precluded the introduction of labour-saving tools and methods in tobacco-cultivation. Unable to develop the productivity of labour through the capitalisation of production, slave-owning planters increased output through geographical expansion. The multiplication of slaves and land, without any substantial change in the ratio of land and labour, resulted in extensive growth in the

---

[89] Berlin 1990, pp.121–3; Gray 1933, I, pp. 217–18, 233–4; Kulikoff 1986, pp. 47–9, 63–4, 92–9, 142–61.
[90] Mann 1990, Chapter 2.
[91] Kulikoff 1986, p. 412.
[92] Kulikoff 1986, pp. 337–40, 392–3, 411–13.

South before independence – growing output without any change in per capita income or output.

Independent household-production in the northern colonies

British settlement of the North-American northern mainland began in the sixteenth century, after Native Americans were forcibly removed from the eastern seaboard.[93] To facilitate colonial settlement and commodity-production, imperial authorities made land grants either to settlers creating townships (New England) or to large mercantile companies that sold land to large landowners (mid-Atlantic). Despite growing social inequality among rural households and the steady increase in the sales of grain, timber and meat to Northern cities and towns and in the plantations of the Caribbean, Northern farmers were *non-capitalist* independent household-producers whose possession of landed property did not depend upon successful commodity-production.[94]

Northern-colonial rural households' capacity to engage in independent household-production (and that of most Southern non-slaveholding rural households) was rooted in the inability of colonial landowners to enforce their legal claims to landed property much beyond the densely settled coastal areas. The existence of unoccupied land within easy reach of most settlers, combined with the inability of landowners to craft state-institutions that could impose legal titles, made the creation of a social monopoly of land impossible in the seventeenth and eighteenth centuries. Most settlers, often migrating with groups of co-religionists, kin, or former neighbours, could not obtain legal title to the land, and illegally occupied ('squatted') on lands owned by private owners. As long as the colonial militias – which were small and composed mostly of small farmers and artisans – could not or would not enforce the legal claims of private owners, rural households were able to establish, maintain, and expand their landholdings without extensive commodity-production.[95]

---

[93] The following paragraphs are based on pp. 57–9 and 73–5 below.
[94] Bidwell and Falconer 1925, pp. 49–62, 115–17, 126–33; Greven 1970; Lockeridge 1970.
[95] Henretta 1991a and 1991d; Nobles 1989, pp. 647–50, 654–61.

The landowners' inability to enforce legal title to land was evident in the countryside surrounding Philadelphia. From the 1690s, the Pennsylvania Assembly attempted to promote an 'orderly settlement' of south-eastern Pennsylvania through the sale of large tracts of land to private landholders, who were expected to resell or lease land to actual settlers. However, none of these attempts succeeded:

> After the turn of the eighteenth century the practices of 'indiscriminate location' and squatting were widespread, and the warrant and survey system came into use. In the back country especially, settlement now preceded survey, and settlers marked out their own land before applying for survey warrants…settlers usually sought survey warrants for their own security. …Acquiring a deed took much longer, however, usually between five and twenty years and sometimes as long as seventy-five years. Although this delay limited the Penns' [the proprietors of the Pennsylvania colony – C.P.] incomes, warrants provided certainty of tenure for settlers.[96]

Squatters' 'claims-clubs' organised land-occupations to resist attempts to force settlers to either purchase land or pay rents in the 1730s, 1740s and 1750s. Colonial and private authorities – land-surveyors, sheriffs, 'rangers', and 'overseers' – were unable to remove the claims-clubs. In 1765, the Penn family and their allies ceased all attempts to enforce their legal title to lands in the hinterland of Philadelphia, and adopted the 'application-system', which gave those occupying land legal title ('warrants') and significantly lowered the price of land.[97]

Brenner[98] and Harriet Friedmann[99] argue that rural household-producers are only compelled to specialise output, accumulate land and capital, and innovate technically when they are compelled to 'sell to survive'. The economic survival of Northern rural households – their ability to obtain, maintain, and expand their possession of landed property – *was not conditioned upon the profitable sale of agricultural goods*. As we have seen in our discussion of the absence of productive specialisation and technical innovation above, the absence of market-based prices or rents for land, high taxes, or debts that

---

96 Lemon 1976, p. 55.
97 Lemon 1976, pp. 49–61.
98 Brenner 1977, pp. 73–5; Brenner 1985a, pp. 46–63.
99 Friedmann 1980, pp. 162–4, 167–8, 170–84.

must be paid in cash with interest allowed Northern independent landowning farmers to engage in 'safety-first' agriculture where they marketed only
physical surpluses.

The social-property relations of independent household-production
provided the material basis for the rural social forms the social historians
described.[100] The ability of rural households to reproduce their possession
of landed property without recourse to commodity-production shaped
exchange-relations with other farmers, artisans and merchants, and the
importance of kinship and community to the social structure of the colonial-
northern countryside. Free from the compulsion to produce for the market
to maintain their land-ownership, northern-colonial farm-households were
able to devote the bulk of their land and labour to production for their own
consumption, providing the basis for the dense web of kinship and communal relations that structured neighbourly exchange of goods and labour
among households. Households and communities, secure in their possession
of landed property, could pursue safety-first agriculture – producing food,
livestock and crafts for their own and their neighbours' consumptions and
marketing only surpluses. Put another way, non-market access to land made
possible both general farming and household-manufacturing.

In the northern-British colonies, independent householders' capacity to
reproduce their landed property independent of commodity-production
exempted them from any compulsion to specialise, innovate, and accumulate.
However, independent household-production was a form of social labour
that that was neither stagnant nor without distinctive social dynamics. The
long-settled regions in the North like most of early-modern Western Europe
outside of England, displayed tendencies toward the parcellisation of land
and social differentiation of rural households.[101] Growing population, partible
inheritance (the division of the family-landholdings among all male heirs),
and the technical stagnation inherent in independent household-production
led to a division and sub-division of landholdings from one generation to
another. This parcellisation of landholding created some plots too small to
support a rural household.[102]

---

[100] Henretta 1991a; Kulikoff 2000; Merrill 1986; Clark 1990.
[101] Brenner 1985a, pp. 54–63; 1985b, pp. 284–319.
[102] Greven 1970; Lockridge 1970; Lemon 1976, pp. 74–92.

As in pre-industrial Western Europe, land-parcellisation and rising land-prices produced inequalities in landholdings among rural households in the long-settled northern British colonies. In many parts of New England and the middle-colonies, landless populations appeared by the early to mid-eighteenth century as the worst-off rural households sold their meagre landholdings to their better-off neighbours.[103] However, social differentiation experienced by rural producers under independent household-production was quite different from that experienced under capitalist production. First, there were clear limits on social differentiation. In the 1740s, after nearly a century of continuous occupation, social inequality in one Massachusetts town was quite limited:

> The richest five percent of the townsmen were still no more than well-off farmers with a few attendant millers or innkeepers, and they owned only about fifteen percent of the property; the richest ten percent of the townsmen owned twenty-five percent [of property].... Born into a family with four or five children, the mythical 'average' man would marry in his middle twenties and die in his fifties. He would know little of plague and less of famine.[104]

Nor did growing social differentiation of rural households lead to consolidation of landholdings, a prerequisite for the introduction of new labour-saving tools and methods. As in pre-industrial Western Europe, large landowners' 'units of property were themselves broken into many, many parcels of cultivation, scattered through the fields, miniscule in size'.[105]

In pre-industrial Western Europe – outside of England, which experienced the breakthrough to capitalist agriculture in the mid-sixteenth century – the parcellisation of landholdings led to declining yields and periodic demographic crises.[106] Independent household-producers in the northern colonies avoided the Malthusian cycle of population-growth/parcellisation of land/demographic collapse through the eighteenth century. However, it was not simply the existence of a low land-to-labour ratio resulting from unoccupied land that allowed Northern farmers to avoid the Malthusian 'B-phase', as the

---

[103] Bidwell and Falconer 1925, pp. 54–9; Greven 1970, Part III; Lockeridge 1970, Chapters 7–8; Henretta 1991e, pp. 176–9.
[104] Lockridge 1970, pp. 141–2.
[105] Brenner 1985b, p. 305.
[106] Hobsbawm 1967; Brenner 1985a and 1985b.

demographic-frontier historians claimed. Rather, it was the ability of rural householders to appropriate this land outside of commodity-production – through squatting and/or at non-market-determined low prices – that allowed migration to the frontier to short-circuit demographic collapse among independent producers in British North America.[107]

In sum, the inability of imperial and colonial landowners and merchants to forge state-institutions that could enforce their legal title to landholdings any distance from the Atlantic seaboard – their inability to establish a social monopoly of landed property – allowed the development of independent household-production in the northern-colonial countryside. With their landholdings unaffected by the travails of market-competition, Northern rural households marketed physical surpluses. Under no compulsion to specialise, innovate, or accumulate, independent household-production in the northern colonies gave rise to *extensive economic growth* – the multiplication of technically unchanging family-farms into the frontier:

> The absence of intensive development did not imply agricultural decline, a subsistence crisis, or an increase in wealth inequality. Rather the Malthusian rates of population increase and the availability of an agricultural frontier resulted in an *extensive* pattern of growth. Farms were hacked continually out of the wilderness for an ever-growing population; the result was a static multiplication of productive units rather than a process of economic development and transformation.[108]

Put simply, the growth of output without increases in per capita income that characterised the northern-colonial countryside flowed from the logic of the *non-capitalist social-property relations* of independent household-production.

IV. Colonial economic development, the American Revolution, and the development of capitalism in the US, 1776–1861

The limits of imperial British power allowed the autonomous development of an independent economy dominated by colonial merchants and planters and short-circuited the development of specifically capitalist forms of

---

[107] Greven 1970, Part III; Lockridge 1968; Lemon 1976, pp. 85–94.
[108] Henretta 1991e, p. 170.

agriculture in British North America. The American Revolution, the product of sharpening tensions between imperial and colonial ruling classes flowing from the colonies' independent economic development, established new state-institutions that could effectively enforce the landowners' legal claims on lands in the interior. The result was sharpening, uneven regional development. In the North, the progressive subordination of rural household-producers to market-compulsion unleashed capitalist industrialisation; in the South, plantation-slavery remained in place, precluding capitalist development in the region.

Over the course of the seventeenth and eighteenth centuries, the British colonies on the North-American mainland developed a distinctive, non-capitalist, and relatively independent economy. The close political and economic ties between the original colonial merchants and landowners and the British state and ruling class of merchants and capitalist landlords 'did not prevent the colonial economy from developing less on the strength of the British domestic market than on the growing interdependence of colonial settlements'.[109] Northern farmers, while maintaining their independence from market-compulsion, produced and sold large surpluses of grains and meat to the northern ports of Boston, New York and Philadelphia and to the growing sugar-plantations of the Caribbean. Southern plantations, while generally self-sufficient in food, sold tobacco in the Caribbean, the northern colonies and Britain.[110]

At the centre of the independent-colonial North-American economy, binding together rural independent household-production and plantation-slavery, was a class of colonial merchants. These merchants first emerged as junior partners of British merchants, who held a monopoly on trade and credit with Britain's colonial empire under the Navigation Acts. Colonial American

---

[109] Wood 2003, p. 107.
[110] Mayer and Fay 1977, pp. 41–84. Mayer and Fay's path-breaking essay was based on a partial translation of Mayer's 1976 dissertation, *Zu Genese des Nationalstaats in America* [The Genesis of the Nation-State in America] (Johann Wolfgang Goethe-Universität, Frankfurt am Main, 1976); later published in 1979 as *Die Entstehung des Nationalstaats in Nordamerika* [The Emergence of the Nation State in North America] (Frankfurt: Campus). Unfortunately, neither the complete dissertation nor book has been translated into English. While Mayer's analysis shapes much of what I argue about the American Revolution and Constitutional Settlement, we differ in our characterisation of northern family-farming. Mayer, incorrectly in our opinion, characterises northern-colonial agriculture as capitalist.

merchants acted as agents of British merchants in the 'triangular trade', organising the import of British manufactures to North America and the Caribbean, and the export of tobacco to Britain.[111] As Northern independent household-producers began to produce surpluses of food for sale to the growing port-cities of North America and the expanding plantation-economies of the Caribbean, colonial merchants organised this inter-colonial, coastal trade. Urban merchants in New York, Philadelphia, and Boston gathered rural surpluses from hundreds of small traders and shopkeepers scattered across the Northern countryside, consolidated them, and shipped them to other parts of colonial North America and the Caribbean.[112]

The development of an independent, non-capitalist colonial economy laid the foundation for the settler-colonists' bid for independence, under the leadership of the merchants:

> ...inevitably, the economic and political connections between colonial America and the imperial power would eventually grow weaker.... At such a great distance, with more or less self-sufficient agriculture and with colonial markets nearer to hand, the colonies were not so easily kept within the economic orbit of the imperial power, and direct political control by the state was even harder to maintain..... A colonial economy with a strong foundation of its own, dominated by local elites with their own distinct interests and enjoying substantial degrees of self-government, was bound sooner or later to break the imperial connection.[113]

Even before independence, colonial merchants in the North and planters in the South were able to exercise political power through elected assemblies in all of the colonies.[114] British imperial attempts to impose new taxes, restrict trade and the geographical expansion of agricultural commodity-production allowed the merchants to forge an alliance of all free people. Under the leadership of the merchant-class, a coalition of slaveholding planters, independent farmers, urban artisans and wage-workers, land-speculators and

---

[111] Brenner 1993, Chapter 12; Kulikoff 1986, pp. 122–31; Gray 1933, I, Chapter 17; Williams 1944.

[112] Matson 1998; Nobles 1989, pp. 655–6; Szatmary 1980, pp. 12–18.

[113] Wood 2003, p. 108.

[114] Mayer and Fay 1977, pp. 53–5.

back-country traders successfully ended British-colonial rule in the American Revolution.

The seven years of revolutionary war profoundly disrupted agricultural production in what became the United States in 1776. In particular, the war disrupted the relationships between Northern-independent farmers and merchants and speculators. State-governments began to purchase food, cloth and other supplies from Northern farm-households at inflated prices to support the war-effort. As a result, farmers began to devote more and more family-labour to the production of commodities. Unable to produce the variety of goods previously manufactured in their self-sufficient communities, rural households borrowed from local storekeepers to purchase US-manufactures during the War, and British manufactures after the War. These debts became particularly burdensome after the War, as newly independent Northern state-governments raised taxes – mostly land-taxes – to fund the enormous public debt accrued to finance the Revolutionary War. The combined growth of debts and taxes forced Northern households to market larger and larger portions of both their subsistence- and surplus-output in order to maintain their landed property in the 1780s.[115]

The wartime-disruption of the balance between production for use and exchange, and the growing burden of debts and taxes were not sufficient to undermine independent household-production. Brenner points out that similar developments during wars in France in the seventeenth century were insufficient to end peasant-proprietorship:

> ...the growth of taxation, especially consequent upon war, meant that greater production was necessary merely to survive (thus, ironically the state which in the first instance provided the primary support for peasant proprietorship was indirectly perhaps also the major source of its disintegration).... It was no accident, moreover, that the greatest number of casualties [loss of land] appears to have occurred in times of war (especially the wars of religions and the Fronde) and of dearth (particularly the subsistence crises of the later seventeenth century) and to have been concentrated in the zones immediately affected by military action (for example, the Paris region and Burgundy). Yet even such long-term pressures and short-term catastrophes

[115] Henretta 1991b, pp. 231–41; Kulikoff 1992, pp. 100–51; Nobles 1990, pp. 12–13; Szatmary 1980, pp. 19–23.

seem to have worked their undermining effects on peasant proprietorship relatively sporadically and slowly over the whole of France.[116]

The French absolutist state's commitment to maintaining the peasantry on the land – in order to protect its independent tax-base – short-circuited the impact of wartime-disruption, taxation, and debt on French agriculture. In the US, however, class-conflicts during the post-revolutionary period created a very different type of state – one committed to and capable of enforcing legal claims on landed property in the countryside.

The Continental Army, the standing army with professional officers that displaced the state-militias, secured US-independence in the early 1780s.[117] The end of the War opened a period of intense social conflict among the classes that made the American Revolution.[118] The colonial merchants and land-speculators sought to create state-institutions that could secure the public debt and re-establish US commercial credit in the Atlantic economy, enforce legal claims to land on the frontier and allow landowners to profit from the sale of these lands. Arrayed against the merchants and speculators were the vast majority of Northern and Southern independent household-producers who feared a strong central state capable of imposing taxes and collecting debts, and slave-owning planters who wanted to exclude all other social classes from interfering with the master-slave relation of production.

During the first decade of independence, US state-institutions embodied the inability of the merchants and land-speculators to establish their political dominance. Under the Articles of Confederation, the US-state was decentralised and the national Congress lacked the independent capacity to levy taxes. Not only was the Confederation incapable of securing the public debt through taxation, it was unable to maintain a peacetime standing army.[119] Their experience with regular British troops during the American Revolution deepened longstanding hostility to a standing among farmers and artisans:

> After 1763, for the first time the British government stationed several
> thousand soldiers in the mainland colonies, and as the agitation increased

---

[116] Brenner 1985a, pp. 60–1.
[117] Kohn 1975, Chapter 1.
[118] The following analysis of the class-conflicts that produced the Constitutional Settlement of 1787 is drawn from Post 1983, pp. 154–95.
[119] Cress 1982, Chapter 2; Weigly 1984, pp. 75–84.

colonials focused much of their discontent on the army as the most visible, crude symbol of British authority. When redcoats suppressed tenant revolts on some of the Hudson River manors in 1766, looting and destroying property, many Americans began to see the analogy between the British army and the standing army of classical theory.[120]

The planters successfully relied on militias made up of non-slave-holding white farmers to control the slave-populations, and had no interest in strengthening the central state with a standing army.

Despite attempts by the political representatives of the merchants to force Congress to maintain and expand the standing army – including an abortive military conspiracy in 1783 – the standing army was effectively disbanded after the Revolutionary War.[121] By 1789, the US-army consisted of a total of 718 men – mostly stationed on the frontier.[122] The tiny army was incapable of either effectively expropriating Native Americans or preventing thousands of squatters from 'pouring into the Ohio Valley, threatening to deter purchase of federal land by speculators and settlers'.[123]

Shays' Rebellion of 1786, the first revolt of Northern farmers against the burdens of debts and taxes that threatened to make their possession of landed property dependent upon successful market-competition, initiated a political realignment among the dominant classes in the US. As armed farmers and artisans closed down courts attempting to collect debts in the fall of 1786, 'the local militia sided with Shays' Rebellion'.

> From September through January reports of the militia's unreliability flowed into the governor's office. Even the militia's successful defence of the Continental arsenal at Springfield was marred when supposedly loyal militiamen joined the ranks of the insurgents during the skirmish. Resistance to constitutional authority was by no means limited to the militia's rank and file. Militia officers discouraged their companies from taking the field, prevented the distribution of powder and supplies, and actively recruited their subordinates for service with the insurgents'.[124]

---

[120] Kohn 1975, p. 5.
[121] Kohn 1975, Chapters 2–4.
[122] US Department of Commerce 1976, Part I, p. 1143.
[123] Kohn 1975, p. 55.
[124] Cress 1982, pp. 95–6.

Planters, frightened by the difficulties the Massachusetts-militia had in suppressing Shays' Rebellion, joined the merchants in demanding a more centralised state. The Constitutional Settlement of 1787 contained a series of
concessions to planters – most importantly preventing any other social classes
represented in the federal government from interfering with the master-slave
relationship in the South. However, the new federal state created in 1787–9
generated a national judiciary, a corps of tax-collectors, centralised control of
the state-militias, and a standing army capable of enforcing the legal claims
of landowners and creditors.[125] By 1794, the regular US-army had grown
from 718 to 3,818 troops and the President had the power to mobilise rebuilt
state-militias.[126]

The new state-institutions allowed merchants and land-speculators to
defeat independent household-producers in the cycle of class-struggles of
the 1780s and 1790s.[127] Independent farmers fought tax-collectors, merchant-
creditors, and land-speculators over the conditions of their economic survival
in a series of armed confrontations across the Northern countryside. Faced
with a merchant-class backed by a standing army, the independent farmers
were defeated.

The new US ruling class demonstrated its military capacity for the first time
during the Whiskey Rebellion of 1794. Western-Pennsylvania farmers, who
marketed their grain-surpluses in the form of whisky, organise armed resistance to the collection of the Federal Whiskey Excise of 1791. In the autumn of
1794, the Washington administration declared the region to be in revolt and
mobilised between 10,000 and 11,000 troops. The Pennsylvania, New Jersey,
Maryland and Virginia militias supplied the troops, mostly recruited from the
urban poor, who were placed under federal commanders. The revolt had all
but collapsed before the arrival of the federalised militia in November 1794.[128]
However, federal forces unleashed a wave of repression in Western Pennsylvania. According to an official US military history of the revolt:

---

[125] Coakley 1988, Chapter 1; Cress 1982, Chapter 6; Weigly 1984; Chapter 5.
[126] US Department of Commerce 1976, Part I, p. 1143.
[127] The following analysis of the destruction of independent household-production
and the emergence of petty-commodity production in the Northern countryside is
drawn from below pp. 75–97.
[128] Coakley 1988, Chapters 2–3; Cress 1982, pp. 123–9; Weigly 1984, pp. 101–3.

Cavalry detachments conducted the rounding up of suspects, which began as scheduled in the wee hours of 13 November and continued for a day or so afterward.... The militia contingents rounded up some 200 people, often mixing suspects and witnesses and including men who were entitled to amnesty.... Men were routed from their beds in the middle of the night amidst threats of hanging made within hearing distance of their wives and children. Some were forced to trot in front of horses along muddy roads to the military encampments, there to be incarcerated under miserable conditions.[129]

The Whiskey Rebellion demonstrated that the new federal régime was able 'to marshal the states' militias to enforce national law'[130] and 'that federal laws would be enforced and that no turbulent faction would set them aside at its whim'.[131] The federal government's use of military force 'inspired respect, even fear, and...established a deterrent atmosphere which could last for years, making another such costly exercise unneeded'.[132] The new régime reinforced these lessons in 1799 when a much smaller army of 500 regular troops and the Pennsylvania-militia crushed Fries Rebellion against federal taxation.[133]

The unintended consequence of closing off access to free or inexpensive land on the frontier, levying burdensome taxes and enforcing the payment of debt in gold or silver, was the transformation of the conditions under which farmers in the North obtained, expanded and maintained landed property. The burdens of mortgages, taxes and debts ensured that Northern farmers marketed both their surplus and portions of their subsistence-output. Put simply, northern-US farmers became dependent upon successful market-production for their economic survival – they became agrarian petty-commodity producers who had to specialise output, accumulate land and capital, and introduce new tools and methods in order to obtain, maintain, and expand landed property.[134]

---

[129] Coakley 1988, pp. 61–2.
[130] Cress 1982, p. 126.
[131] Coakley 1988, p. 67.
[132] Kohn 1975, p. 139.
[133] Coakley 1988, pp. 69–77; Weigly 1984, pp. 103–4.
[134] Additional comparative research is necessary to determine why US-merchants, through the new federal state-apparatus constructed after 1787, were able to impose a

The subordination of Northern rural household-producers to market-compulsion proceeded unevenly over the first four decades of the nineteenth century. Farmers in the north-east increased the time and labour they devoted to commodity-production in the early 1800s. Better-off households were able to maintain and expand their landed property exclusively through farming, while poorer households combined farming and domestic manufacturing organised by merchant-capitalists in increasingly vain attempts to preserve land-ownership. Elements of independent household-production survived in the trans-Allegheny west through the 1830s. However, the extension of federal land-auctions to the north-west raised land-prices at the same time Northern state-governments increased property-taxes, forcing north-western farmers to specialise their output, accumulate land and capital and innovate technically in order to obtain, preserve and expand their landholdings in the 1840s. As rural households became dependent on the market for their economic survival, Northern agriculture became a massive home-market for industrially-produced capital- and consumer-goods, sparking the US industrial revolution of the nineteenth century. In sum, the transformation of social-property relations in Northern agriculture led to the shift from *extensive growth to intensive development – the development of capitalism – in the US-North.*

The American Revolution and Constitutional Settlement did not, however, lead to a capitalist transformation of Southern agriculture.[135] The shift of many Virginia- and Maryland-planters from tobacco-plantations to small grain farms in the face of falling tobacco-prices did not bring about a 'gradual extinction' of slavery. By the early nineteenth century, slave-owning planters had successfully shifted from tobacco to cotton – the most important industrial raw material for capitalist industry in Britain. Slavery's non-capitalist social-property relations remained in place, leading to technical stagnation, self-sufficiency in food-stuffs, and the geographical expansion of plantation-slavery from the Atlantic coast to the plains of east Texas to meet the growing industrial demand for raw cotton. While the expansion of plantation-slavery in the South fuelled capitalist industry in Britain and commodity-production

social monopoly on land. Similar attempts in nineteenth and twentieth century Africa, Asia and Latin America clearly did not produce the same results – the dominance of agrarian petty-commodity production – as in the US.
[135] The following analysis of post-revolutionary Southern plantation-slavery is drawn from pp. 138–54.

in the northern US, slavery's non-capitalist social-property relations under-mined the development of industry in the US-South. The continuity of slave social-property relations led to the *continuity of extensive growth in the US-South.*

By the 1840s, the continued expansion of plantation-slavery threatened the further development of capitalism in the US, which rested on the expansion of agrarian petty-commodity production. The growing contradictions between the social conditions of the development of capitalism and slavery set the stage for the sharp class-conflicts that culminated in the Civil War. Sharpening con-flicts between manufacturers, merchants, farmers, planters and slaves in the 1840s and 1850s over a variety of issues – but especially the class-structure of western expansion – produced a political crisis: the collapse of the bi-sectional Whig and Democratic parties, the increasing sectionalisation of politics, and the secession-crisis that culminated in four bloody years of Civil War. The outcome of the War and nearly a dozen years of tumultuous struggles dur-ing Reconstruction ultimately secured the social and political conditions for industrial-capitalist dominance in the Gilded Age.

Chapter Five

Social-Property Relations, Class-Conflict and the Origins of the US Civil War: Toward a New Social Interpretation

The Civil War in the United States has been a major topic of historical debate for almost one hundred and fifty years. Three factors have fuelled scholarly fascination with the causes and consequences of the War. First, the Civil War 'cuts a bloody gash across the whole record' of 'the American...genius for compromise and conciliation'.[1] The four years of armed conflict undermines claims that US-capitalist democracy has the capacity to peacefully resolve any and all social conflicts. Second, the Civil War marked two major phases in US socio-economic development. Whether described as 'agrarian' and 'industrial' or 'traditional' and 'modern', there is little debate that that production and exchange in the US was radically transformed after the Civil War. Finally, the abolition of slavery during the War altered the social and economic position of African Americans – the origins, course and outcome of the War was intimately linked to the changing character of race and racism in the US.

The existing historical literature on the origins of the Civil War grapples, directly or indirectly, with one central question – why did the existence and

---

[1] Moore 1966, p. 113.

expansion of plantation-slavery become the central and irreconcilable political question in the 1840s and 1850s? Put another way, why had political leaders and the social groups they represented been able to reach enduring compromises, create stable *national* parties which competed for support in both the slave-South and 'free-labour' North, and marginalised debate on slavery and its expansion before the mid-1840s? Why did the question of slavery-expansion became irrepressible afterwards, creating regionally based parties, leading to Southern secession and war?

Charles and Mary Beard produced the first systematic, synthetic *social explanation* of the US Civil War – an explanation that situates the political conflicts culminating in secession and war in socio-economic processes and forces.[2] According to the Beards, the antebellum industrial revolution unleashed a process of economic diversification and growth in the commercial north-east and agrarian north-west, while reinforcing cotton-monoculture and economic stagnation in the plantation-South. The divergent paths of economic development led to conflicts between north-eastern 'business' groups who wanted federally funded transport-construction ('internal improvements'), a national banking and monetary system, public land-policies that discouraged agrarian expansion, and protective tariffs for US-manufacturers; and Southern planters who opposed all these policies. Caught between Northern business and Southern agriculture were the independent, family-farmers of the north-west, who opposed a protective tariff and national banks, but wanted inexpensive land and federally financed transportation-construction.

Prior to the 1840s, the Democratic Party built an agrarian alliance of Southern planters and north-western farmers against north-eastern businessmen grouped in the National-Republican and Whig Parties. After the annexation of Texas in 1844, the Democratic alliance collapsed as the north-west's diversified agriculture was integrated into north-eastern commerce and manufacture. The new economic alignment led the slaveholders to oppose the free distribution of public lands to small farmers (Homestead Act) and federal subsidies of road-, canal- and railroad-construction. The new Republican Party of the 1850s brought together north-eastern business and north-western agriculture on a platform of protective tariffs, free Homesteads, a federally subsidised trans-continental railroad and 'free soil' – a Congressional

---

[2] Beard and Beard 1927, Chapters 15–18.

ban on slavery's expansion into the western territories.[3] The Republicans' victory in 1860 led to the Civil War, which marked the triumph of north-eastern business over both the Southern planters and the north-western farmers.

Beginning in the 1940s, historians identified a number of empirical problems with the Beards' social explanation of the Civil War. Some challenged the Beards' claim that north-eastern business was united in support of national banks, protective tariffs and 'free soil'.[4] Merchants and manufacturers were often on the opposite sides of the debates on monetary policy, tariffs and the expansion of slavery in the 1840s and 1850s. Other historians documented long standing tensions within the Democratic agrarian alliance between Northern family-farmers and Southern slaveholding planters, differences that pre-date and explain the farmers' support for the Republicans in the late 1850s.[5]

Since the 1950s, two non-social explanations of the US Civil War have dominated historical writings. Both the 'revisionist'[6] and 'new-political'[7] historians reject any attempt to provide a social explanation of the US Civil War. For the revisionists, the political conflicts leading to the Civil War were *repressible*. Anti- and pro-slavery agitators forced the question of slavery-expansion on the national political arena. No insolvable conflict – political, ideological or economic – existed between the North and South. The political crisis that culminated in war could have been avoided if moderate and clear sighted political leaders had displaced the 'blundering generation' of demagogic politicians who appealed to 'sectional fanaticism' in the 1840s and 1850s. Such a political leadership could have allowed a peaceful resolution of the minor differences that divided the North and South, avoiding four years of senseless and purposeless carnage.

The 'new-political' historians agree that there was no social foundation for the sectional conflict over the expansion of slavery into the western territories

---

[3] In the United States, new areas annexed through conquest or purchases (or some combination of both) were initially organised as 'territorial governments'. While settlers in these territories elected legislatures, the President appointed territorial governors who had veto-power over territorial laws, and the territories did not have representatives in Congress. After achieving a certain population, territories applied for 'statehood' from Congress, which conferred the right to elect their own governors and legislatures and have representatives in Congress.

[4] Foner 1941; Sharkey 1958; Unger 1964.

[5] Berwanger 1967; Foner 1969; Morrison 1967.

[6] Randall and Donald 1961; Craven 1966.

[7] Holt 1969, 1978, 1999.

in the 1850s. However, they reject the idea sectional tensions that culminated in the Civil War were the result of blundering political leaders. That instead, these historians argue that the sharp increase in Irish-Catholic migration in the two decades before the War produced new, ethno-cultural conflicts. The increasing polarisation of politics in the 1850s over the right of Catholic immigrants to become citizens and hold public office, and restrictions on the production and sale of alcohol destroyed the national Whig Party. While neither nativism nor temperance remained at the centre of political life after 1855, the collapse of the Whigs opened the way to the development of sectional parties – the southern Democrats and northern Republicans. These new parties deepened sectional divisions, allowing Lincoln's election, Southern secession and war.

In the past three decades, there have been some small steps toward the construction of a new social interpretation of the US Civil War. The work of Eugene Genovese[8] on the slave-South inspired new attempts to locate the origins of the Civil War in broad social and economic developments. Eric Foner revealed that the Republican rejection of slavery was rooted in their idealisation of the dynamic Northern-capitalist economy of the 1840s and 1850s.[9] More recently, the work of Charles Sellers[10] on the 'market revolution' of the 1820s and 1830s has inspired Bruce Levine's[11] and Christopher Clark's[12] efforts to revive a social interpretation of the Civil War.

John Ashworth's two-volume *Slavery, Capitalism, and Politics in the Antebellum Republic*[13] marks a qualitative breakthrough in the renewal of a social explanation of the US Civil War. Ashworth makes the regional uneven development of class-relations – plantation-slavery in the South and capitalist manufacture and commercial family-farming in the North – central to his analysis of the political and ideological conflicts that culminate in the Civil War. From his vigorously materialist perspective on politics, he provides a convincing critique of both revisionist and new-political historians. Ashworth

---

[8] Genovese 1967.
[9] Foner 1970.
[10] Sellers 1991.
[11] Levine 1992.
[12] Clark 2006.
[13] Ashworth 1995 – Volume I: *Commerce and Compromise, 1820–1850*; Ashworth 2007 – Volume II: *The Coming of the Civil War, 1850–1861*.

acknowledges that political leaders in the 1840s and 1850s misperceived the motives and goals of their political opponents. However, these errors of perception and the deepening sectional conflict were not random and irrational, but flowed from the political leaders' socially determined world-views. Ashworth also brilliantly analyses the rise and decline of ethno-cultural conflicts in the mid-1850s, demonstrating that these divisions need not have caused the disruption of the national political parties. Instead, the conflict over slavery and its expansion was the root cause of the realignment of political and social forces that led to the War.

Arguing that 'the origins of the Civil War are best understood in terms derived from Marxism but existing Marxist historical writing has not yet adequately considered the problem',[14] Ashworth provides a provocative *political-ideological* explanation of the US Civil War. However, the *absence of a theoretically rigorous and historically concrete analysis of the origins of capitalism in the US ultimately limits Ashworth's magisterial study*. In what follows, we will first summarise Ashworth's complex and original analysis of the social origins of the US Civil War. Next, we will discuss a number of historical and conceptual problems in Ashworth's arguments. Finally, we will present the outlines of an alternative social explanation of the US Civil War based upon the analysis of the origins of capitalism in the US presented in earlier chapters.

I. Ashworth's Social Interpretation of the US Civil War

According to Ashworth, the US Civil War was the inevitable result of a political and ideological polarisation rooted in the growing uneven development between the slave-South and capitalist North over the course of the first half of the nineteenth century. Specifically, the social relations of capitalism and slavery made possible very different forms of *ideological accommodation* of the direct producers (wage-workers and slaves), which led to a sharpening political and ideological conflict in the last decades of the antebellum-republic. Ashworth takes great pains to argue that there were no direct *economic* contradictions between the development of capitalism and plantation-slavery. However, the *political and ideological* conflicts that culminate in secession and

---

[14] Ashworth 1995, p. x.

war 'can only be understood in terms of the differences between capitalist and slave modes of production'.[15]

Ashworth argues that slavery was an inferior form of social labour to capitalism because of the slaves' continuous resistance to their unfree legal status. Bi-sectional political parties (the Democrats and the National-Republicans/ Whigs) were able to contain sectional conflicts over slavery and capitalism during the economic expansion of the 1820s and 1830s. However, that expansion, in particular the impact of the 'market-revolution' in the North, radicalised Northern anti-slavery sentiment to include an embrace of the superiority of wage-labour – not simply 'free-labour' – to slavery. The militant anti-slavery politics of the abolitionists in the 1830s and 1840s produced a defensive Southern radicalisation, leading to the suppression of free speech in the South and the struggle to secure new territories in the south-west for slavery's expansion. The aggressive 'slave-power' and its dominance of the federal government led, according to Ashworth, to a growing radicalisation of Northern public opinion where a majority embraced the call for 'free soil' – the ban on slavery in the western territories – by the 1850s. New patterns of trade marginalised the forces of sectional compromise – the northern Democrats and Conservative Whigs – opening the road to a political polarisation between anti-slavery northern Republicans and pro-slavery southern Democrats. The growing *political-ideological*, but not *economic-material* contradictions between slavery and capitalism culminated in the election of Lincoln in 1860, the slaveholders' bid for political independence and the Civil War – a bourgeois revolution that secured the dominance of liberal-bourgeois politics and ideology in the US.

Slave-resistance

At the heart of the growing political-ideological conflict that culminates in the Civil War was the *weakness* of slavery as a form of social labour. The growing economic gap between the capitalist and family-farming ('free-labour') North and slave-South – whether measured in terms of population-growth, urbanisation or industrialisation – inevitably flowed from the fact that the planters, unlike the Northern manufacturers, 'faced ... the constraint of a resistant

---

[15] Ashworth 1995, p. ix.

workforce'.[16] The slaves' desire for legal and juridical freedom translated into continuous class-resistance to their owners. While this resistance rarely took the form of open revolt, the slaves made their rejection of their enslavement manifest in tool-breaking, collective restrictions of work-effort, feigning illness and flight from the plantations. The slave's resistance led to 'problems in generating a work ethic, a possible reluctance to entrust slaves with expensive tools and machinery...and the tendency toward plantation self-sufficiency in agriculture'.[17] Urban and industrial slaves often lived independently of their masters and had numerous opportunities for 'hiring out' in their free time, providing them with 'too much freedom'.[18] The planters' fears of the effects of city-life and industrial work on the slaves limited urbanisation and industrialisation in the South.

By contrast, the class-relationship between capitalists and legally free wage-workers allowed wage-workers to be reconciled to their exploitation. Under capitalism, 'the proportion of dissatisfied [wage-] workers is likely to be much lower...and...the forms of which resistance to exploitation take, are different and, from the standpoint of the exploiting class, preferable'.[19] Capitalist social relations are reproduced through the impersonal compulsion of the market rather than the personal legal-juridical power of the masters and disguised by the formal equality of the labour-contract. Under capitalism, workers can aspire to individual upward social mobility, and 'the potential hostility between wage-labourer and employer can be mitigated by appeals to shared values'.[20] Thus, capitalists' superior form of exploitation allowed the continuous introduction of new and more complex tools and machinery, urbanisation and industrialisation.

The Missouri Crisis, compromise and the second party-system

Ashworth recognises that sectional political divisions, rooted in the dominance of slavery in the South and 'free labour' (self-employment in agricultur-exc and handicrafts, wage-labour) in the North, existed from the beginnings

---

[16] Ashworth 1995, p. 6.
[17] Ashworth 1995, p. 101.
[18] Ashworth 1995, p. 102.
[19] Ashworth 1995, pp. 197–8.
[20] Ashworth 1995, p. 198.

of the US-republic.[21] However, the gradual abolition of slavery and servitude in the North and the decline of plantation-slavery in the older tobacco-growing regions of Virginia, Maryland and Delaware in the late eighteenth and early nineteenth centuries fuelled Northern hopes that slavery and other forms of unfree labour in the US would eventually disappear. The shift to cotton-cultivation after the War of 1812, and its geographical extension into the trans-Allegheny south-west, undermined Northern hopes for a peaceful end of slavery.

In 1819, the organisation of a state-government that protected slave-property ('slave-state') sparked the 'Missouri Crisis' of 1819–20. The dominant Democratic-Republican Party (the opposition-Federalists had all but disappeared after the War of 1812), split along sectional lines. Northern Republicans argued against the admission of Missouri or any other slave-states now and in the future, and southern members of the Party threatening to disrupt the unity of the US-state ('Union') through secession if Missouri was not admitted as a slave-state. For Ashworth, the Missouri Crisis was a 'dress-rehearsal' for the political crisis of the 1840s and 1850s, highlighting the question of slavery expansion and rehearsing most of the pro- and anti-slavery arguments.

Despite the growing sectional polarisation in 1819–20, the crisis was resolved with a compromise that endured for over two decades – Missouri became a slave-state, Maine a free state, and the unorganised territories obtained from France in 1803 were divided into regions reserved for slavery and free labour. The emergence of a group of northern Democratic-Republicans who came to understand that 'they simply could not have antislavery and the Republican party...and indeed the Union as they had known it'[22] made the passage of Missouri Compromise possible. By the late 1820s, a new political alignment – the second party-system – had emerged pitting 'an essentially pre-capitalist alliance of slaveholders and farmers' in the Democratic Party against 'the

---

[21] Ashworth, however, tends to minimise the impact of slavery on politics before 1820. Robinson 1971, by contrast, documents how the planters' desire to protect their slave-property shaped both the division of authority between the state and central governments ('federalism') in both the Articles of Confederation and the US-Constitution, and the division of the unorganised frontier-territories of the Ohio and Valley into slave- and free regions with the Northwest and Southwest Ordinances of 1787.

[22] Ashworth 1995, p. 73.

advocates and allies of merchant-capital' in the National-Republican and Whig Parties.[23]

Each of these political alliances was bound together by a distinctive ideological world-view and political programme. Ashworth builds upon Edmund Morgan's[24] insight that African slavery was the foundation of political equality among Southern whites. The planters' exploitation of black slaves and wide spread land-ownership among whites allowed slave-owners and non-slave-owning whites to be equal members of the polity, sharing all rights of citizenship including the right to vote. Jeffersonian Republicans and, later, Jacksonian Democrats built a radically egalitarian, democratic and racist 'agrarian' ideology on this foundation, a world-view that systematically promoted the political equality of all landowning white farmers while simultaneously erasing the social and economic differences between slave-owning planters and independent farmers.

The Jacksonian Democrats elaborated a political programme of democratic rights for all (white) men, limited government and 'states rights' – limits on the powers of the federal government, in particular in relation to slavery in the southern states. The Democrats sought to protect what Ashworth describes as 'pre-capitalist commodity-production'[25] – slavery and subsistence-oriented family-farming – from 'aristocratic' government policies – the creation of corporations and banks, tariffs and other forms of taxation. Thus, the Jacksonian Democrats were able to unite slave-owning planters and independent farmers, North and South, into a political bloc around 'the demand that all white men should enjoy the fruits of their labour and be protected in this enjoyment by the possession of political rights',[26] and in opposition to a central bank, protective tariffs, and federally financed transport infrastructure construction

Slavery was either ignored or treated as a 'local matter' state-governments would regulate. Jacksonian Democrats 'were explicitly neither proslavery nor antislavery. So far from their primary goal being the protection of slavery, they were adamant that slavery should play no part in federal politics'.[27]

---

[23] Ashworth 1995, p. x.
[24] Morgan 1975, Chapters 17–18.
[25] Ashworth 1995, p. 315.
[26] Ashworth 1995, p. 76.
[27] Ashworth 1995, p. 336.

While ostensibly neutral on slavery, the Democrats 'insistence upon limited government, and especially on the limited extent of federal power operated to reduce the threat from antislavery sentiment generated outside the South'.[28] The Democrats' control of the federal government through most of the 1820s and 1830s, ensured 'that the slaveholders were the dominant class in the antebellum Republic'.[29]

A very different world-view and programme bound together the minoritarian National-Republican and later Whig Parties' alliance of manufacturers, tobacco-, hemp- and sugar-planters, and Northern and Southern merchants. Like their Federalist forbearers, the National-Republicans and Whigs were political élitists, deeply suspicious of democratic populism (even on a white-supremacist basis) and believed an active government under the leadership of judicious statesmen was a necessary condition for political stability and economic development. While the Democrats sought to 'tame and control commerce',[30] the Whigs were 'eager to promote commerce'.[31] In a society short of both capital and labour, the Whigs advocated a strong central bank to create credit, the creation of corporations to spur investment, maintenance of high public land-prices to limit alternatives to wage-labour and commodity-production, federally funded transportation-projects and a protective tariff.

Although 'the social order that the Whigs desired bears a much closer resemblance to 'capitalism' that the one to which Democrats were committed',[32] the Whigs were not modern liberal advocates of the free pursuit of self-interest in competitive markets. A strong federal government, under the stewardship of prudent leaders, was necessary to maintain harmony among competing interests in US-society. Thus, while many Whigs viewed slavery as 'a blemish on American society', they insisted 'that slavery, at least in the states where it existed, was a legitimate interest'. Whig leaders 'tried to create a harmony of interests between labour and capital, between agriculture and industry, between slave and free-labour'.[33] Not surprisingly, conservative northern and southern Whigs were central to crafting enduring compromises that harmonised

---

28 Ashworth 1995, p. 347.
29 Ashworth 1995, p. 345.
30 Ashworth 1995, p. 307.
31 Ashworth 1995, p. 316.
32 Ashworth 1995, p. 319.
33 Ashworth 1995, pp. 354–5.

the interests of slavery and free labour, and maintained the unity of the US-state before the 1840s.

The economic expansion of the 1820s and 1830s stabilised the second party-system. Political conflict at both the state- and federal level focused on banking, tariffs and the funding of transport infrastructure-projects. Debates about slavery's existence and expansion were marginalised, as political leaders contested whether untrammelled market-competition would allow all (white) men to enjoy the full fruits of their labour (the Democrats) or government regulation was required to harmonise conflicting interests and promote economic development (National-Republicans and Whigs). However, the very success of the market-revolution of the 1820s and 1830s undermined the second party-system and unleashed the political and ideological polarisation that would culminate in the US Civil War.

Wage-labour, abolitionism and pro-slavery radicalism

The Jacksonian market-revolution had contradictory effects in the North and South. Growing global demand for raw cotton consolidated plantation-slavery and fuelled its geographical expansion across the South. In the North, growing markets for foodstuffs and manufactured goods *transformed* the 'free-labour' economy. According to Ashworth, 'the growth of wage-labour' was 'an inevitable effect of the market revolution'.[34] The 'non-capitalist free-labour' of the Northern rural households initially rested on 'a relatively shallow division of labour'[35] which allowed these households to maintain possession of land outside of market-competition. The growth of markets and the deepening division of labour deepened in the 1820s and 1830s, 'accelerated the growth of wage-labour' in the North.[36] The growth of a wage-labour class produced radical shifts in the dominant Northern attitudes towards wage-labour and slavery.

The abolitionist movement's demand for the immediate emancipation of all slaves in the South represented a profound radicalisation of politics of anti-slavery in the US. Abolitionism echoed earlier arguments that the slaves' unfree legal status deprived them of an 'incentive to work' and that slavery

---

[34] Ashworth 1995, p. 79.
[35] Ashworth 1995, p. 115.
[36] Ashworth 1995, p. 493.

condemned the South to economic backwardness.[37] However, their vision of an economically superior free labour went beyond the traditional republican idealisation of independent producers who owned their own means of production and commanded their own (and their families') labour to an *embrace of wage-labour*.

Historically, republican ideology was deeply suspicious of the 'hireling', whose lack of economic independence based in self-earned property made him subject to the influence of his employers and of egalitarian and collectivist demagogues, and thus unfit for the rights of citizenship, in particular the right to vote. According to Ashworth, the abolitionists viewed wage-labour as 'honourable, natural and desirable'.[38] Wage-labourers, while deprived of property in means of production, maintained property in their ability to work and were thus free to develop their individual conscience, nurtured through their autonomous family-households. By contrast, the slave's person was bought and sold, giving another person a 'claim upon the conscience of the labourer'.[39] The slave-owners' denial of the slaves' right to marry and form their own family-households, and the constant threat of family-disruption through the sale of individual slaves were further assaults on the slaves' ability to develop their individual conscience. For the abolitionists, slavery was both economically and *morally* inferior to free wage-labour.

The Republicans of the 1850s deepened and popularised the abolitionists' embrace of wage-labour. Eric Foner, in his classic study of Republican ideology,[40] claimed that most Republicans either maintained traditional republican hostility to wage-labour, or viewed wage-labour as a temporary position in a free-labour society. Ashworth identifies three distinctive positions among Republicans on wage-labour. A minority argued 'that the fewer the wage-earners the better; their goal was a Homestead Act that, by offering free land to actual settlers, would allow more wage-workers to become independent farmers'.[41] A larger group, including Lincoln, accepted wage-labour as temporary position in a society where there were opportunities to become independent producers. However, Ashworth argues that most Republicans

---

[37] Ashworth 1995, p. 157.
[38] Ashworth 1995, p. 165.
[39] Ashworth 1995, p. 185.
[40] Foner 1970, Chapter 1.
[41] Ashworth 2007, p. 267.

'believed...the employee who remained a wage-earner for life was in no sense degraded or dishonoured as a result'.[42]

For Ashworth, the abolitionists and Republicans could accept wage-labour because, 'the equality and freedom contained in the wage relationship was real and important; wage-labour was as a result infinitely more attractive to the wage earner than slavery could ever be to a slave'.[43] The radicalisation of anti-slavery ideology, in particular its embrace of wage-labour, was manifested in a more militant anti-slavery politics after the 1830s. Abolitionists who sought the destruction of slavery in the Southern states remained a small minority in the North before the Civil War. However, the mainstream Free Soil and Republican Parties demanded a Congressional ban on slavery's expansion into the western territories, while their more radical wings sought a 'divorce of the Federal government from slavery' – the abolition of slavery in the District of Columbia and other federal installations and a ban on the interstate slave-trade. Despite the Free Soilers' and Republicans' pledge not to interfere with slavery in the Southern states, most planters 'insisted that free soil and abolition were in effect one and the same, each aiming at the same result even if by different processes and according to different timetables'.[44]

The abolitionist and Republican radicalisation of anti-slavery politics and ideology sparked a defensive political and ideological radicalisation among the slaveholders. According to Ashworth, 'to resist a determined and militant antislavery movement...slaveholders needed to believe in their own cause. The older "necessary evil" argument would no longer suffice'.[45] Before the 1830s, most Southern political leaders argued that slavery's abolition would only lead to the impoverishment of both whites and blacks in the South. After 1830, Southern ideologues argued that slavery was a 'positive good' – a superior form of civilisation to free wage-labour. John C. Calhoun and other Southern radicals believed that economic growth was impossible without a propertyless labouring class. While capitalism produced class-conflict between capitalists and the free and enfranchised wage-labourers, slavery allowed economic growth to coexist with republican institutions. Slavery eliminated class-conflict because:

---

[42] Ashworth 2007, p. 289.
[43] Ashworth 2007, p. 176.
[44] Ashworth 1995, p. 248.
[45] Ashworth 1995, p. 280.

> ...the master and slave had a common interest in securing to labour the full
> fruits of its toil, the master because he owned the title to that labour, the
> slave because he himself would benefit from the generosity of the master...
> the master had an interest in securing the welfare of the slave. The employer
> had no reason to care about the well-being of his employee, but the master
> had a strong motive for maintaining the health and welfare of the slave,
> since a failure to do so would diminish the value of his capital.[46]

If the slaves did not recognise their common interest with their masters and
'worked slowly and badly', it was the result of their *racial inferiority*. 'Some
slaveholders even argued that sullen apathy on the part of their slaves...
was proof that, unlike white men, they were simply unfit for liberty and did
not even aspire to it'.[47]

Calhoun, concerned with the more rapid demographic growth of the
North, ultimately renounced democratic egalitarianism in favour of the rights
of minorities like the planters to nullify majority-decisions that threatened
their interests. However, most antebellum-Southern radicals believed that
slavery was the only basis for stable, democratic institutions. While a legally
free and enfranchised propertyless class in the North constantly threatened
property and stability, slavery produced a republic of white property-owners
that excluded the enslaved and racially inferior labouring class.

Political polarisation: protecting Southern rights v. battling the 'slave-power'

For Ashworth, the slaveholders' inability to acknowledge the weaknesses of
slavery as a form of exploitation weakened pro-slavery arguments and led to
the planters to react defensively to the rise of abolitionism. While proclaim-
ing the superiority of slavery to free labour and the harmonious interests
of masters and slaves, the planters' representatives in Congress – with the
assistance of northern Democrats – moved to restrict the democratic rights
of their opponents. Throughout the 1830s, the slave-owners and their allies
in Congress prevented any discussion or debate on abolitionist petitions
('gag rule') and local postmasters forbid the use of the US-mail to transmit
abolitionist literature in the South.

---

[46] Ashworth 1995, p. 201.
[47] Ashworth 1995, p. 242.

Over the course of the 1840s and 1850s, Southerners took a series of increasingly radical actions in defence of slavery that stimulated Northern hostility to the 'slave-power' – the slave-owners' dominance of the federal government. Fearing the resistance of the slaves themselves, the loss of political support for slavery among non-slave-owning Southern whites, and the growth of Northern hostility to slavery, the representatives of the planters:

> took a further series of actions intended to protect themselves against the threats which surrounded them. The demand for Texas, the drive to plant slavery in Kansas, the proposal to reopen the slave-trade and the pressure for a slave code for the territories – all were an attempt to compensate for the weaknesses of slavery...[48]

While the planters and their representatives 'intended to make the Union safe for slavery', but their actions 'merely served to fuel the political critique of the institution, the claim that the nation was being ruled by a slave Power'.[49] Put another way, the slaveholders' increasingly authoritarian rule in the South and their dominance of the federal government fuelled an increasingly militant Northern opposition to slavery and its expansion.

The two decades leading to the Civil War saw this dynamic produce a profound political polarisation, the collapse of the second party-system, the emergence of the regionally based pro-slavery Democratic and anti-slavery Republican Parties, and the marginalisation of all political forces seeking to find enduring compromises that could maintain the unity of the US-state. The first phase of the crisis began with the war with Mexico, when northern Whigs and Democrats demanded that slavery be excluded from all territories conquered in the war (the Wilmot Proviso). The Compromise of 1850, which avoided a catastrophic crisis, was built on the northern Democrats' formula of 'popular sovereignty', which left the existence of slavery up to the settlers in the southwestern territories. The temporary stabilisation of the second party-system in the early 1850s was rent asunder when the leading northern Democrat, Stephen Douglas applied the popular-sovereignty formula to the organisation of the Kansas- and Nebraska-territories in 1854, effectively

---

[48] Ashworth 2007, p. 332.
[49] Ashworth 2007, p. 334.

repealing the Missouri Compromise ban on slavery in the northern portion of the Louisiana purchase.

The repeal of the ban on slavery in Kansas and Nebraska quickly led to pro- and anti-slavery settlers flowing into Kansas, the creation of rival territorial and state-governments and four years of civil war (1854–8). Between 1854 and 1856, both the Democrats and Whigs suffered massive northern defections to the Republicans. The Whigs collapsed as a national political party, and struggles over slavery and its expansion scuttled the conservative Whigs attempt to build a national nativist party in 1855–6. While the Democrats remained united in 1856 and were able to win the Presidency, their unity was short-lived.

In the late 1850s, northern Democrats' insisted that popular sovereignty gave a *territorial* government the power to ban slavery, as it had in Kansas. Southern Democrats, fearing the containment of slavery, argued that only *state-governments* could exclude slavery. In the absence of state-governments, Congress was obligated to maintain 'Southern rights' in the west through the passage of a Congressional slave-code (the legal-juridical framework for slavery) for the territories. Compelled by the weakness of their form of exploitation, according to Ashworth, the Southern slaveholders' defensive radicalisation led them to abandon their traditional defence of states' rights – no federal interference with the master-slave relation – and demand federal protection of slavery in all the western territories. The result was a sectional schism in the Democratic Party in 1860.

With the Democrats divided and conservative Whigs in the Constitutional Unionist Party pushed to the political periphery, the election of 1860 saw the polarisation of public opinion between the southern Democrats and the northern Republicans. The planters of the Lower South responded to the election of Lincoln with a plurality of the national vote by seceding from the Union and establishing their own, independent Confederate States of America.

The forces of compromise, the northern Democrats and Constitutional Unionists, found themselves increasingly irrelevant in the late 1850s. They continued to advance solutions to the deepening political polarisation over the future of the western territories that had clearly proved to be impractical. For Ashworth, their political insignificance flowed from their ideological indifference to slavery and its expansion as a national issue. Douglas and the northern Democrats advocates of popular sovereignty – leaving the question of slavery to the settlers in a territory – was consistent with both 'Democratic enthusiasm for democracy itself'[50] and the belief 'that soil and climate would determine whether slavery would exist in a territory (or state)'.[51] Put another way, the northern Democrats believed the development of slavery or free labour was simply a matter of relative profitability – itself determined by soil and climate – and was best left to the (white) people most affected – the settlers in a given region.

For the ex-Whigs in the Constitutional Union Party of 1860, 'while there were legitimate differences between North and South, these need not and should not result in antagonism'.[52] In other words, slavery was one of many particular 'interests' that wise 'statesmen' could harmonise. Unfortunately, in the face of deepening polarisation between the demands for Congressional exclusion and protection of slavery in the territories, the northern Democrats and Constitutional Unionists' ideological indifference to slavery-expansion proved thoroughly inadequate.

Economic transformation and political polarisation

The economic changes that accompanied the boom of the 1840s and 1850s made possible growing political and ideological polarisation over slavery, the collapse of national parties and the marginalisation of those forces which sought to defuse the debate on slavery-expansion. On the one hand, the growth in demand for raw cotton in the two decades prior to the Civil War raised the profitability of plantation-slavery. On the other, the economic expansion brought 'increased stability and maturity' to the Northern-capitalist economy.[53] Together, 'the extraordinary growth of the final antebellum years strengthened each section's commitment to its labour system'.[54]

Politically, the vitality of plantation-slavery and the maturation of capitalism greatly reduced the importance of the traditional issues over which the nationally organised Democratic and Whig Parties had struggled in the 1820s and 1830s. In the North, the stabilisation of the banking system after the crisis of 1837–42, the growth of manufacturing, and the development of privately

---

[50] Ashworth 2007, p. 242.
[51] Ashworth 2007, pp. 429–30.
[52] Ashworth 2007, p. 594.
[53] Ashworth 2007, p. 232.
[54] Ashworth 2007, p. 478.

financed canal- and railroad-construction made a national bank, protective tariffs and federally financed internal improvements largely irrelevant.
In the South, the revival of cotton-monoculture undermined proposals for
the region's economic diversification. Deprived of their traditional national
platforms, 'relatively little seemed to separate' the Whigs and Democrats. 'It
was natural that those who wished to see the slavery question at the centre of
political debate, whether to defend or denounce it, should point to the irrelevance of the Jacksonian issues.'[55]

The transformation of patterns of inter-regional trade in the 1840s and 1850s
reduced the political importance of the northern Democrats and Conservative
Whigs:

> There is no question that important changes were taking place in inter-
> regional trade in the 1840s and especially the 1850s...north-east and
> north-west were becoming more closely tied in both absolute and relative
> terms, whereas North and South, in relative terms, were becoming less so.
> Thus the canals that were built in these and the preceding decades were
> overwhelmingly concentrated in the North and they carried freight from
> west to east....The impact of the railroads was similar...increased western
> output (where it did not remain in the West) went not, as historians once
> believed, to the South but overwhelmingly to the East. The South remained
> largely self-sufficient in foodstuffs but the north-east was a food deficit area.
> Moreover when north-eastern manufactured goods left the region, they too
> went not to the South but rather the North-west....These interdependencies
> broadly between an agricultural north-west and an industrial north-east,
> underpinned the demand for Homestead legislation which...was viewed
> both as a means of stimulating western demand for eastern manufactures
> and, at the same time, a way of guaranteeing cheap and plentiful food for
> the East'.[56]

Because 'the economic ties between North and South had traditionally operated as a counter-tendency' to a polarisation over slavery, the weakening of
these economic ties removed 'a barrier to the further growth of anti-slavery

---

[55] Ashworth 2007, p. 485.
[56] Ashworth 2007, p. 621.

in the North was removed'.[57] The social groups enmeshed in these economic ties – primarily Conservative Whigs and northern Democrats – were weakened politically.

The political impotence of the northern Democrats and Conservative Whigs was manifest in their failure to find a compromise solution that could preserve or restore the unity of the US-state during the secession-crisis. At the same time, both Republicans and southern radical Democrats gravely misperceived the strengths and weaknesses of their opponents. Neither Republicans nor southern Democrats were willing to entertain any serious concessions – either a Republican retreat from a Congressional ban on the future expansion of slavery, or a Southern return to the Union. On one side, the Republicans believed that the secessionists were a small and isolated minority in the South, and that a revolt of southern non-slave-owning white Unionists would bring the Lower South back into the Union without any concessions to slavery-expansion. On the other, the southern radicals discounted the possibility of the Republicans launching a war to reunify the US-state, believing that Southern independence had fatally weakened the North.

While both the Republican hope for a southern-Unionist revolt and the Confederate expectation of peaceful separation from the rest of the US were profoundly mistaken, these errors of perception were not random. Instead, they were the rooted in the logic of their socially determined world-views. For the Republicans, the 'free-labour system…was both natural and, potentially at least, harmonious', and slavery 'was both *unnatural* and *disorganizing*':

> Since free labour was the natural system, a slave regime could only by maintained by repressing the nonslaveholding whites (to whom it had nothing to offer and whose aspirations were therefore a profound threat). Only a small minority, the slaveholders (and perhaps their immediate dependents)…could fail to choose free labour over slavery'.[58]

Southern radicals' idealisation of slavery produced systematic political misperceptions as well. Planter-radicals firmly believed that the economic strength of the South, manifest in high profits and strong economic growth in the 1840s and 1850s, was the result of slavery. Slavery, with its propertyless

---

[57] Ashworth 2007, pp. 623–4.
[58] Ashworth 2007, p. 263.

and unfree labour-force, allowed economic growth and class-harmony. By contrast, capitalism's free and enfranchised wage-labourers were a constant source of political conflict and instability. Since the 1830s, southern radicals had claimed that only their wealth and political influence in the Union has prevented the outbreak of class-war in the North. During the secession-crisis, '...some southerners prophesised that the day of reckoning was imminent. ...The war of labour against capital would erupt, and the principal casualty might even be representative government and democratic institutions in the North'.[59] Sanguine in their confidence in the loyalty of their slaves, Confederate leaders believed that the North could not afford to risk unleashing the class-war at home with a war against the South.

The US Civil War as bourgeois revolution

For Ashworth, the US Civil War was the result of socially-determined, materially-rooted *political and ideological conflict*. In 1860, the North and South had 'two different labour systems which generated values, essentially in the realm of political economy, that themselves clashed'.[60] Ashworth insists that there was no direct, *economic* contradiction between capitalism and slavery:

> It as been argued (essentially by those working within the Marxist tradition)[61] that slavery was an impediment to northern capitalism and thus had to be removed. As far as straightforward economic (as opposed to ideological) criteria are concerned, this is an erroneous view. It is abundantly clear that northern capitalism had not come to a grinding halt in 1860, immobilised by the existence of southern slavery...[62]

Slavery's weaknesses, rooted in the slaves' resistance to their enslavement, doomed the Confederacy to military defeat. Southern economic underdevelopment, in particular its relatively low level of industrialisation, placed it at a sharp disadvantage in relation to the North. The slaves' smouldering discon-

---

[59] Ashworth 2007, p. 164.
[60] Ashworth 2007, p. 646.
[61] Ashworth includes our work (Chapter One) among those that argued that 'slavery was an impediment to northern capitalism.' (Ashworth 2007, p. 647, n. 36) As we will argue below, Ashworth misunderstands our argument when he infers that we are among those who believe 'that northern capitalism had...come to a grinding halt in 1860, immobilised by the existence of southern slavery'.
[62] Ashworth 2007, p. 647.

tent with their unfreedom exploded during the War in the form of massive flight from the plantations, further weakening the Confederate war-effort. Despite protestations that their war-aims were limited to the restoration of the unity of the US-state, 'the core belief of the Republican party, the conviction that slavery disorganised the nation' led the Lincoln-administration to abolish slavery in 1863.[63] The Civil War was part of a global movement in the nineteenth century which saw 'unfree-labour systems...being dismantled partly because they were thought to impede economic growth and development'.[64]

For Ashworth, the triumph of a capitalist political-economic world-view made the US Civil War a 'bourgeois revolution'. This revolution did not, as in some variants of Marxism, remove socio-economic obstacles to the development of capitalism. Instead, the Civil War eliminated a rival political-ideological system and its non-capitalist world-view and values:

> After the war northern values became the values of the nation as a whole. ...Indeed the ideology of the victorious North, with its reconciliation of democracy and capitalism became the ideology of Americanism. The tenets of the Republican faith, social mobility, the dignity of labour, equal opportunity, underpinned by the acceptance of wage-labour as a legitimate condition for the worthy citizen have become so integral to the nation's values that it is difficult to perceive that they were ever open to challenge.[65]

II. A critique of *Slavery, Capitalism and Politics in the Antebellum Republic*

John Ashworth's book represents a new benchmark for social historians of the US Civil War. His insistence that social and material factors rooted in the different class-relations of slavery and capitalism led to the political crisis

---

[63] Ashworth 2007, p. 639.
[64] Ashworth 2007, p. 640.
[65] Ashworth 2007, pp. 647–8. Ashworth's account of the Civil War and the abolition of slavery in the US – the result of growing political-ideological conflicts generated by capitalist development, rather than a material economic contradiction between the historical development of capitalism and slavery – mirrors Blackburn's 1988 account of the abolition of slavery in the British and French Caribbean in the nineteenth century. For a critique of Blackburn, see Tomich 1990, Conclusion.

of the 1850s is a welcome alternative to claims that sectional fanaticism or ethno-religious conflicts allowed the slavery-controversy to dominate late antebellum-politics. Recognising that Northern and Southern political leaders seriously misperceived the goals and motivations of their sectional opponents at crucial junctures of the sectional crisis, Ashworth convincingly argues that these misperceptions were rooted in the growing divergences between capitalism and slavery. Similarly, he recognises the sharpening ethno-political conflict of the 1850s, but demonstrates that the slavery-expansion controversy – not the struggles over the naturalisation of immigrants and temperance – fatally disrupted the bi-sectional Democratic and Whig Parties.

Ashworth's nuanced interpretation of the complexity and richness of the political and economic world-views of Democrats, Whigs and Republicans marks a significant advance for materialist social history. In particular, his insight into how Jeffersonian- and Jacksonian-Democratic assimilation of family-farming and plantation-slavery into a common 'agrarian' interest served to mask and promote the class-position of the slaveholders is particularly powerful.

However, key elements of his social interpretation of the origins of the Civil War are conceptually and historically flawed. Ashworth's claim that slavery was an inferior form of exploitation to capitalism because of the slaves' resistance to enslavement is theoretically and empirically questionable. Similarly, his argument that abolitionism and Republicanism embraced wage-labour, radicalising anti-slavery ideology and politics after the 1830s and *unleashing the sectional polarisation of the 1840s and 1850s*, is also open to challenge. Finally, his explanation of the marginalisation of the advocates of sectional compromise is inadequate.

The roots of slavery's 'weaknesses'

Central to Ashworth's social interpretation of the US Civil War is that slavery was 'a weaker form of exploitation than wage-labour' because of the slaves' resistance to their unfree legal status.[66] First, 'the fact that so many slaves did not wish to be slaves, did not wish to see the fruits of their labour appropriated by another, and therefore attempted, in various ways to resist this

---

[66] Ashworth 1995, p. ix.

exploitation' led to Southern economic underdevelopment.[67] The slaves' unwillingness to work and their masters' unease about trusting them with complex tools and machinery blocked technical innovation in plantation-agriculture and limited the use of slaves to simple, repetitive, unskilled tasks. Planters' fears about the lack of supervision of slaves in urban and industrial settings blocked the growth of cities and manufacturing. Second, Ashworth argues that slavery was much more vulnerable to class-conflict than capitalism. While the legal equality of capital and wage-labour masks exploitation and makes all labour appear as *paid* labour, the slaves' unfree legal status makes all labour appear to be *unpaid* labour.[68] Not only do slaves not have the opportunities for individual social mobility available to wage-workers, there is no possibility of masters appealing to their slaves' shared world-view, a shared set of ideological values.

Ashworth's explanation of Southern economic development is a variant of what we have called the 'non-bourgeois civilisation model' of slavery.[69] Like Genovese and others, Ashworth places the slaves' lack of juridical freedom at the centre of his explanation of technical stagnation and economic underdevelopment in the antebellum-South. Unfortunately, the notion that the slaves' unfreedom made them recalcitrant workers, incapable of developing skills, using complex tools or working in non-agricultural pursuits, is not historically accurate. Slaves in both classical antiquity and the plantation-regions of the Americas made up a large proportion and, in some areas, the majority of skilled urban and rural artisans. While sugar- and tobacco-plantations, with their more extensive processing and storage-facilities, required more skilled workers than cotton-plantations, slaves could be found working on almost all New-World plantations as skilled teamsters, blacksmiths, harness-makers, boatmen, stable- and barrel-makers, sawyers and carpenters. On the Caribbean sugar-plantations, slave-artisans directed the complex process of boiling and curing sugar before the introduction of the vacuum-pan in the mid-nineteenth century. All of these crafts required extensive training, considerable technical knowledge and judgement, and often involved the slaves working under their own supervision.

---

[67] Ashworth 1995, p. 92.
[68] Marx 1974, pp. 42–3.
[69] Most of what follows is drawn from pp. 121–31.

Nor did the slaves' unfreedom prevent them from working effectively in non-agricultural pursuits. In ancient Greece and Rome, most slaves were employed in mining and urban handicrafts, where their labour could be utilised year round, rather than agriculture, with its fluctuating seasonal labour-requirements. In the South, nearly one in twenty slaves worked in industrial settings (coal-, lead- and salt-mining, cotton-spinning and weaving, iron-smelting and forging, leather-tanning, tobacco-, hemp- and cloth- and rope-making, lumbering). Not only did they work effectively with industrial machinery, there is little evidence that urban or industrial slaves were any more likely to flee their masters than slaves on rural plantations.

The notion that the slaves' unfree legal status made them recalcitrant, unmotivated and un-trainable workers also tends to *idealise* the condition of legally free wage-workers under capitalism.[70] Unlike household-producers (peasants and artisans), neither slaves nor wage-labourers have control over or an interest in the outcome of the production-process. Both slaves and wage-workers confront a labour-process whose timing, pace and technical character has been organised by the non-producers. Thus, the problems of 'labour-discipline' and supervision – ensuring concerted work – exist under both slavery and capitalism. While the goals and forms of the slaves' struggle differ from those of the wage-worker, many historians have noted the similarities between slaves and workers' struggles in the production-process:

> The conflict between master and slave took many forms, involving the organisation of labor, the hours and pace of work, the sexual division of labor, and the composition of the labor-force – all questions familiar to students of free workers. The weapons that workers employed in such conflicts – feigning ignorance, slowing the line, minimising the stint, breaking tools, disappearing at critical moments, and, as a last resort, confronting their superiors directly and violently – suggest that in terms of workplace struggles, slaves and wage-workers had much in common. Although the social relations of slave and wage-labor differed fundamentally, much can be learned about slave life by examining how the work process informed

---

[70] This is not surprising, given the origins of these arguments in the work of Adam Smith 1937, pp. 365–8, the founder of liberal economics, and John Cairnes 1968, an Irish liberal economist and opponent of British intervention on the Confederacy during the US Civil War.

the conflict between wage-workers and their employers. For like reasons, the processes of production were as much a source of working class culture for slave workers as for free workers.[71]

Wage-workers' lack of motivation, their indifference to the outcome of the production-process has *not* been an obstacle to the introduction of new, complex labour-saving machinery under capitalism. Rather than raising the level of skill and intelligence required of most workers, the division and simplification of tasks and the mechanisation of production have systematically lowered the general level of skill under capitalism over the past four centuries.[72] In sum, the slaves' unfree legal status and her/his lack of motivation and commitment to the labour-process – features shared with wage-labourers under capitalism – cannot explain the absence of technical innovation in agriculture or the relative underdevelopment of urban industry in the antebellum-South.

The claim that the absence of the possibility of individual social mobility under slavery made this form of social labour inferior to capitalism does not withstand historical interrogation. Few if any slaves in the plantation-South could hope to purchase their own freedom and become independent farmers or even slave-owners after 1700.[73] However, there were opportunities for individual slaves to 'rise in the world'. While we need not accept their claim that such opportunities imbued a 'Protestant work ethic' in Southern slaves, Fogel and Engerman point out:

> ...slaves had the opportunity to rise within the social and economic hierarchy that existed under bondage. Field hands could become artisans or drivers. Artisans could be allowed to move from the plantation to town where they would hire themselves out. Drives could move up to the position of head driver or overseer. Climbing the economic ladder brought not only social status, and sometimes more freedom; it also had significant payoffs in better housing, better clothing and cash bonuses.[74]

Ashworth's claim that slavery was an inferior form of exploitation because masters and slaves did not share common ideological values is also open to

---

[71] Berlin 1998, p. 11.
[72] Braverman 1974; Marx 1976, Chapter 15; Montgomery 1992; Thompson 1993.
[73] Breen and Innis 1980 describe one of the last examples of such a transformation before the consolidation of plantation-slavery.
[74] Fogel and Engerman 1974, p. 149.

challenge. In his brilliant study of slave-life and culture, *Roll, Jordan, Roll,*[75] Eugene Genovese persuasively argues that *paternalism* provided a common set of ideological values for both masters and slaves. The planters were able to appeal to their slaves as members of an extended 'family', in which all members of the family had reciprocal, although different responsibilities.[76] Just as capitalist appeals to shared ideological references – equality, freedom, democracy, individual opportunity – do not eliminate working-class resistance and struggle, nor did planters' appeals to their 'black family' eradicate slave-resistance and struggle. Like all *hegemonic* world-views, planter-paternalism attempts to harmonise conflicting classes, but rarely succeeds in eliminating materially-based conflict.

The roots of slavery's weaknesses – technical stagnation in agriculture and underdevelopment of urban industry – are found not in the resistance of the slaves, but in the structure of the master-slave social-property relation.[77] In both slavery and capitalism, the propertyless direct producers have no control over or stake in the outcome of production, making possible and necessary a centralised labour-process under the control of the non-labourers or their agents. The key difference between capitalism and slavery is that capitalists purchase the workers' *labour-power*, their ability to labour for a set period of time; while masters purchase the *labourer*, giving them an unlimited to claim on the slaves' ability to work. Thus, slaves are 'means of production in human form', a *constant* element of the production-process.

The 'capitalisation of labour' has two crucial implications for the labour-process under slavery. First, the slave must be maintained whether or not they labour in order to preserve their value as a form of constant capital. Thus, the threat of unemployment, the main way capitalists discipline wage-labourers, is not available to the masters. Instead, they must rely on physical coercion to ensure that slaves labour. Even more importantly, the master-slave social-property relation makes technical innovation – in particular, the replacement of human labour with new and more complex tools and machinery – an episodic

---

[75] Genovese 1972, Book One.

[76] Ashworth (1995, p. 115) in fact discusses the social foundation for such a world-view in his analysis of the similarities between plantation-slavery and independent household-production: 'The home tends to remain the centre of production, with the characteristics of the family-farm, or plantation.'

[77] This section is drawn from pp. 131–54. The concept of social-property relations is drawn from Brenner 1985.

process at best. Laying off 'redundant workers' and expanding the size of the reserve-army of labour allows capitalists to easily adjust the size of their labour-force in order to adopt labour-saving tools and machinery. By contrast, masters could not easily 'expel labour from production' – they would need to find buyers for any surplus slaves – and adopt labour-saving technology. Put simply, it was the fixed and inflexible costs of reproducing the slave labour-force – not the slaves' reluctance to labour – that prevented relatively continuous technical innovation under slavery. Generally, the introduction of new crops or expansion to new regions provided masters with the only opportunity to introduce labour-saving technology, fundamentally altering the relatively fixed relationship between labour, land and tools.

The structure of the master-slave social-property relation, rather than slave-resistance to bondage, also explains the underdevelopment of Southern cities and manufacturing. The absence of continuous technical innovation in plantation-slavery severely limited the market for manufactured tools and machinery in the South. The masters' need to ensure that their slaves' were constantly working, even in the 'slack-seasons' between cotton-crop cycles, encouraged plantation self-sufficiency in food and other consumer-goods. The resulting absence of a 'home-market' for industrial production, not the masters' fears of an urban environment, prescribed the growth of industry and cities in the South.

The distinctive structure of the master-slave social-property relation shaped 'rules of reproduction' of this form of social labour that led, inexorably, to the geographical expansion of plantation-slavery.[78] Unable to reduce the amount of necessary-labour the slave performed through mechanisation, the planters had few options to increase the volume of production or reduce costs in the face of world-market competition. On the one hand, the planters could attempt to increase the intensity and pace of work by increasing the acreage each slave or slave-gang tilled in a given period of time. On the other, the planters could add more slaves and more land (preferably more fertile lands) in order to increase output and reduce costs. In sum, *geographical expansion was the necessary form of the expanded reproduction of the master-slave relation of production.*

---

[78] Brenner 1989.

Ashworth points out that the planters articulated their struggle to secure the political and legal conditions for slavery's geographical expansion in very different terms. While the planters correctly equated the geographical containment of slavery with its eventual destruction, they argued this on ground of political representation – 'the political need for additional slaves states' and profitability:

> ...the slave-population was increasing at a rate which, in some parts of the South at any rate, was highly alarming....They had serious doubts whether the anticipated number of slaves, if confined to the present boundaries of the South, could be profitably used by their masters.[79]

Ashworth, however, doubts whether the geographical expansion of slavery was either *necessary* or *possible* in the late antebellum-period. Geographical expansion was unnecessary because 'vast supplies of land were available in the South in 1860'.[80] Ashworth also questions the *possibility* of slavery-expansion because of natural conditions:

> Only where large-scale agriculture was possible, in highly favourable climatic conditions and where there was massive overseas demand for the staple-crops produced, did the institution thrive and expand. Thus it proved unable to compete across much of the West even where white opinion was utterly indifferent to the welfare of the African-American population.[81]

The 'vast supplies of land available in the South' were primarily in the 'upcountry' (hill and mountain) and pine-barrens. The inferior soil-fertility and rough terrain made large-scale plantation-agriculture difficult, leading the planters to leave these areas to non-slaveholding white farmers who engaged in subsistence-production before the Civil War.[82] Nor were there any 'natural limits' of climate and soil to slavery. Slavery, in both classical antiquity and the Americas, had been utilised successfully in a wide variety of crops, including grains, in the grazing of livestock, and mining. While the western territories may not have been suitable for cotton, tobacco or hemp, there were ample opportunities for masters' to use slaves in ranching and

---

[79] Ashworth 2007, p. 49.
[80] Ashworth 2007, p. 148.
[81] Ashworth 2007, p. 634.
[82] Hahn 1983, Part I.

mining.[83] In sum, the geographical expansion of slavery into the western territories – and beyond to Cuba and Central America – was both *possible and necessary* for the future of slavery as a distinct form of social labour.

Abolitionism, republicanism and wage-labour

For Ashworth, the abolitionist and Republican embrace of wage-labour as compatible with republican institutions produced a more aggressive and radical-Northern antislavery-sentiment and politics, *which sparked the growing polarisation over the geographical expansion of slavery in the two decades before the Civil War.* For Ashworth, 'the growth of capitalism in the North generated the economic critique of southern slavery' that brought a radical ideological and political shift – away from viewing wage-labour as 'wage-slavery', a social form incompatible with the stability of republican institutions.[84]

Ashworth's case concerning the abolitionists rests on a rather thin foundation. He cites only one abolitionist – Lydia Maria Child – who explicitly speaks about 'labourers' who work for wages as distinct from self-employed artisans and farmers.[85] His case for the Republicans rests on stronger evidence. Most Republicans, like Lincoln, viewed wage-labour as superior to slave-labour because free workers could rise into the ranks of the self-employed. However, Ashworth cites other Republicans who argued that whether or not workers remained wage-labourers their entire life, wage-labour was superior to slavery and a sound foundation for republican institutions.[86]

Ashworth is quite explicit that the Republican vision of capitalism and wage-labour was not that or large-scale, mechanised industry with armies of unskilled workers. Instead:

> When Republicans extolled their society as one in harmony with human nature, it was the small shop, the village artisan and the small-scale manufacturing enterprise with an average of perhaps ten employees, they had in mind. This was the wage-labour system as Republicans understood it on the eve of the Civil War.[87]

---

[83] Genovese 1967, pp. 251–64 presents the classic critique of the 'natural-limits' thesis.
[84] Ashworth 1995, p. 115.
[85] Ashworth 1995, pp. 165–8.
[86] Ashworth 2007, pp. 267–97.
[87] Ashworth 2007, p. 298.

However, the Republican vision of a 'free-labour' society not only envisioned *small-scale* production, but *manufacturing*, where skilled workers still organised and controlled the labour-process. In his study of debates in antebellum political economy, Allen Kaufman argues that 'the economists of the American school' – Daniel Raymond, Matthew Carey and Henry Carey who helped shape Whig and Republican economic ideology and politics – did not equate the promotion of *manufacture* with what we understand as *industrialisation*:

> Both processes conjure in our imagination the emergence of the factory system, the formation of an industrial working class.... But the crucial distinction between the American school's concept of that process and our own (which consequently differentiates their notion of promoting manufacturing from our notion of industrialization) is that for the American school the *laborer was not separated from the direct control of the production-process*. Certainly, these theorists accepted the accumulation of land and capital as a natural consequence of increasing wealth and in so doing underwrote the formation of the working class. However, they hoped to prevent the development of an impoverished working class by restricting and ensuring its skill composition. The American school could thus assume that, over time, independent labor would fundamentally structure the economy. In this theory capital neither organized production for its own profit nor acquired any productive characteristics ...[88]

Put another way, it was not the small-scale of production that Republicans idealised, but the skilled workers' control over the labour-process – their *independence* from capital in the organisation of production. The degradation of slavery was not simply the slaves' unfreedom or their inability to experience individual upward social mobility, but that they were subject to the will of their masters in the plantation labour-process.

The Republican vision of skilled wage-labour as a form of *independent labour* was an accurate 'mental road map of lived experience'[89] of capitalist manufacture – with its *formal subsumption of labour to capital*[90] – in the antebellum-US. With the exception of the cotton-textile industry, skilled

---

[88] Kaufman 1982, pp. 43–4. (Emphasis added.)
[89] Fields 1990, p. 110.
[90] Marx 1976, Chapter 14, Appendix.

workers organised and directed almost all of antebellum-Northern capitalist manufacturing.[91] Even more importantly, the vast majority of antebellummanufacturers emerged from the ranks of the artisanal petty producers.[92] Even after the Civil War, skilled workers often controlled the labour-process and hired and supervised apprentices and helpers in the production of iron, steel and machinery.[93]

For the Republicans, the containment of slavery, a homestead-act and a protective tariff would promote the growth of manufacturing – ensuring the continued independence of the skilled worker in command of the labour-process, and short-circuit the emergence of a permanent, potentially politically radical proletariat in the US. According to Beckert, most manufacturers in New York and the rest of the North embraced this vision in the 1850s:

> believed in the mutual interest of capital and labor, a belief that came naturally to a group of employers in close contact with their workers. They expected that for skilled, temperate, and native-born workers, wage-labor was to be merely a way station en route to economic independence. If jobs were lacking, agricultural expansion in the West would provide a new route to realize their independence. As long as there was opportunity, there would be no permanent proletariat, and, correspondingly, no permanent poverty. Opportunity, as industrialists saw it, was a right of the citizens of the republic.[94]

The emergence of specifically capitalist social-property relations in the North did not create a radically new critique of slavery. Most of the abolitionist and Republican political, economic and moral arguments against slavery were present in the debates over the admission of Missouri in 1819–21. However, the development of capitalism in the North – *the result of the transformation of Northern-rural household-production* – made anti-slavery arguments and *the demand for the geographical containment of slavery* the 'common sense' of the majority of Northern farmers, manufacturers, artisans and skilled workers. These new social relations of production also created an irreconcilable political conflict over the future class-relations of the geographical expansion of

---

[91] Taylor 1951, pp. 207–20; Clark 1929, pp. 367–76.
[92] Beckert 1993, Chapter 2, Livesay and Porter 1971, Wilentz 1984, Chapter 3.
[93] Clawson 1980; Montgomery 1992.
[94] Beckert 1993, p. 73.

commodity-production. While Ashworth is generally a consistent materialist, his explanation for growth of Republican anti-slavery ideology in the North ignores their roots in the antagonism between the *conditions of reproduction* of Northern-capitalist manufacturing and petty-bourgeois agriculture, and Southern plantation-slavery.

Economic transformation and political crisis

Ashworth argues that, while the economic expansion of the 1820s and 1830s allowed 'sectional peace' and the marginalisation of debate on slavery's existence and expansion on a national level, the growth of the 1840s and 1850s thrust this debate to the centre of the political stage and marginalised all political forces seeking 'sectional' compromise. The growth of commerce, the 'market-revolution' of the 1820s and 1830s, 'inevitably' brought the growth of capitalism in the North, while reinforcing the dominance of slavery in the South.[95] By the 1840s and 1850s, the growing economic gap between the North and South fuelled both pro- and anti-slavery political agitation. By that point, the patterns of interregional trade had also shifted as a result of canal- and railroad-construction, strengthening ties between eastern industry and western agriculture. While sharpening regional uneven development bolstered a sharpening polarisation between Republican defenders of capitalism and southern-Democratic advocates of slavery; the changed direction of interregional trade economically and politically marginalised northern Democrats and Conservative Whigs.

Ashworth's argument that the growth of markets inevitably led to the development of capitalism in the North essentially reserves the historical and theoretical sequence of causation – *it was the growth of capitalism that generated the growth of markets, not vice-versa.* Although he never explicitly discusses the mechanism by which commercial development leads to capitalism, Ashworth's descriptions of how expanding markets lead to wage-labour is compatible with what Brenner[96] and Wood[97] have called the 'neo-Smithian' or 'commercialisation'-model of the origins of capitalism. In this model, the growth of trade provides new opportunities for independent producers –

---

[95] Ashworth 1995, p. 79.
[96] Brenner 1977.
[97] Wood 1999.

land-owning farmers unencumbered by legal restrictions on their freedom (serfdom) – to specialise output, introduce labour-saving technology and accumulate land, animals and tools in order to maximise income and reduce costs. As these profit-maximising farmers specialise output, they cease to produce much of their own subsistence (other than food), creating markets for manufacturers of consumer-goods. The farmers' continuous search for labour-saving tools and machinery also creates markets for specialised producers of capital-goods. Competition leads to deepening social inequality in the countryside, with successful farmers accumulating land and capital and unsuccessful farmers losing land and becoming wage-labourers in agriculture and industry.

The historical record of 'peasant-agriculture' in pre-industrial Europe (and most of the world prior to the late twentieth century) and the colonial and antebellum-US directly contradicts the causal predictions of the 'neo-Smithian' or 'commercialisation'-model.[98] As long as the independent farmers are able to obtain, maintain and expand landed property outside of market-competition, they are under no compulsion to specialise output, introduce new techniques or accumulate land and capital. When prices are rising, independent household-producers increase the production of physical surpluses which they sell in the market to purchase the items of consumption they or their neighbours cannot produce themselves. When prices fall, such producers simply cut back the production of surpluses and restrict their consumption. They are, however, under no threat of losing their possession of landed property if they fail to specialise output, introduce cost- (and labour-) saving tools and machinery, and accumulate land and capital. Only when the conditions under which household-producers obtain, maintain and expand landholdings are transformed – when producers are compelled to 'sell to survive' – do household-producers specialise, innovate and accumulate. Such 'precapitalist commodity-production' – independent household-production – was the dominant form of rural production in much of the rural North before the 1840s. As we will see, the transformation of this form of social labour into petty-commodity production – where household-producers were subject to 'market-coercion' – was not the 'inevitable' consequence of the growth of

---

[98] For pre-industrial Europe, see Brenner 1985b. For the colonial and antebellum-US, see Chapters Two and Four below.

commerce, but of class-conflicts over conditions of landownership that began in the 1780s and culminated in the 1830s.

Ashworth's analysis of shifts in interregional trade in the 1840s and 1850s, which explains the growing irrelevance of the northern Democrats and Conservative Whigs is also open to historical challenge. Ashworth essentially reprises Douglas North's thesis that Southern export of cotton fuelled economic growth in the US in the 1820s and 1830s:

> ...a major consequence of the expansive period of the 1830's was the creation of conditions that made possible industrialisation in the North-east. Transport facilities developed to connect the East and West more efficiently; a new market for western staples developed in the rapidly industrialising East and, sporadically, in Europe. The dependence of both the North-east and the West on the South waned.[99]

Albert Fishlow's[100] research, which Ashworth cites,[101] challenged North's claim that the completion of canals and railroads in the late 1830s shifted the main axes of interregional trade from west-south (food-cash) and south-east (cotton-shipping) to west-east (food-manufactured goods). Fishlow discovered, first, the bulk of western foodstuffs marketed during the 1820s and 1830s were destined for eastern urban markets. The Southern plantations were already self-sufficient in foodstuffs. Food shipped down the Mississippi River was re-exported from the port of New Orleans to New York, Boston and Philadelphia. Even more important, investments in railroads and other transportation-facilities tended to follow, rather than lead to increased commodity-production in agriculture. Put another way, the building of railroads and canals did not *cause* the growth of markets and commodity-production, instead they were its *consequence*.

In sum, Ashworth's analysis of the social roots of the growing political and ideological polarisation over slavery-expansion is highly problematic. Slavery's economic weaknesses were not rooted in the resistance of the slaves, but in the structure of the master-slave social-property relation – whose 'rules of reproduction' made *geographical expansion* the necessary form of the expanded reproduction of this form of social labour. Nor did the abolitionists

---

[99] North 1961, pp. 69–70.
[100] Fishlow 1965a, Chapters 3–4; 1965b, pp. 187–200.
[101] Ashworth 2007, p. 621, n. 294.

and Republicans substantially alter anti-slavery arguments with an embrace of wage-labour and spark the sectional polarisation of the 1840s and 1850s. The Republicans preserved the traditional republican hostility toward a propertyless, impoverished class of wage-labourers subject to the will of others in their work lives. Their innovation, following the American-school economists, was to envision a society where manufacturing – in which skilled labourers organised and controlled the labour-process – prospered under the protection of tariffs and a homestead-act. Put simply, neither the planters' weakness in relation to their slaves, nor the Northern embrace of wage-labour and fully-blown capitalism explain the political crisis of the 1850s. The development of Northern capitalism was not the 'inevitable' result of the growth of trade. Nor did patterns of interregional trade change in the way Ashworth asserts in his account of sectional polarisation and the marginalisation of the forces of compromise. Ultimately, all of these problems flow from the absence of a *theoretically rigorous and empirically detailed analysis of the origins of capitalism in the US*. Lacking such an analysis, Ashworth's important insights into the political and ideological dimensions of the conflicts leading to the Civil War remain unexplained.

III. Toward a new social interpretation of the US Civil War

The transformation of Northern agriculture[102]

The roots of the catastrophic class-polarisation over the social character of the expansion of commodity-production in the US during the 1840s and 1850s are found in the transformation of Northern-rural household-production between 1800 and the late 1830s. As Wood[103] points out, the British expansion into the Americas in the seventeenth and eighteenth centuries was the first example of specifically capitalist imperialism – where the reproduction of capitalist social-property relations governed the process of geographical expansion. However, the first experiment in capitalist imperialism *was unable to recreate capitalist social-property relations in British North America*. Although

---

[102] This section is based on Chapters Two and Four in this volume.
[103] Wood 2003, Chapters 4–5.

the British state granted legal title to wide swathes of land in the North-American colonies to private individuals and corporations, the undeveloped colonial state-institutions, in particular the military, made it impossible for land-owners to effectively enforce their claims to landed property. As a result, the majority of rural households in the North (and the majority of non-slave-holding households in the South) were 'squatters' – occupying land without legal title or payment. Even when landholders were able to force squatters to purchase land, the relative strength of the farmers rather than market-forces set the price of land. As a result, most rural households were able to obtain, maintain and expand landholdings without successfully competing in the market. In sum, while large-scale commodity-production on the basis of plantation-slavery was established in the British Caribbean and southern mainland-colonies by 1700, the British were *unable to reproduce capitalist social-property relations in the Northern-colonial countryside.*

Free from 'market-coercion', rural households in the Northern-British main-land-colonies organised production the way peasants – independent house-hold-producers – had for millennia. Northern farmers engaged in 'safety-first' agriculture, raising a wide variety of crops and animals for the consumption of themselves and for non-market-exchange with their neighbours, market-ing only physical surpluses. Technological change was highly episodic, with North-American farmers using tools and methods that contemporary capital-ist farmers in Britain had already abandoned. Landholdings tended to become fragmented over time as land was divided among adult sons who formed their own households. Only the relatively continuous expropriation of Native Americans, which provided new lands for European-colonial settlement, prevented the sorts of demographic collapses that resulted from fragmented landholdings in continental Europe in the seventeenth century. In sum, the Northern farmers' ability to obtain, maintain and expand landholdings with-out successful commodity-production, freed them from any compulsion to specialise output, introduce labour-saving tools and methods, and accumu-late land.

Colonial merchants and land-speculators constantly sought to increase the Northern farmers' volume of commodity-production and enforce legal claims to lands on the frontier – to augment mercantile profits from buying and sell-ing agricultural goods and land – before the American Revolution. However, as long as the colonial militia remained small and staffed mostly by small farmers, independent household-producers were able to obtain and keep land at no or minimal cost. Thus, they were able to continue marketing only the physical surpluses they and their neighbours did not consume.

The American Revolution and its immediate aftermath radically changed the relationship between the Northern farmers and the merchants and speculators. The War itself, in particular state-government requisitions of food, cloth and other supplies, usually produced and consumed in Northern-rural households, temporarily disrupted their non-market reproduction. More and more Northern farmers fell into debt to local merchants to purchase goods they had previously produced themselves. These debts became particularly burdensome after the War, as newly independent Northern state-government raised land-taxes to fund the enormous public debt accrued to finance the Revolutionary War. The combined growth of debts and taxes forced Northern households to market larger and larger portions of both their subsistence- and surplus-output in order to maintain their landed property in the 1780s.

The threat of the loss of possession of landed property as the result of debts and taxes produced a wave of rural unrest in the 1780s and 1790s. Beginning with Massachusetts' Shays' Rebellion in 1787, Northern farmers physically confronted local and federal courts, tax-collectors and land-speculators in defence of their self-earned – non-market appropriated – landed property. The new federal state, the product of the merchant and planters' 'Constitutional Settlement', was able to create a national army capable of defeating the Northern independent household-producers and *enforcing legal claims to landed property*. By closing off access to cheap or inexpensive land on the frontier, the merchants' newly established political hegemony ensured that the farmers marketed both the 'surplus' and portions of their 'subsistence'-output. Put simply, farmers in the north-eastern US became dependent upon successful market-competition for their economic survival – they became agrarian petty-commodity producers in the last two decades of the eighteenth century.

The class-struggles of the 1780s and 1790s effectively ended independent household-production in the original area of colonial settlement, but did not spell the end of this form of social labour in the US. As we will see, the dominance of plantation-slavery in the South allowed the reproduction of independent household-production among non-slaveholders in the region. In the

Ohio Valley and Great Plains, independent production developed as Native Americans were 'removed' and white settlers occupied land at little or not cost. Even when the federal public land-system gave legal title to land companies, 'squatters' were able to organise 'claims-clubs' to force landowners to sell the land to the settlers well below market-prices. As a result, most farmers in the north-west prior to the 1830s were able to market only physical surpluses and produce most of their own food, clothing and simple tools.

However, the outcome of the class-conflicts of the 1780s and 1790s sharply limited the reproduction of independent household-production in the north-west. In particular, the development of the federal public land-system transformed the conditions under which household-producers obtained, maintained and expanded landed property in the first four decades of the nineteenth century. As Native Americans were expelled, the federal public land-office surveyed and auctioned land in the trans-Allegheny west. While minimum-prices and acreage were progressively reduced during the antebellum-period, no maximum price or acreage limits were ever imposed. Federal land-auctions promoted successive waves of land-speculation during the antebellum-period, as land-companies, railroad- and canal-companies and wealthy individuals bought up large tracks of land for profitable resale to actual settlers. Particularly in the 1830s, settlers found themselves either having to obtain mortgages to purchase land (older farmers with some capital), or become temporary tenants in order to accumulate enough cash for a down-payment (younger farmers with no capital).

The commercial depression of 1837–42 not only left most farmers in the north-west with crushing debts accrued to obtain land, but produced a sharp increase in state-taxation. Most northern state-governments had subsidised canal- and railroad-construction with public funds. As railroad- and canal-companies failed, state-governments were forced to raise taxes – in particular, taxes on landed property – and expand the numbers of tax-collectors and assessors in order to fund their public debts in the 1840s.

Increased land-prices and growing debts and taxes completed the transformation of Northern-rural household-production. Payment of debts and taxes became the conditions for obtaining, maintaining and expanded landed property in the Ohio Valley and Great Plains 1840s and 1850s. To obtain sufficient cash to meet obligations, farmers were compelled to specialise output, introduce new and labour-saving tools and methods and accumulate landholdings. Put another way, north-western rural households in the two decades before the Civil War found themselves in the same position as north-eastern farmers after 1800 – they had to engage in successful market-competition in order to survive as property-owning agrarian producers. The result was the 'agricultural revolution' of the 1840s and 1850s – the growth in the size and proportion of output produced as commodities, increasing specialisation in cash-crops, rising labour-productivity with the introduction of new seeds, fertilisers and improved implements and machinery, and growing social inequality among farm-households.

The completion of the transformation of Northern farmers from independent-household to petty-commodity producers was the main cause of the sharpened pace of capitalist manufacturing growth in the two decades before the Civil War. As Northern farmers were compelled to 'sell to survive', they became a growing home-market for capitalist produced consumer- and capital-goods. Family-farmers specialising in cash-crops found themselves purchasing a wide variety of consumer-goods (cloth, shoes and boots, etc.) they and their neighbours had previously produced. In their struggle to reduce production-costs through technical innovation, farmers began to purchase the most advanced tools and machinery rather than producing these implements themselves or procuring them from local blacksmiths. The importance of the rural home-market on capitalist industrialisation is evident in development of the US 'agro-industrial complex.'[104] Unlike Britain, cotton-textile and shoe- and boot-production were not central to the US industrial revolution. Instead, industries producing farm-machinery, tools and supplies, and processing agricultural raw materials (meat-packing, leather-tanning, canning, flour-milling, baking, etc.) were the axis of US-industrialisation in the mid-nineteenth century.

From merchant- to industrial capital

The transformation of Northern agriculture – the subordination of rural household-production to the discipline of competitive markets – and the subsequent formation of a home-market for industrial capital also brought about a radical alteration in the structure of the US-economy as a whole. Before

---

[104] Headlee 1991, pp. 28–38; Post 1983, pp. 121–6; Pudup 1983.

the crisis of 1837–42, the dominance of non-capitalist forms of social production in all regions of the US – plantation-slavery in the South, independent household-production in the North – made the activities of merchant-capital the main stimulus to commodity-production and circulation. Northern and Southern merchants and bankers financed slave-based cotton-cultivation and organised the sale of raw cotton to textile-manufacturers in New England and Great Britain.[105] Small and medium-merchants across the North gathered up agricultural surpluses for shipment, directly from the north-east and through New Orleans from the north-west, to the eastern urban centres.[106] Land-speculators purchased land from the federal government at public auction and resold to family-farmers in the North and planters in the South.[107]

The dominance of merchant-capital in the US prior to the 1840s was rooted in the non-capitalist character of commodity-production and the resulting shallow social division of labour.[108] The dominance of merchant-capital requires no specific social-property relations, only the production and circulation of commodities. As a result, the geographical expansion of plantation-slavery was a *spur* to the growth of commodity-circulation in the US before the mid-1840s.[109] Growing exports of slave-produced cotton to Britain allowed Northern merchants to accumulate capital directly from the cotton-trade, and to import British capital. The accumulated merchant-capital fuelled the continued geographical expansion of commodity-production in the US through the 1830s, as merchants financed the purchase of land and slaves in the South and provided capital for land and transport-infrastructure speculation in the North.[110]

The fruit of land-speculation in the north-west was the completion of the subordination of rural household-producers to 'market-discipline' in the 1840s and 1850s. The dominance of agrarian petty-commodity production in the North created a home-market for industrial capital – *qualitatively transforming the US-economy as a whole*. Put another way, the *unintended consequence* of the merchants' pursuit of their own, *non-capitalist* strategy for reproduction – buying land cheap and selling it dear – created the condition for the devel-

---

[105] Foner 1941, Chapters 1–2; Woodman 1968, pp. 30–50.
[106] Clark 1966, Chapters 1–2; Fishlow 1965b.
[107] Opie 1991, Chapters 4–5.
[108] Marx 1981, Chapter 20.
[109] Fox-Genovese and Genovese 1983, pp. 3–25.
[110] North 1956; 1960, Chapter 7.

opment of industrial capitalism in the US. After c.1837–42, the activities of manufacturers and commercial family-farmers became the main stimulus of commodity-production and circulation. The geographical expansion of agrarian petty-commodity production encouraged the growth of capitalist manufacturing of capital and consumer-goods, while the growth of manufacturing and cities induced further rural specialisation, innovation and accumulation. These new social-property relations not only stimulated increased investment in railroads, but transformed the role of Northern rural merchants. Large, specialised grain- and livestock-merchants located in the growing rail-, river- and lake-cities of the Ohio Valley and Great Plains displaced local merchant shop-keepers who had gathered up marketable surpluses and often prepared them for shipping (milling, meat-packing). The new western grain- and livestock-merchants often became agents of manufacturing capitalists in flour-milling and meat-packing during the 1840s and 1850s.[111]

The transformation of Northern social-property relations deepened the social division of labour and led to the subordination of merchant- to industrial capital. After the crisis of 1837–42, Northern merchants increasingly became agents of manufacturing capitalists and manufacturers became financially independent of the merchants, with banks becoming the main source of credit for both manufacturers and farmers.[112] While the merchant-capitalist's condition of existence was the exchange of commodities independently of social-property relations, the dominance of industrial capital required *capitalist* or *petty-commodity* social-property relations. Thus, as industrial capital became the dominant form of capital in the 1840s and 1850s, the geographical expansion of plantation-slavery became an *obstacle* to the development of capitalism in the US.

The social origins of the sectional crisis

The roots of the catastrophic political crisis that culminated in the US Civil War are found in the conflict between the social and political conditions of the continued development of capitalist manufacturing and plantation-slavery after 1840. The development of capitalism in the US rested on *the continuous*

---

[111] Clark 1966, Chapter 3–7, 10–13.
[112] Livesay and Porter 1971.

expansion of agrarian petty-commodity production – household-production subject to 'market-coercion' that compelled producers to specialise, innovate and accumulate, providing a mass home-market for industrial capitalist production. The expansion of plantation-slavery – *the necessary form of the expanded reproduction of this form of social labour* – was incompatible with the development of petty-commodity and capitalist production in the regions where it was dominant. In sum, the social and economic contradictions between the development of capitalism and slavery after 1840 produced the growing radicalisation of Northern and Southern public opinion, the marginalisation of the advocates of sectional compromise and the collapse of the nationally organised Whig and Democratic Parties.[113]

As we have seen, the structure of the master-slave social-property relation was inimical to the growth of industry in the South. On the one hand, the slaves' status as 'means of production in human form' made it difficult for masters' to expel labour in order to introduce labour-saving tools and machinery, limiting the market for industrially produced capital-goods. On the other, the masters' need to continuously employ their slaves encouraged plantation self-sufficiency in food and clothing, limiting the market for industrially produced consumer-goods. Nor was the dominance of plantation-slavery compatible with the development of commercial family-farming – agrarian petty-commodity production. The planters were able to use their superior financial resources to appropriate the most fertile and best located lands, leaving only the hill-regions and pine-barrens available at no or low cost to non-slave-owning white family-farmers. As land-owners, the planters

---

[113] While Ashworth characterises plantation-slavery as a 'mode of production', we follow Ellen Meiksins Wood 1988, Chapter 1, in viewing slavery as a form of social labour whose 'logic of process' differs depending on the social forms in which it was embedded. While we are agnostic on the *historical* debate between Wood 1988, Chapter 2 and de Ste. Croix 1981, Part III, over whether slavery was the dominant form of social labour in the ancient Greek city-states, it is clear that the historical dynamics of ancient and modern slavery were different. One could argue that slave-owning planters in the Caribbean and southern colonies responded *more directly* to market-imperatives emanating from capitalist Britain than the independent household-producers in the northern British colonies. Clearly, the slave-plantation economies responded to these market-imperatives in a *non-capitalist* manner. However, their subordination to a capitalist world-market clearly marked these societies. In sum, we identify a *specific historical contradiction* between the social conditions of the expanded reproduction of plantation-slavery and capitalism *in the US in the mid-nineteenth century*, rather than a timeless, structural antagonism between slave- and capitalist modes of production. We thank Ellen Wood, whose comments on an earlier draft of this essay brought this issue to our attention.

sought to maintain low land-taxes in the South. As a result, Southern family-farmers were under no compulsion to specialise output, technically innovate or accumulate. Put simply, the geographical expansion of plantation-slavery would have prevented the development of agrarian petty-commodity production in the western territories, retarding the development of capitalism in the United States.

To be clear, this argument does not imply either 'that northern capitalism had...come to a grinding halt in 1860, immobilised by the existence of southern slavery'[114] or that the continued existence of plantation-slavery *where it existed* in 1861 would have led to a crisis of Northern capitalism.[115] Our thesis is that the *continued* development of capitalism and slavery were incompatible after 1840. On the one hand, the continued development of slavery *required* geographical expansion into new territories – a geographical expansion that knew no 'natural limits'. On the other, US-capitalism's expanded reproduction *required* the geographical expansion of petty-commodity social-property relations in agriculture. Put directly, the social-property relations of plantation-slavery and agrarian petty-commodity production *could not coexist*. One or the other set of social-property relations had to dominate the geographical expansion of agricultural production in the US after 1840, making the question of the social character of geographical expansion an explosive and irresolvable issue on the political terrain in the 1840s and 1850s.

Mercantile hegemony and the second party-system, c. 1828–44

If we view the economy as a matrix of social relations – between people and between people and nature – then:

> The historical development of the relations of production and exchange formed a field of constraint and possibility within which political interests and action took shape. It permitted a wide range of perception, motive, and choice and a sphere of action that is properly political. Political action and ideology were neither simply contingent nor the expression of idealised 'material interests' but resulted from the active response of historical actors to these complex and evolving processes.[116]

---

[114] Ashworth 2007, p. 647.
[115] Ashworth (2007, p. 647, n. 36) mistakenly attributes these arguments to us.
[116] Tomich 1990, p. 286.

Before the 1840s, merchant-capital's dominance in the US social formation made possible the specific alliances of class-forces organised in the
Democratic and National-Republican/Whig Parties and the marginalisation
of national debate on slavery-expansion. The resulting political hegemony of
the merchant-class permitted them to impose their structural *indifference* to
the social relations of commodity-production on national politics, suppressing any debate on the potentially disruptive question of slavery's existence
and expansion after the Missouri crisis.

The Jacksonian Democrats included within their alliance not only the Northern independent household-producers and Southern small and medium-
planters, but Northern land-speculators.[117] The speculators' disinterest in
whether family-farmers or slave-owning planters purchased land and produced
commodities melded well with the Jacksonian world-view which erased the
class-distinctions among 'agrarians'. Politically, states' rights, the abolition of
the Bank of the US,[118] low land-prices (but not the abolition of the sale of public
lands) and opposition to protective tariffs united the Democratic alliance. The
Democrats' opposition to federal-government regulation (banks and corporations, state-rights) and embrace of geographical expansion made 'freedom'
the continual duplication of a 'timeless present' without 'customary restraints'
across space. Such a world-view captured the lived experience of *extensive
growth* of the various non-capitalist social groups – land-speculators, middling
planters and subsistence-farmers – that made up the Democratic coalition.[119]

The National-Republican and Whig Parties brought together a political
alliance of manufacturers, urban artisans, commercial farmers, and large
cotton-, tobacco- and hemp-planters under the leadership of Northern and
Southern merchants and bankers. The Whig notion that slavery, although
inferior morally and economically to free labour, was one of a number of
diverse interests that needed to be harmonised was quite compatible with

---

[117] Pessen 1978, Chapter 11; Hammond 1957, Chapter 12.

[118] Land-speculators and subsistence-farmers had very different goals in their struggle to abolish central banking in the US in the 1820s and 1830s. Like the Democratic
planters, the subsistence-farmers believed that the destruction of the Bank of the
United States would be the first step toward the end of all banks, paper-money and
the scourge of land- and commodity-speculation. The land-speculators, however,
wanted to end central banking restrictions on state-banks in order to increase the
money-supply and promote the inflation of land and commodity-prices.

[119] Wilson 1967.

the merchants' *indifference* to the social relations of commodity-production in the antebellum-US. The 'American System', which called for an interventionist state to establish a new central bank, levy protective tariffs and raise land-prices to ensure that only rural households with capital engaged in agriculture, spoke to the demands of the diverse social groups enmeshed in commodity-production.[120] The Whigs' world-view envisioned the encouragement and deepening of freedom over time, in which the 'federal government...was a corporate instrument for realising a larger positive good. Qualitative change through time rather than quantitative growth across space marked the true destiny of a nation of freemen.'[121] Just as the Democratic vision of a spatial expansion of timeless freedom captured the planters, subsistence-farmers and speculators' experience of *extensive growth*, the Whig vision of a qualitative deepening of freedom over time corresponded to the merchants, manufacturers and commercial farmers' experience of *intensive growth*.

First schisms in second party-system: 1841 Pre-Emption Debate

The stability of the Whig and Democratic Parties depended on the economic and political hegemony of merchant-capital in the US. The indifference of *all* merchants to the social relations of commodity-production allowed different groups of merchant-capitalists to cement alliances with different segments of the slave-owning class in each party, preventing any debate over the existence and expansion of slavery in the federal government. The changed field of constraint and possibility that emerged with the dominance of industrial capital after 1840 undermined the ability of merchants in the Democratic and Whig Parties to impose lasting compromises concerning the social character of the geographical expansion of commodity-production on their respective social allies. Instead, *the incompatibility of the expansion of slavery and petty-commodity and capitalist production* radicalised the political demands of Northern manufacturers and farmers, and induced the planters to make increasingly militant demands in defence of the existence and expansion of their form of social labour.

---

[120] Van Dusen 1958, 1973; Sellers 1969.
[121] Wilson 1967, p. 624.

The first fissures in the second party-system emerged during the debate on public-land policy, rather than slavery-expansion. The Democrats had traditionally advocated the rapid geographical expansion of both plantation-slavery and independent household-production through lower minimum-prices for public land. The Whigs, as advocates of the 'planned colonisation' of the west by 'improving farmers' generally advocated higher minimum-prices for western lands. By the early 1830s, western farmers began to demand a general and permanent 'pre-emption' – the right of those settlers who had occupied public land to buy their land at federal minimum-prices outside of the public-auction system. Democrats had generally been favourable to limited pre-emption laws, but opposed a permanent law which would have effectively abolished the auction-system which nurtured land-speculation. The Whigs tended to oppose the sale of land to 'squatters' below market-prices before the crisis of 1837, and, instead, advocated the distribution of public land-sale revenues to the state-governments to finance transport-infra-structure projects.[122]

The crisis and depression of the late 1830s and early 1840s fed renewed agitation among western farmers, now subject to 'market-coercion', for a general and permanent pre-emption law.[123] The Whigs' victory in the Presidential election of 1840 and their capture of a majority north-western House- and Senate-seats, set the stage for the Congressional debate on land-policy in the summer of 1841.[124] The northern Whigs reversed their opposition to pre-emption, introducing a bill that combined pre-emption and distribution. In the debate, northern Whigs no longer argued against 'anarchic' and 'unplanned' settlement in the west, but praised the geographical expansion of commercial household-production for stimulating both agriculture and industry.[125] They met opposition not only from southern Democrats and a minority of northern Democrats who opposed distribution, but from a number of prominent south-ern Whigs. While most of the opposition to distribution centred on concerns that Congress would have to increase tariffs to compensate for distribution,

---

[122] Hibbard 1924, pp. 56–115; Robbins 1976, pp. 3–50.
[123] US Congress 1837, S. doc. 248, 25th Cong., 2d Sess.; H. doc. 178, 25th Cong., 2d Sess.
[124] Robbins 1976, pp. 80–91; Stephenson 1917, pp. 44–65. US Congress 1841, pp. 10–12 for a listing of the party-affiliations of various House- and Senate-delegations.
[125] See for example, US Congress 1841, p. 10: 443.

a number of prominent southern Whigs and Democrats attacked distribution as a violation of states' rights, an 'unconstitutional' centralisation of power and a danger to the region's 'peculiar institution'.[126]

The House vote of 6 July 1841 on the combined pre-emption- and distribution-bill clearly indicates a sharp *sectional* division on public land-policy.[127] All the Northern Whigs, whether from the manufacturing east or agricultural west, voted in favour of the bill. By contrast, the majority of southern representatives, Whig and Democratic, opposed the legislation. Only nine of sixteen Upper-South Whigs supported the bill, while fourteen of sixteen Lower-South Whigs voted against. In sum, the alignment around the Pre-Emption Act of 1841 *prefigures* the *sectional polarisation* of the later 1840s and 1850s. The political spokespersons of manufacturers and farmers stood together to promote the spread of capitalist and petty-commodity production. Opposed to them were the relatively unified representatives of the planters who perceived a threat to the master-slave social-property relation from the use of federal funds to build transport-infrastructure. Similar divisions, focusing on the southern Democrats continued opposition to federally-financed transport-infrastructure projects sought by Northern farmers, increased tensions within the Democratic Party in the early 1840s.[128] The root of these tensions was the same – the completion of the transformation of Northern farmers into petty-commodity producers, which altered the attitude of many eastern Whigs toward the expansion of family-farming; and the growing incompatibility of the expansion of slavery and capitalism, which fuelled planters' fears of a centralised federal government.

---

[126] See for example, US Congress 1841, p. 10: 400.

[127] US Congress 1841, p. 10: 156. House-votes generally give a better indication of the alignment of different social groups on key policy-issues because representation in the lower chamber was based on population. This was especially true in this case because the Senate-bill contained an amendment ending distribution of land-revenues to the states if the tariff had to be raised – a provision making it more palatable to southern Democrats. US Congress 1841, pp. 10: 364–70.

[128] Foner 1969.

Class-conflict over the social character of the geographical expansion of commodity-production, c.1844–61[129]

The sharpening political conflicts and ideological polarisation of the 1840s and 1850s, so well described by Ashworth, were rooted in the incompatibility of the expansion of social-property relations of plantation-slavery on the one hand, and agrarian petty-commodity production and capitalist manufacture on the other. The growing radicalisation of Northern public opinion in the late 1840s and 1850s, manifested in the defections of Whig and Democratic farmers, manufacturers, artisans and urban professionals to the Free Soil and Republican Parties,[130] was not simply a product of their idealisation of the Northern free-labour society, or a response to the perceived threat of the slave-power. While the threat of the slave-power and free-labour ideology canalised Northern opposition to slavery-expansion, the increasingly militant refusal of the Republican majority of the Northern society to countenance any further expansion of plantation-slavery *corresponded to the social position* of manufacturers and commercial farmers in the North. Beckert argues that manufacturers in New York and other parts of the North understood that 'the westward expansion of slavery was a threat both to their own well being and to the Republic':

> American industry had experienced rapid growth, and railroads, together with increased immigration, had helped settle the West, resulting in an expansion of prairie agriculture based on free labor. The advent of new economic structures facilitated the emergence of new segments of the economic elite, who based their businesses not on the export of agricultural commodities produced by slave labor but instead on domestic industrialisation, import substitution, and the export of agricultural commodities (especially wheat) grown by free farmers.... Free labor needed free soil, a political programme that brought these businessmen into increasing conflict with an expansionist South and into coalition with other social groups in the North.[131]

Put simply, the continued development of the manufacturers' form of social labour after c.1837–42 *required* the containment of slavery to the areas it was

---

[129] The following is a summary of the much more detailed argument in Post 1983, Part III.

[130] Beckert 1993, pp. 89–97; Blue 1973; Foner 1970.

[131] Beckert 1993, pp. 89–90.

already dominant. Any further expansion of slavery would have undermined the spread of agrarian petty-commodity production, and with it, capitalist industry. The reproduction of the class-position of the manufacturers and farmers made Republicans commitment to 'free soil' *necessary*. Whatever illusions the Republicans had about the strength of southern Unionism during the secession-crisis of 1860–1, their refusal to countenance any expansion of plantation-slavery into the western territories was a *rational* expression of their social position.

Similarly, the increasing radicalism of the planters organised in the Democratic Party was not simply a defensive reaction to the slaves' resistance to bondage, the planters' inability to ideologically defend their form of social labour, or concerns about the political loyalty of non-slave-owning white farmers.[132] Instead, the radical planters' refusal to countenance any restriction on the expansion of slavery, their advocacy of US-expansion into the Caribbean and Central America, and their championing of the demand for a Congressional slave-code for the western territories flowed from the *social requirements* of the reproduction of their form of social labour. Geographical expansion – the addition of more slaves and more fertile land – was the *most rational and efficient* way to increase output and raise productivity under plantation-slavery. Because small and medium-planters had little land in reserve and were often the first to seek new and more fertile lands for their operations, it is not surprising that they were in the vanguard of Southern radicalism.[133] However, even larger planters, with large 'private frontiers' of uncultivated land, would not accept any limits on the spatial extension of their form of social labour.[134] Just as the future development of capitalism in the North required reserving the western territories for petty-commodity and capitalist producers, the future of plantation-slavery depended upon securing, either within the US-state or in an independent state of their own, the legal-political conditions for the spread of slavery to new territories. According to Schoen:

---

[132] Barney 1972.

[133] Gates 1960, pp. 142–4; Genovese 1967, Chapter 4.

[134] Contrary to Ashworth's claim (1995, p. 491) that the large planters' commitment to Whig ideology militated against their embracing southern radicalism, it was their large reserves of uncultivated land that made them relatively inured to the need for geographical expansion in the short term.

Some voices in the Lower South, particularly in South Carolina and former Whig circles, believed slavery's expansion a chimera perpetuated by opportunistic Democrats. Diverse reasons led many more to the conclusion that southern society and regional interest actually depended on...more land suitable for slavery. Simple political arithmetic suggested a contained Slave South might not survive an expanding free soil American empire. Amateur demographers, especially in the black belt, argued that without a vent for rapidly reproducing slave-population in the region would soon be on the brink of racial warfare. Proud men, and not a few women, believed on principle that taking their property anywhere in federal territories remained a natural right, the relinquishing of which would make them second-class citizens. Others just wanted to prop up their proslavery belief that race-based slavery could adapt to all climates and businesses. To this traditional list must be added slaveholders' desire, largely economic in origin, to ensure that their progeny would have the cheap land, labor supply, and access to commercial opportunities necessary to fulfil the Lower South's version of the American dream.[135]

The changing matrix of social relations of production and exchange, the subordination of merchant- to industrial capital, also doomed the force of sectional compromise – the Democratic land-speculators and the Whig merchants and large planters – to irrelevance in the political crisis of the 1840s and 1850s. The northern Democrats' world-view, which collapsed family-farming and plantation-slavery into an undifferentiated 'agrarian' interest and their embrace of 'states' rights' and white male democracy were not the main reasons they embraced 'popular sovereignty' and reduced the choice of class-relations in new territories to a matter of soil and climate determined relative profitability. Nor was the conservative Whigs' (and later Americans and Constitutional Unionists) belief that the role of statesmen was to balance the diverse interests in society the main reason they strenuously argued that slavery was not a concern of the federal government. These political and ideological stances were the 'road map of the lived experience' of merchant-capital's *structural indifference* to the social relations of commodity-production. The inability of either the northern Democrats or the Conservative Whigs to

---

[135] Schoen 2009, pp. 212–13.

impose enduring compromises on the question of slavery-expansion after 1850[136] was the unavoidable consequence of the subordination of merchant- to industrial capital in the US-economy, which made the expansion of slavery and capitalism irreconcilable.

The US Civil War: a bourgeois revolution?

While the changing structure of the social relations of production and exchanged created the class-conflicts that ultimately led to the disruption of the unity of the US-state and the Civil War, neither the outcome of the military conflict nor the social relations that would emerge after the War were predetermined. Instead, they were determined by the *unpredictable* and *historically contingent* outcome of class-conflict. For Ashworth, slavery's weaknesses – 'the comparative lack of manufacturing and the heavy reliance on a single crop, the weak financial infrastructure, and the inferior transport network together inflicted immense damage upon the Confederate war effort and played a key role in bringing about Union victory'.[137] He clearly recognises that the North's economic superiority did not *guarantee* military victory. Of equal importance was the sharpening of class-conflict *within the South* during the War – between planters and non-slave-owning farmers who bore the financial and military brunt of the War, and most importantly between masters and slaves. The growing refusal of slaveless whites to continue fighting in the Confederate army gravely weakened the Southern war-effort. The mass-flight of slaves from the plantations as the Union-army advanced dealt a death blow to the Confederacy after 1863.

Ashworth's explanation of Lincoln and the Republican's decision to issue the Emancipation Proclamation, which encouraged an even larger exodus of slaves from their masters' control, and to recruit former slaves as labourers, spies, and eventually soldiers, which helped turn the tide of the War, is also flawed. Ashworth recognises that military considerations were one determinant of Lincoln's decision to abolish slavery in Confederate-controlled territories. However, he argues:

---

[136] Becker 1993, pp. 78–93, Chapter 3; Foner 1941, Nichols 1948.
[137] Ashworth 2007, pp. 632–3.

To a lesser extent, it was a reflection of the concern held by some Republicans, including Lincoln himself, for the welfare of the African Americans held in bondage. Above all, however, it was a recognition that the struggle upon which the North had now embarked was so profound, the sacrifices made by ordinary northerners already so vast, that to restore slavery when the War was won, would be a palpable absurdity....Slavery had now brought about a Civil War, the ultimate form of national disorganisation and for this reason it had to be ended.[138]

It is indisputable that the radical wing of the Republican Party, which enjoyed the support of most Northern manufacturers[139] and whose strength was growing during the War, began to agitate for the abolition of slavery soon after the beginnings of hostilities. Both military considerations and radical anti-slavery and racially-egalitarian ideas motivated the radicals. However, it is unclear whether the majority of Northern public opinion supported emancipation before 1863. Even more importantly, there was no guarantee that Lincoln and the majority of the moderate and conservative Republicans would have ever abandoned their initial war-aims of restoring of the antebellum *status quo, if the struggle of the slaves' themselves had not compelled them.* Put simply, it was the combination of the military necessity of disrupting the Southern economy, the slaves' seizure of the opportunity to bid for freedom presented by changed relationship of forces during the War,[140] and growing discontent with declining living standards and a class-biased draft among Northern workers that forced the Lincoln-administration to abandon its original war-aims, issue the Emancipation Proclamation and recruit approximately 185,000 former slaves into the Union-army.[141]

Ashworth concludes that the US Civil War was a bourgeois revolution because it made 'the ideology of the victorious North, with its reconciliation of

---

[138] Ashworth 2007, p. 638.

[139] Beckert 1993, Chapter 4; Montgomery 1967, pp. 72–89.

[140] Genovese (1979, pp. 15–18) argues that, unlike in some Caribbean islands, white slave-owners and non-slave-owners outnumbered slaves in most of the US-South, creating an unfavourable relationship of forces for open, large-scale slave-revolts in the region. The Union-army's incursions into the South during the Civil War changes this relationship of forces and makes possible the 'general strike' of the slaves – the mass-flight from the plantations.

[141] DuBois 1969, Chapters 4–5; Foner 1988, Chapter 1.

democracy and capitalism...the ideology of Americanism'.[142] His privileging of the removal of ideological obstacles to the dominance of capitalism is based on a rejection of our thesis that the continued geographical expansion of slavery was an impediment to the continued development of capitalism in the US. From our point of view,[143] the US Civil War removed the single most important hindrance to the expansion of capitalism – the territorial extension of plantation-slavery to the western territories. Although the class-struggles during the Reconstruction-period did not result in the emergence of either capitalist plantation-agriculture or a class of African-American petty-commodity producers; the non-capitalist form that replaced slavery – share-cropping – did not share slavery's spatially imperialist tendencies. While share-cropping condemned the South to continued economic underdevelopment,[144] it did not pose an obstacle to capitalist expansion in the rest of the US.

What then is the theoretical and historical status of the notion of the bourgeois revolution? As both Wood and Brenner have argued, the notion of the bourgeois revolution is rooted in the early Marx's vision of the transition to capitalism.[145] Marx's original analysis (which he abandoned in his mature writings of the 1850s and 1860s), drew on Adam Smith's vision of the development of 'commercial society'. In *The German Ideology* and *The Communist Manifesto*, Marx argued that capitalism began in the medieval cities with the activities of merchants and artisans. The growing cities provided both a haven for peasants escaping serfdom and a market for agricultural goods. The growth of markets encouraged peasants to specialise output, innovate technologically and accumulate land and tools. Precapitalist propertied classes' hold on political power maintained old and created new impediments (legal coercion of direct producers, state-taxation and monopolies, etc.) to the deepening of markets. The bourgeoisie, the ascending class in production, leads its revolution and destroys these precapitalist remnants, allowing the free development of their new mode of production.

We have already discussed the theoretical and historical criticism of this 'Smithian' vision of the transition to capitalism – that the growth of market-'opportunities' are not sufficient to disrupt the 'rules of reproduction' of

---

[142] Ashworth 2007, p. 647.
[143] See pp. 32–5 below.
[144] Ransom and Sutch 1977.
[145] Brenner 1989; Wood 1995, Chapter 4.

non-capitalist social-property relations. Instead, the *unintended consequences* of non-capitalist social classes pursuing the reproduction of their forms of social labour in very specific conditions of crisis and sharpened class-conflict potentially lead to the emergence of capitalist social-property relations.[146] As Brenner points out, the notion of the 'bourgeois revolution' rooted in the commercialisation-model actually 'renders revolution unnecessary in a double sense':

> First, there really is no *transition* to accomplish: since the model starts with bourgeois society in the towns, foresees its evolution as taking place via bourgeois mechanisms, and has feudalism transcend itself in consequence of its exposure to trade, the problem of how one society is transformed into another is simply assumed away and never posed. Second, since bourgeois society self-develops and dissolves feudalism, the bourgeois revolution can hardly claim a necessary role.[147]

The critique of the 'neo-Smithian' analysis of the origins of capitalism has led to a re-evaluation of the notion of the bourgeois revolution. Brenner has developed a new social interpretation of the English Revolution of the seventeenth century.[148] English agriculture was capitalist a full century before the Revolution of the 1640s and 1650s. The class-conflict between English landlords and peasants took a very different trajectory from the conflict in western Europe. Like the peasants in Western Europe, English peasants were able to gain their legal freedom in the fifteenth century. However, the English landlords, alone in Europe, were able to impose commercial leases on their tenants in the sixteenth century, thereby making the latter's continued possession of landed property dependent upon successful market-competition. The revolution of the seventeenth century did not pit capitalists landlords and farmers against precapitalist aristocrats, but a new merchant-class enmeshed in the English capitalist economy leading an already capitalist landlord- and farmer-class against the monarchy and merchants who depend upon royal monopolies.[149]

---

[146] Brenner 2007.

[147] Brenner 1989, p. 280.

[148] Brenner 1993.

[149] Comninel's 1987 analysis of the French Revolution of the eighteenth century concludes that the 'bourgeoisie' that led this revolution was in no sense a capitalist class. French agriculture remained thoroughly non-capitalist and most of the urban merchants and professionals remained dependent on the French absolutist state.

Ashworth's analysis of the US Civil War as a 'bourgeois revolution' suffers from the same theoretical problems as the classical schema. Ashworth denies any material, economic contradiction between the expansion of slavery and capitalism in the mid-nineteenth-century US. The Civil War was the product of sharpening political and ideological conflicts – no material obstacles existed to capital's triumph. No arguments are offered to demonstrate how the politics and ideology of slavery was a substantial impediment to the development of capitalism. The Civil War – like other 'bourgeois revolutions' – was unnecessary to the triumph of an already extant and robust capitalist mode of production.

By contrast, our analysis of the social origins of the US Civil War indicates that it, almost alone among the 'bourgeois revolutions' identified by the historical-materialist tradition, actually fits the classical schema. The geographical spread of a non-capitalist form of social labour, plantation-slavery, constituted an obstacle to the future expansion of a vibrant capitalism. Capitalist manufacturers and commercial family-farmers, organised in the Republican Party, take the lead in organising the political and military struggle to remove the impediment posed by slavery and its expansion. The classical schema, however, remains highly problematic. The origins of capitalist social-property relations in the US – the subordination of Northern-rural household-producers to 'market-coercion' in the late eighteenth century – was the *unintended consequence* of the class-conflicts that followed the American Revolution of 1776–83.[150]

The first American Revolution, at best, fits a *minimal definition*[151] of the bourgeois revolution – a revolution that creates state-institutions capable of promoting the development of capitalist social-property relations. This definition requires no prior development of capitalist social-property relations, no precapitalist obstacles to capitalist development, nor a class-consciousness capitalist class in the lead of the revolution. A revolution is *bourgeois* only to

---

[150] See pp. 184–93 below.
[151] Mooers 1991, pp. 1–4, 33–40. Mooers effectively uses this 'minimal' definition to argue that the English Revolution of the seventeenth century and German unification in the nineteenth century were 'bourgeois revolutions' – revolutions that created states the advanced capitalist development. However, his analysis of the outcomes of the French Revolution of 1789–94, the Napoleonic Empire and the Revolution of 1848 indicates the preservation of precapitalist state-structures, in particular tax-farming. In our opinion, it was the Second Empire (1850–71) that established a viable capitalist state in France.

the extent that it, *intentionally or unintentionally*, advances capitalist development in a given society.

The colonial economy was *non-capitalist*, based in independent household-production in the North and plantation-slavery in the South. The activities of a class of colonial merchants bound together various non-capitalist forms of social labour. As these merchants organised the growing export of Northern surpluses of grain and meat to the South and the Caribbean and of Southern tobacco, rice and indigo to Europe, they laid the basis for an independent non-capitalist economy and a bid for political independence in the 1770s and 1780s. Put simply, the American Revolution was not the struggle of a capitalist class to free themselves and their form of social labour from pre-capitalist restrictions. Rather, it marked the success of precapitalist merchants and agricultural classes to establish an independent state for their increasingly autonomous pre capitalist economy.

Nor did the dominant merchants and land-speculators in the post-revolutionary period seek to free capitalist production from non-capitalist fetters. Instead, the merchants and speculators sought to *promote their position as land- and commodity-traders*. In the 1780s and 1790s, the merchants, with the support of the planters after Shays' Rebellion, constructed state-institutions and a standing army that was capable of enforcing their legal claims to landed property – not in order to establish capitalist production, but to allow themselves to reproduce themselves as buyers and sellers of land. The *unintended consequence* of the speculators' successful struggle to enforce legal titles on land – the creation of the social monopoly of land – was to fundamentally alter the conditions under which Northern households obtained, maintained and expanded landholdings. The result was the disruption of the rules of reproduction of independent household-production and the consolidation of the rules of reproduction of agrarian petty-commodity production and capitalist manufacture. As we have argued, the subordination of Northern farmers to 'market-coercion' through the actions of speculative merchant-capitalists in the first four decades of the nineteenth century established the conditions for the subordination of merchant- to industrial capital and made the further expansion of slavery and capitalism incompatible.

The American Revolution and Civil War can, at best, be viewed as bourgeois revolutions because they established and consolidated state-institutions that helped secure the political and juridical conditions for the development of capitalism in the US. Only the unintended outcomes of a revolution led by a non-capitalist merchant-class – the development of petty-commodity production and capitalist manufacturing in the North and the preservation of plantation-slavery in the South – allowed the US Civil War to assume the form of a 'classic' bourgeois revolution led by a self-conscious class of capitalist manufacturers and commercial farmers struggling to remove the obstacle posed by the geographical expansion of plantation-slavery.

Conclusion

Democracy Against Capitalism in the Post-Civil-War United States

In the late nineteenth and early twentieth centuries, Russian Marxists grappled with what appeared to them a rather unique historical situation. On the one hand, Russia was experiencing rapid capitalist development, creating a large and concentrated urban proletariat. On the other, the Tsarist state remained a feudal-absolutist state and elements of non-capitalist landownership survived in the post-Emancipation Russian countryside. Utilising a concept Marx had appropriated from the Scottish Enlightenment and French materialist historiography to analyse the revolutions of 1848,[1] most Russian Marxists argued that the coming revolution would be a *bourgeois revolution* – a revolution that would overthrow the Tsarist autocracy and create a state that would remove all obstacles to capitalist development.

In their debates on the respective role of capitalists, workers and peasants in this revolution, Russian Marxists spoke of a 'bourgeois-democratic' revolution – a revolution that would simultaneously establish the conditions of the expanded reproduction of capitalism and a democratic form of the capitalist

---

[1] Nygaard 2006.

state.[2] The model of the bourgeois-democratic revolution was the French Revolution of 1789–99, which swept away feudalism and absolutism, established democracy and, purportedly, promoted the development of capitalism.[3] In more recent years, Marxists have viewed the class-struggles during the US Civil War and Reconstruction through the prism of the (albeit 'incomplete') 'bourgeois-democratic revolution' – a revolution that destroyed slavery in the South, made four million African-American ex-slaves citizens and voters, and allowed the continent-wide expansion of capitalist social-property relations.[4]

In recent years, the notion of the bourgeois revolution generally, and the bourgeois-democratic revolution specifically have come under theoretical and historical criticism. Both Robert Brenner and Ellen Meiksins Wood have argued that the notion of the bourgeois revolution – in which an already existing bourgeoisie removes political and economic obstacles to the free development of capitalist production – is rooted in Marx's initial appropriation of Adam Smith's analysis of the origins of 'commercial society'.[5] Both the Smithian vision of the spread of markets inevitably leading to the capitalist dynamic of producers' specialising output, innovating technologically, and accumulating land, tools and labour; and the classical vision of the bourgeois revolution *assume* what they need to explain – the origins of capitalist social-property relations. Historically, George Comninel has demonstrated that the 'classic' bourgeois-democratic revolution – France in the late eighteenth century – actually threw up major obstacles to capitalist development in France.[6] In fact, all the *democratic* advances of the French Revolution – all the manifestations of a substantive popular power in the towns and countryside – led to *anticapitalist policies*: urban price-controls that set maximums on the price of bread and other necessities, and guarantees of peasant-proprietorship regardless of the rural households' ability to compete successfully in the marketplace.

Wood, in her *Democracy Against Capitalism*,[7] provides a more theoretically rigorous and historically insightful framework to analyse the relationship between democratic political forms and capitalist social-property relations.

---

[2] Trotsky 1941 provides a useful summary of the differing uses of the 'bourgeois-democratic' revolution among Russian Marxists.

[3] Soboul 1975 is a good example of this analysis.

[4] Novack 1961; Gaido 2006, Chapter 3.

[5] Brenner 1989; Wood 1995, Chapter 4.

[6] Comninel 1987.

[7] Wood 1995, Chapter 7.

Drawing on her work on ancient Athens, Wood points out that 'democracy' originally referred to *substantive popular power* – 'rule by the *demos*'.[8] In Athens, peasant-citizens' 'political participation – in the assembly, in the courts, and in the street – limited their economic exploitation' through taxation and rent.[9] In contrast, capitalism is the first form of social labour in which the process of exploitation takes place through the operation of the market – the buying and selling of labour-power – rather than the exercise of legal and juridical power. On the one hand, the absence of extra-economic coercion *makes possible* citizenship and suffrage for the direct producers. On the other, capitalism requires that working-class citizenship and voting rights do not 'significantly modify class inequality'.[10] Historically, capitalist republics initially disenfranchised the propertyless. However, the rise of popular and labour-movements made the permanent exclusion of the working class from suffrage impossible.

To reconcile capitalism and democratic forms, capitalists radically transformed the meaning and scope of democracy. Wood points out that it was the US-republic that pioneered the limitation of popular power in a 'democratic' state. Unable to exclude the politically active mass of farmers and artisans from the suffrage after the Revolution:

> The framers of the Constitution embarked on the first experiment in designing a set of political institutions that would both embody and at the same time curtail popular power, in a context where it was no longer possible to maintain an exclusive citizen body. Where the option of an active but exclusive citizenry was unavailable, it would be necessary to create an inclusive but passive citizenship with limited scope for its political powers.[11]

The notion of a 'representative democracy' was born, in which popular power was alienated to the 'men of property and intelligence' who would represent the 'people' in the new US-state. As suffrage spread in the nineteenth-century US, first to propertyless white men and later to propertyless black men, the concept of democracy was transformed again, into *liberal democracy*:

---

[8] Wood 1988.
[9] Wood 1995, p. 212.
[10] Wood 1995, p. 213.
[11] Wood 1995, p. 214.

The effect was to shift the focus of 'democracy' away from the active exercise of popular power to the passive enjoyment of constitutional and procedural safeguards and rights, and away from the collective power of subordinate classes to the privacy and isolation of the individual citizen. More and more, the concept of 'democracy' came to be identified with *liberalism*.[12]

The era of Reconstruction in the United States was the crucible of the birth of liberal democracy as both capitalist world-view and restructured political institutions. The tumultuous class-conflicts of this era – between capitalist manufacturers and workers in the North, and landowning planters and their ex-slaves in the South – reshaped the theory and practice of democracy in the United States. In these class-struggles, every advance of the substantive democratic power of workers or former slaves challenged capitalist dominance. The stabilisation and establishment of capitalist social-property relations required the *radical restriction of democracy*, in the form of liberalism in the North, and legal racial segregation, disenfranchisement and racial terror in the South.[13]

I. Democracy against capitalism in the North: radicalism, class-struggle and the rise of liberal democracy, 1863–77

The Civil War produced a profound radicalisation in the United States. At the beginning of the War, the Radical Republicans – a small minority of the party based among successful commercial farmers and small-town professionals[14] – alone advocated a revolutionary war which would abolish chattel-slavery in the South. The dominant moderate Republicans, with their close ties to the Northern manufacturers,[15] sought to pursue a 'limited war' in 1861 and early 1862. They were convinced that the 'southern rebellion' was a minoritarian conspiracy of the planters and that a 'unionist majority' of slave-less white farmers would quickly rally to the Union after a series of limited military incursions into the South. As a result, the Lincoln-administration initially relied on a mostly volunteer, relatively poorly trained, equipped

---

[12] Wood 1995, p. 227.
[13] Blackburn 2010, while focusing on the postbellum labour-movement's trajectory, puts forward a similar analysis to ours.
[14] Foner 1970, Chapter 4.
[15] Beckert 1993, Chapters 3–4.

and organised army to defeat the Confederacy without overthrowing the Southern state-governments or undermining plantation-slavery. Military set-backs in 1861 and early 1862 forced the moderate Republicans to shift their strategy to 'total war' – the mobilisation of Northern productive resources for the war-effort, mass military conscription and large-scale incursions into the South that undermined the social foundations of the Southern plantation-economy.[16]

Military imperatives alone did not propel this change of strategy – the slaves' struggles forced the Lincoln-administration to radicalise its war-aims.[17] Even during the period of 'limited war' in 1861–2, thousands of slaves took advantage of the presence of federal troops to flee their masters' plantations and join the invading armies. While the Lincoln-administration initially ordered federal commanders to return runaway-slaves to their masters, the numbers of slaves fleeing the plantations and seeking refuge with Union-troops led to a sharp shift of policy, culminating in the 'Emancipation Proclamation' that declared all slaves in Confederate-controlled territories free as of 1 January 1863. The Proclamation and Union-victories unleashed a massive flight of slaves from the plantations, a veritable 'general strike' that involved 500,000 slaves and paralysed the Southern economy. After the July 1863 New York city-riots against the class-biased federal draft, Lincoln overcame his hesitation to arm runaway-slaves and enlisted 180,000 African Americans in the Union-army, albeit in segregated units under white commanders.

The War necessitated a radical *centralisation* of the US-state.[18] Before the War, issues of taxation, banking policy, and the legal status of labourers were left to state-governments. Federal protective tariffs and national taxes on consumption and income provided the revenues necessary to finance, and a national draft provided the manpower required to raise and equip huge armies capable of waging 'total war'. For the first time in US-history, the federal government produced a national paper-currency – the 'greenbacks'. The War ended with the ratification of the Thirteenth Amendment to the Constitution, which made legal-juridical freedom the *national* legal frame-work for labour. The destruction of slavery through the self-activity and

---

[16] Barney 1975, Chapters 1–3; McPherson 1988, Chapters 10–27.
[17] DuBois 1969, Chapters 4–5; Foner 1988, pp. 1–11.
[18] Foner 1988, pp. 1–18, 18–24; Montgomery 1967, pp. 45–8.

self-organisation of the slaves also *radicalised* Northern public opinion. Before the War, most Northern whites, including most radical opponents of slavery and its expansion, viewed African Americans as weak, cowardly and incapable of asserting their independent 'manhood' under slavery. African Americans' military service, however:

> helped transform the nation's treatment of blacks and blacks' conception of themselves....For the first time in American history, large numbers of blacks were treated as equals before the law – if only military law...military service has often been a politicising and radicalising experience....Union soldiers...debated among themselves the issues of war and emancipation. As the army penetrated the heart of the Deep South and encountered the full reality of plantation slavery, soldiers became imbued with abolition sentiment...[19]

At the centre of this radicalisation were the Radical Republicans – the most consistent defenders of the Northern 'free-labour' system. In the North, the Radicals sought to preserve and expand a social order based in small-scale manufacturing employing skilled labour and market-driven household-based agricultural production. While a minority of Radicals joined Conservative merchants and bankers in opposing inflationary paper-money and the protective tariff, the majority believed the tariff and 'greenback'-currency would allow US manufacturing to pay high wages, avoid the type of mechanisation that would reduce skilled workers to 'mere operatives', and allow 'thrifty and sober workmen' to become self-employed.[20] In the South, the Radicals were united in support of measures that guaranteed the mass of African-American freedmen 'full self-ownership', in particular federally-protected citizenship- and voting rights. Only a minority considered the possibility of confiscating the lands of the former planters and distributing them to the freedpeople. However, all Radicals believed that black plantation-workers in a truly free labour-market – one free of any legal and juridical coercion of the workers – would be able to earn wages that would allow them to save and become independent farmers or artisans.[21]

---

[19] Foner 1988, pp. 8–9.
[20] Montgomery 1967, pp. 81–9.
[21] Foner 1988, pp. 62–8, 174–8.

The instrument of this radical transformation of social relations was the centralised and democratised national state. The Radicals had led the war-time revolution that consolidated the nation-state 'while identifying that state, via emancipation, with the interests of humanity in general'.[22] Militant nationalists and utilitarians, the Radicals embraced a vision of *substantive* democracy as popular power unrestrained except for the wishes of the majority:

> ...neither the vested rights of states nor the vested rights of one group of men in the subordination of another was to withstand the 'sovereignty of the people...the powers of popular government were and should have been unlimited...it was ridiculous to circumscribe the power of democratic government in the name of safeguarding liberties....As the people were sovereign...so the good of the people was the only criterion by which the activity of the state could be measured.[23]

The Radicals drew support from a wide variety of social forces in the post-war North. Native-born Protestant skilled workers, urban professionals and the prosperous family-farmers of the upper Midwest all gravitated to the Radicals' vision of a 'free-labour' society that provided all men with full 'self-ownership', and preserved and expanded the opportunities for all men to rise into the ranks of petty proprietors. However, it was the manufacturers who were at the centre of the Radicals' political alliance:

> While the Radicals expressed this egalitarian ideal in the name of 'the people', they saw the people's needs and desires through the eyes of the vigorous new elite of manufacturers and promoters....Like the entrepreneurs, they envisioned the 'self-made' man as the most trustworthy and proper spokesman for the community as a whole...their disdain for 'the mercantile classes'...the hireling masses at the other end of the social spectrum were equally unfit to lead the nation....Only men of property could possess the free will, the intelligence, and the disposition to be true revolutionaries. But they assumed, of course, that in a 'purified Republic' of equal opportunity, 'merit and conduct' alone would determine who rose to acquire property.[24]

---

[22] Foner 1988, p. 29.
[23] Montgomery 1967, pp. 79–80.
[24] Montgomery 1967, pp. 73–4.

The manufacturers were drawn to Radicalism not simply because most Radicals defended inflationary monetary policy and the protective tariff. The manufacturers embraced the Radicals' vision of a world in which universal freedom, protected by a substantive democracy based on national male citizenship and suffrage, would allow all to rise into the ranks of the self-employed through hard-work and thrift.[25] Such a world-view was a viable 'mental road map of the lived experience'[26] of a class of small capitalists only one generation removed from the ranks of self-employed craftsmen.[27]

'Class-conflict' in the North was 'the submerged shoal on which' the Radicals' vision of a harmonious society of small producers and upwardly-mobile skilled workers 'foundered'.[28] Despite their hopes that tariffs and inflationary paper-money would allow high wages and social mobility to short-circuit the development of a permanent class of wage-earners, the resulting development of capitalist manufacturing deepened class-divisions in the North. While the typical manufacturing firm employed an average of 8.15 workers in 1869,[29] nearly two thirds of the total working population in 1870 were wage-workers – with 27.4% manufacturing workers.[30] Workers, skilled and unskilled, laboured on the railroads and in mines, mills and factories in small and medium-towns and cities across the Ohio-Valley/Great-Lakes and New-England regions. While divided along lines of skill, ethnicity, race and politics, large segments of the working class sought to use the democratic state to promote their own vision of Reconstruction.[31]

Almost immediately upon the end of the War, workers in the North launched new struggles to realise their vision of 'freedom' and 'full self-ownership'. Skilled workers in printing, machine-making, iron-production, shoe-making, and urban construction set about reorganising their craft-unions. Local unions would collectively set wage-rates and work-rules, and used strike-action to impose the 'union-shop' on recalcitrant employers. Competition among small manufacturers and contractors made these tactics relatively successful before 1870, after which employers began to co-ordinate

---

[25] Beckert 1993, pp. 135–44, 163–170; Montgomery 1967, pp. 73–8.
[26] Fields 1990, pp. 1–10.
[27] Beckert 1993, Chapter 2; Livesay and Porter 1971; Wilentz 1984, Chapter 3.
[28] Montgomery 1967, p. x.
[29] Montgomery 1967, p. 8.
[30] Montgomery 1967, p. 30.
[31] Foner 1988, pp. 461–9; Montgomery 1967, pp. 25–44.

their resistance to skilled workers' unions. Unskilled workers in mining, textiles, longshore and other industries fought against wage-cuts and speed-up through mass, community-based mobilisations in support of strikes. While most unskilled workers were unable to create lasting unions, skilled workers had established twenty-one national craft-unions and dozens of municipal labour-councils by 1870.[32]

The organisation of unions and frequent strikes raised serious challenges to the Radical manufacturers' belief 'that liberty rested on ownership of productive property, and that working for wages was merely a temporary resting place on the road to economic autonomy'.[33] Even more threatening was the growing agitation for 'eight-hour legislation' in the late 1860s and early 1870s. Cotton-textile, building-trades, printing, shipyard-, and iron-workers across the North attempted to win the eight-hour day through direct industrial action. Through the National Labour Union and local and state labour-reform parties, workers agitated for democratic state-governments to limit the working day to eight hours.[34]

The manufacturers were nearly unanimous in their opposition to the eight-hour day – whether achieved through strike-action or, worse, legislation.[35] However, individual Radical Republicans supported eight-hour laws that lacked any enforcement mechanisms in Congress and Northern state-legislatures after the War. The workers' appropriation of Radical ideology to argue for the legal limitation of the working day presented an even more profound challenge for the manufacturers. According to labour-radicals like Boston's Ira Steward, popular, democratic government was obligated to protect and promote the interests of the labouring majority. The legal limitation of the working day would free workers from 'wage-slavery' and give them true 'self-ownership'. On the one hand, the additional free time workers would enjoy would give them the leisure and educational opportunities required of 'virtuous' and 'independent' citizens of the Republic. On the other, Steward argued that shorter hours would raise wages, increase demand and expand economic opportunities for all:

---

[32] Foner 1988, pp. 475–8; Montgomery 1967, pp. 135–70.
[33] Foner 1988, p. 477.
[34] Montgomery 1967, pp. 177–95, 237–49, Chapters 7–8.
[35] Montgomery 1967, pp. 232–6.

> Once the state had established a legal definition of the working day dividing
> the waking hours of the workers equally between himself and the purchaser
> of his work, Steward assigned it no further task. Subsequently, society would
> become harmonious by it own unaided evolution.[36]

While labour-reformers would continue to deny the realities of class-conflict through the end of Reconstruction, the manufacturers found the Radicals' vision of a democratic state promoting a harmonious society of petty proprietorship and social mobility an inadequate 'mental road-map' of the lived experience of class-warfare in the late 1860s and early 1870s. Radicalism ceased to be the dominant trend in the Republican Party after the nomination of Grant in 1868, as the Radicals lost support among the manufacturers and their programme for the South – nationally guaranteed citizenship and voting rights for the freedmen – was realised with the election of Republican state-governments across the former Confederacy.[37]

A new layer of Republican politicians emerged during the Grant administration – the 'Stalwarts'. While committed to defending the civil and political rights of African Americans in the South and preserving protective tariffs and inflationary paper-money, the Stalwarts were political pragmatists whose main goals were winning and maintaining public office. Under their leadership, the Republican Party shifted:

> from an ideological to an organisational mode of politics...government less
> an instrument of reform than a means of obtaining office and mediating
> the rival claims of the diverse economic and ethnic groups that made up
> northern society.[38]

The manufacturing capitalists found the Stalwarts' rule, at best, a temporary political home. The Stalwarts were quite willing to use federal and state-funds to subsidise railroad-construction, charter private corporations, and otherwise promote capitalist development. However, while the Stalwarts 'served business', they 'also preyed upon it'.[39] The rampant corruption of the Grant years, combined with the Stalwarts' willingness to court the vote of workers

---

[36] Montgomery 1967, pp. 259–60; 252–60.
[37] Foner 1988, pp. 333–45, 479–88; Montgomery 1967, pp. 335–60.
[38] Foner 1988, p. 484.
[39] Foner 1988, p. 486.

with promises of pro-labour legislation, led the manufacturers to gravitate toward different political ideas in the 1870s.

The depression of 1873, which marked the end of the long boom that had begun in the mid 1840s, and the subsequent sharpening of class-struggle in the North pushed the industrial capitalists to embrace a new world-view – *liberalism*. While the sharp economic contraction destroyed the urban trades' assemblies and national unions of skilled workers, it aroused mass-movements of the urban unemployed across the North. Urban political machines, Democratic and Republicans, found themselves caught between workers demanding public works and relief, and Northern industrial and banking capitalists' insisting on cutting public expenditures and taxes. The cyclical recovery that began in 1875 led to renewed union-struggles against wage-cuts and the intensification of work. The coal-miners' strike for the restoration of wage-cuts during the first half of 1875 was defeated, but new union-organisation emerged among iron- and steel- and railway-workers. The post-depression cycle of industrial struggles culminated with the railway-workers' uprising in 1877. Faced with renewed employer demands for wage-reductions, rail-workers launched national strikes, which rapidly attracted the active support of workers in major towns and cities across the US. The dispatch of federal troops against workers, for the first time since the Jackson-administration, crushed the rail-workers.[40]

Liberal Republicanism emerged, at first as a trend among former Radical intellectuals, in the late 1860s and early 1870s. Faced with widespread political corruption, both North and South, and the eruption of militant working-class struggles, the Liberals rejected the equation of democracy with the substantive and unrestrained power of the majority. Widespread corruption 'underscored the dangers of unbridled democracy and the political incapacity of the lower orders'.[41] In both the North and South, the Liberals called for 'limited government' – a deflationary monetary policy, reductions in tariffs, lower taxes and public expenditures, and an end to all the dangerous 'social experiments' of the Reconstruction-era. While some Liberals' vision of a restricted suffrage based on education and property was never realised in the North, Liberals demanded the reduction in the number and powers of elected officials,

---

[40] Beckert 1993, Chapter 7; Foner 1988, pp. 510–15, 582–7.
[41] Foner 1988, p. 497.

shorter legislative sessions and lower salaries for legislators, the substitution of competitive examinations for political appointments of civil servants, the abolition of special corporate charters in favour of general-incorporation laws, and legal limits on public expenditures, taxation and debt. In sum, the Liberals redefined 'democracy' to mean 'the passive enjoyment of constitutional and procedural safeguards and rights'[42] and freedom to mean 'not economic autonomy or the right to call upon the aid of the activist state, but the ability to compete in the marketplace and enjoy protection against an overbearing government'.[43]

Liberalism provided the Northern-industrial capitalists with a mental road-map adequate to their struggles with the industrial working class. They rejected the vision of an activist state based in substantive democratic power creating and maintaining a harmonious society of petty producers and skilled workers. The Liberals embraced the division of society between capital and labour as 'natural', sought to remove the 'corrupting influence' of the lower classes on government, and restore the proper independence of the market as the regulator of economic and social life. Their élitism and commitment to the rule of 'men of property and intelligence' justified the restructuring of state-institutions in the North so they could more adequately defend capitalism against the 'democratic mob'. The Liberals' ascendancy had even more disastrous effects in the South, unleashing the planter-merchant counter-revolution that crushed the African-American and poor whites' 'peasant-democracy' in the late 1870s.

II. Democracy against capitalism in the South: the rise and fall of peasant-citizenship, 1865–77

The incompatibility of substantive democracy and the development of capitalist social-property relations were nowhere more evident than in the postbellum US-South. In the aftermath of the collapse of slavery in 1863, the Lincoln-administration, military officials and the Freedmen's Bureau pursued contradictory policies regarding the future of agricultural class-relations in

---

[42] Wood 1995, p. 227.
[43] Foner 1988, p. 498. On Republican Liberalism generally, see Beckert 1993, Chapters 6–7; Foner 1988, pp. 488–94, 499–510; Montgomery 1967, pp. 380–6.

the South. On the one hand, some army, and Freedmen's Bureau officials carried out local experiments distributing abandoned or confiscated lands to freedpeople in forty-acre lots.[44] On the other hand, most federal officials sought to restore land to its former owners and re-establish plantation-agriculture on the basis of the freely contracted wage-labour of the freed-people. The majority of Northern capitalists, led by the Conservative cotton-textile industrialists and merchants and bankers enmeshed in the global cotton-trade, correctly feared that any distribution of land to the ex-slaves would lead to the development of a subsistence-peasantry as it had in the post-emancipation Caribbean. By the end of the War in April 1865, the federal officials committed themselves to restoration of the plantations on the basis of legally-free wage-labour.[45]

While the planters were quite happy that the federal government had restored their property and supported the transformation of the ex-slaves into wage-labourers, the planters had no intention of relying on the unfettered operation of the labour-market in their struggle to create capitalist plantation-agriculture in the South. Not only did they impose year-long contracts with payment of wages in the form of a share of the crop only after the harvest in order to guarantee the stability of their labour-force through the crop-cycle, but the planters sought to restore corporate punishment as a means of ensuring that the work-gangs laboured from 'sunrise to sunset'. The planters also attempted to restrict the geographical movement of their new employees in order to prevent them from seeking other employment, and sought to force all members of the freedpeople's households, including women and children, to labour in centralised gangs under their direction. Most of the labour-contracts in 1865 were verbal, and did not 'specify the days and hours of work, the rules of on-the-job conduct, or the penalties for unsatisfactory work or misbehavior'.[46] The endemic paramilitary violence that marked the South in 1865 was a central component of the planters' struggle to impose capitalist social-property relations in agriculture:

---

[44] Foner 1988, pp. 50–3; Hahn et al. 2008, pp. 18–20.
[45] Foner 1988, pp. 53–60, 66–8, 158–61; Hahn et al. 2008, pp. 14–20, 27–8, 49–53; McFeely, 1970.
[46] Hahn et al. 2008, p. 32. See also pp. 30–9; Foner 1988, pp. 123–35.

Freedmen were assaulted and murdered for attempting to leave plantations, disputing contract settlements, and not laboring in the manner desired by their employers, attempting to buy or rent land, and resisting whippings.[47]

In late 1865, the planters, deprived of the personal authority they wielded over their slaves, 'turned to the state to reestablish labor discipline'.[48] Conservative Republicans in the Johnson-administration facilitated a rapid restoration of the Southern state-governments, granting a broad amnesty to former Confederate officials, and permitting white voters alone to elect state-constitutional conventions. These conventions accepted the abolition of slavery, but extended neither citizenship nor the suffrage to the freedmen.[49] New state-legislatures, dominated by former Whig large planters now organised in the Democratic Party, promulgated the 'Black Codes' in early 1866, legislation designed to compel the freedpeople to sell their labour-power and toil under the command of their former masters. While the particular provisions varied from state to state, the Black Codes generally included anti-vagrancy laws, which threatened unemployed African Americans with fines and imprisonment; 'anti-enticement' laws that limited competition for labour-power by forbidding employers to offer employment to freedpeople already under contract to another planter; and laws that forbade African Americans from buying or leasing land, carrying arms, testifying in court or serving on juries. In addition, new legislation banned grazing, fishing and hunting on privately owned land, and gave creditors and landlords, rather than labourers, the first 'lien' or claim on crops.[50]

The planters justified their reliance on extra-economic coercion to establish and maintain capitalist social-property relations with the racist claim that people of African descent would labour effectively only under compulsion.[51] However, juridical-legal coercion has always been a *necessary* element of the establishment of capitalist social-property relations – imposing a social monopoly of landed property and compelling propertyless workers to labour

---

[47] Foner 1988, p. 121.
[48] Foner 1988, p. 198.
[49] No significant forces in the Republican Party after the Civil War supported the extension of voting rights to women, either black or white.
[50] DuBois 1969, pp. 153–75; Foner 1988, pp. 197–216.
[51] Hahn et al. 2008, pp. 21–2.

in situations where alternative forms of subsistence are possible.[52] Put simply, the operation of the market cannot establish capitalist social relations – the markets' regulation of production.[53] Capitalist agriculture, with its disjunction between production and labour-time in the form of 'slack-seasons' between planting and harvesting, has often relied on legally coerced wage-labour to secure labour year-round.[54] In the US-South in 1865, the planters also faced the organised resistance of the freedpeople to wage-labour. The wartime-experiences of self-emancipation through the mass-flight from the plantations and Union military service raised the political and social confidence of the freedpeople. The South saw a veritable explosion of self-organisation among the freedmen in the summer and fall of 1865. Former slaves pooled resources and built their own churches and schools, while:

> A host of fraternal, benevolent, and mutual-aid societies also sprang into
> existence…burial societies, debating clubs, Masonic lodges, fire companies, drama
> societies, trade associations, temperance clubs, and equal rights leagues.[55]

Freedpeople, under the leadership of Union-veterans and skilled artisans, organised 'Union Leagues' across the South, to challenge the planters' command of the plantation labour-process and to contest for civil and political rights.[56]

The lived experience of plantation-slavery shaped the freedpeople's vision of freedom – a vision at odds with both the planters and Northern manufacturers and merchants. The slaves' place in the plantation labour-process as a 'means of production in human form', and the disjuncture between production and labour-time in agriculture together compelled slave-owning planters across the Americas to make their plantations self-sufficient in food and other productive inputs.[57] In order to realise their investment in the slaves as fixed capital, the slaves had to labour all year-round. Agriculture, as a natural-biological process, with its slack-seasons, is not well suited to providing year-round, continuous work. Planters across the Americas put their slaves to

---

[52] The classic discussion of extra-economic coercion in the process of 'the primitive accumulation of capital' is Marx 1976, Chapters 26–8, 33.
[53] Wood 1999.
[54] Mann 1990, pp. 28–46.
[55] Foner 1988, p. 95.
[56] Foner 1988, pp. 89–102, 110–9; Hahn 2002.
[57] This section is drawn from pp. 141–4 below.

work growing food and making tools and handicrafts during the slack-season for their staple-crops. In the antebellum cotton-South, slaves grew corn in centralised gangs under the direction of their masters. However, as in the rest of the Americas, most cotton-planters granted garden-plots of approximately one acre to each slave-household. The slaves organised their own independent production of food, poultry and handicrafts during their free time, selling any surplus beyond what the slave-household consumed.

Much of the day-to-day class-struggle between masters and slaves in the antebellum-South focused on the division of working time between centralised gang-labour producing staple-crops for the world-market under the command of the masters, and self-directed, independent production of food and handicrafts primarily for the slaves' own consumption. Put simply, the experience of the socially linked, but *spatially and temporally distinct realms* of plantation-slavery and independent production led African-American freed-people to identify *slavery* with the production of cotton in planter-directed gangs, and *freedom* with the production of their own means of subsistence in autonomous household-labour. Thus, it is not surprising that the freedpeople viewed capitalist plantation-agriculture as the *re-imposition of slavery*, while demanding land on which they and their families could pursue subsistence-oriented independent production as the *condition of freedom*.[58]

Various wartime-experiences raised the former slaves' expectations for a radical land-reform in 1865–6. As early as 1861–2, federal troops assented to the freedpeople's' seizure of abandoned plantations and the distribution of land to their households on the South Carolina Sea Islands, where they 'commenced planting corn and potatoes for their own subsistence, but evinced considerable resistance to growing the "slave crop", cotton'.[59] In parts of Virginia and North Carolina, Sherman's army divided abandoned plantations and leased household-plots to former slaves. The Freedmen's Bureau initially had authority over confiscated and abandoned lands in the South. Bureau Commissioner Howard's 'Circular 13' of July 1865 ordered lands under his control sold or leased to the freedpeople. While the Johnson-administration overruled Howard, ordering land to be returned to its former Confederate

---

[58] Foner 1988, pp. 103–10; Hahn et al. 2008, pp. 24–7.
[59] Foner 1988, p. 51.

owners, African Americans across the South believed that a radical land-reform was immanent in late 1865 and 1866.[60]

Refusing to return to conditions they associated with slavery and encouraged by rumours of a federal land-reform, freedmen organised to undermine capitalist plantation-agriculture in the first three years after the end of the War. First, the freedmen withdrew female and juvenile labour-power from plantation-labour. Under slavery, planters utilised the labour of all the slaves – men, women and children. With emancipation, only adult men made themselves available for work on the cotton-plantations. The resulting 28–37% drop in number of hours rural African Americans worked created a severe labour-shortage, giving the former slaves considerable leverage. They routinely left employers during the harvest, despite fines and loss of wages, because they were able to gain significantly higher wages from other employers.[61] The freedmen organised proto-trade-unions to bargain over wages, hours and working conditions, and engaged in short strikes during the time-sensitive harvests to enforce their demands. Organised in kin-based 'Associations' and 'Companies', freedmen 'met, marched, and drilled in pursuit of their aspirations'.[62] These Associations often became the Union Leagues, the backbone of the Republican Party in the South:

> League council enabled and encouraged freedpeople to negotiate better contracts, contest the abuses of their employers, engage in strikes and boycotts, claim their just wages and shares of the crop, and generally alter the balance of power on the land. How much League activities contributed to the overall transition from gang-labor to tenancy and sharecropping is a matter of some conjecture, but there can be little doubt that the League helped rural laborers achieve greater bargaining leverage, improved terms and more independence. [63]

Northern Republicans and the merchants and manufacturers they represented responded ambivalently to development of legally coerced wage-labour in the South. On the one hand, Conservative merchants and cotton-textile

---

[60] Cox 1958; Hahn et al. 2008, pp. 17–20, 23–7, 49–53; Foner 1988, pp. 80–8.
[61] Ransom and Sutch 1977, pp. 65–7, 232–6.
[62] Hahn 2002, p. 119.
[63] Hahn 2002, p. 125. On African-American resistance to capitalist plantation-agriculture, 1865–8, see DuBois 1969, pp. 128–82, 230–5; Foner 1988, pp. 135–42; Hahn 2002; Hahn et al. 2008, pp. 40–6.

manufacturers wanted a rapid restoration of plantation-production and only a small minority of Radical manufacturers supported the distribution of land to the freedpeople, which they understood would produce subsistence-oriented household-agriculture. On the other hand, the Radicals and Conservatives rejected any and all legal-juridical coercion of the freedmen and were appalled at the rise of paramilitary violence in the South, which they saw as a violation of the free-labour system's most basic tenets. The uncertainty of the northern ruling class was reflected in the vacillations of Freedmen's Bureau policies in the immediate postwar-years. The Bureau was committed to restoring land to the planters and enforcing labour-contracts which gave the planters command of the rural labour-process. However, the Bureau attempted to mitigate the most egregious forms of extra-economic coercion, demanding written contracts that specified wages and hours of work, banning the use of corporal punishment to enforce labour-discipline, imposing a labourers' lien on the crop to guarantee the payment of share-wages, and establishing courts to adjudicate contract-disputes.[64] In sum, Northern capitalists and the federal government hoped that Southern cotton-production would resume rapidly on the basis of wage-labour, but eschewed the legal-juridical coercion *necessary* to impose capitalist social-property relations.

The persistent violence against the freedpeople and the passage of the Black Codes provided the opening for the Radicals to overturn Johnson's 'Presidential Reconstruction'. Believing that black wage-workers with full civil and political rights could take full advantage of the free labour-market, the Radicals pressed for Congressional action to establish *national* citizenship and voting rights for African Americans in the South. Despite their concerns about reviving cotton-production, most Republican Conservatives followed the lead of the Radicals in 1866 and 1867. First, Congress passed, over Johnson's veto, the Civil Rights Act of 1866, which defined all persons born in the US (with the exception of Native Americans) citizens and established legal equality regardless of race, and authorised federal officials to enforce these laws. The Fourteenth Amendment, approved by Congress in June 1866, placed national citizenship 'beyond the reach of Presidential vetoes and shifting political majorities',[65] and made representation of a state in Congress dependent upon

---

[64] Foner 1988, pp. 66–8, 142–53, 155–8, 161–70, 216–39; Hahn et al. 2008, pp. 31–9.
[65] Foner 1988, p. 251.

the number of adult males enfranchised. Finally, the Reconstruction Act of 1867 placed the South under military occupation and made the reintegration of Southern state-governments into the Union dependent upon 'the writing of new constitutions providing manhood suffrage, their approval by a majority of registered voters, and ratification of the Fourteenth Amendment'.[66]

'Congressional Reconstruction' had its intended effect in the South in late 1867 and early 1868. A wave of new political agitation spread across the South, as freedmen in the cotton-South and upcountry white farmers formed Union Leagues. Over 700,000 newly enfranchised African Americans – the majority of voters in Alabama, Florida, Louisiana, Mississippi and South Carolina – went to the polls. The new state-conventions were elected in the autumn of 1867, met in early 1868, and drafted constitutions that guaranteed universal male suffrage and citizenship. The Republicans swept to power across the South, with the exceptions of violence-ridden Georgia and Louisiana, in Spring 1868 on the votes of newly enfranchised freedmen and white yeoman-farmers. The new Southern governments repealed the Black Codes and began to radically re-organise social relations in the South.[67]

Congressional Reconstruction, however, had a major *unintended* consequence. Rather than realising the *utopian* vision of a capitalist plantation-agriculture based on juridically free labour, Republican dominance in the South led to the break-up of the plantations and the emergence of a new, *non-capitalist* form of social labour, share-cropping tenancy. By the spring of 1866, planters were facing difficulties enforcing 'anti-enticement' laws that sought to limit competition among planters for labourers. Increasingly, planters across the cotton-belt competed with one another for labour, leading to a rise in wages. They contracted with self-organised groups of freedmen, who negotiated wages and conditions of work and appointed one of their numbers as supervisors. In the late 1860s, the planters began to abandon centralised gang-labour on the basis of wage-labour, leasing land in forty- to eighty-acre lots to freedmen and their families. The planter-landlord provided land, tools, seed, fertiliser and work-animals to the freedmen, who organised their

---

[66] Foner 1988, p. 277. On Congressional Reconstruction see DuBois 1969, pp. 325–79; Foner 1988, pp. 242–79.
[67] Foner 1988, pp. 281–345.

households' labour and paid a share of the crop to the landlord at harvest-time. Although planter-landlords dictated the crop-mix, with cotton as the dominant crop, the freedmen enjoyed patriarchal command of their house-hold-members' labour, often using corporal punishment to discipline women and children.[68] In sum, sharecropping embodied a class-compromise between the planters' desire to continue the production of cotton as a cash-crop under their command, and the freedmen's aspiration to produce their own subsistence independently:

> Planters strongly resented the sense of 'quasi-proprietorship' blacks derived
> from the arrangement – the notion that sharecropping made the tenant 'part
> owner of the crop' and therefore entitled to determine his family's own pace
> of work.... While sharecropping did not fulfil blacks' desire for full economic
> autonomy, the end of the planters' coercive authority over the day-to-day
> lives of their tenants represented a fundamental shift in the balance of power
> in rural society, and afforded blacks a degree of control over their time,
> labor, and family arrangements inconceivable under slavery.[69]

Although the majority of elected and unelected positions in the new Southern governments went to white Republicans from the North, the reliance of the new régimes on the votes and political activity of the freedmen and upcountry-whites gave these Reconstruction-governments a radical, *anticapitalist* character. The Southern peasant-citizens used their substantive political power, in ways reminiscent of the peasant-citizens of ancient Athens, to defend their class-positions against the landlords.[70] Across the South, Republican governments built public schools, hospitals, orphanages and asylums. While these public institutions were *de facto* segregated by race, formal racial segregation of public institutions, accommodations and transport was illegal across the South before the 1890s. The new state-governments also repealed discriminatory poll-taxes and licenses, and established property-

---

[68] Foner 1988, pp. 399–409; Ransom and Sutch 1997, pp. 68–72, 90–4, 97–9; Mann 1990, Chapter 4.

[69] Foner 1988, p. 406.

[70] The reality of an active and organised peasant-citizenry defending itself against the Southern landlord-class is the 'rational kernel' of DuBois' (1969, p. 345) claim that the Reconstruction-governments were a form of the 'dictatorship of labor'. As we will see, the peasant-citizens did not aspire to collective and democratic control of productive resources, but to the defence and extension of *non-capitalist* household-based production.

taxes on landed property. 'Homestead exemptions' and 'stay laws' protected upcountry-farmers from losing their land through excessive taxation, shifting the tax-burden to planters. Lien-laws gave first claim on the crop to farmers and labourers, protecting white yeoman-farmers and black sharecroppers from the landlords and merchants.[71]

The most radical anticapitalist measures were taken at the local level, where African Americans dominated public office in the cotton-belt. Drawn from the ranks of artisans, shopkeepers, small landholders, ministers and teachers, most black officeholders were justices of the peace who 'generally ruled on minor criminal offences as well as a majority of civil cases', sheriffs who 'enforced the law, selected trial jurors, and carried out foreclosures and the public sales of land', and county-commissioners who 'established tax rates, controlled local appropriations, and administered poor relief'.[72] Through these offices, freedmen were able to insure that African-American sharecroppers were not taxed, received their fair share of the crop and public spending, and did not suffer retribution or victimisation in the hands of their landlords or vigilantes.[73]

The rule of the peasant-citizens in the postbellum-South was short-lived. As the Northern manufacturers became increasingly conservative in response to sharpening class-confrontations with the Northern working class in the 1870s, they progressively abandoned the freedmen. The Liberals' élitist hostility toward white wage-workers in the North extended toward African-American sharecroppers and farmers in the South. After 1872, Liberals called for universal amnesty for former Confederates, viewing 'southern men of property and culture as allies of the northern counterparts in a common struggle against corrupt mass politics'. During the second Grant-administration, the Liberals effectively blocked Congressional renewal of the Enforcement Acts, which had allowed the federal military to repress the Klan in 1871, or the passage of new civil-rights legislation. The new Republican leaders believed that the violence of the Klan and the White Leagues were justifiable 'reactions of society's legitimate leaders against usurpers of political power'.[74]

---

[71] DuBois 1969, Chapters 10–12, 15; Foner 1988, pp. 316–33, 364–76.
[72] Foner 1988, p. 355.
[73] Foner 1988, pp. 351–6, 363–4.
[74] Montgomery 1967, p. 385; Foner 1988, pp. 452–9, 525–34, 554–63.

At the same time, their Northern-capitalist allies abandoned them, the southern-Republican alliance of black sharecroppers and white upcountry-farmers was strained. The white Republicans who controlled the most important public offices in the South, like Republicans in the North, issued bonds and allocated funds to build railroads across the South in the late 1860s and early 1870s. As in the North, the result was widespread corruption of government-officials, rising public debt and new taxes. Especially after the depression of 1873, Republican state-governments in the South raised property-taxes, often eliminating homestead-exemptions and stay laws which had protected white, upcountry independent farmers. Faced with the threat of losing their landed property to pay back-taxes, the white yeoman-farmers were open to the planter-landlords' appeals for racial solidarity in the struggle to re-establish 'white supremacy' in the South.[75]

With Congress unwilling to send additional federal troops to defend the civil and political rights of the freedmen after 1874, the planters and their allies unleashed a reign of terror in the South. The revived Klan, the White Leagues and other racist paramilitary organisations broke up Republican meetings, assassinated white and black Republican leaders, and intimidated African-American voters across the South. By the Fall of 1877, Democratic 'Redeemers' held power in all the Southern state-governments except South Carolina and Louisiana. The contested Presidential election of 1876, in which the Democrat Tilden received a majority of popular votes in the midst of massive violence and electoral fraud in the South, marked the end of Reconstruction in the South. The 'Compromise of 1877' placed the Republican Hayes in the White House, in exchange for the final withdrawal of federal troops and the installation of Redeemer-governments in Louisiana and South Carolina, and the return of 'home-rule' – giving the Southern landlords and merchants a free hand in organising class- and racial relations in the region.[76]

---

[75] Foner 1988, pp. 536–45.
[76] DuBois 1969, pp. 379–86; Foner 1988, pp. 547–53, 568–85; Woodward 1951, pp. 23–50.

III. The defeat of populism, 'Jim Crow' and the establishment of capitalist plantation-agriculture in the South, 1877–1900

The Redemption-governments were neither able to deprive African Americans of citizenship or suffrage, nor impose capitalist plantation-agriculture in the South in the 1870s and 1880s. However, with the Republican Party effectively dismantled, the Democratic representatives of the planters and merchants rolled back key advances of the Reconstruction-government. First, the Redeemers cut government-spending, reducing funding for the public schools and hospitals both black and white farmers had relied upon. While reducing taxes on landed property, the Democratic Southern governments repealed homestead-exemptions and stay laws that protected upcountry-farmers; implemented new crop lien-laws giving merchants and landlords, rather than farmers and tenants, first claim on the cotton-crop; and reinstated fence-laws making it impossible for small farmers and tenants to graze livestock on uncultivated fields. Finally, they made local sheriffs, justices of the peace and county-commissioners appointed, rather than elected, officials, effectively purging African Americans from these positions and removing the checks these black peasant-citizens had imposed on the planters and merchants in their dealings with their sharecropping tenants. [77]

The new relationship of forces between the landlords and merchants on one side and the African-American sharecroppers and white upcountry-farmers on the other resulted in profound changes in rural social-property relations across the South in the 1870s and 1880s. The end of plantation-slavery coincided with the collapse of the fatorage-system of merchant-credit that had financed cotton-production before the Civil War. [78] Endemic shortages of cash had compelled planters to offer wages in the form of a share of the crop in the immediate postbellum-period, and led to the emergence of local landlord-merchants who established territorial monopolies in the Southern countryside under sharecropping. The landlord-merchant would provide food, clothing and agricultural supplies the sharecropper needed to initiate and survive the agricultural production cycle. In exchange, the landlord-merchants, who were usually the only source of credit and goods in a region, would charge inflated prices and usurious interest. Under the new lien-laws, the merchants

---

[77] DuBois 1969, Chapter 16; Foner 1988, pp. 412–24, 588–93.
[78] Woodman 1968.

had first claim on the tenant's share of the crop. Each year, the sharecroppers found themselves with little or no surplus after the sale of the cotton-crop. Between their rent-payment (usually half the crop) and payments of interest (approximately 14% of crop) and principal, the sharecroppers were left with little beyond their own subsistence.[79]

In the upcountry, rising taxes compelled independent white farmers to devote more and more land and labour to the cultivation of cotton. As they were no longer able to produce the majority of their food, clothing and house-hold-items, they were forced to borrow from local merchant-creditors to purchase these items. Like the African-American sharecroppers in the black belt, the upcountry-white farmers were charged inflated prices for consumer-goods and usurious rates of interest by local merchant-monopolists. By the late 1870s and early 1880s, a substantial portion of independent-white farmers had lost title to their lands and were reduced to cash-tenants or sharecroppers of the merchant-landlords of the upcountry-South.[80]

For the first time since Bacon's Rebellion of 1676, the majority of poor whites and African Americans occupied the same class-position – they were tenant-farmers. Their common class-position produced the southern Farmers' Alliance, the most important multiracial social movement the South had ever experienced. The Southern People's Parties and Farmers' Alliances demanded new homestead-exemptions on small property, government-owned banks and new paper-money to provide inexpensive credit, and government-owned railroads that would lower freight-rates for farmers. The possibility of a populist coalition of Northern industrial workers and Southern black and white farmers in the 1880s and 1890s sparked a new planter counter-offensive, supported by Northern capital. Using the divisions between primarily African-American sharecroppers and mostly white cash-tenants, the plant-ers and merchants imposed legal segregation of public facilities, disenfran-chised African Americans and a substantial minority of poor whites through poll-taxes and literacy-tests, and maintained order in the plantation-districts through lynch-law and Klan-terror.[81]

---

[79] Ransom and Sutch 1977, pp. 81–170.
[80] Hahn 1983, Chapters 4–5; Wiener 1978; Wiener 1979. A discussion of the 'rules of reproduction' of sharecropping and debt-peonage and its impact on southern economic development is beyond the scope of this essay. See Post 2006.
[81] Davis 1986, pp. 29–40; Foner 1988, pp. 592–8; Woodward 1955.

In the wake of the defeat of the southern Farmers' Alliance and the imposition of Jim Crow in the South, planters were able to begin to reorganise cotton-production along capitalist lines. According to Wright, by the late 1870s:

> Throughout most of the plantation South, however, the coexistence of sharecropping and wage-labor prevailed not just between districts but within each plantation. The typical planter divided his total acreage into portions assigned to sharecroppers, portions rented out to tenants, and a portion retained for himself and cultivated by wage labor…[82]

This balance began to shift in favour of centrally supervised wage-labour after 1890. While planters continued to refer to their wage-labourers as 'croppers' and even 'tenants' – often providing a cabin and garden-plot and paying them with a share of the crop after the harvest – these workers did not supervise their own and their households' labour in independent labour-processes. Instead, they were working under the supervision of the planter and his agents in centralised labour-gangs.[83] In the first four decades of the twentieth century, the planters' ability to organise the labour-process under their command and fire workers at will allowed them to progressively mechanise southern agriculture.[84]

The establishment and expanded reproduction of capitalist social-property relations in the US required the radical curtailment of *substantive* popular power and democratic rights for the vast majority of direct producers. In the North, the labour-capital struggle led the manufacturers' to embrace *liberal democracy* – universal suffrage was preserved, but the scope of activity of the democratic state was limited to the preservation of individual property-rights. In the South, the development of a substantive peasant-democracy in the late 1860s and 1870s consolidated the *non-capitalist* social-property relations of sharecropping. Only the destruction of that radical-plebeian democracy and the creation of a racially-exclusive suffrage, backed up by legal and extra-legal violence and terror, allowed the consolidation of capitalist social-property relations in Southern agriculture after 1890. In sum, the actual historical evolution of capitalism and democracy in the post bellum-US seems to contradict the possibility of a 'bourgeois-democratic revolution' – a revolution that promotes both capitalism and democracy.

---

[82] Wright 1986, pp. 90–1.
[83] Reidy 1992, Chapter 9; Wright 1986, Chapter 4.
[84] Mann 1990, Chapter 5.

References

Adreano, Ralph L. (ed.) 1966, *The Economic Impact of the Civil War*, Boston: Schenkman Publishers.

Aglietta, Michel 1978, 'Phases of US Capitalist Expansion', *New Left Review*, I, 110: 17–28.

Aitken, Hugh G.J. (ed.) 1971, *Did Slavery Pay? Readings in the Economics of Black Slavery in the United States*, Boston: Houghton Mifflin.

Anderson, Perry 1974, *Passages from Antiquity to Feudalism*, London: New Left Books.

Anderson, Ralph V. and Robert E. Gallman 1977, 'Slaves as Fixed-Capital: Slave Labor and Southern Economic Development', *Journal of American History*, 64, 1: 24–46.

Appleby, Joyce 1982, 'Commercial Farming and the "Agrarian Myth" in the Early Republic', *Journal of American History*, 68, 4: 833–49.

Ashworth, John 1995, *Slavery, Capitalism, and Politics in the Antebellum Republic*, Volume I: *Commerce and Compromise*, Cambridge: Cambridge University Press.

—— 2007, *Slavery, Capitalism, and Politics in the Antebellum Republic*, Volume II: *The Coming of the Civil War, 1850–1861*, Cambridge: Cambridge University Press.

Aston, T.H. (ed.) 1967, *Crisis in Europe*, Garden City: Doubleday Books.

Aston, T.H. and C.H.E. Philpin (eds.) 1985, *The Brenner Debate: Agrarian Class Structure and Economic Development in Pre-Industrial Europe*, Cambridge: Cambridge University Press.

Atherton, Lewis E. 1971 [1939], *The Frontier Merchant in Mid-America*, Columbia, MO.: University of Missouri Press.

Atack, Jeremy and Fred Bateman 1987, *To Their Own Soil: Agriculture in the Antebellum North*, Aimes: University of Iowa Press.

Aufhauser, R. Keith 1973, 'Slavery and Scientific Management', *Journal of Economic History*, 33, 4: 811–24.

Balibar, Etienne 1970, 'Basic Concepts of Historical Materialism', in *Reading 'Capital'*, by L. Althusser and E. Balibar, London: New Left Books.

Barney, William L. 1972, *The Road to Secession: A New Perspective on the Old South*, New York: Praeger.

—— 1975, *Flawed Victory: A New Perspective on the Civil War*, New York: Praeger Publishers.

—— 1982, 'Towards the Civil War: The Dynamics of Change in a Black Belt County', in *Class, Conflict and Values: Antebellum Southern Community Studies*, edited by Orville Vernon Burton and Robert C. McMath, Jr., Westport,: Greenwood Press.

Barrett, Ward 1965, 'Caribbean Sugar Production Standards in the Seventeenth and Eighteenth Centuries', in *Merchants and Scholars: Essays in the History of Exploration and Trade*, edited by John Parker, Minneapolis: University of Minnesota Press.

Bateman, Fred and Thomas Weiss 1981, *A Deplorable Scarcity: The Failure of Industrialization in the Slave Economy*, Chapel Hill: University of North Carolina Press.

Battalio, Raymond C. and John Kagel 1970, 'The Structure of Antebellum Southern Agriculture: South Carolina, A Case Study', *Agricultural History*, January, 44, 1: 25–37.

Beard, Charles A. and Mary R. Beard 1927, *The Rise of American Civilisation*, New York: MacMillan.

Beckles, Hilary McD. 1989, *White Servitude and Black Slavery in Barbados, 1627–1715*, Knoxville: University of Tennessee Press.

Beckert, Sven 1993, *The Monied Metropolis: New York City and the Consolidation of the American Bourgeoisie, 1850–1896*, Cambridge: Cambridge University Press.

Bell, Michael M. 1989, 'Did New England Go Downhill?', *Geographical Review* 79, 4: 450–66.

Bergad, Laird W. 1990, *Cuban Rural Society in the Nineteenth Century: The Social and Economic History of Monoculture in Mantanzas*, Princeton: Princeton University Press.

Bergad, Laird W., Fe Iglesias Garcia and Maria Del Carmen Barcia 1995, *The Cuban Slave Market, 1790–1880*, Cambridge: Cambridge University Press.

Berlin, Ira 1998, *Many Thousands Gone: The First Two Centuries of Slavery in North America*, Cambridge, MA.: Harvard University Press.

Berlin, Ira and Philip D. Morgan 1993, 'Labor and the Shaping of Slave Life in the Americas', in *Cultivation and Culture: Labor and the Shaping of Slave Life in the Americas*, edited by I. Berlin and P.D. Morgan, Charlottesville: University Press of Virginia.

—— (eds.) 1991, *The Slaves' Economy: Independent Production by Slaves in the Americas*, London: Frank Cass.

Bernstein, Henry 1977, 'Notes on Capital and the Peasantry', *Review of African Political Economy*, 10: 60–73.

Berwanger, Eugene 1967, *The Frontier Against Slavery: Western Anti-Negro Prejudice and the Slavery Extension Controversy*, Chicago: University of Illinois Press.

Bidwell, Percy and John I. Falconer 1925, *History of Agriculture in the Northern United States, 1620–1860*, 2 Volumes, Washington, DC.: The Carnegie Institution of Washington.

Birch, Brian P. 1985, 'A British View of the Ohio Backwoods: The Letters of James Martin, 1821–1836', *Ohio History*, 94: 149–57.

Blackburn, Robin 1988, *The Overthrow of Colonial Slavery, 1776–1848*, London: Verso.

—— 1997, *The Making of New World Slavery: From the Baroque to the Modern, 1492–1800*, London: Verso.

—— 2010, 'State of the Union: Marx and America's Unfinished Revolution', *New Left Review*, II, 61: 153–74.

Blue, Frederick J. 1973, *The Free Soilers: Third Party Politics, 1848–1854*, Chicago: University of Chicago Press.

Bogart, Ernest L. 1912, *Financial History of Ohio*, Urbana-Champaign: University of Illinois Press.

Bogue, Allen G. 1951, 'The Land Mortgage Company in the Early Plains States', *Journal of American History*, 25, 1: 20–33.

—— 1958, 'The Iowa Claims Clubs: Symbol and Substance', *Mississippi Valley Historical Review*, 45, 2: 231–53.

—— 1963, *From Prairies to Corn Belt: Farming on the Illinois and Iowa Prairies in the 19th Century*, Chicago: University of Chicago Press.

—— 1976, 'Land Credit for Northern Farmers 1789–1940', *Agricultural History*, 50, 1: 68–100.

Botwinick, Howard 1993, *Persistent Inequalities: Wage Disparity Under Capitalist Competition*, Princeton: Princeton University Press.

Braverman, Harry 1974, *Labor and Monopoly Capital: The Degradation of Work in the Twentieth Century*, New York: Monthly Review Press.

Breen, T.H. and Stephen Innes 1980, *'Myne Owne Ground': Race and Freedom on Virginia's Eastern Shore*, Oxford: Oxford University Press.

—— 1985, *Tobacco Culture: The Mentality of the Great Tidewater Planters on the Eve of Revolution*, Princeton: Princeton University Press.

Brenner, Robert P. 1977, 'The Origins of Capitalism: A Critique of Neo-Smithian Marxism', *New Left Review*, I, 104: 27–92.

—— 1985a, 'Agrarian Class Structure and Economic Development in PreIndustrial Europe', in Aston and Philpin (eds.) 1985.

—— 1985b, 'Agrarian Roots of European Capitalism', in Aston and Philpin (eds.) 1985.

—— 1989, 'Bourgeois Revolution and Transition to Capitalism', in *The First Modern Society*, edited by A.L. Beier, D. Cannadine and J.M. Rosenheim, Cambridge: Cambridge University Press.

—— 1993, *Merchants and Revolution: Commercial Change, Political Conflict, and London's Overseas Traders, 1550–1653*, Princeton: Princeton University Press.

—— 2007, 'Property and Progress: Where Adam Smith Went Wrong', in *Marxist History Writing for the Twenty-First Century*, edited by C. Wickham, London: Oxford University Press for The British Academy.

Brindley John E. 1911, *History of Taxation in Iowa*, Iowa City: The State Historical Society of Iowa.

Brooke, John L. 1989, 'To the Quiet of the People: Revolutionary Settlements and Civil Unrest in Western Massachusetts, 1774–1789', *William and Mary Quarterly*, 3rd Series, 46, 3: 426–62.

Bushman, Richard L. 1967, *From Puritan to Yankee: Character and the Social Order in Connecticut: 1690–1765*, Cambridge, MA.: Harvard University Press.

Cairnes, John E. 1968 [1862], *The Slave Power: Its Character, Career, and Probable Designs: Being an Attempt to Explain the Real Issues Involved in the American Contest*, New York: A. Kelley.

Campbell, John 1993, 'As "A Kind of Freeman"?: Slaves' Market-Related Activities in the South Carolina Up Country, 1800–1860', in *Cultivation and Culture: Labor and the Shaping of Slave Life in the Americas*, edited by I. Berlin and P.D. Morgan, Charlottesville: University Press of Virginia.

Cardoso, F.H. and E. Faletto 1979, *Dependency and Development in Latin America,* Berkeley: University of California Press.

Cayton, Andrew R.L. 1986, *The Frontier Republic: Ideology and Politics in the Ohio Country, 1780–1825*, Kent: Kent State University Press.

Chandler, Alfred D. 1965, *The Railroads: The Nation's First Big Business*, New York: Harcourt, Brace & World.

Clark, Christopher 1978, 'The Household Mode of Production – A Comment', *Radical History Review*, 18: 166–71.

—— 1979, 'Household Economy, Market Exchange, and the Rise of Capitalism in the Connecticut Valley, 1800–1860', *Journal of Social History*, 13, 2: 169–89.

—— 1990, *The Roots of Rural Capitalism: Western Massachusetts, 1780–1860*, Ithaca: Cornell University Press.

—— 2006, *Social Change in America: From the Revolution Through the Civil War*, Chicago: Ivan R. Dee.

Clark, John G. 1966, *The Grain Trade in the Old North-West*, Urbana: University of Illinois Press.

Clark, V.S. 1929, *History of Manufactures in the United States*, Volume I, *1607–1860*, New York: Peter Smith.

Clawson, Dan 1980, *Bureaucracy and the Labor Process: The Transformation of American Industry, 1860–1920*, New York: Monthly Review Press.

Clemens, Paul G.E. and Lucy Simler 1988, 'Rural Labor and the Farm Household in Chester County, Pennsylvania, 1750–1820', in *Work and Labor in Early America*, edited by Stephen Innes, Chapel Hill: University of North Carolina Press.

Coakley, Robert W. 1988, *The Role of Federal Military Forces in Domestic Disorder, 1789–1878*, Washington, DC.: Centre of Military History/United States Army.

Cochran, Thomas C. 1961, 'Did the Civil War Retard Industrialization?', *The Mississippi Valley Historical Review*, 48, 2: 197–210.

Coclanis, Peter A., 1989, *The Shadow of a Dream: Economic Life and Death in the South Carolina Low Country, 1670–1920*, Oxford: Oxford University Press.

Cole, A.H. 1963, 'Cyclical and Seasonal Variations in the Sale of Public Lands, 1816–1860', in *The Public Lands: Studies in the History of the Public Domain*, edited by V. Carstensen, Madison: University of Wisconsin Press.

Cohen, Ira J. 1981, 'Introduction: Max Weber on Modern Capitalism', in *General Economic History*, by Max Weber, New Brunswick: Transaction Press.

Comninel, George C. 1987, *Rethinking the French Revolution: Marxism and the Revisionist Challenge*, London: Verso.

Conrad, Alfred H. and John R. Meyer 1955, 'The Economics of Slavery in the Ante Bellum South', *Journal of Political Economy*, 66, 2: 95–130.

Cooper, J.T. 1985, 'In Search of Agrarian Capitalism', in Aston and Philpin (eds.) 1985.

Countryman, Edward 1976, '"Out of the Bounds of the Law": Northern Land Rioters in the Eighteenth Century', in *The American Revolution: Explorations in the History of American Radicalism* edited by Alfred F. Young, DeKalb: Northern Illinois University Press.

Cox, Lawanda 1958, 'The Promise of Land for the Freedmen', *Mississippi Valley Historical Review*, 45, 3: 413–40.

Craton, Michael and James Walvin, 1970, *A Jamaican Plantation: The History of Worthy Park, 1670–1970*, Toronto: University of Toronto.

Craven, Avery 1966, *The Coming of the Civil War*, Chicago: University of Chicago Press.

Cress, Lawrence Delbert, 1982, *Citizens in Arms: The Army and the Militia in American Society to the War of 1812*, Chapel Hill: University of North Carolina Press.

Curtin, Phillip, 1990, *The Rise and Fall of the Plantation Complex: Essays in Atlantic History*, Cambridge: Cambridge University Press.

Danhof, Clarence H. 1941, 'Farm-Making Costs and the "Safety-Valve": 1850–1860', *Journal of Political Economy*, 49, 3: 317–59.

—— 1969, *Changes in Agriculture: The Northern United States, 1820–1870*, Cambridge, MA: Harvard University Press.

—— 1970, 'Economic Validity of the Safety-Valve Doctrine', in *Essays in American Economic History*, edited by A.W. Coats and Ross M. Robertson, New York: Barnes & Noble.

—— 1979, 'The Farm Enterprise: The Northern United States, 1820–1860s', *Research in Economic History*, 4: 127–91.

David, Paul A. 1967, 'The Growth of Real Product in the United States Before 1840: New Evidence, Controlled Conjectures', *Journal of Economic History*, 27, 2: 151–97.

—— 1971, 'The Mechanisation of Reaping in the Antebellum Midwest', in *The Reinterpretation of American Economic History*, edited by Robert W. Fogel and Stanley L. Engerman, New York: Harper Collins Publishers.

David, Paul A. et al. (eds.) 1976, *Reckoning with Slavery: A Critical Study in the Quantitative History of American Negro Slavery*, Oxford: Oxford University Press.

David, Paul A. and Peter Temin 1976, 'Slavery: The Progressive Institution?', in David et al. (eds.) 1976.

Davies, K.G. 1952, 'The Origins of the Commission System in the West India Trade', *Transactions of the Royal Historical Society*, Fifth Series, 001–2: 89–107.

Davis, David Brion, 1966, *The Problem of Slavery in Western Culture*, Ithaca: Cornell University Press.

—— 1975, *The Problem of Slavery in the Age of Revolution: 1770–1823*, Ithaca: Cornell University Press.

Davis, Lance 1960, 'The New England Textile Mills and the Capital Markets: A Study in Industrial Borrowing', *The Journal of Economic History*, 20, 1: 1–30.

Davis, Mike 1978, '"Fordism" in Crisis: A Review of Michel Aglietta's *Régulation et Crises*', *Review* (Binghamton), 2, 2: 207–69.

—— 1986, 'Why the American Working Class is Different', in *Prisoners of the American Dream*, London: Verso.

Dawley, Alan 1976, *Class and Community: The Industrial Revolution in Lynn*, Cambridge, MA: Harvard University Press.

Degler, Carl N. 1959, *Out of Our Past: The Forces that Shaped Modern America*, New York: Harper Collins.

de Ste. Croix, G.E.M. 1981, *The Class Struggle in the Ancient Greek World*, Ithaca: Cornell University Press.

Dobb, Maurice 1947, *Studies in the Development of Capitalism*, New York: International Publishers.

—— 1976, 'A Reply', in *The Transition from Feudalism to Capitalism*, edited by Rodney Hilton, London: New Left Books.

Domar, Evsey D. 1970, 'The Causes of Slavery and Serfdom: A Hypothesis', *Journal of Economic History*, 30: 18–32.

Drescher, Seymour 1986, 'The Decline Thesis of British Slavery Since *Econocide*', *Slavery and Abolition*, 7, 1: 3–23.

Dublin, Thomas 1979, *Women at Work: The Transformation of Work and Community in Lowell, Massachusetts, 1826–1860*, Cambridge: Cambridge University Press.

—— 1991, 'Rural Putting-Out Work in Early Nineteenth Century New England: Women and the Transition to Capitalism in the Countryside', *New England Quarterly*, 64,4: 531–73.

Dubois, W.E.B. 1969 [1935], *Black Reconstruction in America: An Essay Toward a History of the Part Which Black Folk Played in the Attempt to Reconstruct Democracy in America, 1860–1880*, New York: Russel & Russel.

Ellison, Thomas 1968 [1886], *The Cotton Trade of Great Britain*, New York: Augustus M. Kelley.

Ely, Richard T. 1888, *Taxation in American States and Cities*, New York: Thomas Y. Crowell & Co.

Engelbourg, Steven 1979, 'The Economic Impact of the Civil War on Manufacturing Enterprises', *Business History* 20, 2: 148–62.

Engels, Friedrich 1981, 'Law of Value and Rate of Profit', in Marx, *Capital*, Harmondworth: Penguin.

Ennew, Judith, Paul Hirst, Keith Tribe 1977, '"Peasantry" as an Economic Category', *Journal of Peasant Studies*, 4, 4: 295–322.

Faragher, John Mack 1985, 'Open-Country Community: Sugar Creek, Illinois, 1820–1850', in *The Countryside in the Age of Capitalist Transformation: Essays in the Social History of Rural America*, edited by Steven Hahn and Jonathan Prude, Chapel Hill: University of North Carolina Press.

—— 1986, *Sugar Creek: Life on the Illinois Prairie*, New Haven: Yale University Press.

Ferris, William G. 1988, *The Grain Traders: The Story of the Chicago Board of Trade*, Lansing: Michigan State University Press.

Fields, Barbara J. 1990, 'Slavery, Race and Ideology in the USA', *New Left Review*, I, 181: 95–118.

Finley, Moses I. 1982, 'Technical Innovation and Economic Progress in the Ancient World', in *Economy and Society in Ancient Greece*, New York: Viking Press.

Fishlow, Albert 1965a, *American Railroads and the Transformation of the Antebellum Economy*, Cambridge, MA: Harvard University Press.

—— 1965b, 'Antebellum Interregional Trade Reconsidered', in *New Views in American Economic Development*, edited by R.L. Andreano, Cambridge, MA.: Schoken.

Fleisig, Heywood 1976, 'Slavery, the Supply of Labor, and the Industrialisation of the South', *Journal of Economic History*, 36, 3: 572–97.

Fogel, Robert 1989, *Without Consent or Contract: The Rise and Fall of American Slavery*, New York: W.W. Norton & Co.

Fogel, Robert W. and Stanley L. Engermann 1974, *Time on the Cross: The Economics of American Negro Slavery*, Boston: Houghton Mifflin.

Foner, Eric 1969, 'The Wilmot Proviso Revisited', *Journal of American History*, 56, 2: 262–79.

—— 1970, *Free Soil, Free Labor, Free Men: The Ideology of the Republican Party before the Civil War*, Oxford: Oxford University Press.

—— 1980, 'The Causes of the Civil War: Recent Interpretations and New Direction', and 'Politics, Ideology and the Origins of the American Civil War', in *Politics and Ideology in the Age of the Civil War*, Oxford: Oxford University Press.

—— 1988, *Reconstruction: America's Unfinished Revolution, 1863–1877*, New York: Harper & Row.

Foner, Philip 1941, *Business and Slavery: The New York Merchants and the Irrepressible Conflict*, Chapel Hill: University of North Carolina Press.

Foust, James D. and Dale E. Swan 1970, 'Productivity and Profitability of Antebellum Slave Labor: A Micro-Approach', *Agricultural History*, 44, 1: 48–54.

Fox-Genovese Elizabeth and Eugene D. Genovese 1983, *Fruits of Merchants Capital: Slavery and Bourgeois Property in the Rise and Expansion of Capitalism*, Oxford: Oxford University Press.

Frank, Andre Gunder 1967, *Capitalism and Underdevelopment in Latin America: Historical Studies of Chile and Brazil*, New York: Monthly Review.

Friedenberg, Daniel M. 1992, *Life, Liberty, and the Pursuit of Land: The Plunder of Early America*, Buffalo: Prometheus Books.

Friedmann, Harriet 1980, 'Household Production and the National Economy: Concepts for the Analysis of Agrarian Formations', *Journal of Peasant Studies*, 7, 2: 158–84.

Furtado, Celso 1971, *Development and Underdevelopment: A Structural View of the Problems of Developed and Underdeveloped Countries*, Berkeley: University of California Press.

Gaido, Daniel 2006, *The Formative Period of American Capitalism: A Materialist Interpreation*, London: Routledge.

Galenson, David W. 1981, *White Servitude in Colonial America: An Economic Analysis*, Cambridge: Cambridge University Press.

—— 1984, 'The Rise and Fall of Indentured Servitude in the Americas: An Economic Analysis', *Journal of Economic History*, 64, 1: 1–26.

Gallman, Robert E. 1966, 'Gross National Product, 1834–1909', in *Output, Employment and Productivity in the United States After 1800*, edited by Dorothy S. Brady, Washington, DC.: National Bureau of Economic Research.

—— 1970. 'Self-Sufficiency in the Cotton Economy of the Antebellum South', *Agricultural History*, 44, 1: 5–23.

—— 1972, 'The Pace and Pattern of American Economic Growth', in *American Economic Growth*, edited by Lance Davis, Richard Easterlin and William Parker, New York: Harper & Row.

Galloway, J.H. 1989, *The Sugar Cane Industry: An Historical Geography From Its Origins to 1914*, Cambridge: Cambridge University Press.

Garrett, Richard D. 1978, 'Primitive Accumulation in the Antebellum Cotton South', Ph.D. Diss.: New School for Social Research.

Gates, Paul W. 1936, 'The Homestead Act in an Incongruous Land System', *American Historical Review*, 41, 4: 652–81.

—— 1942, 'The Role of the Land Speculator in Western Development', *The Pennsylvania Magazine of History and Biography*, 66, 3: 314–33.

—— 1943, *Frontier Landlords and Pioneer Tenants*, Ithaca: Cornell University Press.

—— 1960, *The Farmer's Age: Agriculture 1815–1860*, New York: Holt, Rinehart & Winston.

—— 1973, *Landlord and Tenants on the Prairie Frontier: Studies in American Land Policy*, Ithaca: Cornell University Press.

Genovese, Eugene D. 1967, *The Political Economy of Slavery: Studies in the Economy and Society of the Slave South*, New York: Vintage Books.

—— 1972, *Roll, Jordan, Roll: The World Slaves Made*, New York: Vintage Books.

—— 1979, *From Rebellion to Revolution: Afro-American Slave Revolts in the Making of the Modern World*, New York: Vintage Books.

Godelier, Maurice 1972, *Rationality and Irrationality in Economics*, London: New Left Books.

Grant, Charles S. 1961, *Democracy in the Connecticut Frontier Town of Kent*, New York: W.W. Norton & Co.

Gray, Lewis Cecil 1933, *History of Agriculture in the Southern United States to 1860*, 2 volumes, Washington, DC.: The Carnegie Institution.

Greven, Philip J. 1970, *Four Generations: Population, Land, and Family in Colonial Andover, Massachusetts*, Ithaca: Cornell University Press.

Gutman, Herbert 1973, 'Work, Culture and Society in Industrializing America, 1815–1919', *American Historical Review*, 78, 3: 531–88.

—— 1975, *Slavery and the Numbers Games: A Critique of 'Time on the Cross'*, Urbana: University of Illinois Press.

—— 1977, 'The Reality of the Rags to Riches "Myth": The Case of Patterson, New Jersey Locomotive, Iron and Machinery Manufacturers, 1830–90', in *Work, Culture and Society in Industrializing America*, New York: Vintage Books.

Hacker, Lewis M. 1947, *The Triumph of American Capitalism: The Development of Forces in American History to the End of the Nineteenth Century*, New York: Simon & Schuster.

Haig, Robert Murray 1914, *A History of the General Property Tax in Illinois*, Urbana: University of Illinois Press.

Hahn, Steven F. 1983, *The Roots of Southern Populism: Yeoman Farmers and the Transformation of the Georgia Upcountry, 1850–1890*, Oxford: Oxford University Press.

—— 2002, 'The Politics of Black Rural Laborers in the Postemancipation South', in *The American South and the Italian Mezzogiorno: Essays in Comparative History*, edited by E. Del Lago and R. Halpern, New York: Palgrave.

Hahn, Steven F. et al. 2008, *Freedom: A Documentary History of Emancipation, 1861–1867. Selected from the Holdings of the National Archives of the United States*, Series 3: Volume 1: *Land and Labor, 1865*, Chapel Hill: University of North Carolina Press.

Hammond, Bray 1957, *Banks and Politics in America from the Revolution to the Civil War*, Princeton: Princeton University Press.

Hammond, Matthew B. 1897, *The Cotton Industry, An Essay in American Economic History*, Part I, *The Cotton Culture and Cotton Trade*, New York: Macmillan for the American Economic Association.

Harris, Nigel 1987, *The End of the Third World: Newly Industrializing Countries and the Decline of an Ideology*, New York: Penguin Books.

Hartz, Louis 1955, *The Liberal Tradition in America*, New York: Harcourt, Brace & World.

Hazard, Blanche 1921, *The Organization of the Shoe and Boot Industry in Massachusetts Before 1875*, Cambridge, MA.: Harvard University Press.

Headlee Sue E. 1991, *The Political Economy of the Family Farm: The Agrarian Roots of American Capitalism*, Westport: Praeger.

Henretta, James A. 1991a, 'Families and Farms: *Mentalité* in Pre-Industrial America', in *The Origins of American Capitalism: Collected Essays*, Boston: North-Eastern University Press.

—— 1991b, 'The War for Independence and American Economic Development', in *The Origins of American Capitalism: Collected Essays*, Boston: North-Eastern University Press.

—— 1991c, 'The Morphology of New England Society in the Colonial Period', in *The Origins of American Capitalism: Collected Essays*, Boston: North-Eastern University Press.

—— 1991d, 'The Transition to Capitalism in America', in *The Origins of American Capitalism: Collected Essays*, Boston: North-Eastern University Press.

—— 1991e, 'Wealth and Social Structure', in *The Origins of American Capitalism: Collected Essays*, Boston: North-Eastern University Press.

Hibbard, Benjamin J. 1924, *A History of Public Land Policy*, New York: MacMillan.

Hilliard, Sam Bowers 1972, *Hog Meat and Hoecake: Food Supply in the Old South, 1840–1860*, Carbondale: Southern Illinois University Press.

Hilton, Rodney (ed.) 1976, *The Transition from Feudalism to Capitalism*, London: New Left Books.

—— 1985, 'A Crisis of Feudalism', in Aston and Philpin (eds.) 1985.

Hindess, Barry and Paul Q. Hirst 1975, *Pre-Capitalist Modes of Production*, London: Routledge & Kegan Paul.

Hobsbawm, Eric J. 1967, 'The Crisis of the Seventeenth Century', in *Crisis in Europe*, edited by T. Aston, Garden City: Doubleday Books.

—— 1969, *Industry and Empire*, Harmondsworth: Penguin Books.

Holt, Michael F. 1969, *Forging a Majority: The Formation of the Republican Party in Pittsburgh, 1848–1860*, New Haven: Yale University Press.

—— 1978, *Political Crises of the 1850s*, New York: J. Wiley and Sons.

—— 1999, *The Rise and Fall of the American Whig Party: Jacksonian Politics and the Onset of the Civil War*, Oxford: Oxford University Press.

Hunter, Louis C. 1929, 'The Influence of the Market Upon Technique in the Iron Industry in Western Pennsylvania up to 1860', *Journal of Economic and Business History*, 1: 241–81.

Inikori, Joseph E. and Stanley L. Engerman (eds.) 1992, *The Atlantic Slave Trade: Effects on Economies, Societies, and Peoples in Africa, the Americas, and Europe*, Durham, NC.: Duke University Press.

Jensen, Joan M. 1986, *Loosening the Bonds: Mid-Atlantic Farm Women, 1750–1850*, New Haven: Yale University Press.

Jensen, Merrill 1969, 'The American Revolution and American Agriculture', *Agricultural History*, 43, 4: 107–24.

Jones, A.H.M. 1956, 'Slavery in the Ancient World', *Economic History Review*, New Series, 9, 2: 185–99.

Kaufman, Allen 1982, *Capitalism, Slavery, and Republican Values: Antebellum Political Economists, 1819–1848*, Austin: University of Texas Press.

Kelly, Kevin D. 1979, 'The Independent Mode of Production', *Review of Radical Political Economics*, 11, 1: 38–48.

Kerridge, Eric 1969, *Agrarian Problems in the Sixteenth Century and After*, London: George Allen & Unwin.

Kim, Sung Bok 1978, *Landlord and Tenant in Colonial New York: Manorial Society, 1664–1775*, Chapel Hill: University of North Carolina Press.

Kohn, Richard H. 1975, *The Federalists and the Creation of the Military Establishment in America, 1783–1802*, New York: The Free Press.

Knight, Franklin 1970, *Slave Society in Cuba During the Nineteenth Century*, Madison: University of Wisconsin Press.

Kula, Witold 1976, *An Economic Theory of the Feudal System*, London: New Left Books.

Kulik, Gary 1985, 'Dams, Fish, and Farmers: Defence of Public Rights in Eighteenth-Century Rhode Island', in *The Countryside in the Age of Capitalist Transformation: Essays in the Social History of Rural America*, edited by Steven Hahn and Jonathan Prude, Chapel Hill: University of North Carolina Press.

Kulikoff, Allan 1986, *Tobacco and Slaves: The Development of Southern Cultures in the Chesapeake, 1680–1800*, Chapel Hill: University of North Carolina Press.

—— 1989, 'The Transition to Capitalism in Rural America', *William and Mary Quarterly*, 3rd Series, 46, 1: 120–44.

—— 1992, *Agrarian Origins of American Capitalism*, Charlottesville: University of Virginia.

—— 2000, *From British Peasants to Colonial American Farmers*, Chapel Hill: University of North Carolina Press.

Laclau, Ernesto 1971, 'Feudalism and Capitalism in Latin America', *New Left Review*, I, 67: 19–38.

Landes, David 1972, *The Unbound Prometheus: Technological Change and Industrial Development in Western Europe from 1750 to the Present*, Cambridge: Cambridge University Press.

Lewis, Ronald L., 1979, *Coal, Iron, and Slaves: Industrial Slavery in Maryland and Virginia, 1715–1865*, Westport: Greenwood Press.

Lemon, James T. 1967, 'Household Consumption in the Eighteenth Century and its Relationship to Production and Trade: The Situation among Farmers in Southeastern Pennsylvania', *Agricultural History*, 41, 1: 59–70.

—— 1980a, 'Early Americans and Their Social Environment', *Journal of Historical Geography*, 6, 2: 115–31.

—— 1980b, 'Comment on Henretta', *William and Mary Quarterly*, 3rd Series, 37, 4: 688–96.

Lenin, Vladimir I. 1974, *The Development of Capitalism in Russia*, Moscow: Progress Publishers.

Lewis, Ronald L. 1979, *Coal, Iron, and Slaves: Industrial Slavery in Maryland and Virginia, 1715–1865*, Westport: Greenwood Press.

Levine, David F. 1975, 'The Theory of the Growth of the Capitalist Economy', *Economic Development and Cultural Change*, 24: 47–74.

Levine, Bruce 1992, *Half Slave and Half Free: The Roots of the Civil War*, New York: Hill and Wang.

Lindstrom, Dianne 1970, 'Southern Dependence Upon Interregional Grain Supplies: A Review of the Trade Flows, 1840–1860', *Agricultural History*, January, 44, 1: 101–13.

Livesay, Harold C. and Glen Porter 1971, *Merchants and Manufacturers*, Baltimore: The Johns Hopkins University Press.

Lockridge, Kenneth 1968, 'Land, Population and the Evolution of New England Society, 1630–1790', *Past and Present*, 39: 62–80.

—— 1970, *A New England Town: The First Hundred Years*, New York: W.W. Norton & Co.

Loehr, Raymond C. 1952, 'Self-Sufficiency on the Farm', *Agricultural History*, 26, 2: 37–41.

Luxemburg, Rosa 1968, *The Accumulation of Capital*, New York: Monthly Review Press.

Lynd, Staughton 1967, *Class Conflict, Slavery and the United States Constitution*, Indianapolis: Bobbs Merrill.

Main, Jackson T. 1965, *The Social Structure of Revolutionary America*, Princeton: Princeton University Press.

—— 1973, 'The Anti-Federalist Party', in *History of U.S. Political Parties*, Volume I, *1789–1860: From Factions to Parties*, edited by Arthur M. Schlesinger, Jr., New York: Chelsea House Publishers.

Mandel, Ernest 1968, *Marxist Economic Theory*, Two Volumes, New York: Monthly Review Press.

—— 1991, *Beyond Perestroika: The Future of Gorbachev's USSR*, London: Verso Books.

Mann, Susan Archer 1990, *Agrarian Capitalism in Theory and Practice*, Chapel Hill: University of North Carolina Press.

Marx, Karl 1970, 'Preface', in *A Contribution to the Critique of Political Economy*, New York: International Publishers.

—— 1974, *Value, Price and Profit*, New York: International Publishers.

—— 1976, *Capital*, Volume I, Harmondsworth: Penguin Books.

—— 1981, *Capital*, Volume III, Harmondsworth: Penguin Books.

Matson, Cathy 1998, *Merchants & Empire: Trading in Colonial New York*, Baltimore: The Johns Hopkins University Press.

May, Robert E. 1973, *The Southern Dream of a Caribbean Empire, 1854–1861*, Baton Rouge: Louisiana State University Press.

Mayer, Margit and Margaret A. Fay 1977, 'The Formation of the American Nation State', *Kapitalistate*, 6: 39–90.

McCusker, John J. and Russel R. Menard 1985, *The Economy of British America, 1607–1789*, Chapel Hill: University of North Carolina Press.

McGrane, Reginald C. 1935, *Foreign Bondholders and American State Debt*, New York: Macmillan.

McFeely, William S. 1970, *Yankee Stepfather: General O.O. Howard and the Freedmen*, New York: W.W. Norton & Co.

McPherson, James M. 1988, *Battle Cry of Freedom: The Civil War Era*, Oxford: Oxford University Press.

Medick, Hans 1976, 'The Proto-Industrial Family Economy: The Structural Function of Household and Family During the Transition from Peasant Society to Industrial Capitalism', *Social History*, 1, 3: 291–315.

Menard, Russel R., 1977, 'From Servants to Slaves: The Transformation of the Chesapeake Labor System', *Journal of Southern Studies*, 16: 335–90.

—— 2006, *Sweet Negotiations: Sugar, Slavery, and Plantation-agriculture in Early Barbados*, Charlottesville: University of Virginia Press.

Mendels, Franklin 1972, '"Proto-Industrialisation": The First Phase of the Industrialisation Process', *Journal of Economic History*, 32, 1: 241–61.

Merrill, Michael 1976, 'Cash is Good to Eat: Self–Sufficiency in the Rural Economy of the United States', *Radical History Review*, 3, 4: 42–72.

—— 1986, 'Self–Sufficiency and Exchange in Early America: Theory, Structure, Ideology', Ph.D. Diss.: Columbia University.

Miller, Steven F. 1993, 'Plantation Labor Organisation and Slave Life on the Cotton Frontier: The Alabama-Mississippi Black Belt, 1815–1840', in *Cultivation and Culture: Labor and the Shaping of Slave Life in the Americas*, edited by I. Berlin and P.D. Morgan, Charlottesville: University Press of Virginia.

Mintz, Sidney W., 1985, *Sweetness and Power: The Place of Sugar in Modern History*, Harmondsworth: Penguin Books.

Montgomery, David 1967, *Beyond Equality: Labor and the Radical Republicans, 1862–1872*, Chicago: University of Illinois Press.

—— 1992, *Workers' Control in America: Studies in the History of Work, Technology, and Labor Struggles*, Cambridge: Cambridge University Press.

Mooers, Colin 1991, *The Making of Bourgeois Europe: Absolutism, Revolution and the Rise of Capitalism in England, France and Germany*, London: Verso Books.

Moore, Barrington 1966, *Social Origins of Democracy and Dictatorship: Lord and Peasant in the Making of the Modern World*, Boston: Beacon Press.

Moore, John, 1988, *The Emergence of the Cotton Kingdom in the Old Southwest: Mississippi, 1770–1860*, Baton Rouge: Louisiana State University Press.

Moreno Fraginals, Manuel, 1976, *The Sugarmill: The Socioeconomic Complex of Sugar in Cuba, 1760–1860*, New York: Monthly Review Press.

Morgan, Edmund S. 1975, *American Slavery, American Freedom: The Ordeal of Colonial Virginia*, New York: W.W. Norton & Company.

Morrison, Chaplain W. 1967, *Democratic Politics and the Wilmot Proviso Controversy*, Chapel Hill: University of North Carolina Press.

Murray, Martin J. 1980, *The Development of Capitalism in Colonial Indochina (1870–1940)*, Berkeley: University of California Press.

—— (ed.) 1982, *South African Capitalism and Black Political Opposition: Essays on Capitalist Development in South Africa*, Cambridge, MA.: Schenkman Publishing Co.

Mutch, Robert E. 1977, 'Yeoman and Merchant in Pre-Industrial America: Eighteenth Century Massachusetts as a Case Study', *Societas*, 7, 4: 279–302.

—— 1980, 'The Cutting Edge: Colonial America and the Debate About the Transition to Capitalism', *Theory and Society*, 9: 847–63.

Newman, James J. 1988, 'To Plough the Same Five Times': Estate Management and Agricultural Change in the Genessee Valley of New York State, 1810–1865', Ph.D. Diss.: University of Rochester.

Nobles, Gregory H. 1989, 'Breaking into the Backcountry: New Approaches to the Early American Frontier, 1750–1800', *William and Mary Quarterly*, 3rd Series, 46, 4: 641–70.

—— 1990, 'The Rise of Merchants in Rural Market Towns: A Case Study of Eighteenth Century Northampton, Massachusetts', *Journal of Social History*, 24, 1: 5–23.

North, Douglass C. 1956, 'International Capital Flows in the Development of the American West', *Journal of Economic History*, 41, 4: 493–505.

—— 1961, *The Economic Growth of the United States, 1790–1860*, New York: Harper & Row.

Novack, George 1961, 'The American Civil War: It's Place in History', *International Socialist Review*, 22, 2: 48–52. Available at: <http://boston.marxists.org/archive/novack/works/1961/x03.htm>.

Nove, Alec 1989, *An Economic History of the USSR*, London: Pelican Books.

Nygaard, Bertel 2006, 'Bourgeois Revolution: The Genesis of a Concept', Unpublished Paper presented to the *Historical Materialism Conference*, London. Available at: <http://mercury.soas.ac.uk/hm/pdf/2006confpapers/papers/Nygaard.pdf>.

Oakes, James 1982, *The Ruling Race: A History of American Slaveholders*, New York: Random House.

—— 1990, *Slavery and Freedom: An Interpretation of the Old South*, New York: Alfred A. Knopf.

O'Connor, James 1975, 'The Twisted Dream', *Monthly Review*, 26, 10: 41–54.

—— 1976, 'A Note on Independent Commodity-Production and Petty Capitalism', *Monthly Review*, 28, 1: 60–3.

Okada, Yasuo 1985, 'The Economic World of a Seneca County Farmer, 1830–1880', *New York History*, 5–28.

Olmstead, Alan L. 1975, 'The Mechanisation of Reaping and Mowing in American Agriculture, 1833–1870', *Journal of Economic History*, 35, 2: 327–52.

Opie, John 1991, *The Law of the Land: Two Hundred Years of American Farmland Policy*, Lincoln, NB.: University of Nebraska Press.

Parker William N. and Judith L. Klein 1966, 'Productivity Growth in Grain Production in the United States, 1840–1860 and 1900–1910', in *Output, Employment, and Productivity in the United States after 1800*, edited by Dorothy S. Brady, Washington, DC.: National Bureau of Economic Research.

—— 1970, 'Slavery and Southern Economic Development', *Agricultural History*, 44, 1: 115–25.

—— 1987, 'New England's Early Industrialization: A Sketch', in *Quantity and Quidity: Essays in U.S. Economic History*, edited by Peter Kirby, Middletown: Wesleyan University Press.

Pessen, Edward 1978, *Jacksonian America: Society, Personality, and Politics*, Homewood: The Dorsey Press.

Phillips, Ulrich B. 1905, 'The Economic Cost of Slaveholding in the Cotton Belt', *Political Science Quarterly*, 20, 2: 257–75.

Post, Charles 1983, 'Primitive Accumulation, Class Struggle and the Capitalist State: Political Crisis and the Origins of the US Civil War, 1844–1861', Ph.D. Diss.: SUNY–Binghamton.

—— 2006, 'Review of Ransom and Sutch's *One Kind of Freedom*', *Historical Materialism*, 14, 3: 283–94.

Poulantzas, Nicos 1975, *Classes in Contemporary Capitalism*, London: New Left Books.

Price, Jacob M. 1991, 'Credit in the Slave Trade and Plantation Economies', in *Slavery and the Rise of the Atlantic System*, edited by B. Solow, Cambridge: Cambridge University Press.

Pruitt, Bettye Hobbs 1984, 'Self-Sufficiency and the Agricultural Economy of Eighteenth Century Massachusetts', *William and Mary Quarterly*, 3rd Series, 41: 333–64.

Pudup, Mary Beth 1983, 'Packers and Reapers, Merchants and Manufacturers: Industrial Structuring and Location in an Era of Emergent Capitalism', MA Thesis, University of California-Berkeley.

—— 1987, 'From Farm to Factory: Structuring and Location of the U.S. Farm Machinery Industry', *Economic Geography*, 63, 3: 203–22

Quataert, Jean 1988, 'A New View of Industrialisation: "Proto-Industry" or the Role of Small-Scale, Labor Intensive Manufacturing in the Capitalist Environment', *International Labor and Working Class History*, 33: 3–22.

Ransom, Roger L. and Richard Sutch 1977, *One Kind of Freedom: The Economic Consequences of Emancipation*, Cambridge: Cambridge University Press.

Randall, J.G. and David Donald 1961, *The Civil War and Reconstruction*, Boston: D.C. Heath and Co.

Rasmussen, Wayne D. 1969, 'The American Revolution and American Agriculture: A Comment', *Agricultural History*, 43, 4: 125–8.

Ratchford, B.U. 1941, *American State Debts*, Durham, NC.: Duke University Press.

Reidy, Joseph P. 1992, *From Slavery to Agrarian Capitalism in the Cotton Plantation South: Central Georgia, 1800–1880*, Chapel Hill: University of North Carolina Press.

Robbins, Roy M. 1976, *Our Landed Heritage: The Public Domain, 1776–1790*, Lincoln: University of Nebraska Press.

Robinson, Donald L. 1971, *Slavery in the Structure of American Politics, 1765–1820*, New York: Harcourt, Brace.

Rhodes, Robert I. (ed.) 1970, *Imperialism and Underdevelopment: A Reader*, New York: Monthly Review.

Ross, Steven J. 1984, *Workers on the Edge: Work, Leisure, and Politics in Industrialising Cincinnati, 1788–1890*, New York: Columbia University Press.

Rothenberg, Winifred B. 1981, 'The Market and Massachusetts Farmers, 1750–1855', *Journal of Economic History*, 41, 2: 283–314.

—— 1984, 'Markets, Values and Capitalism: A Discourse on Method', *Journal of Economic History*, 44, 1: 174–8.

—— 1985, 'The Emergence of a Capital Market in Rural Massachusetts, 1730–1838', *Journal of Economic History*, 45, 4: 780–807.

—— 1988, 'The Emergence of Farm Labor Markets and the Transformation of the Rural Economy: Massachusetts, 1750–1855', *Journal of Economic History*, 48, 3: 537–66.

—— 1992, *From Market Places to a Market Economy: The Transformation of Rural Massachusetts, 1750–1850*, Chicago: University of Chicago Press.

Salsbury, Stephen 1966, 'The Effect of the Civil War on American Industrial Development', in *The Economic Impact of the American Civil War*, edited by R.L. Andreano, Boston: Schenkman Publishers.

Scarano, Francisco A., 1984, *Sugar and Slavery in Puerto Rico: The Plantation Economy of Ponce, 1800–1850*, Madison: University of Wisconsin Press.

Scheiber, Harry N. 1969, *Ohio Canal Era: A Case Study of Government and the Economy*, Athens, OH.: Ohio University Press.

Schmidt, Louis B. 1939, 'Internal Commerce and the Development of a National Economy Before 1860', *Journal of Political Economy*, 47, 6: 798–822.

Schob, David C. 1975, *Hired Hands and Plowboys: Farm Labor in the Midwest, 1815–1860*, Urbana: University of Illinois Press.

Schlotterbeck, John T. 1982, 'The 'Social Economy' of an Upper South Community: Orange and Greene Counties, Virginia, 1815–1860', in *Class, Conflict and Consensus: Antebellum Southern Community Studies*, edited by Orville Vernon Burton and Robert C. McMarth, Jr., Westport: Greenwood.

Scott, Rebecca J. 1985a, *Slave Emancipation in Cuba: The Transition to Free Labor, 1860–1899*, Princeton: Princeton University Press.

—— 1985b, 'Explaining Abolition: Contradiction, Adaptation, and Challenge in Cuban Slave Society, 1860–1886', in *Between Slavery and Free Labor: The Spanish-Speaking Caribbean in the Nineteenth Century*, edited by Manuel Moreno Fraginals, Frank Moya Pons, and Stanley L. Engerman, Baltimore: The Johns Hopkins University Press.

Schoen, Brian 2009, *The Fragile Fabric of Union: Cotton, Federal Politics, and the Global Origins of the Civil War*, Baltimore: The Johns Hopkins University Press.

Schumacher, Max G. 1948. 'The Northern Farmer and His Markets During the Late Colonial Period', Ph.D. Diss.: University of California-Berkeley.

Sellers, Charles 1969, 'Who Were the Southern Whigs?', in *New Perspectives on Jacksonian Parties and Politics*, edited by E. Pessen, Boston: Allyn & Bacon.

—— 1991, *The Market Revolution: Jacksonian America, 1815–1846*, Oxford: Oxford University Press.

Severson, Robert F., James F. Niss and Richard D. Winkelman 1966, 'Mortgage Borrowing as a Frontier Developed: A Study of Mortgages in Champaign County, Illinois, 1836–1895', *Journal of Economic History*, 26, 2: 147–68.

Shaikh, Anwar M. 1978, 'Political Economy and Capitalism: Notes on Dobb's Theory of Crisis', *Cambridge Journal of Economics*, 2: 233–51.

—— 1980, 'Marxian Competition versus Perfect Competition: Further Comments on the So-Called Choice of Technique', *Cambridge Journal of Economics*, 4: 75–83.

Shammas, Carole 1982, 'How Self-Sufficient Was Early America?' *Journal of Interdisciplinary History*, 12, 2: 247–72.

Sharkey, Robert P. 1958, *Money, Class and Politics: An Economic Study of Civil War and Reconstruction*, Baltimore: The Johns Hopkins University Press.

Sherry, Robert 1976, 'Comments on O'Connor's Review of *The Twisted Dream*: Independent Commodity-Production versus Petty-Bourgeois Production', *Monthly Review*, 28, 1: 52–60.

Singer, Daniel 1981, 'The Soviet Union: The Seeds of Change', in *The Road to Gdansk: Poland and the USSR*, New York: Monthly Review Press.

Slaughter, Thomas P. 1986, *The Whiskey Rebellion: Frontier Epilogue to the American Revolution*, Oxford: Oxford University Press.

Smith, Adam 1937 [1776], *An Inquiry into the Nature and Causes of the Wealth of Nations*, New York: Modern Library.

Smith, Alan K. 1991, *Creating a World Economy: Merchant Capital, Colonialism, and World Trade, 1400–1825*, Boulder: Westview Press.

Smith, Daniel Scott 1972, 'The Demographic History of Colonial New England', *Journal of Economic History*, 32, 1:165–83.
—— 1980, 'A Malthusian-Frontier Interpretation of United States Demographic History Before c.1815', in *Urbanisation in the Americas: The Background in Comparative Perspective*, edited by W. Borah, J. Hardoy, and G.A. Stelter Ottawa, Canada: History Division, National Museum of Man.
—— 1982, 'Early American Historiography and Social Science History', *Social Science History*, 6, 3: 267–91.
Soboul, Albert 1975 [1962], *The French Revolution, 1787–1799: From the Storming of the Bastille to Napoleon*, New York: Random House.
Solow, Barbara L. and Stanley L. Engerman (eds.) 1987, *British Capitalism and Caribbean Slavery: The Legacy of Eric Williams*, Cambridge: Cambridge University Press.
Sowers, Don C. 1914, *The Financial History of New York State: From 1789 to 1912*, New York: Columbia Studies in Social Science.
Spark, Earl Sylvester 1932, *History and Theory of Agricultural Credit in the United States*, New York: Thomas Y. Crowell Company.
Starobin, Robert S. 1970, *Industrial Slavery in the Old South*, Oxford: Oxford University Press.
Stephenson, George M. 1917, *The Political History of the Public Lands, 1840–1862*, Boston: Richard Badger.
Sweezy, Paul 1976a, 'A Critique', in Hilton (ed.) 1976.
—— 1976b, 'A Rejoinder', in Hilton (ed.) 1976.
Swierenga, Robert P. 1968, *Pioneers and Profits: Land Speculation on the Iowa Frontier*, Ames: University of Iowa Press.
Szatmary, David P. 1980, *Shays' Rebellion: The Marking of An Agrarian Insurrection*, Amherst: University of Massachusetts Press.
Tadman, Michael 1989, *Speculators and Slaves: Masters, Traders, and Slaves in the Old South*, Madison: The University of Wisconsin Press.
Taylor, Alan 1989, '"A Kind of Warr": The Contest for Land on the North-Eastern Frontier, 1750–1820', *William and Mary Quarterly*, 3rd Series, 46, 1: 3–26.
Taylor, George W. 1951, *The Transportation Revolution, 1815–1860*, New York: Holt, Rhinehart and Winston.
Therborn, Göran 1976, *Science, Class and Society: On the Formation of Sociology and Historical Materialism*, London: New Left Books.
Thompson, Edward P. 1993, 'Time, Work-Discipline and Industrial Capitalism', in *Customs in Common: Studies in Traditional Popular Culture*, New York: The New Press.
Thompson, Paul 1989, *The Nature of Work: An Introduction to Debates on the Labor Process*, London: Macmillan.
Tinzmann, Otto John 1986, 'Selected Aspects of Early Social History of De Kalb County, Illinois', Ph.D. Diss.: Loyola University of Chicago.
Tomich, Dale 1988, 'The "Second Slavery": Bonded Labor and the Transformation of the Nineteenth Century World Economy', in *Rethinking the Nineteenth Century: Contradictions and Movements*, edited by Francisco O. Ramirez, Westport: Greenwood Press.
—— 1990, *Slavery In the Circuit of Sugar: Martinique and the World-economy, 1830–1848*, Baltimore: The Johns Hopkins University Press.
Trotsky, Leon 1941, 'Three Concepts of the Russian Revolution', in *Stalin: An Appraisal of the Man and his Influence*, New York: Harper & Brothers. Available at: <www.internationalist.org/three.html>.
Turner, Fredrick Jackson 1893, 'The Significance of the Frontier in American History', available at: <http://polaris.anaheimaltschools.org/ourpages/auto/2009/2/11/45478901/Fredrick%20Jackson%20Turner%20essay.pdf>.
Tyron, Rolla M. 1917, *Household Manufactures in the United States, 1640–1860*, Chicago: University of Chicago Press.
Unger, Irwin 1964, *The Greenback Era: A Social and Political History of American Finance, 1865–1879*, Princeton: Princeton University Press.
US Congress 1837, *Serial Set*, Washington, DC.: Government Printing Office.

—— 1841, *Congressional Globe: Proceedings and Appendices*, Washington, DC.: Government Printing Office.

US Department of Commerce, Bureau of the Census 1865, *Manufactures of the United States in 1860: Compiled from the Original Returns of the Eighth Census*, Washington, DC.: Government Printing Office.

—— 1872, *Ninth Census, 1870 Volume III: The Statistics of Wealth and Industry in the United States*, Washington, DC.: Government Printing Office.

—— 1884, *Tenth Census of the United States; Valuation, Taxation, and Public Indebtedness*, Washington, DC.: Government Printing Office.

—— 1976, *Historical Statistics of the United States: Colonial Times to 1970*, Two Volumes, Washington, DC.: Government Printing Office.

Van Duesen, Glyndon G. 1958, 'Some Aspects of Whig Thought and Theory in the Jacksonian Period', *American Historical Review*, 63, 2: 304–22.

—— 1973, 'The Whig Party', in *History of US Political Parties*, Volume I: *1789–1860: From Factions to Parties*, edited by A. Schlesinger, New York: Chelsea House Publishers.

Verthoff, Rowland and John M. Murrin 1973, 'Feudalism, Communalism, and the Yeoman Freeholders: The American Revolution Considered as a Social Accident', in *Essays on the American Revolution*, edited by Stephen G. Kurtz and James H. Hudson, Chapel Hill: University of North Carolina Press.

Vickers, Daniel 1990, 'Competency and Competition: Economic Culture in Early America', *William and Mary Quarterly*, 3rd Series, 47, 1: 3–29.

Wade, Richard C. 1964, *Slavery in the Cities: The South 1820–1860*, Oxford: Oxford University Press.

Wallenstein, Peter 1984, '"More Unequally Taxed" than any People in the Civilised World": The Origins of Georgia's Ad Valorem Tax System', *Georgia Historical Quarterly*, Winter, 64, 4: 459–87.

Wallerstein, Immanuel 1974, *The Modern World System*, New York: Academic Press.

—— 1976, 'American Slavery and the Capitalist World-Economy', *American Journal of Sociology*, 81, 5: 1199–213.

Walsh, Lorena S. 1993, 'Slave Life, Slave Society, and Tobacco-production in the Tidewater Chesapeake, 1620–1820', in *Cultivation and Culture: Labor and the Shaping of Slave Life in the Americas*, edited by I. Berlin and P.D. Morgan, Charlottesville: University Press of Virginia.

Warren, Bill 1980, *Imperialism: Pioneer of Capitalism*, London: Verso Books.

Watts, David 1987, *The West Indies: Patterns of Development, Culture and Environmental Change Since 1492*, Cambridge: Cambridge University Press.

Ward, J.R. 1978, 'The Profitability of Sugar Planting in the British West Indies, 1650–1834', *Economic History Review*, 31, 2: 197–213.

Weber, Max 1958, *The Protestant Ethic and the Spirit of Capitalism: The Relationship Between Religion and the Economic and Social Life in Modern Culture*, New York: Charles Scribner and Sons.

—— 1978, *Economy and Society: An Outline of Interpretive Sociology*, I, Berkeley: University of California Press.

—— 1981, *General Economic History*, New Brunswick: Transaction Books.

Weiman, David F. 1985, 'The Economic Emancipation of the Non-Slaveholding Class: Upcountry Farmers in the Georgia Cotton Economy', *Journal of Economic History*, 45: 71–93.

—— 1987, 'Farmers and the Market: A View from the Georgia Upcountry', *Journal of Economic History*, 47: 627–47.

—— 1988, 'Urban Growth on the Periphery of the Antebellum Cotton Belt: Atlanta, 1847–1860', *Journal of Economic History*, 48: 261–72.

—— 1989, 'Families, Farms and Rural Society in Preindustrial America', *Research in Economic History*, 10, Supplement 5: 255–77.

Wessman, James W. 1979–80, 'A Household Mode of Production – Another Comment', *Radical History Review*, 22: 129–39.

Westermann, William L. 1955, *The Slave Systems of Greek and Roman Antiquity*, Philadelphia: The American Philosophical Association.

Whartenby, Franklee Gilbert 1963, 'Land and Labor Productivity in United States Cotton Production, 1800–1840', Ph.D. Diss.: University of North Carolina.

Wickham, Chris (ed.) 2007, *Marxist History-Writing for the Twenty-First Century*, London: The British Academy/Oxford University Press.

Weigly, Russel F. 1984, *History of the United States Army*, Bloomington: Indiana University Press.

Wiener, Jonathan M. 1978, *Social Origins of the New South: Alabama, 1860–1880*, Baton Rouge: Louisiana State University Press.

—— 1979, 'Class Structure and Economic Development in the American South, 1865–1955', *American Historical Review*, 84, 4: 97–992.

Weiss, Thomas 1993, 'Long-Term Changes in US Agricultural Output per Workers, 1800–1900', *Economic History Review*, 46, 2: 324–41.

Wilentz, Sean 1984, *Chants Democratic: New York City and the Rise of the American Working Class*, Oxford: Oxford University Press.

Williams, Eric 1944, *Capitalism and Slavery*, Chapel Hill: University of North Carolina Press.

Wilson, Major L. 1967, 'The Concept of Time and the Political Dialogue in the United States, 1828–48', *American Quarterly*, 19, 4: 619–44.

Winters, Donald L. 1978, *Farmers Without Farms: Agricultural Tenancy in Nineteenth-Century Iowa*, Westport: Greenwood Publishing Group.

Wood, Ellen Meiksins 1988, *Peasant-Citizen and Slave: The Foundations of Athenian Democracy*, London: Verso Books.

—— 1995, *Democracy Against Capitalism: Renewing Historical Materialism*, Cambridge: Cambridge University Press.

—— 1999, *The Origins of Capitalism*, New York: Monthly Review Press.

—— 2003, *The Empire of Capital*, London: Verso.

Woodman, Harold 1968, *King Cotton and His Retainers: Financing and Marketing the Cotton Crop of the South, 1800–1925*, Lexington: University of Kentucky Press.

Woodward, C. Vann 1951, *Origins of the New South, 1877–1913*, Baton Rouge: Louisiana State University Press.

—— 1955, *The Strange Career of Jim Crow*, Oxford: Oxford University Press.

Wright, Gavin 1970, '"Economic Democracy" and the Concentration of Agricultural Wealth in the Cotton South, 1850–1860', *Agricultural History*, 44, 1: 63–93.

—— 1978, *The Political Economy of the Cotton South: Households, Markets, and Wealth in the Nineteenth Century*, New York: W.W. Norton & Co.

—— 1986, *Old South, New South: Revolutions in the Southern Economy Since the Civil War*, New York: Basic Books.

Index